# Travel and Tourism

written by
**Mike Bottomley Renshaw**
**Huw Evans**
**Lesley France**
**Amanda Greason**
**Barbara Harrison**
**Ken Harrop**
**David Hind**
**Joan Henderson**
**David Holding**
**Philip Long**
**John Towner**
*with contributions from*
*Niall Mackel*

edited by
**Paul Callaghan**

**BUSINESS EDUCATION PUBLISHERS LIMITED**
*in association with*
**THE CENTRE FOR TRAVEL AND TOURISM**

**1989**

© Paul Callaghan, Mike Bottomley Renshaw, Huw Evans, Lesley France, Amanda Greason, Barbara Harrison, Ken Harrop, David Hind, Joan Henderson, David Holding, Philip Long, John Towner and Niall Mackel 1989

ISBN 0-907679-27-7


Cover and Maps by Richard Draper


Published in Great Britain by Business Education Publishers Limited, Leighton House, 10 Grange Crescent, Stockton Road, Sunderland, Tyne and Wear.

Tel: 091 567 4963

Printed in Great Britain by Athenaeum Press Limited, Unit 3, Mill Lane Industrial Estate, Newcastle upon Tyne.

Tel: 091 273 7737

# Preface

Travel and Tourism is one of the fastest growing industries in the world and has shown remarkable growth in the last twenty years. Such expansion requires a trained and educated workforce and in response to this need there has been established a wide range of courses allowing students to achieve qualifications recognised by bodies such as the City and Guilds of London Institute, BTEC and the CNAA. The industry itself, under the auspices of the ABTA National Training Board, continually strives to ensure that the standard of Travel and Tourism education is maintained and improved.

This book was specifically written for students studying Travel and Tourism on recognised courses at all levels. It will also be of considerable interest to those working in the industry who wish to gain a greater insight into the workings of the travel and tourism business.

With such a wide readership in mind the authors have consciously adopted a style which is both lively and accessible and have structured the content so that readers with no previous knowledge of the travel and tourism industry can confidently use the text as a valuable learning resource.

The book covers the nature of tourism; its history and development; its contemporary importance; the structure of the industry and the operation of its component parts, concentrating specifically on transport, accommodation, retail travel, tour operation and public sector tourism. The final chapter examines the role of marketing in travel and tourism.

Finally case studies looking at various aspects of the industry have been included to provide the student with a realistic insight into the operation of the business. They are also designed to be used by lecturers as the basis of a case study based assignment programme.

# Acknowledgements

In producing this book there have been contributions from a number of people whose efforts we would like to acknowledge.

The editorial process has involved contributions from Caroline White, Tom Harrison, Michael Ayton, Niall Mackel, Mike Robinson, Peter Hughes, Bernie Callaghan, Ray Hopper and Lucy Berrington. Our thanks to all of them for their suggestions and improvements.

The production team included Moira Page and Kathryn Martin who have diligently typeset the manuscript. The maps and illustrations were produced by Richard Draper whose imaginative approach has added much to the book.

We must also thank Joan Taylor of New College Durham and Malcolm Martin of Newcastle Polytechnic for their continued support for the Centre for Travel and Tourism.

Finally our sincerest thanks must go to the ABTA National Training Board and in particular to Norman Richardson, Don Calder and Kevin McGrath who have always been extremely supportive of the efforts of our two institutions in the furtherance of Travel and Tourism education.

# The Centre for Travel and Tourism

This book has been published by Business Education Publishers Limited in association with the Centre for Travel and Tourism. The Centre is a body established by New College Durham and Newcastle Polytechnic with the aim of promoting research, consultancy and publications in the field of Travel and Tourism. All of the authors are members of the Centre.

# The Authors

## Chapters

☐ Tourism and Tourists

*by Lesley France*

☐ The History and Development of Tourism

*by John Towner and Huw Evans*

☐ The Importance of Tourism

*by Lesley France, John Towner and Huw Evans*

☐ The Structure of the Travel and Tourism Industry

*by Joan Henderson*

☐ Transport in Travel and Tourism

*by David Holding*

☐ Tourist Accommodation

*by Barbara Harrison*

☐ Retail Travel Agency

*by Mike Bottomley Renshaw*

☐ Tour Operations

*by Mike Bottomley Renshaw*

☐ Government and Tourism

*by Ken Harrop and Philip Long*

☐ The Marketing of Travel and Tourism

*by David Hind*

## Case Studies

☐ Continental Coach Holidays after 1980

*by David Holding*

☐ Strategy Changes at Sealink after Privatisation

*by David Holding*

☐ British Airways Air Fares and Liberalisation in Europe

*by David Holding*

☐ Westworld Travel

*by Joan Henderson*

☐ The Neilson Leisure Group

*by Amanda Greason*

☐ Miles Better

*by Joan Henderson*

☐ The North of England Open Air Museum at Beamish

*by Ken Harrop*

# Table of Contents

# Chapter 1

---

# ☐ Tourism and Tourists

## Introduction

Travel and tourism are complex activities undertaken by people worldwide for a variety of reasons. A detailed understanding of these reasons demands careful study, not only of tourism statistics and travel destinations, but also, for example, of psychological motives and social trends.

Peoples'perceptions of travel and tourism differ. To the consumer travel and tourism may be: a necessary evil to be endured in the course of business life; a means of being re-united with friends and relatives; or an escape from the monotony of daily life to an environment created to satisfy dreams. To a person who works in the business of travel and tourism, it is their job and their livelihood. To the person studying travel and tourism, it is a multi-million pound international industry, the growth of which has been dramatic. It provides direct employment for millions of people in a variety of occupations, and indirectly affects the lives of many others. Indeed it makes an important contribution to the incomes of both individuals and nations.

The spectacular growth experienced by the travel and tourism industry since the Second World War has slowed, particularly in Europe. However, there still remain areas in which potential for expansion exists. Despite, or perhaps because of, changes in the nature of the activities it undertakes, the future of this complex industry seems assured. In order to understand the travel and tourism phenomenon, we need to understand the scope and meaning of the term, together with its antecedents.

## Why study Travel and Tourism ?

It is important to recognise that the area of relaxation and pleasure, which includes travel and tourism, is a subject for academic study and theoretical debate. However, it is not the intention of this book to view travel and tourism simply from an academic standpoint. Whilst the industry needs to be examined in a structured and analytical way, we also need to see it in a practical sense, affecting the lives of millions throughout the world. With this in mind, travel and tourism can usefully be placed within the framework of play, recreation and leisure.

# What is meant by Play, Recreation and Leisure?

One way of looking at tourism is to consider it as an aspect of 'play', 'recreation' or 'leisure'. Play, the action of "amusing oneself" (as defined by the Concise Oxford Dictionary, 1964), is an integral part of the lives of people in a wide range of societies. In many societies, including that of the U.K., people expect to engage in recreation and play. The portion of their lives normally reserved for these activities is termed leisure time. The Oxford English Dictionary (1933) defines leisure as "the state of having time at one's disposal; time which can be spent as one pleases; free or unoccupied time." Webster's Dictionary (1971) offers a more specific definition of leisure as "time free from work or duties".

These fairly precise and restricted meanings are clear and easy to understand but are frequently confused in common parlance. Dictionary definitions tend to get ignored, and the terms 'leisure' and 'recreation' are often treated as being interchangeable. In the context of this book, the terms are used in their more precise sense.

# The Development of Play, Leisure and Recreation through History

The ideas conveyed by the terms 'play', 'leisure' and 'recreation' are deeply embedded within world cultures. Throughout history people have attempted to bring enjoyment into their lives. In pre-industrial European societies there was little separation of work from pleasurable activities. To attend the local market might have been considered a chore imposed by an employer. Yet such visits would vary the routine of a person's daily life, bringing contact with other people, providing opportunities for the exchange of news and gossip, for personal shopping and, indeed, for a wide range of diversions defined by Dr Johnson in his dictionary as 'play': to play is "to do something not as a task, but for pleasure" (Armitage, 1977).

Pleasures were woven into the fabric of everyday existence. There was an unconscious acceptance of the need for a departure from routine work. This was acknowledged by Henry Peacham in his English Recreations of 1641, where he said: "For such is our nature...we must have our relaxations as well of mind, as of body..." (Armitage, 1977).

The industrial revolution dramatically changed this free and easy attitude towards work and leisure. Work became more highly structured. People flocked from the countryside to work in factories set in grimy, overcrowded towns. The monotonous production process was carried on unceasingly by people working long hours on a shift system. Time available for leisure was scarce and the pursuit of recreation activities with which to fill that leisure time occurred well away from the daily work environment. In response to poor working conditions and poor pay, workers combined to form trade unions. Unions were able to negotiate better working conditions, better pay, a shorter working day, and annual holidays. Through the nineteenth century, leisure time lengthened, affluence grew and new forms of recreation emerged.

Initially, the use of this new-found leisure time was constrained by attitudes derived from the Protestant Reformation. Such constraints included:

    (i)  severe restrictions upon alcohol, dancing and many other forms of enjoyment;

    (ii)  the imposition of strict rules of behaviour on Sunday, which was seen as a day of worship and rest;

    (iii)  the all pervasive influence of the so called 'Protestant work ethic'.

Wherever Protestantism was powerful, strong pressures were placed upon the population to conform to strict moral and legal restraints (Chubb and Chubb 1981).

The influence of the Industrial Revolution on the availability of leisure time, and Protestant attitudes toward recreation, have together shaped the way in which modern British society views enjoyment. Even in the late 1980s there is a common belief that many forms of recreation should be less frivolous. The protracted struggle over Sunday trading shows that many people adhere to the vestigal remains of Protestant attitudes.

As hours of work shortened and wages improved, an increasing number of people had the time, energy and income to devote to recreation. In response to the demand, an industry was gradually developed to service the needs of travellers, tourists and day trippers. Small at first, this industry grew rapidly in size and complexity as demand escalated. Its modest beginnings involved taking factory workers to the newly developing coastal resorts, and on educational trips perhaps to London or Paris. The travel and tourism industry grew by propagating a desire to travel for pleasure, and by offering people the means by which they could fulfil this desire.

# Defining Travel and Tourism

We can see that an increase in people's leisure time enabled them to engage in travel and tourism. Yet other factors were also important. Higher incomes gave people the means and motivation to travel and tour. The development of an efficient infrastructure increased comfort and social fashions helped determine who travelled, to where and for how long. It is clear that given such a range of variables, a full definition of travel and tourism is likely to be complex.

To travel, as defined by the Concise Oxford Dictionary (1964), is to

> *"make a journey, especially one of some length to distant countries";*

The same dictionary describes tourism as

> *"organised touring" or "making a journey through a country from place to place".*

Webster's International Dictionary (1961) and the Oxford English Dictionary (1933) both offer more useful definitions of tourism. The former suggests that the tourist is someone who makes:

*"a circular trip usually for business, pleasure or education during which various places are visited and for which an itinerary is usually planned".*

The latter states that a tourist is

*"one who (makes a tour) for recreation...one who travels for pleasure or culture".*

These somewhat general definitions have been refined as the study of travel and tourism has highlighted the need for a more precise use of such terms. It is now commonly accepted that a tourist, as opposed to a day-visitor, is someone who spends at least 24 hours (that is overnight), away from home, even though both categories of visitor might engage in similar activities. Although there is no generally accepted maximum time-limit for a tourist visit, it is normally accepted that a tourist is away from home for a relatively short period. Similarly the money spent on the trip by a tourist would be earned at home and not at the place visited (Mathieson and Wall, 1982).

The United Nations definition of tourism, adopted by the United Nations Conference on Travel and Tourism in 1968, recognises a tourist as:

*"any person visiting a country other than that in which he has his usual place of residence, for any reason other than following an occupation remunerated from within the country visited" (Murphy, 1985).*

This goes a stage further by combining the earlier ideas of Mathieson and Wall, and also offers an insight into the activities of tourists. Using this approach, it is possible to identify different types of tourist.

The perspective taken above is not the only way of approaching the difficult task of defining tourism. Pearce (1982) stresses the need for what he describes as an 'experiential' definition of tourists and tourism. He suggests that visitors become tourists when they feel that they are engaging in tourism. Therefore on occasions, business visitors could become true 'holiday' tourists while taking part in recreation activities at their destination during a period of time when they felt 'at leisure'. Such a definition, while more complex than those used in compiling the official statistics, and one for which it would be almost impossible to calculate with any degree of accuracy, is perhaps more realistic than traditional attempts to define tourism.

Many of the recreational activities with which we fill our leisure, while time-consuming if taken together, individually rarely occupy more than a full day. Knitting, playing football, watching television, driving into the countryside to admire the scenery and have a picnic on a fine summer Sunday, are all relatively short-term activities. Travel and tourism demands a block of leisure time longer than, say, an afternoon: usually a weekend or the annual holiday. That we have so much leisure time today is largely the result of the nineteenth-century struggle between employers and unions, where workers sought to improve their conditions and create opportunities to escape from the dull and depressing daily round of life in an urban, industrial environment.

# The Reasons why People Travel

Tourism is concentrated into weekend and holiday periods and is frequently linked with travel outside the local community. Whilst much tourism is recreational, there are other reasons why people travel. People travel on business, go shopping for exotica, visit friends and relatives, make pilgrimages and take educational journeys. So although travel can be recreational, it can also be part of some other aspect of life. It may thus be difficult to classify the tourist activity of a person, given that people often have mixed motives for travelling. They may, perhaps during a business trip, visit a relative, look in at a local religious shrine, indulge in a boat excursion, attend a theatre performance and do some shopping.

A problem encountered in trying to evaluate and quantify why people travel, is the way in which tourist statistics are collected. Tourist statistics are often derived from the number of people who enter a country, or the numbers who stay in hotels. Both methods incorporate numbers of travellers whose motives may be mixed. In being so imprecise, neither method differentiates between the various types of tourism. So although the main focus of this book is on holiday tourism, it is important to recognise that people travel for a wide variety of reasons, and that they make use of the same forms of transport and accommodation.

These definitions and concepts offer a starting point in any attempt to understand the travel and tourism industry. The industry depends on the desire of individuals and groups to travel for business or pleasure. In this context, people's motives for travel become crucial, as do the ways in which people try to satisfy their needs through the travel experience.

# The Characteristics of Tourists

Political, social and industrial changes in twentieth-century Britain (and other parts of the world) have brought about substantial increases in leisure time and the redistribution of wealth, leading to major changes in the patterns of recreation and tourism in the developed world. All but the very poor have been able to enjoy the forms of play that were once restricted to the privileged few. Indeed, apart from there having been a major shift in their socio-economic profile, tourists in the past were, as Swinglehurst (1982) points out, much like tourists now:

> *"They enjoyed...freedom...away from the domestic environment, they revelled in the attentions of foreign Romeos, they swooned romantically at scenery, they complained about the food, they distrusted foreigners. The main difference...lies in their numbers."*

In essence, then, the behaviour of tourists remains basically unchanged. It is the scale of their movements that has made them more noticeable and magnified their impact.

Inevitably, the kind of 'play' a person chooses "depends upon his nature, his environment, his mood and his age" (Armitage, 1977). Those who are young, fit, extrovert and normally tied to a dull urban job may seek escape into a rural or coastal setting in which they can expend their excess energy in a variety of active pursuits. Evidence suggests that people who have experienced higher education and who are often engaged in professional occupations are more likely to have the income, mobility and inclination to enjoy travelling and holidays. In contrast, pensioners, who have ample leisure, may have restricted incomes and may not be fit enough to enjoy active leisure pursuits and so take part in more passive forms of recreational activity. They are less likely to want to suffer the discomfort of long-distance travel and so may holiday nearer home.

In addition to focusing on the type of holiday in terms of its destination, length and on the characteristics of tourists (notably their income group, social status and educational background), many classifications consider a number of other factors. These include:

(i) the nature of the organisations with which people travel;

(ii) the type of visit they make, for instance, whether it involves individual arrangements or a package tour;

(iii) the person's motivations for the trip;

(iv) the facilities the tourist uses, such as the mode of transport and type of accommodation. (de Kadt 1976).

Both Cohen (1972) and Plog (1972) have sought to categorise tourists in terms of their attitude towards their trip, their expectations and the role that such an experience would play within their lives.

Consider the following two extremes:

(a.) Some people prefer to identify completely with the culture and environment they choose to visit, becoming absorbed into their surroundings and living with the local inhabitants whose life-style they imitate. So far as the majority of societies are concerned, only relatively small numbers of such adventurers could be absorbed without creating a significant impact on those societies. These people would tend to reject familiar attitudes and material goods in favour of new and strange experiences. Independent and often solitary, they frequently avoid organised forms of travel and tourism, preferring to make their own arrangements.

(b.) At the other end of the scale are people who dislike contact with unfamiliar environments, which they fear and distrust. Unadventurous, they enjoy travelling as a group. They like their tours to be organised for them in considerable detail. For such people, the travel and tourism industry provides holidays which mirror the attitudes and life-styles they have left behind at home. From this secure base, the 'mass tourist' rarely ventures out into local society. The only contact with the indigenous population is through organised events, such as an evening barbecue in a 'typical' hill village attended by hundreds of fellow tourists, who enjoy an experience which reflects what they perceive of as reality, but which is often far from a true reflection of local life.

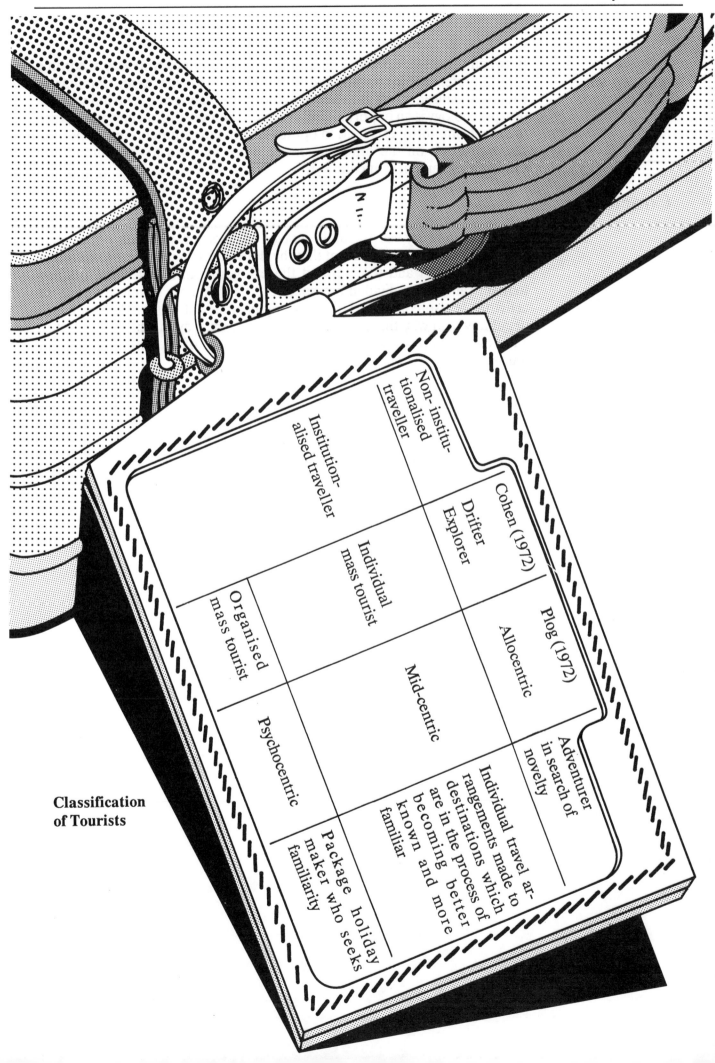

**Classification of Tourists**

| | Cohen (1972) | Plog (1972) | |
|---|---|---|---|
| Non-institu-tionalised traveller | Drifter Explorer | Allocentric | Adventurer in search of novelty |
| Institution-alised traveller | Individual mass tourist | Mid-centric | Individual travel arrangements made to destinations which are in the process of becoming better known and more familiar |
| | Organised mass tourist | Psychocentric | Package holiday maker who seeks familiarity |

Between these two extremes lie a range of tourist types who vary according to their preference for novelty and risk as opposed to security and familiarity, and for organised travel as opposed to footloose wandering. The individual's own psychology is an important influence on their position at any point along the spectrum. Introverts tend to opt for secure environments and experiences. Extroverts on the other hand, are more inclined to seek unfamiliar surroundings and new encounters.

## Conclusion

The travel industry has gradually evolved to cater for the needs of this wide variety of tourists. It is apparent that the definitions which relate to different aspects of travel and tourism and the categories into which tourists and tourism can be sub-divided are complex. The industry which serves these activities is also complex. The following chapters of this book examine in detail how and why this industry has evolved, the way in which it operates, and how it aspires to meet the needs and desires of the different types of tourist.

# Chapter 2

## ☐ The History and Development of Tourism

## A Historical Perspective on Tourism

The spectacular growth of tourism which has occurred in western societies, particularly since the 1960s, may serve to distort our understanding of tourism's historical development. It may appear that tourism is a fairly new development in western societies and that present patterns are the inevitable result of recent social and economic change. This, however, is not so. Tourism, albeit on a smaller scale, has been a feature of many different societies throughout different periods of history. Tourism in the late twentieth century appears to be new because of the sheer volume of tourists and the growing number of destinations involved. In order properly to understand the nature of tourism, however, we have to gain a historical perspective upon it and this means appreciating its significance for tourists themselves. Five days holiday in Blackpool for a Lancashire mill worker in the 1870s was probably as significant as two weeks on the Costa del Sol would be for his or her modern counterpart.

The basic factors and processes which underlie tourism have remained much the same throughout history. Tourism, in any age, can operate only within a broader environment which embraces a number of important cultural, social, economic, political and technological conditions. Within this broad environment, certain basic enabling factors must exist for there to be tourism:

A significant section of society must have:

>   (i) adequate leisure time;

>   (ii) sufficient wealth; and

>   (iii) the desire to travel.

Within the society as a whole there must be:

>   (i) a reasonable level of political stability (and this, of course, applies equally to destination countries); and

(ii) an acceptable travel infrastructure which provides a minimum basic standard of transport and accommodation.

Leisure time and wealth reflect the economic and social environment, security the political environment, transport the technological environment, and the desire to travel the cultural environment.

These interrelated factors have varied in importance for different social groups in different societies in different periods of history. Some conditions have tended to remain fairly constant whilst others have fluctuated considerably. Two brief examples illustrate how such changes have taken place at differing rates:

1. The technological aspects of travel remained significantly the same for many centuries. The speed and distance of travel were limited by the stamina of a horse on land, and by the vagaries of wind and tides at sea. The Romans (who came to Britain in AD 70) used draught animals to pull carts, and sailing ships to travel overseas. Some 1,800 years later, these technologies were still in common use throughout nineteenth century Britain. Highlighting Britain's previous social stability, the construction of steam railways (Stockton and Darlington Railway, 1825), engine-propelled boats (Brunel's 'Great Britain'), motor cars (Hans Otto, Germany circa 1880) and aircraft (the Wright brothers, Kitty Hawk, USA circa 1903) revolutionised travel times and costs.

2. Conversely, economic, social and cultural conditions in Britain have varied dramatically over the centuries. In western societies the opportunities for tourism for more people are now greater than they have ever been. By contrast, traditionally agricultural societies, to which the majority of the world's population belongs, have never offered many opportunities for tourism, if any at all. Thus the numbers of people able to engage in tourism have varied over different historical periods. In addition, there have been significant changes in those social groups which have been able to travel. Tourism has rarely been confined to one social group, but there have generally been significant differences between social groups in the forms of tourist activity undertaken and in the destinations chosen.

Historical knowledge relating to tourism is generally biased towards European and North American developments, and usually towards the activities of the more affluent social groups. Because of these factors, the idea has developed that tourism originated solely in Western Europe (with its development often credited to Britain) and from there it spread to other parts of the world. A more informed examination of the facts shows that such ideas are simplistic. It is important to recognise that societies in other parts of the world, in the past as well as the present, have also experienced tourism movements.

As our knowledge is incomplete, it would be inappropriate to try to trace the history of tourism throughout every age. (For the reader interested in this area, general studies of tourism are listed in the references at the end of the book.) In this chapter a number of periods in history will be examined which both reflect various aspects of the development of tourism and illustrate some aspects of the historical research which has been carried out. A broad perspective is taken in order to situate tourism within the structure and culture of a society and it is assumed, too, that there is a relationship between leisure, recreation and tourism. This relationship is explored in each case.

It is worth mentioning also at this stage that inventions and innovations have been and remain a critical influence in shaping society and hence the physical and cultural parameters of 'play'. Inventions, such as the steam engine or the telephone, change the relationship between people and the physical environment around them. Further, the coming together of particular inventions can transform that relationship. The individual inventions of the electric dynamo and the radio transmitter are important in their own right but when combined they form the basis for radio, television and radar. Society is shaped culturally, psychologically, socially and economically by the impact of technology.

# Tourism in Ancient Times

The origins of tourism are likely to lie in those societies in which agricultural productivity was sufficient for a social elite to have leisure time. Ancient civilisations of the Middle East, with their more-than-adequate food supplies supporting non-productive, wealthy people, may have generated the first tourists. A number of ancient civilisations which flourished around the Mediterranean have in fact left written and archaeological evidence of the types of tourism in which they engaged. Let us examine some examples of tourism in ancient times.

## Ancient Egypt

Some of the first clear signs of tourism are to be found in Ancient Egypt from around 1500 BC. A number of factors helped to create tourism in Egypt:

(i) the social and economic environment of the country at this time was suitable for tourism, since there was a high level of prosperity and since strong political control was exercised by the so-called 'New Kingdom' during the period from 1600 to 1200 BC;

(ii) travel by boat was comparatively easy on the River Nile;

(iii) a range of attractions appealed to the wealthy classes. For example, by this period the great pyramids and the Sphinx at Gizeh were already over 1,000 years old.

Pre-echoes of the modern tourist can be traced in the graffiti left on the monuments. One inscription, dated to 1244 BC, records that

> *Hadnnakhte, scribe of the treasury...came to make an excursion and amuse himself on the west of Memphis, together with his brother Panakti, scribe of the Vizier.*

> *(Casson, 1974)*

Tourism was not confined to the social elite. Religious festivals were of the utmost importance in this society, and the River Nile enabled enormous numbers of people, perhaps several thousand at a time, to journey to sacred sites on the occasion of the deity's festival. Religion and pleasure were intermixed. As the Greek historian Herodotus later noted:

> *The Egyptians meet to celebrate festivals not once a year but a number of times. The biggest and most popular is at Bubastis...they go there on the river, men and women together, a big crowd in each boat. As they sail, some of the women keep clicking castanets and some of the men play on the pipes and the rest, both men and women, sing and beat time with their hands.*
>
> *(Casson,1974 )*

Although physical mobility was generally not a problem for these 'mass tourists', the necessary services for accommodation and food do not seem to have existed for these occasions: the travellers camped in the open, and fed themselves as best they could.

# The Roman Empire

Tourism prospered during certain periods of the Roman Empire. This was for a number of factors:

(i) the first two centuries AD were economically prosperous for the Roman Empire, with wide sectors of society enjoying relative affluence and leisure time;

(ii) there was a considerable degree of political stability within the Empire itself;

(iii) an immense network both of seaways and of secure roads for horses, carts, carriages and litters criss-crossed the Empire. Conditions for travel in Europe were better over a wider area than they were at any time until the nineteenth century, as the following quotation illustrates:

> *... the tourist could make his way from the shores of the Euphrates to the border between Britain and Scotland without crossing a foreign frontier, always within the bounds of one government's jurisdiction. A purse full of Roman coins was the only kind of cash he had to carry; they were accepted or could be changed anywhere. He could sail through any waters without fear of pirates, thanks to the emperor's patrol squadrons. A planned network of good roads gave him access to all major centres, and the through routes were policed well enough for him to ride them with little fear of bandits. He needed only two languages - Greek would take him from Mesopotamia to Yugoslavia, Latin from Yugoslavia to Britain.*
>
> *(Casson,1974)*

**Some Roman Tourist Centres in Italy**

Vicarello
Sabine Hills
Rome
Alban Hills
Puteoli
Cumae
Naples
Baine
Sorrento
Capri

**The Roman Empire c116AD**

Hadrian's Wall
London
Bath
Aix
Rome
Naples
Segesta
Lipari
Corinth
Delphi
Athens
Troy
Olympia
Sparta
Epidaurus
Babylon
Alexandria
Memphis
R. Nile

Rome was a tourist attraction to people living in the provinces both in Italy and elsewhere in the Empire. The city possessed monumental buildings and boasted a range of festivities unrivalled in the ancient world. During the second century AD, 130 days out of the year were holidays dedicated to lavish public entertainments such as chariot racing, boxing and theatrical performances. There were so many visitors, either for pleasure or on business, that other cities elsewhere in the Empire maintained offices in the forum to help their citizens find accommodation and to advise them in other ways.

Elsewhere in Italy there were tourist locations catering for different social groups. The wealthy leisured elite of Rome annually left the city in the spring on their peregrinatio to escape the heat. First of all they visited their villas scattered along the coast of the Bay of Naples from Cumae to Sorrento. As the wealthy Symmachus wrote to a friend:

> *I've passed a few days on this shore...where the healthy air and cool waters are such an inducement to linger...I have a steady stream of friends dropping in on me. I'm not afraid that you'll think of me idling away my time in such delightful surroundings amid such good things.*

> *(Casson, 1974)*

Late in the summer, the leisured elite moved on to their villas in the cool of the Alban and Sabine hills to the east of the capital, before returning to the city in the autumn.

Tourism was also enjoyed by other social groups. Even the middle classes could afford second houses in times of economic prosperity, and the seaside resorts that grew up along the coast around the Bay of Naples catered for all types of visitors from a wealthy villa-owner to a tradesman renting a room in a boarding house at Baiae, Puteoli or Naples. Baiae, with its baths, beach, two amphitheatres, tree-shaded park, restaurants and souvenir shops, became Rome's most popular summer resort.

As with Britain's seaside resorts in the nineteenth century, each resort had its own distinctive character and catered for particular social classes and activities. Baiae was the venue for pleasure-seekers: "Why must I look at drunks staggering along the shore or noisy boating parties?", grumbled one Roman. Puteoli was a more sedate resort adjoining an important commercial harbour, while Naples, originally a Greek city, attracted the intellectual visitor with contests for poets and musicians. The city also became a retirement centre for the elderly.

Italy also possessed a great range of spas for health-related tourism. These included Vicarello on Lake Braccione near Rome, the spas in Sicily at Segesta, Selinus and Himera and the island of Lipari. Elsewhere in the Empire, there were spas at centres such as Vichy, Bath, Wiesbaden and Aix-en-Provence. All probably combined health with pleasure activities.

Travel abroad was confined to the wealthy, although the mechanics of travel were comparatively straightforward. A popular destination was Egypt, with visits being undertaken to the monuments of its past glory. A fast grain ship could be taken from Rome's port at Ostia directly to Alexandria, and from there it was possible to sail up the Nile. Another favourite trip was to Greece, a culture that was then past its peak. The journey could be made by sea from Rome to Corinth or Athens. An established itinerary included visits to Corinth, Athens, Delphi, Epidaurus, Olympia and Sparta. Further afield, the legendary site of Troy, the city from which the Romans traced their origins, was a popular destination.

In some ways the interests of the Roman tourists and the facilities they used were similar to those of present-day tourists. As well as having a taste for the seaside and other entertainments, tourists were interested in the art and architecture of other cultures such as Egypt, where Alexandria, Memphis and the pyramids were popular tourist destinations, and Greece, where Athens, Corinth and Olympia attracted many tourists. The Romans were also keen to visit centres associated with historical events, such as Marathon, Troy and Babylon, centres famous for mythology, and also oracles such as those at Delphi and Delos. The landscapes they seem to have enjoyed were those associated with forms of divinity: springs, grottoes and groves, and the charms of pastoral scenes. Unlike modern tourists, the ancient Romans do not seem to have derived aesthetic pleasure from mountains and other wild landscapes.

The essential infrastructure of tourism resembled that of today. Although travel was by foot, litter, carriage or on horseback, other facilities were much the same as today. Inns existed along the main routes and in the main centres. They bore familiar names: the Elephant, the Hind, the Cock. Outside the Mercury and Apollo in Lyons, the innkeeper, Septumanus, wrote:

> *Here Mercury promises you wealth, Apollo health, and Septumanus room and board. Whoever comes will be the better for it afterwards. Traveller - keep an eye on where you put up!*
>
> *(Casson 1974).*

Handlists were available showing the location of these inns. Owners of private houses would also rent out rooms, and it was possible to eat in a range of restaurants. In many tourist centres, guides were available, and their activities were sometimes the butt of satirical plays and poems. Cheap souvenirs were also abundant. Archaeologists have uncovered a wide range of these. In the Bay of Naples small glass vials with pictures entitled 'Lighthouse', 'Palace', 'Theatre', 'Nero's Pool' and 'Oyster Beds' have been found, and antique buying was common in the larger cities such as Rome.

With the break-up of the Roman Empire from the fifth century AD, social organisation and travel conditions deteriorated sharply. Tourism, which flourished in a prosperous, politically stable environment, contracted accordingly. There was an element of continuity, however, in the form of religious pilgrimages. The Roman Empire had been converted to Christianity in the fourth century AD, and travellers increasingly visited Palestine to see places associated with their new religion, including Jerusalem, Bethlehem, Bethany and Hebron. This tour became known as the peregrinatio ad loca sancta, and a series of hospices were created for accommodation on this journey (Hunt,1978).

This practice of travelling to religious shrines persisted throughout the Middle Ages, with pilgrimages to Jerusalem and to Rome as well as to other centres such as St James a Compostello in Spain and the shrine of Thomas a Becket at Canterbury. Political and religious conflicts, especially the Crusades, frequently placed enormous barriers to this form of travel, and the social and economic system of the Middle Ages, feudalism, was inimical to tourism. It can be assumed that travel for pleasure during the Middle Ages was far less common than it had been during the Roman Empire.

# Leisure and Tourism in the Middle Ages

A central problem of Northern European life in medieval times was that of devising technologies which sustained a permanent population in a self-contained agricultural life-style when land was no longer abundant. In England, the basic system which emerged was called the 'manorial system'. The essence of this system was a highly ordered and structured economy and society which enabled land to be farmed in such a way that an agricultural surplus was produced and the fertility of land holdings restored or maintained. The manorial system was successful in that it was sustained over a considerable period of time. Between Domesday (1086 AD) and the first outbreak of the Black Death (1348 AD) the population of England increased from around one million to some four million people.

## Leisure

Almost all aspects of life in medieval Britain were directly related to the seasonal pattern of agricultural life, and this included play. Festivals and holidays were related to the annual rhythm of the agricultural year, and in pre-Christian times these involved ceremonies intended to win the favour of the gods who controlled the natural elements upon which success or failure depended. A series of festivals were associated with ploughing time, seed time, first life (early growth), harvest, and mid-winter (when people implored the gods to allow the sun to return and bless them). Later, Christian symbolism became attached to these originally pre-Christian festivals. Hence the Saxon 'Yule' (Midwinter feast) became Christmas, the spring festival (Easter) came to incorporate a Christian notion of rebirth and harvest took on Christian symbolism. To these major periods of leisure (Christmas was celebrated for some fourteen days and Easter for seven) were added a large number of 'Saint's days' and, of course, fifty-two Sundays. These were not the only 'holydays', there were secular holidays too, including 'Ales days', generally organised by the lord of the manor as fund-raising occasions, and fair days in local market towns. Play was important in medieval life, and leisure time came in traditional 'chunks' of time including a large number of staccato breaks throughout the year. In all societies, play through its various expressions takes place mostly in the home or local community. In Medieval times the community dominated: miracle plays, mummings, fairs, football, wrestling, morris dancing, bear baiting and so on provided a relatively rich diet of community leisure and recreation. What, then, of tourism?

# Medieval Pilgrimage

The nearest thing there was to modern tourism in medieval times was the pilgrimage. How like the modern tourist was the medieval pilgrim? Christopher Holloway has written that two categories of conditions have to be met before private travel is encouraged:

> a) 'enabling conditions' or 'travel facilities' (which include time and money); and
>
> b) motives for travel.

# Travel Facilities

Modern scholars have been able to learn a good deal about Medieval travel facilities from contemporary reports contained in the writings of a fifteenth century Dominican friar, Brother Felix Fabri of Zurich.

Places of pilgrimage were the tourist resorts of their time. It is interesting to note that there were not only recognised places of pilgrimage, but also established ways of getting to them. British pilgrims favoured the journey to Santiago de Compostela, in North West Spain, where the body of St James was supposed to be buried. The established route was for the traveller to embark for Normandy or Bordeaux, and then cross France on one of the well-established pilgrim ways. All the pilgrim routes converged on St Jean Pied-de-Port, from where the pilgrim crossed by way of Cise and Roncevaux into Spain. Thence the pilgrim made his way along the northern pilgrim route to Santiago. By the fifteenth century, a network of travel facilities had built up along the route, including inns and hospices which catered specially for the pilgrim. It is interesting to note that a guide book of sorts was also available, though how pilgrims came to know of its contents is difficult to imagine. The book called the'Guide du Pelerin' was written by a twelfth-century monk named Aymery Picaud, who provided all kinds of useful advice about the journey, including methods of protecting oneself from horse flies when crossing the marshy and low-lying 'Pays de Landes' of Southern France, and warnings of areas where thieves and toll officials were likely to be lurking. (Mullins, 1974)

On the prestigious pilgrim routes, the supporting infrastructure was even more elaborate. The Knights of Malta were originally formed to establish and run rest houses for pilgrims in Jerusalem, and the Knights Templar also offered help and protection to pilgrims. They eventually became so skilful in general financial and currency arrangements that they became the bankers of Europe. Monastic orders provided an elaborate network of hospices and gave succour and shelter to all pilgrims, although Fabri notes that the best rooms, food and plate were reserved for those who could pay for them. If tourism brought an entrepreneurial spirit to the monasteries it also gave rise to numerous small businesses, inns, shipping agents, land carriers and guides, as well as a host of persons providing souvenirs and relics of doubtful value.

Fabri and others have described these enterprises, as well as the characteristics of pilgrims who 'chipped off fragments of buildings to take home with him'. Fabri himself admits to having collected a little bag of pebbles from Mount Sion and the Mount of Olives as well as the thorns which grew on the hedgerows (Gordon, 1972). The modern package tourist might well sympathise with the medieval pilgrim who was conducted around every place that had the least connection with the Scriptures or was forced to choose between half-day excursions to Bethlehem or the Dead Sea. The comparison between the medieval pilgrimage and the modern tourist industry can be elaborated, and is the more convincing the more detailed it becomes.

When journeying to Rome and the Holy Land, pilgrims were likely to be routed via Venice. Venice gained valuable commercial advantages from its location on the pilgrim route, and took seriously its responsibilities to the pilgrims. Venice regarded itself as the watchdog of fair trading and passed laws to ensure the pilgrim got what the various entrepreneurial agents in the city promised to deliver. In Venice inns were licensed by the state, and had to conform to set standards. 'Piazza guides', too, had specified duties which included acting as a pilgrim information bureau offering advice on language, currency and many other problems. The location and opening hours of Piazza guides were also specified. Similarly, regulations were laid down to try to control the business behaviour of transporting agents such as ships' captains. Strict rules were enforced to prevent the overloading of ships. Legal contracts between ship captains and their passengers were encouraged. Fabri records many details of the difficult and elaborate preparations which pilgrims had to make at Venice. Thirty to sixty ducats covered the cost of the return fare to Jaffa, two hot meals with good wine, and the arranging of transport and safe conduct on arrival. (Gordon, 1972) Is this the complete package with a 'no-surcharge' guarantee?

These expensive and exotic journeys represented the apex of a fairly well established hierarchy of pilgrimages. Domestic pilgrimages were undertaken by a wider spectrum of people whose pockets were smaller or whose travel characteristics were less adventurous. Pilgrimages to Canterbury, York, Durham, Ty Ddewi and other places were a common if not an everyday feature of medieval Britain. Chaucer's pilgrims in 'The Canterbury Tales' give some impression of the nature, spirit and purpose of the medieval pilgrimage.

# Motives for Travel

People travel on any one occasion for more than one reason. For most people, travel and tourism results from a combination of motives. The different motives people have for travelling suggest a classifying of tourism into business tourist travel, health tourist travel, incentive tourist travel, etc. Setting the travel motives of a medieval pilgrim in a religious framework is appropriate not only in terms of the individual, but also in terms of the general cultural perspectives of the pre-Renaissance Christian world. Within this cultural framework, many social and psychological needs akin to, or even identical with, those of the modern tourist are evident:

(i) The exploration, evaluation and subsequent enhancement of one's self would have been satisfied by the search for new experiences.

(ii) The cultural motivations which today draw many modern tourists to the classical sites of Greece, Rome and

Renaissance Europe would have led the medieval traveller to focus upon places which then dominated legend and folklore.

(iii) The need for personal and social esteem would be strong in an age when any pilgrimage (let alone a distant one) was rare, and, on his return, the pilgrim was listened to as a holy man.

(iv) The search for 'a good time' (a context which allowed less restrained behaviour than would be tolerated at home) seems to have been an increasingly important motive for travel as time went on. Some medieval pilgrims may have sought the salvation of their souls or the restoration of their health, but many, it seems, lost their moral restraints and 'made a journey into the arms of the devil'. (Gordon, 1972)

In general, therefore, consideration of leisure and tourism in the Middle Ages reveals a society in which play was important and one which provided a relatively rich variety of leisure and recreation at home. Those who 'played' away from home, though few in number, stimulated the growth of a general level of organisation similar to that on offer to the modern tourist. The sixteenth century, however, saw the virtual disappearance of pilgrimage as a significant element of the play and leisure pattern.

# Sixteenth, Seventeenth & Eighteenth Centuries

## Social and Technological Changes in Britain

As we considered in chapter 1 the Play, Leisure, Recreation and Travel (PLRT) pattern of tourists is an extremely important factor in determining the nature of tourism development. The PLRT pattern of the Middle Ages shows that certain elements of leisure were much as they are today. Something akin to modern tourism is recognisable. What forces modified the medieval pattern? From around 1500 to 1840 a variety of important processes altered the PLRT pattern. Changes in home-based leisure and recreation gathered pace during this period, and the effect of significant technological changes became more pronounced. These changes cannot be dated precisely because the process was gradual. Until the late eighteenth century, the basic pattern of pagan inheritances such as holy days, ale days, fairs and wakes still operated in what was essentially a rural society which changed very slowly. The rhythm and customs of the agricultural year were modified, but the broad framework of rural leisure remained intact. The main pastimes were still dancing, football, boxing, wrestling, foot racing and animal sports; in fact it was not until the eighteenth century that a new game called cricket emerged. Animal sports included cock fighting, horse and dog racing, otter baiting and dog fighting.

Of the economic changes that took place during the sixteenth and seventeenth centuries, a few tended to strengthen and sustain these medieval leisure patterns. Cottage industries, for example, left peasant workers still largely in control of their own time, and the public house remained the local organising centre for the recreational activities of a male-dominated society. The majority of the changes, however, tended to alter the patterns. The enclosure of common land and the consolidation of holdings tended to swell the ranks of the paupers. The game laws became more severe, and changes in religious practices, especially the rise of Methodism and Sabbath societies, altered the nature of Sundays. The social separation of the ruling class into a separate 'estate' with its own distinctive pattern of leisure including horse racing, shooting and hunting, combined with the development of an urban middle class interested in theatre, music  and literature, created social changes which were to become very significant in later years. Perhaps most significantly of all, life in the new factory and mill communities which were emerging at 'water-power sites' in Northern England and elsewhere laid stricter demands of space and time upon the workers. By the second half of the nineteenth century, under the dramatic influences of technological changes, these new constraints were to make a basic contribution to the transformation of PLRT patterns.

# The Importance of Britain in the Development of Travel and Tourism

Britain is often regarded as having played a crucial role in the development of modern tourism. A number of important factors are quoted as justification for this:

> (i) the institution of the Grand Tour of Europe;
>
> (ii) the rise of spas and seaside resorts;
>
> (iii) the growth of working-class tourism;
>
> (iv) the impact of Thomas Cook's innovations on organised tourism.

All of the above are frequently cited as uniquely British and, more specifically, English, contributions to the evolution of tourism. The economic prosperity of Britain in the eighteenth and nineteenth centuries certainly permitted more of its citizens to engage in tourism than was the case in other European countries, but the apparent uniqueness of Britain's contribution to tourism can be exaggerated, and it would be wrong to see tourism as an exclusively British invention.

Research into tourism in British society in the past has so far concentrated on two main phases. These are:

> (i)  the growth from the sixteenth to nineteenth centuries of tourism abroad undertaken by a social elite: this became known as 'the Grand Tour';
>
> (ii) the development of spas and seaside resorts in Britain during the eighteenth and nineteenth centuries.

Other forms of tourism, such as tours around Britain and cheap alternative holidays to the seaside, have not yet been studied in any great detail.

# The Grand Tour

The best-known form of tourism engaged in by the British from the seventeenth to the early nineteenth century was their Grand Tour of Europe. It

was the most prestigious form of travel and was confined to the ranks of the wealthy elite in society. Essentially, the Grand Tour was a circuit of Western Europe undertaken for culture, education and pleasure. It is worth remembering, however, that the British were not the only nationality to have made the Grand Tour. Wealthy people from France, Germany and Russia also toured Europe, but never in such large numbers as British people.

Most of the British Grand Tourists were drawn from the ranks of the landed classes of peers and gentry. This group had the time and money for touring. Their wealth was generally derived from the rents from the large landed estates they owned. As the British economy expanded during the eighteenth century, more middle-class people undertook the Grand Tour as their share of wealth increased. Of course, these social groups were only a small minority of the total population. In the eighteenth century the landed classes comprised some 2.5% of the population, while the middle classes accounted for some 4-6%. High incomes were concentrated in the hands of these groups, however. The landed classes possessed around 14-15% of the national income and the middle classes about 13-17%.

The majority of Grand Tourists were men in their late teens or early twenties. During the eighteenth century, as more middle-class travellers made the tour, the average age of Grand Tourists rose. The reasons for their undertaking the tour were many and varied. During the seventeenth century, some were seeking potential training in diplomacy for a career in government, others to improve their social skills in dancing, riding, fencing or to improve their knowledge of the world. Later on, the dominant interest was probably in cultural pursuits such as art and architecture, or in enjoying the freedom that distance from home can bring. Other tourists travelled to the warmer climates of Southern Europe in an effort to improve their health. For most, a whole range of motives underlay their decision to tour abroad, not least the desire to acquire the social prestige to be derived from so spectacular a show of expenditure.

The general cultural environment in Britain and Europe was important for the Grand Tour. There was an increasing interest in the fine arts and, for the British Grand Tourist, the best examples of art and architecture were to be found abroad, in France, and above all in Italy. A strong taste for the antiquities of the Roman Empire was combined with an admiration for the styles of the Renaissance. The country seats of the landed classes reflected these tastes. The classical architecture of the stately home echoed the styles of Italy, whilst inside, the rooms became repositories for art treasures purchased during a Grand Tour.

The itinerary of the Grand Tour remained remarkably constant over the centuries. Paris was the dominant cultural and political centre of Europe in the seventeenth and eighteenth centuries, and was generally the first centre visited on the tour. From there, the Roman antiquities at Vienne, Orange and the Pont du Gard in the lower Rhone Valley might be visited before the traveller crossed the Alps to Turin and Milan. Italy was always the principal goal of the Tour and it was there that the most clearly defined route patterns were found. The major circuit was to Florence, Rome and Naples, the traveller returning northwards through Rome again and so on to Venice. From Venice the tourist could come home via Switzerland and Germany, visiting centres such as Dresden and Vienna and perhaps using the River Rhine as a convenient routeway to the Low Countries. This tour could take anything from two to four years, sometimes even longer.

In the later eighteenth century, cultural tastes diversified to a certain extent, with a growing interest being taken in mountains and picturesque scenery as well as in medieval architecture. Grand Tourists of the later eighteenth and early nineteenth centuries, therefore, increasingly visited the scenic splendours of Switzerland (and developed resorts such as Chamonix) as well as exploring the picturesque medieval towns of central Italy such as Arezzo and Perugia.

The travel infrastructure that the Grand Tourists used remained, until the nineteenth century, much the same as it had been for centuries. Thus, transport systems and accommodation created for all forms of travel were used, and there was little specifically devoted to the tourist. Accommodation consisted of the hostels, inns and post houses established for generations of pilgrims and merchants. Major centres generally offered a range of rooms that could be rented for longer periods. During the seventeenth and eighteenth centuries, some centres became increasingly famous for the size and quality of their accommodation and catered specifically for the tourist. Florence and Frankfurt am Main possessed some of the best hotels in Europe, and districts such as the Faubourg St Germain in Paris and the Piazza di Spagna in Rome became dominated by hotels and lodgings.

Grand Tourists made up one part of the regular clientele of the extensive transport services that existed throughout Europe. Regular passenger services could be found on most of the major rivers, such as the Rhine, Rhone, Danube, Po and Loire, as well as on the canals. The canal system in the Low Countries was especially well regulated, with timetables and fixed fares. On land, the post system, with relays of horses, extended throughout much of Europe by the late sixteenth century. Regular stage-coach services operated in France and parts of Italy and Germany from the mid-seventeenth century and became widespread by the mid-eighteenth century. Tourists could also make use of the veturino system (as it was called in Italy), or the voiturier system (as it was called in France). Here, a contract was made between the traveller and a horse-and-carriage dealer who would accompany the traveller for a fixed period or between specified places.

Gradually, the volume of wealthy tourists travelling in Europe resulted in some services being organised exclusively for their use. By the mid-eighteenth century, at Dessein's 'Hotel d'Angleterre' in Calais, travellers could hire or buy a carriage for their European tour. Outside Geneva, another 'Hotel d'Angleterre' arranged for the transport of passengers arriving from London, Paris, Switzerland and Italy. By the early nineteenth century, a Mr Emery at the White Bear in Piccadilly was arranging 'package tours' of Europe. He undertook to transport passengers to Switzerland in sixteen days, with two days in Paris, including all lodgings, food and transport, incorporated in the price.

The volume of tourists also made an impact in a number of ways upon the host countries. In Switzerland, by the 1830s innkeepers were estimated to be among the wealthiest and most influential inhabitants in some cantons. It also seems that prices had a tendency to rise when wealthy British tourists arrived in an area. The fashionable health resort of Montpellier was considered very expensive in the 1760s, as was Naples later in the century. Sometimes, prices would vary with the tourist season. In Rome, prices rose during Easter when the city was full of visitors, but they could fall by one half during the summer months when the city was abandoned by the tourists. The major centres on the Grand Tour had a range of souvenirs on sale, and some shops catered for their English customers by stocking goods from London.

As the number of middle-class tourists from Britain making the Grand Tour increased, so the landed classes moved away from the traditional itinerary and visited more isolated areas such as Greece, the Middle East and Portugal. For them, the social prestige of visiting Paris and Rome was gone, and ever more exotic places were visited, where the attractiveness of a region was in inverse proportion to the number of tourists from other social groups. By the 1820s and 1830s, the Grand Tour of Europe as an institution for the social elite in Britain had disappeared.

As tourism abroad was possible for the British landed classes and later on for sections of the middle classes, so certain locations within Britain became established as tourist centres. A greater range of social groups participated in this domestic tourism, because, of course, the demands on time and pocket were not so great as for travel abroad. Social group differences were, however, illustrated by the different resorts within Britain frequented by each social class.

## Spas and Seaside Resorts in Britain

A number of important factors helped the growth of spas and seaside resorts:

(i) Those same social and economic conditions which formed the background to the Grand Tour also affected developments within Britain. Leisure time and wealth enabled the landed classes to be the first to visit both spa centres and seaside resorts and, as with the Grand Tour, they were followed, from the later eighteenth century, by the expanding middle classes of an increasingly prosperous Britain. Indeed, by the nineteenth century a degree of wealth and leisure time had filtered through to some sections of the working classes and this enabled them to participate in some forms of tourism.

(ii) The cultural environment produced a desire to seek health cures, and the existence of this desire helped to promote the development first of the spa centres and later of the seaside resorts. In both cases, the health motive was quickly superseded by the inclination towards activities associated more with pleasure, and the spas and seaside resorts outside London became centres of fashion.

**Some Important Spas in England and Wales**

Harrogate
Ilkley
Scarborough
Llandrindod Wells
Llanwyrtyd Wells
Builth Wells
Buxton
Boston Spa
Tenbury
Matlock
Droitwich
Woodhall Spa
Llangammarch Wells
Hotwell
Malvern
Bath
Cheltenham Spa
Leamington Spa
London
Sadlers Wells
Islington Spa
Epsom
Dulwich
Tunbridge Wells

(iii) A changing technological environment helped the development of resorts. Road travel improved during the eighteenth century, and from the mid-nineteenth century rail travel revolutionised access to tourism centres, particularly those on the coasts. Thus an improving travel infrastructure served to open up tourist locations to a wider range of social groups who were able to engage in tourism because of increased wealth and a trend towards holidays with pay.

In tracing the development of spa and seaside resorts it is possible to identify three main eras:

(a.) The mid-sixteenth century to the 1780s saw the growth and popularity of spas for the social elite.

(b.) From the 1780s, seaside resorts became increasingly fashionable, first for the elite and later for the middle classes.

(c.) After the 1870s, seaside resorts experienced their heyday, with visitors drawn from both the middle and the working classes. Different resorts tended to cater for different social groups.

## British Spas

The medieval pilgrim looking for a miracle health cures gradually gave way to the spa-visitor. People visited spas because the medical and (quasi-) scientific notions of the time held that drinking or bathing in mineral-rich waters was health-giving. During the sixteenth century, springs at places such as Bath and Buxton were developed for the sick by town corporations. Gradually, a range of entertainments, such as plays, tennis or bowls, came to be provided for convalescents. The transition from health to pleasure was hardly perceptible, but from the 1660s, with the restoration of the monarchy, pleasure was in fashion for the social elite. By 1700, Bath, Tunbridge Wells and Epsom were the main spas, but there were over 100 scattered throughout the country. The transformation of squalid, unfashionable springs into elegant resorts for a fashion-conscious elite following the pleasant routines of well-conducted soirées, was associated with entrepreneurs, of whom Richard (Beau) Nash is the most famous. Spas became fashionable, with royal or aristocratic patronage playing a key role in establishing which spas were in fashion at any one time.

Degree of access from London helped to define a social hierarchy at the spas. Bath and Buxton were sufficiently distant to attract only the wealthy, but around London greater differences could be seen. As Daniel Defoe noted in 1724:

> *As the nobility and gentry go to Tunsbridge, the*
> *Merchants and Rich Citizens to Epsome, so the*
> *Common People go chiefly to Dullwich and Stretham.*
> *(Pimlott 1947)*

The most famous spa was Bath. Royal approval came with visits from Queen Anne in 1702 and 1703. In 1705, Beau Nash became 'Master of Ceremonies' and helped to create a range of attractions such as the Assembly Rooms and

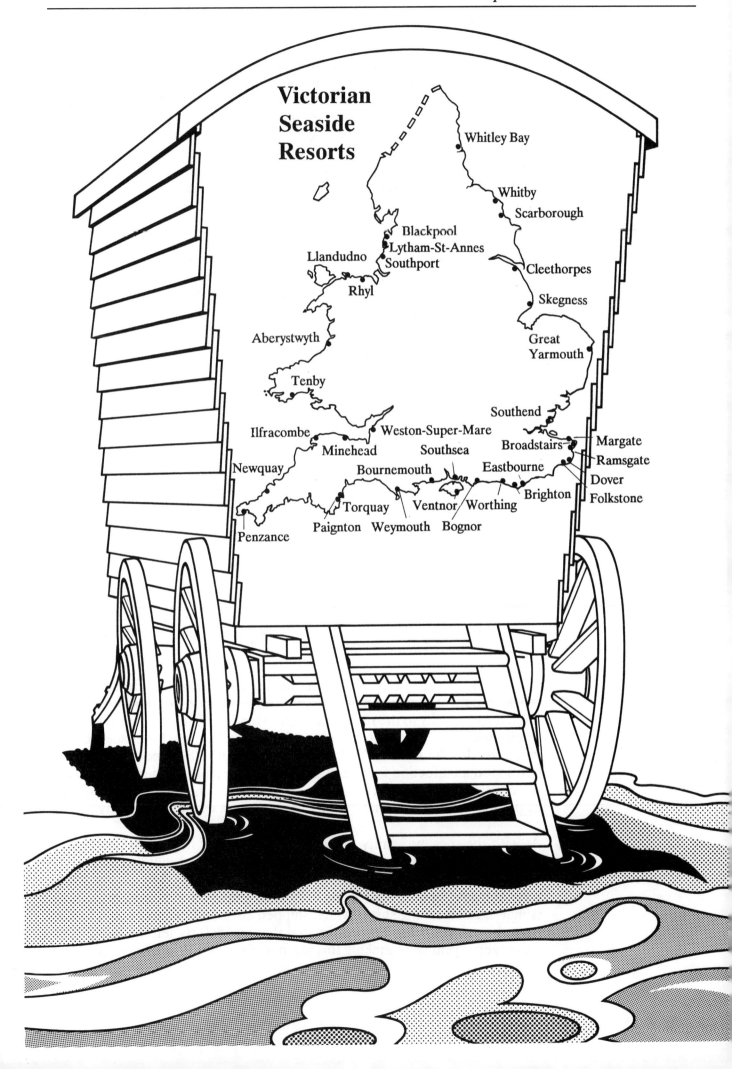

**Victorian Seaside Resorts**

Whitley Bay
Whitby
Scarborough
Blackpool
Lytham-St-Annes
Llandudno
Southport
Cleethorpes
Rhyl
Skegness
Aberystwyth
Great Yarmouth
Tenby
Southend
Ilfracombe
Weston-Super-Mare
Broadstairs
Margate
Minehead
Southsea
Ramsgate
Newquay
Bournemouth
Eastbourne
Dover
Brighton
Folkstone
Torquay
Ventnor
Worthing
Paignton
Weymouth
Bognor
Penzance

Pump Room, as well as providing street lighting and improving the road from London. His regulations for admission to the spa helped to maintain the resort's social exclusiveness. Bath was the prototype for other spas, developing relaxing and gentle patterns of 'play' which remain part of the holiday image even today. By the later eighteenth century increasing numbers of middle-class tourists were able to visit the spas and imitate the activities of the landed classes. Improved transport helped to accelerate this process. In the 1750s it took three days to travel from London to Bath; by 1827, the coach took only twelve and a half hours.

The later fortunes of the spas were nevertheless various. Cheltenham became highly fashionable in the 1780s; Leamington in the 1820s and 1830s. In fact, spas probably did not decline as much as has been thought. They certainly lost their fashionable exclusiveness, but in terms of numbers of tourists attracted they probably remained very significant centres throughout the nineteenth century. Some spas were revived, for the middle classes, when the railways came, for example Buxton in 1867 and Llandrindod Wells in 1866. Woodhall Spa in Lincolnshire developed as a middle-class wateringplace as late as the 1890s. It is interesting to note that an English obsession with the activities of the aristocracy can often distort our views of what are significant social trends.

## British Seaside Resorts

The first seaside resorts originated, like the spas, as a result of health considerations. Sea bathing was held to be therapeutic in accordance with the already perceived value of mineral waters, while from the earliest years of the eighteenth century medical treatises had drawn attention to the health-giving properties of cold sea-water baths.

Scarborough, Margate and Brighton had limited sea-bathing seasons by the 1730s. By 1800, seaside resorts had become a small but significant element in the PLRT pattern. Such resorts were modelled on the elegant lines of the inland spas. Royal and aristocratic patronage helped to create a fashionable image. The Duke of Gloucester, for instance, visited Brighton in 1765, the Prince Regent in 1783. The pavilion was started in 1784, and Brighton soon replaced Bath as the fashionable leisure centre outside London. Weymouth owed its prosperity to the recommendation made to King George III that he would find some restoration of his sanity by sea bathing. He made his first visit after his initial attack of mental illness in 1789, and subsequently developed an affection for the place. The fashionable elements of London society flocked to take a house at Brighton for the season, and by the beginning of the nineteenth century the town was expanding rapidly.

As with the spas, proximity to London was another important factor. The Kent resorts such as Margate and Ramsgate developed rapidly in the early 1800s, attracting an ever-widening range of social groups. Margate began to receive from London, boat loads of holiday-makers travelling on the hoys (single-masted sailing ships) which shipped corn and general cargo to and from the capital. It has been estimated that by 1800 something like 20,000 passengers a year were making this journey (Gordon, 1972). Later, pleasure steamers brought cheap and quick access to the South East coast for Londoners, whether for a day excursion or a more prolonged visit.

The coming of the railways accelerated the growth of the coastal resorts and helped to promote certain seaside resorts when they arrived in the town. For example, the railway came to Cleethorpes in 1846 and to Skegness in 1871. Many resorts developed a distinctive 'social tone' the exact cause of which it is often difficult to explain. In Kent, Sheerness was seen as humble and cheap, Broadstairs was essentially middle-class, while Folkestone was regarded as rather fashionable. Some resorts maintained a degree of social exclusiveness by limiting their range of facilities, for instance Lytham St Annes near Blackpool. Others, such as Bournemouth, could rely on distance from London to maintain a more 'respectable' air.

Improved transport was a key to the development of these play-places. Indeed it could be said that the single most important factor in the development of modern tourism has been technological change. It is important for the student of tourism to recognise how vital a role man's inventions have played in determining the ways in which modern recreation and tourism have developed.

## The Emergence of the Industrial Age

Many of the changes which took place in Britain in the first half of the nineteenth century subsequently brought about the industrial society of the second half of the century. This change in society was accelerated by the remarkable spate of inventions which occurred in the early nineteenth century. These inventions were to have a profound effect on society in general and, of particular interest here, in the ability of people to travel. These inventions followed from the invention of the steam engine, and its subsequent introduction into an entirely new type of environment concentrated on the coalfields. This new environment created many changes in society.

(i) There was a total change in the PLRT pattern of these new coalfield societies. The dominance of the factory and mill destroyed old rhythms and created new ones. Industrial society imposed new demands on people which affected their disposable time and discretionary income. Once the versatility of the steam engine had been established the changes came quickly. By 1850 more people in Britain lived in towns and cities than lived outside the urban areas, and 30% of the work force were employed in manufacturing as opposed to 20% in agriculture. In the new industrial towns, leisure diminished at first, not only because the new factories demanded long hours of labour (often seventy hours in a six-day week) and employed men, women and children, but also because the social infrastructure of play had disintegrated. Clarke and Critcher (1985) state that it was during this period that leisure came to be recognised as a discrete area of human activity. 'The form industrialisation took in the mid nineteenth century ensured that what was an artificial imposition would be taken for granted by succeeding generations ... ' This 'artificial imposition' was the notion of leisure as the antithesis of work and as a compensation for labour.

(ii) There was a time lag or delay in the change of work and living patterns leading to a decrease in 'play'. If a decrease in time for 'play' was the immediate effect of the industrial age, this was followed in the period between 1870 and 1914 by an increase in leisure.

One important change in this period, resulting from the development of the economic system which began with the new industrial societies of nineteenth century Britain, was that people increased their demand for marketable goods and services. Increased consumption made the system work.

Two major stages in this pattern can be seen. First, there was a delay before the inventions which stimulated the economic changes had their effect on the economy. Hence, in the first industrial revolution, significant inventions such as Darby's coke-smelting process for iron (1709), Cromption's mule (1779), Cartwright's power loom (1785) and the steam locomotive (Trevithic 1820 and Stevenson 1825) sometimes considerably preceded the establishment of the new industrial complexes on the coalfields of Britain, though they were very important elements in them. Second, there was a further delay before the new industrial society created as a result of these inventions was able to adjust its patterns of Play, Leisure, Recreation and Travel to meet the new situation.

Whilst a decrease in leisure time was characteristic of the earlier stages of industrial expansion, the period from about 1870 saw some increase in leisure provision. As we noted earlier, this may have been because the new system demanded an increasing consumption of marketable goods and services. Alternatively the increase in leisure could have been linked to the need to keep the new industrial classes happy and to establish patterns of social control and stability in the new urban concentrations. Whatever the reasons, the effects were clear enough. Real working-class income rose by 90% between 1840 and 1900, new patterns of wholesaling and retailing emerged including the introduction of co-operative and multiple stores, and new transport systems such as railways and urban tramways were developed. Hence not only did disposable income increase but this was accompanied by changing conditions which allowed people to travel more. Legislation which shortened the working day such as the Factory Acts of 1850, 1867 and 1874 and the Bank Holiday Acts of 1871 and 1875 gave Parliamentary approval to the notion of leisure time. Organised games, often nurtured in the public schools and eagerly embraced by the reform churches, emerged at this time. The first rules of football were drafted in Cambridge in 1862, and the Football League was founded in 1888; the Rugby Union was founded in 1871 and the Rugby League in 1895. Newly established local authorities found themselves involved in the provision of open spaces, public parks and swimming pools. Public library provision became widespread, and choral societies and brass bands became characteristic features of industrial towns and villages. It became necessary to license all public houses and public places of entertainment, and concern over the dominance of licensed pubs and music halls led to the emergence of Temperance Clubs and working men's clubs, which by the 1880s had half a million members.

This period also saw the beginning of a new leisure movement as an increasing number of people sought to escape from the new conurbations to the countryside. Cycling clubs and ramblers' associations owed their origins to the urban middle class but became increasingly important features of working-class leisure.

This period also saw the beginnings of a very rapid growth in tourism, which was related both to the changing leisure patterns discussed above and to the revolution in transport. Steam boats began to replace the old Margate hoys in the 1820s, and between 1800 and 1835 the number of passengers had increased five-fold to some 10,000 people, but it was the new steam locomotive which principally served to step up travel. The railway system was established at an extraordinary speed. In the twenty-five years after the successful establishment of the Stockton and Darlington railway, some 7,000 miles of railway track were laid and eighty million passenger journeys were made each year (Gordon 1972). The cost of rail travel decreased rapidly in real terms between 1840 and 1860, and excursion trains began to be a feature of the life of the industrial conurbation. In 1845 the excursion trains from Manchester carried 15,000 passengers on Whit Monday, and enterprising businessmen such as Thomas Cook began to hire excursion trains at their own risk and offer tickets for sale to the general public.

At this point it is worth considering two important developments in tourism which both occurred at approximately the same time and which both had significant influences on tourism in this country and abroad. These are the development of organised tours by Thomas Cook and the emergence of tourism in North America.

# Thomas Cook

In Britain organised 'package tours' for tourists going abroad had begun to emerge in an embryonic form by the 1820s and 1830s. This development has generally been attributed to Thomas Cook, but it seems more likely that Cook adapted and promoted a travel infrastructure that was already in existence. The history of Thomas Cook is not the whole history of travel abroad in the nineteenth century. In fact, the firm's archives, although rich in its advertising literature, tell us little of the company's economic history. Nevertheless, the expansion of Cook's enterprise can be seen as symbolic of the growth of tourism abroad in the nineteenth century.

Cook began in 1841 with a small temperance excursion on the Midland railway from Leicester to Loughborough. (It is interesting to note the connection between the temperance movement and the early excursionists. Most of Thomas Cook's early enterprises were organised for temperance societies. John Frame's popular 'Highland's' also had temperance connections, and Sir Henry Lunn's entry into the tourist business arose out of a religious conference in Grindelwald in 1892.) Cook developed his plans for organised, inclusively priced excursions on a rapidly expanding scale. In 1845, 350 people were taken to Liverpool and then on to Caernafon and Yr Wyddfa (Mount Snowdon). In 1846, a trip was made to Glasgow and Edinburgh. Cook devised a Circular Ticket whereby the traveller purchased tickets for specific routes of his own devising, using them as required and returning any unused tickets at the end of the tour. By the 1850s, these were selling well to visitors to the seaside resorts.

The most popular destination for these excursions was the seaside, and the period saw the mushrooming of resorts around the British coast. A whole panoply of seaside attractions quickly established themselves: piers, pier-theatres, camera-obscuras, weighing machines, peep shows, slot machines, picture postcards and ice cream rapidly became the standard provisions of the seaside resorts. The seaside holiday, with stays as long as a week, was almost entirely restricted to the middle class, but by the turn of the century some working-class families, led by those from the Lancashire mills with their traditional Wakes Week, could afford to stay at the new seaside boarding houses. Blackpool was the first resort to develop this type of holiday, and other resorts quickly followed suit.

Some discerning tourists sought solitude and peace in the Lake District or the Scottish Highlands, while the disenchanted aristocracy, perceiving their seaside resorts swamped by trades people and factory workers, looked further afield for their holiday pleasures. The establishment of a continental railway system in the late nineteenth century drew the aristocracy to the Riviera, where small towns like Cannes and Nice flourished and grew. Monaco offered the opportunity to relocate the elegance of the Beau Nash salon with all its gambling excitement. Switzerland, which had long been famous for health holidays, also became a holiday playground for the rich British tourist who had developed a modish taste for remote mountain scenery. The Alpine Club had been established as early as 1850.

Gradually, Cook turned his attention to catering for the growing numbers of professional middle-class tourists and their increasing tendency to travel abroad. A trip to the Paris Exhibition in 1855 was followed by one to Switzerland in 1863. This was an excursion of 21 days, including a visit to Paris. The following year Cook moved on to Italy. By 1866 he was in North America, and by 1872 he had organised his first round-the-world tour.

Many regions felt the impact of Cook's ventures. India, Australia, the Middle East, the Holy Land and South Africa were included and the whole of his 'empire' was linked from the later nineteenth century by the coming of the telegraph. Offices throughout the world were able to organise and serve the needs of the Cook's tourist.

Cook's, however, were not the only tour agents operating. Firms such as Dean and Dawson's, Frame's and Sir Henry Lunn developed during the later nineteenth century. Some were not purely commercial. The Polytechnic Touring Association, established in 1872, and the Co-operative Holidays Association begun in 1891, had social and educational aims, and were concerned with improving the quality of holidays for working people. These firms may not have had the glamour of some of the Thomas Cook enterprises, but they nevertheless represented significant developments in the increased organisation of tourism. There has been a tendency for tourism to become increasingly 'industrialised', with tourist flows depending more upon the decision of tourist firms than the whims of the individual tourist. Today, most tourists select 'packages' from firms who have organised the transport, itinerary and accommodation in advance. This development clearly has its roots in the nineteenth century, when an expanding tourist population enabled companies to specialise in catering for their different travel and tourism needs.

# The Emergence of Tourism in North America

The development of tourism in the nineteenth century was not confined to Britain. Similar patterns of growth can be seen in other countries, both in Western Europe and in North America. In the early nineteenth century, North American seaside resorts catered, like their British counterparts, for the wealthier classes. Newport, Rhode Island, Nahant, Massachusetts, and Cape May on the New Jersey shore were similar to Brighton and Eastbourne. There were also spa resorts, such as Saratoga Springs in upstate New York. By the 1850s, however, a broader social involvement in tourism was apparent, and wealthy Americans began to travel to the cultural centres of Europe. Their motives were similar to those of the Grand Tourists, and their itinerary resembled that of the Grand Tour. At the same time, resorts like Atlantic City were catering for other classes now able to travel by cheap and quick rail journey from the main urban centres.

In Canada, major urban centres were also generating tourists. The wealthy of Toronto, who lived by Lake Ontario, travelled to the resorts of the St Lawrence or to the Atlantic seaside resorts in Maine. More local holidays took them to Niagara to admire the Falls or to St Catherine's to take the waters. By the 1870s, excursion steamers were traversing the Great Lakes, while proliferating rail routes and improved road conditions were opening up the forests and the Lakes of the Canadian Shield to the north of Toronto. Steamers and a hotel appeared on the Muskoka Lakes in the late 1860s, and by the late 1880s wealthy visitors from Southern Ontario were buying handsome villas on islands in the Lakes.

One difference between American and British resorts was that the American centres consciously saw themselves as catering for all social groups. The citizens of Atlantic City liked visitors to regard their resort as 'a thoroughly democratic place'. A guidebook in 1895 claimed that it was

> *no uncommon sight to see the children of millionaires*
> *and the little ones of laboring men riding happily on the*
> *merry-go-round at the same time and perhaps to find the*
> *parents fraternizing on the Switchback Railway.*
> *(Lewis, 1980)*

Problems arose, however, through racial prejudice. Black people in Atlantic City were restricted to the 'negro pier', and there were race riots in Chicago when black people used a white bathing area on Lake Michigan.

Perhaps the egalitarianism of North American society was more apparent than real. Just as in Britain, the geographical location of tourist centres revealed social differences. For Torontonians, relatively inaccessible resorts such as Muskoka, Thirty Thousand Islands and Stony Lake in the Kawarthas were socially select, whereas Scarborough Beach on Lake Ontario was more proletarian.

# Leisure and Tourism Patterns from 1850 until the First World War

It is the range of social groups engaging in it which makes the development of nineteenth-century British tourism so interesting. Too often, it is thought that tourism has spread to the great mass of people only since the Second World War. Yet significant groups of working-class people participated in tourism before then, even though on a more limited scale. A social survey of York in 1901 revealed that over 50% of its working-class population took a few days summer holiday away from the city. This general trend was the result of a number of factors:

a. Statutory holidays with pay were introduced.

b. The 1871 Bank Holiday Act not only sanctioned some of the traditional holidays, but added to them.

c. This was carried further in 1875 with the Holidays Extension Act. *The Times* noted in 1871 that there had been 'an increasing tendency of late years among all classes to find excuses for Holydays'.

One of the first areas in Britain to experience working-class tourism on an appreciable scale was the Lancashire coast, with visitors going there from the nearby textile towns in the south and east of the county. From the 1870s, the Lancashire cotton towns created Britain's first specialised working-class resort development, with Blackpool as the pre-eminent resort.

For working-class people to be able to engage in tourism, a number of conditions had to be present:

(i) with limited time and money available for holidays, working-class people had to have access to cheap and rapid transport to the coast, and this was provided by the coming of the railways in the 1850s;

(ii) working-class people also had to earn a reasonable income in order to save money for holidays, as holidays with pay were rare in the mid-nineteenth century;

(iii) in addition, a series of consecutive days' holiday was needed, and this depended on the approval of employers;

(iv) also, the industrial labour force had to have the desire to spend its time and money at the seaside instead of in alternative ways;

(v) finally, the resorts themselves had to be geared to coping with the demands of a particular clientele. Blackpool, for instance, responded fully to the new challenge, while Southport resisted popular amusements and cheaper accommodation and retained a more middle-class image.

Wage levels in the cotton industry were relatively high and young men could set aside reasonable amounts of money for recreation. Families with teenage children had additional sources of income as wages were relatively generous for adolescents. In the weaving towns of Lancashire wages for women workers were among the highest in the country. Furthermore, employment in the cotton industry was fairly stable and so money could be assigned to holidays. One way of doing this was through a network of saving and mutual insurance schemes. By the 1880s 'going off' clubs were well established in many Lancashire towns. In 1889, Oldham achieved for itself a full week's holiday in the summer and £40,000 was saved through clubs. Three years later, about £80,000 was saved.

Although many industrial workers had very limited amounts of free time, from the 1840s employers in the cotton industry began to allow holidays in an effort to improve productivity and reduce absenteeism. It was better to close a mill for an agreed period in the summer than suffer constant disruption. Oldham and Darwen acquired a week's holiday in 1889 and were later followed by Chorley and Nelson. Different towns took their holidays at different times throughout the summer, and this had the effect of producing a prolonged season for the seaside resorts. Blackpool, Rhyl, Douglas, New Brighton and Scarborough all responded to this demand. Trips were often organised at street level or through Sunday schools, pubs or sports clubs, and relatives and neighbours would stay in the same boarding house. Some industrialised towns were said to be virtually empty during the holiday period. Tourism was obviously important in the lives of these industrial workers and their families. In the 1890s, an Oldham mule spinner allocated £15 a year for expenses out of an income of £206 'especially for holiday during factory holidays for self and family' (Pimlott,1947).

The initial growth in working-class seaside holidays may have begun in Lancashire, but the West Riding wool towns soon followed Lancashire's example, as did the steel town of Sheffield. By the 1880s, skilled workmen from Birmingham were visiting North Wales and Blackpool for 4-5 days' holiday. Elsewhere, however, growth was slower. In some areas, workers adhered to the traditional holidays scattered throughout the year rather than combining them to provide opportunities for tourism. Thus the Potteries and the Black Country lagged behind other regions as their local culture did not adapt so readily to the changing times.

By the turn of the century a new pattern of leisure and recreation had been established in Britain and though it was to undergo major modifications, it was in essence to be adopted by every major industrialised country in the world.

# Tourism's 'Drive to Maturity' - 1920-1960

We have seen that the period between 1850 and 1918 was one in which the new industrial society emerged and new patterns of leisure and tourism developed. The period which followed it from about 1920 to 1960 has been described as tourism's 'Drive to Maturity'.

During the period following the First World War, a transformation was brought about by the impact of a series of new inventions. What is noticeable about these inventions is that they all took place during the second half of the nineteenth century or in the earliest years of the twentieth century.

Again, there was a delayed response in the economic and social reaction to these inventions. One major economic change affected the distribution of the industrial world's population. With the invention of electricity and the motor car, industry was technically free to locate almost anywhere, yet what actually resulted was 'new concentrations of industry and services and population away from the coalfields, in the great metropolitan regions' (Hall, 1966). The reason for this was that although industry itself might be free to decentralise, the offices which administered industry were not. Companies established their head offices next to financial institutions and banking centres. The support services which established around these generated a massive expansion in white collar employment. These commercial centres subsequently attracted particular kinds of manufacturing industries associated with the new technology and the growing retail market. This pattern is the prime cause of the growth of new metropolitan centres in the early twentieth century.

The new technology brought with it new forms of leisure. While sporting events remained a mass recreational activity, by 1926 the cinema had attracted over 20 million people weekly to the 3,000 or so cinemas up and down Britain. In the 1930s and 1940s, cinema audiences continued to grow. Listening to the radio became a national pastime, with under thirty thousand licences held in 1922 but over two million by 1926 and nearly ten million by 1939. Family-centred leisure grew in importance in the new dormitory housing estates within commuting distance of the new metropolitan business centres.

During the inter-war period, a remarkable range of holidays became available to a steadily increasing public. Although seaside holidays remained the mainstay of working and middle-class tourism, new activity holidays became important. The popularity of the walking tour led to the foundation of the Youth Hostel Association in 1930 on the model of the successful German Youth Inns. The older generation was catered for by organisations such as the Holiday Fellowship and the Co-operative Holidays Association, while the more wealthy were able to buy and rent cottages in the green country-side of the Home Counties or the Yorkshire dales. Excursions into the suburban countryside, offering itself to a mobile urban population transported now not only by train but also coach and bus, became a feature of the leisure and holiday scene. When the motor-bike and small cheap car (though cars were affordable only by the well off until after the Second World War) appeared on the market, exploration of the countryside increased at an even faster pace. By 1939 there were over three million registered vehicles in the United Kingdom, and RAC and AA boxes had become familiar features of the rural landscape.

Just two years previously, in 1937, the first Butlins holiday camp was opened in Skegness. The holiday camp may be regarded as the harbinger of the age of mass consumption in holidays, and after the 1939-45 war Butlins camps boomed. Some camps, claiming to offer everything that the holiday-maker needed, could accommodate over 5,000 people, and a rash of caravan and chalet settlements sprang up along the British coastline.

Overseas tourism expanded after 1946, largely because of the expansion of air services. World War Two set up conditions extremely favourable for the expansion of civil aviation. A large body of experienced pilots was created, and thousands of airports had been built over much of the world. Not only had aircraft, navigational equipment and knowledge of weather forecasting improved, but a large assortment of surplus aircraft were available for purchase and conversion to civilian use. Perhaps most important of all, public acquaintance with aviation had increased enormously, and ordinary people were ready to regard aircraft as a mode of transport they were likely to use. By the early 1960s, the charter flight (in so many ways the re-enactment of Cook's railway excursions) opened the door to cheap, long distance flights and the period of mass consumption overseas tourism had arrived. This may be seen as part of a wider pattern of mass consumption of consumer durables, based on the twin foundations of real increases in disposable income (which doubled from 1951 to 1972) and consumer credit.

# The 1960s and the Growth of Mass International Tourism

The 1960s saw an enormous increase in the development of overseas tourism following the introduction of charter flights and economy class fares. International tourist arrivals increased from 25 million in 1950 to 183 million in 1970 and subsequently to some 300 million by the late 1980s. In Britain the percentage of holidays taken overseas has risen in the same period from 5% to over 20%.

Surveys of hobbies and recreational activities suggest that they have changed less dramatically than tourism patterns. Recreation in Britain still follows much the same pattern as that which developed as a response to the technological advances described earlier. A recent list (G J Ashworth, 1984) of leisure activities in England and Wales shows that the only new feature is the emergence of television as a leading leisure element. There are certainly interesting changes in participation rates in certain activities, such as the emergence of squash as a popular sport but, generally speaking, it is the informal recreational activities which have increased in popularity. This trend has strengthened the position of the family as the cornerstone of contemporary leisure patterns, whether it is in the planned used of a newly built leisure centre or the provision of the family annual holiday.

Yet as we have seen, each era in the development of our current industrial society has generated inventions and innovations which have been at the root of changes which have transformed the economic and social structure of society. Some authors, such as Brzezinski and Toffler, have suggested that the impact of new technologies, especially micro-computers, automation and cybernetic systems, will bring about a transformation more dramatic in its historic and human consequences than any previously experienced by mankind. Visions of the future are necessarily speculative, but there is already enough evidence from changes which have taken place to date to show that the introduction of new technologies will affect population distribution, leisure and holidays. Brzezinski's predictions are especially interesting. He presents a detached picture of a society in which every aspect is influenced culturally, psychologically, socially and economically by the impact of technology and electronics. In such a society, leisure will become the normal practice, and active work the exception 'bestowed as a privilege' upon the most talented, capable of managing and developing the complex technology. The picture Brzezinski presents of a leisure-focused society in the USA 'where spectator spectacles such as mass sports and TV provide the opiate for increasingly purposeless masses' seemed highly improbable in 1965, but is perhaps a more realistic vision today. It is certainly worth speculating what the effects of massively increased leisure and tourism will be on host communities and on the natural environment. Many regions are finding that there capacity for tourists is almost exceeded and consequently the quality of the tourist experience has declined. J. Krippendort (1986) has recently pointed out that there are signs that the present system of tourism provision does not satisfy the needs of the traveller. He argues that recreation and tourism are 'integral parts of the whole industrial scene' and that structural strains and changes in the industrial scene will stimulate changes in patterns of leisure and tourism. 'Viewed thus', tourism, so successful in the past two decades, seems clearly doomed to radical change'. He calls for a more integrated synthesis of 'work, habit, recreation and life as a whole'. Perhaps more like the medieval society.

# Summary

In selecting a few episodes from the history of tourism, this chapter has attempted to emphasise that tourism has existed in societies in the past where the basic enabling factors of sufficient leisure time, wealth, security and a travel infrastructure have combined with a favourable cultural, social, economic, political and technological environment. Where and when such tourism has existed, there has also had to be present among the members of those societies the desire to travel.

We have also tried to emphasise that tourism in the past was not always confined to a wealthy social elite. It is important to remember that the information that is available concerning the activities of tourists tends to distort the picture in favour of the affluent and famous. Thus, far more is known about the travels of the wealthy villa-owners in Ancient Rome and of the Grand Tourists of the eighteenth century than about less prestigious forms of tourism.

Just as the history of tourism in western societies remains fragmented and loaded towards events in Britain and North America, so there is an even more incomplete picture of events in other parts of the world. A true understanding of the nature of tourism and its development requires an historical perspective, and history emphasises that society and its activities are never static but are instead in the process of constant change.

# Chapter 3

## ☐ The Importance of Tourism

## The World Scale

Identifying the overall pattern of development, and the significance, of world tourism is not straightforward, because trends in Europe have historically dominated world tourism. There are a number of reasons for this domination:

1. Europe is a small continent, divided into many countries which are often little bigger than states within other nations such as the United States, Australia or the Soviet Union. However, movements between European nation-states have international status and are therefore classified as international tourism. By contrast, movements on a similar scale within large countries such as the United States are counted as domestic tourism.

2. The number of short-distance international tourism movements in Europe are large because the continent is densely populated. As a consequence, large numbers of people frequently cross international boundaries for business, family or holiday purposes.

3. Europe, like all continents, enjoys a rich diversity of physical environments (terrain, climate, fauna, flora etc.). European social cultures, like cultures throughout the world, have developed over centuries, resulting in a fascinating legacy of customs and traditions. What distinguishes Europe, however, is that, collectively, these physical and cultural resources have been intensively promoted by the travel and tourism industry as a means of encouraging tourism to a great number of destinations within Europe.

4. In North West Europe and North America, an industrial society grew and developed earlier than in other parts of the world. An advanced industrial society makes available wealth and leisure which are preconditions for the initial generation of mass tourism. In Chapter 1 it was noted that increased leisure time, and particularly the growth of holidays with pay,

in conjunction with a rise in disposable income, were major factors leading to the growth of tourism. Europeans initially tended to restrict their travel to within Europe. In contrast, many North Americans, particularly those of European origin, travelled to Europe on holiday.

The effect of international tourism in Europe on the world pattern of tourism means that a simple description of the world situation alone would be insufficient. Restricting an examination of world tourism to general trends masks detailed trends and deviations. In order to avoid superficial generalisations, only a brief world overview is attempted here. To illustrate more effectively the importance of travel and tourism, we shall focus in greater depth upon tourism in a number of specific countries. Examples will be taken from both the Developed and the Third World. Comparisons regarding tourism will be made between countries under different political regimes, and also between countries in which tourism can be found from an early date and those to which it is a relative newcomer. Descriptions of these case studies, drawn from across the globe, will be followed by a detailed examination of tourism in Britain.

# The Growth in Tourist Numbers

There has been a dramatic increase in international tourist numbers since the end of the Second World War. In 1950, only 25 million international tourists were recorded world-wide, yet by 1986 that figure had risen to approximately 340 million. This growth has been moderately steady, although there have been a number of periods in which it was interrupted. These were:

## (a) 1968-1969

The lower rates of growth in tourism during this period were associated with the downturn in the U.S. economy and the adverse economic effects of U.S. involvement in the Vietnam War. This had repercussions on the economies of a number of the major tourist-generating countries of Western Europe and led to a general fall in tourist numbers.

## (b) 1973-74

Following the 1973 Arab-Israeli war, OPEC substantially increased the price of oil. The consequences of this price rise for tourism were most pronounced in North America. In Europe, the effect was temporarily to reduce the rate of growth of tourism rather than to cause an actual decline in international arrivals.

## (c) The early 1980s

This period was characterised by more fundamental economic problems. For several years during the economic recession of the early 1980s the rate of international tourism growth levelled off. By 1984 it had begun to rise again, and that rise continued into the late 1980s.

Overall the decade from 1970 to 1980 was the most significant post-war period in terms of world-wide increase in international tourist numbers.

# The Growth in the Financial Receipts from Tourism

Parallelling the growth in the numbers of tourists has been the increase in financial receipts from international tourism. Steady growth during the decade 1960-70 was followed by a considerable increase between 1970 and 1980. The subsequent decline in real terms which occurred between 1980 and 1984 was associated with two factors:

    (i) the world economic recession;

    (ii) the growing proportion of mass tourists coming from lower income brackets whose per capita expenditure at their destination was relatively low.

This latter trend has been most notable in Europe, particularly when European tourism is compared with tourism in Central and South America, the Caribbean and the Middle East, which are venues where high-spending, allocentric visitors still form the majority of tourists. However, even in parts of the Caribbean (traditionally at the luxury end of the holiday market) charter flights from Britain, introduced in May 1987 and expanded dramatically in the summers of 1988 and 1989, have led to an increase in the number of lower-spending mass package tourists whose mid- and psycho-centric demands are rather different from those of their allocentric, high-spending counterparts.

The pattern of exports has tended to follow that of international tourist receipts. The only notable exception was the marked rise in value in 1973 and 1974, undoubtedly associated with price rises resulting from the world oil crisis.

Although Europe still dominates international tourism in terms of receipts and numbers of arrivals, this pattern is slowly changing. Since the end of the 1970s, the Americas, East Asia and the Pacific have experienced rapidly rising numbers of tourists and growing income from visitors. By contrast, despite an overall net increase in international visitor arrivals in Europe, the rate of increase has fallen, and there has also been a decline in receipts from international tourism. These trends are reinforced by significant relative changes in the proportion of the population employed in tourism in different parts of the world. The marked increase in the significance of tourism-related employment in the Americas, East Asia and the Pacific has been parallelled by relative stagnation in Europe.

The world pattern of international tourism, then, appears to be undergoing gradual change. The dominance of Europe, while still apparent, is waning as new areas assume increasing importance. It is obvious nonetheless that tourism flourishes only under conditions of economic and political stability. If such circumstances occur in these 'new' tourist areas, the trends identified may continue. But as the following case studies illustrate very clearly, international tourism is a highly substitutable commodity, and even small adverse political, social or economic events can interrupt hitherto well-established patterns of growth.

# Tourism Statistics

Throughout this book tables and graphs, of tourism statistics are used to illustrate significant features of the tourist industry. However, it is important to stress that the validity of international tourism statistics is notoriously suspect, and only general conclusions should be drawn from the data produced here. Despite the efforts of the World Tourism Organisation (WTO) and the Organisation for Economic Co-operation and Development (OECD), significant variations in definitions and methods of accounting still exist between different countries.

Two main types of statistics are available for the assessment of international tourism:

(a.) Those based on an attempt to record every arrival, either at the frontier or at registered tourist accommodation within the destination country.

(b.) Those based on sample surveys of visitors departing from/arriving at their destination or country of origin.

The statistics published by the WTO are generally of the first sort. Figures from each destination country belonging to the WTO are collected. The aggregate figures for all countries then give a reasonable picture of the total volume of world tourism, but at the regional and national level the detailed statistics are suspect. The problems here include:

(i) The same visitor being counted at every frontier crossing.

(ii) Failure to distinguish between short-stay, long-stay and transit visitors.

(iii) Visits to friends and relatives or stays in non-registered centres being missed if registered accommodation returns are used.

(vi) Variations in methods of collecting tourist receipts. Some countries base their estimates on central banks' returns of foreign exchange transactions rather than on controlled visitor surveys.

The second approach to collecting tourism statistics, based on sample surveys, has the advantage of consistency since a standardised procedure is followed. In the UK, the International Passenger Survey (IPS) is based on a stratified random sample of passengers entering and leaving the UK at the main air and sea outlets. This produces what is probably the best set of routine national statistics in the world. However, even here there are problems. The sampling error varies with the size of the sample. Thus in 1983, the sampling error for all UK residents going abroad was ±0.8%, and for France ±2.1%, but for Tanzania, ±59.8%. Establishing the volume of UK tourists to individual Third World countries, for example, is therefore extremely difficult.

Finally, in order to reinforce the need for caution regarding tourism statistics, it is possible to look at China. China's statistical system was ruined between

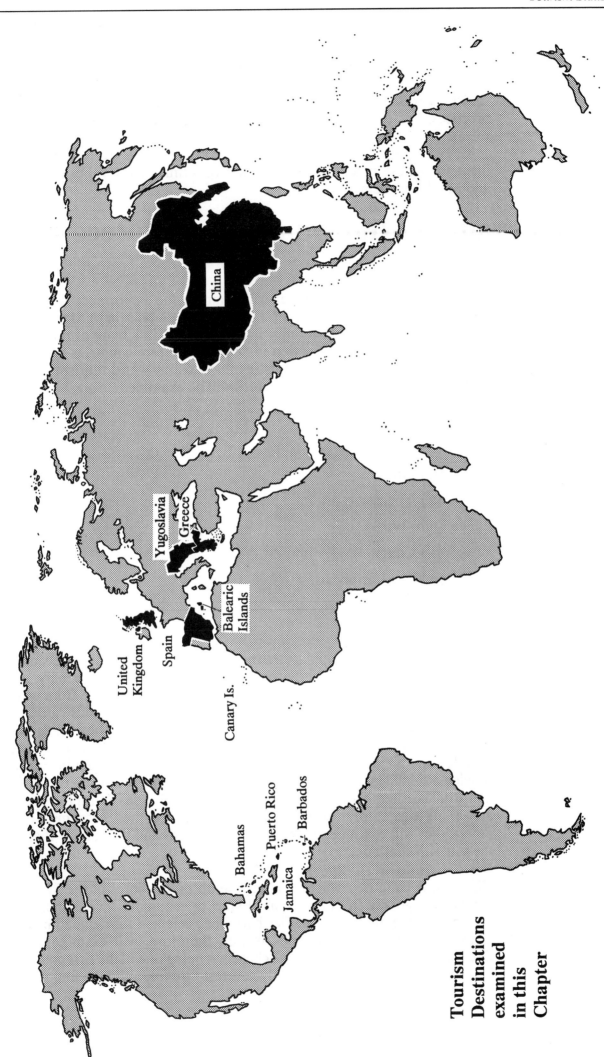

China

Yugoslavia
Greece

United
Kingdom

Spain

Balearic
Islands

Canary Is.

Bahamas

Puerto Rico

Barbados

Jamaica

**Tourism
Destinations
examined
in this
Chapter**

1958 and 1978 as a result of the upheavals of the Cultural Revolution. Even given the recent restoration of greater order, it is difficult to be sure that statistical concepts and methodologies conform to standard international practices. For example, as late as 1982 the Chinese government did not release any information about visitor expenditure at all, and even when, in 1985, visitor expenditures in the Guangzlion area were given, one government source estimated expenditure at 4 or 5 times the level estimated by another department!

# The Importance of Individual Tourist Receiving Areas

The next section of this chapter will examine the importance of specific tourist-receiving areas in terms of the volume of tourists they attract and the revenue which tourism generates. It is impossible in a book of this sort to examine every tourist destination in detail. Therefore countries have been selected which illustrate the contrasts that exist in world tourism and the trends that prevail. The following areas will be examined:

1. The Mediterranean

    (a.) Spain

    (b.) Greece

    (c.) Yugoslavia

2. The Third World

    (a.) China

    (b.) The Caribbean

# 1. The Mediterranean

Southern Europe is a popular international tourist destination because it offers a markedly different environment in terms of climate, scenery, artifacts and attitude to that of the countries in Northern Europe from which the majority of tourists originate. In addition, North Europeans can easily reach Southern Europe by road or by a short flight. It has been suggested that Europe needs its periphery for its physical and mental well-being (Seers, Schaffer and Kiljunen, 1979). The northern shores of the Mediterranean provide a suitable venue to which large numbers of people from the cooler industrial northern parts of Europe can escape. As long as South Europeans are willing to cater for the ever-increasing demands of these escaping Northerners, they will continue to reap financial rewards and the annual 'flight to the sun' will continue.

Since those countries which lie along the northern shores of the Mediterranean vary greatly from the point of view of economic development and political regime, three case studies have been selected for detailed investigation. The next section of the chapter, therefore, will examine Spain, Greece and Yugoslavia. Spain was chosen as being one of the first countries in which mass tourism emerged. By contrast Greece, although undergoing similar phases of tourism development, has seen them occur at a much later date. Both these countries are now members of the European Economic Community. Yugoslavia was chosen because it differs from Spain and Greece in that its political system, and its economic and cultural links, ally it more closely with the East European bloc than with the West. Nevertheless it is within those constraints that tourism in Yugoslavia has become an important economic activity.

## (a.) Spain

Although domestic tourism had begun to emerge among the wealthier members of Spanish society by the late nineteenth century, few foreign tourists were prepared to make the long and difficult journey to Spain until the beginning of the twentieth century. Tourism retained its exclusive character at this time, with only an estimated 195,000 foreigners visiting Spain annually in the early 1930s. War, both within and outside the country, brought the incipient tourist industry to an abrupt halt. Tourism recommenced in the 1950s, when favourable conditions in the main tourist-generating countries of North West Europe were paralleled by efforts within Spain to encourage visitors to take advantage of the abundant physical and cultural resources for tourism Spain had to offer. Post-war rises in incomes and in the length of annual paid-holidays, together with low-cost charter flights encouraging the desire to seek out novel destinations, led many North West Europeans to look overseas for new holiday experiences. A number of factors established Spain as a major tourist venue, including:

(i) A convenient location.

(ii) A series of government measures, associated with the Stabilisation Plan of 1959, including the abolition of entry visas for tourists from Europe.

(iii) The maintenance of a favourable rate of exchange for the Spanish currency.

(iv) Advantageous credit terms for hotel construction.

(v) Improved co-ordination and marketing which followed the establishment of a new ministry to develop tourism in 1962.

As a result of these and other events, the number of international arrivals into Spain increased by 145% between 1958 and 1963. This massive growth continued into the 1970s.

This progressive rise in tourism was finally halted by the oil crisis of 1973-4, when the number of visitors fell sharply and then stagnated for three years before once more beginning to increase. The 1980s economic recession again interrupted the pattern of growth. The Spanish tourist industry's apparently rapid recovery from these ills in the late 1980s can be ascribed partly to many visitors to Spain having sacrificed other forms of consumption, or personal savings, in order to ensure a Spanish holiday. Behind this phenomenon, however, lies a more fundamental change in the structure of tourism demand. Increasingly, visitors to Spain opted for cheaper types of accommodation, including self-catering apartments instead of hotels. Lengths of stay have become shorter. These trends are reflected in the reduction in real incomes received from tourism by Spain. These fell by 37% between 1973 and 1976. Not until 1983 did revenue from tourism again recover its 1973 level again. Since then, both the numbers of visitors and the revenue from tourism have fluctuated in response to social, economic and political events, such as:

(i) higher prices in Spain;

(ii) competition from rival tourist destinations;

(iii) Basque terrorist threats;

(iv) crimes of robbery and violence.

Nevertheless, it must be stressed that despite the undoubted importance of foreign tourists to Spain, such visitors are not the only category of tourist. The Spanish economic miracle of the 1960s, when rapidly rising economic growth rates were experienced, led to a massive increase in disposable incomes within Spain, which stimulated domestic tourism. The market is now divided fairly evenly between foreign and domestic tourists. In 1982, they together generated employment for 20% of Spain's working population, with 2,148,000 people involved in jobs related to tourism.

The geographical spread or spatial distribution of tourism in Spain is most clearly revealed through the pattern of accommodation provision. By 1984, there were over 1.5 million registered accommodation spaces in Spain. These were both geographically concentrated and, in the main, located along the coast. Although Spain is a large country containing a wide variety of physical and cultural environments which offer considerable potential for tourism development, the main focus has been upon the Mediterranean coasts and the islands. Some ski resorts have developed, both in the Pyrenees and the Sierra Nevada, the latter until the late 1980s largely frequented by domestic tourists. The countryside, which is little spoiled by modern developments, and the comparatively undiscovered historic cities are often poorly served by the modern tourism industry from the point of view of accommodation provision, and are subject to exploitation by international tour operators.

In 1984, 90% of all registered accommodation spaces were located in the coastal provinces of Spain, while 69% were clustered in the Balearic and Canary Islands, along the coasts of Catalonia, Alicante and Malaga, and in the capital Madrid. It is interesting to note that hotel capacity in the Balearics alone is almost equal to that of the whole of Greece. These islands are a relatively new tourist destination, having gained their popularity only in the past twenty-five years and have, encouraged by changes in fashion and by the promotion efforts of the major tour operators, attracted a growing proportion of mass tourists seeking their traditional goals of sun, sea, sand and a change of environment.

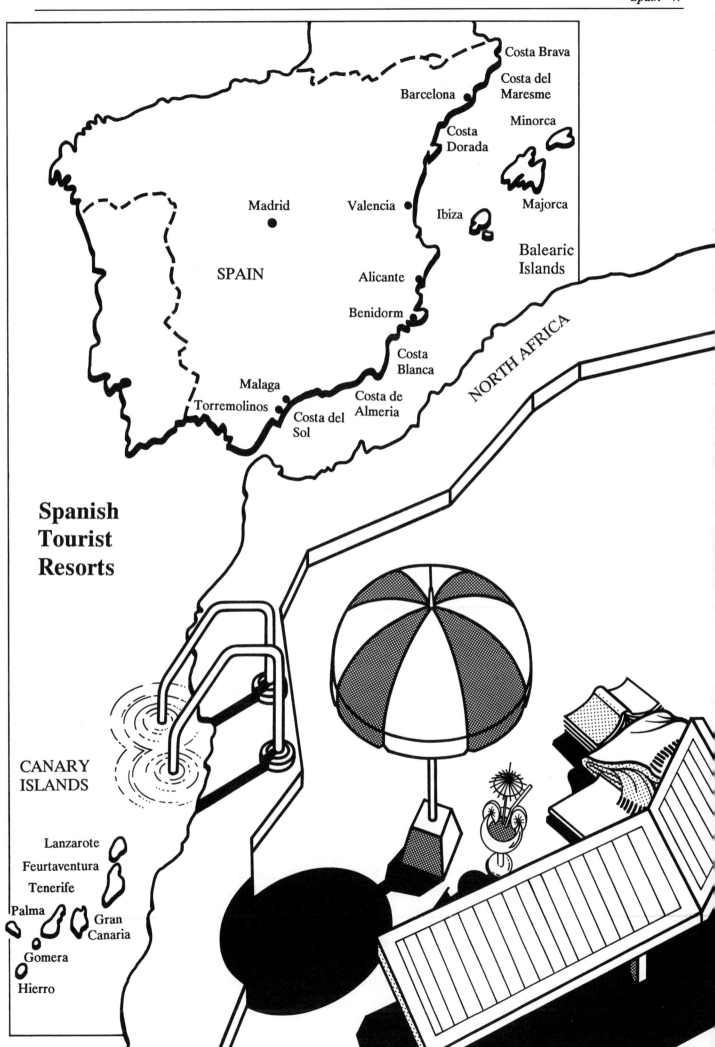

**Spanish Tourist Resorts**

SPAIN

Madrid

Valencia

Barcelona

Costa Brava

Costa del Maresme

Minorca

Costa Dorada

Ibiza

Majorca

Balearic Islands

Alicante

Benidorm

Costa Blanca

Malaga

Torremolinos

Costa del Sol

Costa de Almeria

NORTH AFRICA

CANARY ISLANDS

Lanzarote

Feurtaventura

Tenerife

Palma

Gran Canaria

Gomera

Hierro

It was the growing tourist industry that transformed small fishing villages like Torremolinos, formerly a weekend retreat for the wealthy from Malaga, into large international resorts. The effects of such transformations, repeated along all the 'sunshine' coasts of mainland Spain and the Spanish islands, have been dramatic. Not only has the population living in coastal municipalities such as Malaga increased rapidly, but the distribution of tourism has also led to a change in the pattern of regional incomes, as the economic stimulus provided by tourism has widened the local economic base and improved levels of income, consumption and employment.

Foreign tour operators have played an important part in organising the marketing of Spain and the flow of foreign tourism. Income derived from tourism was initially a useful economic prop for the Spanish government of General Franco, and was encouraged. Profitable land speculation and development on the part of private enterprise went largely unchecked by a weak planning system. This resulted in a haphazard, sprawling, urbanised landscape in many of the resorts, and a sadly deficient infrastructure. Clearly, unless tighter planning control is imposed in current tourist areas, visual, noise and water pollution may lead to tourists deserting Spain in favour of less spoiled alternative destinations.

# The Balearic Islands

The Balearics are a microcosm of the pattern of tourism growth in Spain. Because they are islands and because access is more difficult than it is to mainland Spain, most international tourists arrive by air. Tourism growth in the islands began early in the 1960s. Rapid increases in the numbers of international arrivals occurred during the late 1960s and early 1970s, interrupted only by the 1973-4 oil crisis. Further growth again suffered a slight set-back associated with the 1980 world economic recession. Since then, tourist numbers have increased more slowly, and fluctuations can be identified. It is noticeable that the individual islands were developed for tourism at different dates.

(a) Mallorca, the largest and most popular island, was already well established as a tourist destination by the late 1960s.

(b) Ibiza came to greater prominence early in the 1970s.

(c) Menorca, always a less important tourist destination than the other two islands, saw the importance of tourism increase as the 1970s progressed.

As the most visited island, Mallorca was most affected by the economic problems of 1973-4 and 1980. By contrast, Menorca was affected only minimally during both these periods of crisis and this is illustrated in the figure below. Because tourism on the Balearics has recovered after these economic difficulties, the same trend can be identified there as is apparent elsewhere in Spain, with more and more new apartment blocks being built instead of more hotels, in response to a demand for cheaper and more flexible forms of accommodation. Again, these are concentrated into predominantly coastal locations where the major resorts are to be found. Greater congestion at these sites has lowered the quality of the holiday experience and led to a increased likelihood of alternative venues being chosen, particularly by allocentric and mid-centric tourists from North West Europe.

# (b.) Greece

The evolution of tourism in Greece has followed a similar pattern to that identified in many other Southern European countries. Only the timing of the main thrust of tourism development differs among these nations which border the Mediterranean Sea.

A relatively small number of high-spending, allocentric tourists visited Greece before the Second World War. Subsequently, visitors have been drawn increasingly from a wider spectrum of socio-economic groups in the originating countries in North West Europe and North America as Greece has become a mid-centric or even a psycho-centric destination with the growth of mass package tourism. Only 37,464 foreign tourists visited Greece in 1950, and even by 1960 international arrivals were a mere 371,330. In contrast to Spanish tourism, tourism in Greece was still at an early stage of evolution. This was due to a number of factors:

(i) Greece was relatively remote from the main tourist-generating areas;

(ii) at that time, Greece had a low level of economic development and consequently a poor infrastructure;

(iii) tourism demand within Europe in the early 1960s was not so high that it had become necessary for tour operators to search further afield in order to exploit new destinations;

(iv) because of relatively low economic development it would have been more expensive to develop Greece than economically more advanced, traditional holiday locations such as Spain, Switzerland and Italy.

Although growth began during the 1960s, internal political events within Greece, which led to the military coup in 1967, interrupted the broad pattern of tourism growth and led to a 12% reduction in international arrivals in that year. Similarly, the more rapid expansion of tourism in Greece during the 1970s was abruptly halted by the invasion of Cyprus by the Turkish army in 1974, which had repercussions throughout the eastern Mediterranean. Nevertheless, despite the fluctuation in international arrivals caused by political instability, tourist movements to Greece have expanded rapidly, with particularly good growth during the late 1970s and 1980s, when mass package tourism became dominant.

The pattern of tourism development in Greece, then, is similar to that of Spain, the growing numbers of foreign tourists being associated with a change from individual movements of high-spending visitors largely engaged in cultural tourism, to mass movements of sun-seeking tourists exploiting budget-priced package tours. This latter trend is revealed most clearly by an examination of the average expenditure of tourists. The average amount each tourist spends has varied between 1960 and the early 1980s. At constant 1980 prices, there was initially a fairly high level of individual expenditure followed by a gradual reduction until the early 1970s, when a brief rise in per capita spending was followed by a dramatic fall. This rapid change in the mid-1970s was probably associated with a change from individual to mass tourism, the package industry having penetrated into Greece in search of new destinations for a larger North European market looking for new holiday experiences. During this period, the composition of the tourist population began to change, with a higher proportion of tourists drawn from low income brackets. However, the further decline in per capita spending by foreign tourists between 1980 and 1982 was more closely allied to the world economic recession than to a reconstituted tourist population whose increasingly psycho-centric demands and consequent impact on the country were rather different from those of earlier visitors.

Receipts from tourism grew at an average annual rate of 16.9% between 1960 and 1982. This compares favourably with the country's second major source of income, merchandising, the growth of which averaged only 14.3% per year over the same period. These growth rates, however, give a false impression. In real terms, the expansion of tourism in Greece, and of its export value to the Greek economy, was not as spectacular as it appears. While international tourist arrivals increased fifteen-fold between 1960 and 1979, receipts rose only nine-fold and exports grew by a factor of only five. This was largely the result of market segmentation in Greece having changed in the latter half of the 1970s.

By 1985, visitor arrivals continued to rise, and average expenditure levels to decline. Although this growth in visitor arrivals reflected the continuing movement in the pattern of tourists towards the lower-spending section of the market, the influence of economic and political events both within and outside Greece have been important contributory factors to this rise in visitor numbers. Other such factors included:

    (i) The devaluation of the drachma.

    (ii) A rapid reduction in the numbers of relatively high-spending U.S. visitors consequent upon the TWA hijack at Athens in June 1985. Fear of terrorist reprisals for U.S. military action against Libya also contributed to the nervousness of U.S. tourists to Europe and led to a further decline in their numbers in 1986.

Tourism is now the most important invisible export earner in Greece and makes a substantial contribution to the economy. It also affects the incomes of those who work in the industry, those who offer associated services, including suppliers of food and beverages, and those in the construction industry. By 1982, 523,000 people were engaged in tourism-related employment. This accounted for 15% of total employment, and proves a useful additional indicator of the importance of tourism in Greece.

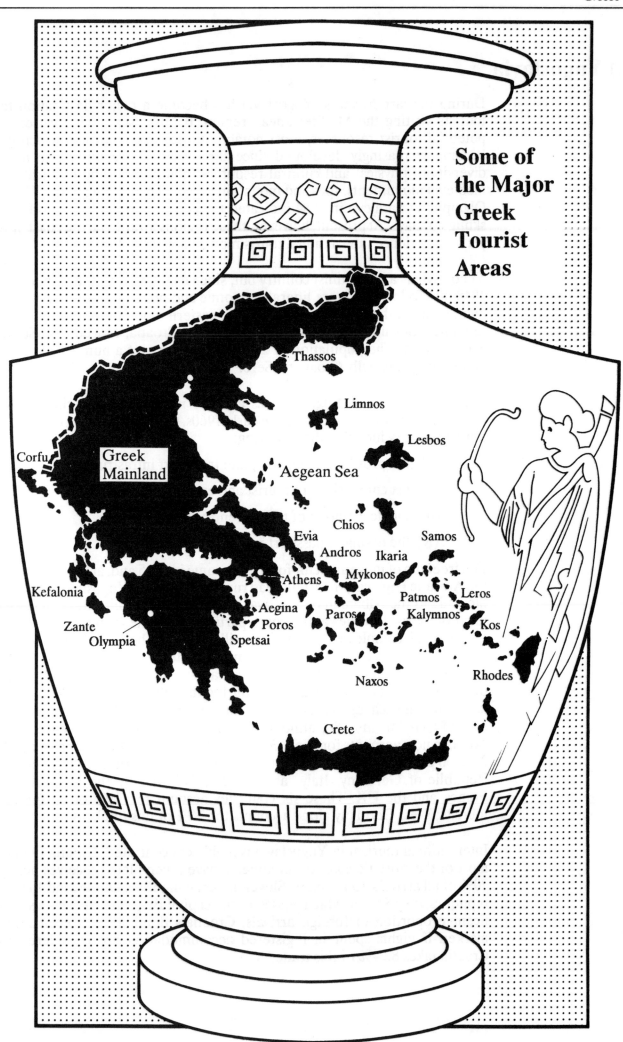

Some of
the Major
Greek
Tourist
Areas

Thassos

Limnos

Lesbos

Corfu

Greek
Mainland

Aegean Sea

Chios

Samos

Evia

Andros        Ikaria

Athens        Mykonos

Kefalonia                           Patmos        Leros

Aegina              Paros        Kalymnos

Zante          Poros                              Kos

Olympia              Spetsai

Naxos                    Rhodes

Crete

# (c.) Yugoslavia

During the last 30 years, Yugoslavia has become a major destination for tourists visiting the Mediterranean region. It possesses a wide variety of potential tourist resources, most notably its Adriatic coastline, which has become increasingly developed since the 1960s. The country also has a diversity of physical and cultural resources inland, including classical and medieval monuments, spas and mountain ranges. The holding of the Winter Olympics at Sarajevo in 1984 indicated the country's potential for offering skiing holidays. At present, however, those regions away from the coast have yet to experience international tourism on an appreciable scale.

Yugoslavia is a communist country but, since its break with the Comicon in 1948, has followed a more liberal economic and political route to development compared to other countries of the eastern bloc. It is composed of six republics, Bosnia-Hercegovinia, Montenegro, Croatia, Macedonia, Serbia and Slovenia. The population of 22 million consists of a number of ethnic groupings, principally Croat and Serb.

The development of Yugoslavia as a major international destination for tourists began in earnest during the early 1960s. Government support for the tourist industry included the following:

> (i) the provision of an adequate transport infrastructure;
>
> (ii) tax concessions to tourist and catering organisations;
>
> (iii) the devaluation of the currency;
>
> (iv) the easing of passport regulations.

Full freedom of movement for foreigners came in 1965 and, at the same time, the Adriatic Highway, the trunk road running along the Yugoslav coast from Slovenia to the Albanian border, was opened. This permitted the development of tourist facilities at the coast, particularly in the republic of Croatia. Large hotel complexes and holiday villages were built and now occupy extensive areas between Split, Dubrovnik and Montenegro in the south. The numbers of foreign tourists increased dramatically in the 1960s, although overall growth rates have slackened during the late 1970s and 1980s. Similarly, foreign exchange receipts from tourism rose from US$14.2m in 1960 to US$1,114.7m in 1980, although earnings have eased back since then. Tourism now accounts for about 3% of GNP and is thought to employ about 220,000 people. The principal countries generating tourists are the Federal Republic of Germany, Italy and Austria, followed by the Netherlands, France and the UK. These six countries account for 71% of all foreign tourists; West Germany alone accounts for 34% of this total.

International tourism in Yugoslavia is highly concentrated. Croatia (where most of the Adriatic coast developments have taken place) receives nearly 70% of all arrivals, followed by Slovenia, receiving 13%. Of the land-locked republics, only Serbia, which possesses the capital Belgrade, attracts a significant proportion of foreign arrivals. Croatia's dominance is even more marked if nights spent in registered accommodation are considered as Croatia takes 82.4% of this trade.

Slovenia

Ljubljana

Porterez

Umag

Porec

Vrsar

Rijeka

Pula

Zagreb

Croatia

Bosnia-
Hercegovinia

Split

Sarajevo

Novi Sad

Belgrade

Serbia

Dubrovnik

Montenegro

Titograd

Skopje

Macedonia

**Yugoslavian
Tourist
Areas**

The nature of Yugoslavia's international tourist trade presents a number of problems for the country. As has been seen, Yugoslavia relies on a very small number of countries for the bulk of its tourist trade, which makes it vulnerable to changing circumstances. For example, an economic setback in West Germany in 1982 resulted in a 17% fall in German visitors, which hit the industry badly. Also, much of Yugoslavia's tourism is now of the mass packaged type. This means that Yugoslavia is competing with other Mediterranean countries offering similar products, such as Spain, Greece, Turkey and some North African countries.

Many of the distinctive areas of Yugoslavia are to be found inland, where relatively few foreign tourists go. A pronounced regional economic imbalance means that not only is the full tourist potential of the country not being realised, but also inter-regional tensions are being exacerbated within the country. Croatia and Slovenia dominate the tourist trade, yet they have long been the most economically privileged republics. While it can be argued that tourism has benefited the backward and isolated coastal zones within those two republics, a country that has long experienced tension between its constituent areas cannot afford to allow tourism to heighten those differences.

Planning for tourism development in Yugoslavia has to some extent taken account of these problems. The state's Social Plan includes a major drive towards diversifying the range of tourist attractions. These include:

    (i) the promotion of hunting;

    (ii) the provision of conference centres and spas;

    (iii) packages for older travellers;

    (iv) the introduction of winter sports holidays.

The developments at Sarajevo, connected with the Olympics, represented one part of a general strategy of distributing tourists and the benefits created by tourism over a wider area of the country. Given the competitive nature of international tourism, Yugoslavia will need to promote its full tourism potential if it is to derive substantial benefit from this trade in the 1990s.

# 2. Tourism and the Third World

The growth of international tourism to countries in the Third World has been a significant development in recent years. About 17% of all international tourists are estimated to visit Third World destinations, and this proportion has doubled in the past ten years.

Third World countries offer the tourist warm climates, exotic landscapes and a diversity of local cultures. Social prestige and a feeling of 'difference' enjoyed by the visitor are also associated with visits to these destinations.

There are many benefits which Third world countries may reap from tourism. These include:

    (i) the economic development which can result from the inflow of valuable foreign exchange;

(ii) the diversification of the country's economic base;

(iii) the creation of employment.

Recently, however, there has been considerable debate concerning whether tourism does bring significant benefits to the developing world.

The Third World embraces countries varying greatly in their social, economic and political structures. This chapter examines two contrasting areas: China, a socialist planned economy where international tourism has become significant only during the past ten years, and the Bahamas, with a capitalist economy and a well-developed tourist industry.

# (a.) China

In looking at China as a tourist destination we have chosen a third world country with enormous tourist potential. Its tourist industry had begun to flourish in the 1980s and the future looked promising. As we note at the end of this section such optimistic predictions must now be seen in the light of the events of the summer of 1989 when the government mercilessly crushed the flowering democracy movement in the full glare of the western media. The immediate impact was an almost total end to incoming tourists. Whether the passage of time and the changing political climate will encourage tourism to flourish again remains to be seen but we shall nevertheless consider what China has to offer to the tourist world should its political situation once more encourage visitors.

The Peoples' Republic of China has an abundance of potential tourism resources, both cultural and physical. The Great Wall of China, the terracotta army of the Emperor Qinshihuang at Xi'an and the forbidden city in Beijing are world-renowned. In addition, landscapes such as the limestone rock formations at Greilin, the West Lake at Hangzhon and the Stone Forest in Yunan are of outstanding scenic interest.

International tourism to China, however, has developed on an appreciable scale only since 1978. This was the year that the Chinese government began its policy of opening up the country to the international community, a process which included the development of tourism. Before 1978, limited exchanges with a few politically compatible countries such as USSR, Mongolia and some east European states had taken place, but even this trade virtually ceased during the upheavals of the Cultural Revolution during the years 1967 to 1976. Since 1978, however, tourism has been developed dramatically according to the principle of 'friendship and economic benefit, with the emphasis on the former' (Uysal et al., 1986), and the government tourism organisation, the State Administration for Travel and Tourism (SATT), has been made into a government ministry.

The political and economic framework within which the tourist industry has been developed is extremely fluid. Essentially, the industry is a state-operated monopoly, the state having almost total control of all aspects of the tourist sector. Nevertheless, the Chinese government has been experimenting with policies that range from socialism to western capitalism. At present, the overall economic policy seems to be moving from a centrally planned economy to one that includes elements of enterprise and market demand.

Visitor arrivals in China have increased steadily since 1978 and there are two distinct components to these arrivals. The dominant group of visitors are the Chinese from nearby Hong Kong and Macau visiting friends and relatives on the mainland. Their numbers have increased substantially: from just over 1 million in 1978 to nearly 12 million by 1984. The other group of tourists are classified as foreign visitors, and their numbers have increased from 230,000 in 1978 to over 1.3 million by 1985. The majority of these visitors come from Japan and the USA. Foreign visitors account for fewer than 1 in 10 arrivals, and this proportion has declined in recent years. In fact, the annual growth rate in foreign visitors declined from 57% in 1979 to a low of 14% in 1983. It has, however, been increasing again since.

Data on tourist expenditure has only recently become available and making estimates is somewhat hazardous. Total foreign exchange earnings from international tourism were estimated in 1984 at US$ 1.13 billion, a rise of over 20% on the previous year. The number of people employed in the tourist industry is thought to be at present about 110,000.

There are a number of major tourist areas in China. The province of Jiangsu, on the eastern edge of the country, lies on the route from Shanghai to Beijing and contains a number of important tourist destinations including Shanghai itself, Wuxi, Suzhon and Nanjing. The nearby city of Hangzhon in Zhe Jiang province is also an important centre. In the south east of the country, the port of Guangzhon, formerly known as Canton, benefits from its proximity to Hong Kong. Further inland, the capital Beijing (Peking), which remains the premier tourist destination, Xian and Guilin form other centres.

The tourism industry has tried to keep pace with the growth of tourist arrivals. By 1985, there were over 700 hotels, 200 of which were built since 1980, with a total capacity of about 120,000 guest rooms. China has experienced some difficulties in its tourist development. These include:

(i) an acute shortage of accommodation in Beijing, Shanghai, Guilin and other major centres;

(ii) a lack of carrying capacity on domestic air flights;

(iii) a decline in interest in China after the initial novelty value wore off.

It is noticeable that, apart from visitors from Japan, the USA, Australia and Canada, many foreign visitors, including British, French and German ones are expatriates living in Asia, emphasising the fact that China has still to penetrate other long-distance markets.

In an effort to meet present and possible future demands, estimated at 3 million foreign visitors by 1990, the Chinese government plans to expand the tourist infrastructure considerably. A national programme for tourism development from 1986 to 2000 was adopted in January 1986. This plan has the following main aims:

Great Wall

Beijing

Xi'an

Nanking    Suzhou

Emperor's        Shanghai
Warriors

Hangzghou

Guilin

Guangzhou

Aainan Island

**China's
Major
Tourist
Areas**

(i) Manpower, funds and materials are to be concentrated in a few centres. These include six cities (Beijing, Shanghai, Xi'an, Guilin, Hangzhon and Guangzhon), Aainan Island and Jlangsu province.

(ii) More hotels will be built in these centres, raising capacity from 120,000 rooms to 180,000.

(iii) There are plans to increase the domestic airline fleet by expanding routes and increasing frequency of service.

(iv) The construction of new airports and the improving of existing ones is also scheduled.

(v) Training of tourism manpower is also identified as a priority.

(vi) There are two departments and an expansion in numbers of tourism graduates is being planned.

Although overall policies and planning remains within a central government framework, the encouragement of tourism developments has necessitated certain policy changes. For instance, until 1982, separate travel permits in addition to the usual entry visas, were required for visits to every city on an itinerary. Thirty cities were exempted from this restriction in 1983, 107 were freely accessible by 1985, and this number has now been expanded to 244. The way in which tours are sold has also necessarily changed. When all sales were centralised in Beijing there were considerable hold-ups, but when sales were decentralised, there were problems of over-booking. Now, annual sales plans are centralised, but with quotas for different areas. Within these quotas, local officials are allowed to make contracts directly with tour operators in other countries.

Tourism development in China still faces a number of problems. For instance:

(i) New hotels may fail to reach international standards due to poor construction or poor maintenance.

(ii) Hotel workers tend to be poorly paid compared with other groups, and therefore lack the motivation to improve standards.

(iii) The partial decentralisation of tour sales will present formidable problems of organisation and management before difficulties with over-booking and service standards can to be resolved. While the first foreign tourists to China were prepared to endure these setbacks, the second wave of tourists may be less tolerant.

(iv) If China moves into the mass tourist market, it will have to compete with a range of alternative destinations, where service standards may be higher.

(v) Considerable investment will be needed in expensive facilities for relatively low-spending visitors.

Whether to embrace this form of tourism or to focus on attracting a lower volume of higher spending tourists is a problem facing not only China but, also many other developing countries who wish to use tourism as an agent in economic growth. For China, this is a problem that has yet to be resolved.

The self imposed isolation of the Peoples Republic of China following the Cultural Revolution created images of oppression and social deprivation sufficient to persuade even the most adventurous of Western Tourists to look elsewhere for holiday destinations. Over the last decade however, the more relaxed policies of the Communist administration in Beijing have seen an increase in international tourism initiatives inspired and directed by the Party and targeted at the more liberal and wealthy nations of the West.

Exploiting to a great extent the publicity vehicle of the international news media, the Chinese authorities have been able to market their country, not as oppressed and deprived, but as ancient, mystical and unique. This policy has been increasingly successful in attracting the more allocentric of Western tourists eager to explore China's history and culture.

However, the same international media which helped fuel the growth in China's tourist industry, reported to the West scenes of social chaos and dictatorial violence which may in the space of a few days, have totally erased the progress made in Chinese Tourism since 1978. The events in Beijing, and in particular Tiananmen Square, on and around the 4th June 1989 filled television screens the World over with images of a country in turmoil and a regime as oppressive and intolerant.

It would appear that the interests of the Chinese Tourist Industry and the insecurity of the Chinese Communist Party will for some time at least, be in conflict with one another. The tourist industry requires more 'openness' to attract western visitors and their money, but marginal reforms such as these, in the best traditions of revolution, will create a hunger within the Chinese population for greater and 'constitutional' changes.

Against this background, any study of the development of Chinese Tourism, including the account presented in this book, is perhaps limited in its significance as a pointer to how this development may continue in the future as it is impossible to say whether the progress made since 1978 will have any influence over developments in the unpredictable post - Tiananmen years.

Nevertheless, the Chinese experience from 1978 to June 1989 provided an excellent example of a Third World Nation investing in the exploitation of its history and unique image in order to ply a trade in tourism.

# (b.) The Caribbean

Political fragmentation, geographical isolation and similarity of resource endowment are all characteristic of the small islands of the Caribbean. In terms of both population and land area some of the islands are very small indeed. However, population density is generally high, especially where cultivatable land is available. Mineral resources are largely absent, except in Trinidad and Jamaica. The economies of the islands are very open, and there is a limited potential for the development of manufacturing industry. Against such a background, tourism grew very readily, owing to the following factors:

(i) relative proximity to North America;

(ii) considerable natural endowments in the form of the 'basic' tourist assets of sun, sea and sand;

(iii) other tourist resources, such as culture, history and a prestigious 'image';

(iv) effective promotion and marketing.

The Caribbean began to emerge as a tourist area in the 1950s and was one of the prime destinations in the mass package boom of the mid 1960s and early 1970s. Jamaica was typical in this respect. The island was a favoured location for the jet set in the 1950s when the high cost of holidays helped to maintain its exclusivity, and its reputation as a 'high class' venue eliminated competition with many other places which all offered the same basic attractions.

Alongside Jamaica, Bermuda and the Bahamas were major early destinations for visitors from outside the Caribbean, with Trinidad attracting visitors from within the Caribbean Basin. This development was based on a number of important criteria:

(i) The early provision of hotels and tourist infrastructure such as bars, water-sports and yachting facilities.

(ii) The surfeit of excess aircraft in the post-war period and subsequent technical advances in air transport, meaning that travel was relatively easy.

(iii) The growth of charter tours, leading to an increase in general accessibility to Caribbean destinations.

Efforts to foster tourism began in the late 1960s in the Eastern Caribbean, with Barbados making early progress. By the early 1970s, the oversupply of aircraft capacity was beginning to be a problem and, given also the large oil price rises implemented by OPEC in 1973, the situation became critical. Some recovery from this downturn took place in the late 1970s, but aviation difficulties were compounded in the early 1980s when major charter companies such as Laker Airways and Suntours went bankrupt. Changing circumstances thus forced visitors to lower their thresholds of acceptance, and at the same time former minor competitors in the Eastern Caribbean managed to make their venues more attractive by the provision of hotel beds, better water supplies etc. This led to greater competition.

In addition, the Caribbean Basin was overshadowed by a series of political, social and natural events which on certain islands inhibited tourism temporarily. In chronological order these were as follows:

(i) In the early 1960s the Cuban revolution occurred and political unrest was experienced in the Dominican Republic. By comparison the Commonwealth Caribbean seemed very attractive.

(ii) By 1971 Trinidad had its revolution, and the Carnival Festival there was postponed due to unsatisfactory public health conditions.

(iii) There were volcanic eruptions in St Vincent.

(vi) By the late 1970s Jamaica was being condemned in the United States on account of 'left-wing leanings' and a deterioration in social life.

(v) Dominica had internal security problems.

(vi) The emergence of the Bishop government in Grenada in 1979 was the culmination of a set of changes which took place in the 1970s and which gave the region a 'bad product' image.

(vii) Hurricane 'Gilbert' brought widespread damage to a number of islands, including Jamaica, in 1988.

The Caribbean was seen as offering less and less to visitors from outside the region. The effects of these changes were difficult to counter. There has been a fluctuation in the pattern of tourism development in the Caribbean as a whole, but it is only in the past twenty years that the tourist industry has reached any significant size in the smaller islands of the region. Growth rates in visitor arrivals of 15-20% per year, with corresponding growth in tourist receipts, were common in the smaller islands during the first half of this period. Since that time growth has slowed, although recently there has been wide variation from +50% to -20.8% among the islands. These changes relate to 1985-86 and are based on figures provided by the Caribbean Tourism Research and Development Centre. There was an increase in the total number of tourist arrivals of 6.2% between 1985 and 1986. The Bahamas, Jamaica and Puerto Rico, the three main tourist destinations, reported increases of 0.5%, 16.1% and 1.8% respectively. Increases of 10% or more were recorded by a number of countries among them Cuba, Dominica and St Lucia. Of total tourism inflows in the Caribbean, 94% are derived from the stay-over tourist sector and 6% from day trippers, arriving usually on cruise ships.

In general, the most important source of visitors to the Caribbean has been North America, which provided 69.8% of total visitor arrivals in 1986. In recent years numbers of visitors from Europe have risen, although such visitors still only comprise a relatively small proportion of the market, 9% in 1986.

# The Bahamas

Tourism did not begin to develop on the island of New Providence in the Bahamas (shown in the map below) until piracy was eliminated during the 1720s. By 1740 the mild winter climate had already led to the island's development as a health resort for wealthy Americans, despite the difficulties of the journey and the relative lack of accommodation. It was not until the 1840s that accommodation in private houses in Nassau was supplemented by the construction of four guest houses. Increasing numbers of visitors, who engaged in a wide range of recreational pursuits, stimulated the establishment of improved sea links between New York and Nassau in 1859. In the same year, construction began on the first hotel, which was completed in 1861 at a time when the enterprise could be financed out of revenue from blockade-running during the American Civil War. During the 1860s and

1870s, tourism became a small but significant industry, with nearly 500 visitors to Nassau in 1873.

Towards the end of the nineteenth century, further expansion occurred in both steamship services and hotel accommodation provision. This led to a growth in tourist numbers, particularly in the winter season. By 1937 there were over 34,000 international arrivals in New Providence, a figure which exceeded the total population of the island. The Second World War interrupted this pattern of growth, and visitors were slow to return during the early post-war period, with only 32,000 arrivals in 1949. However, during the early 1950s increasing time for holidays, higher incomes and the desire on the part of many Americans to travel, together with cheaper and more reliable air services and the introduction of air conditioning in the Bahamas (which alleviated the worst effects of high temperatures and humidity during the summer months), changed the nature of tourism.

The Bahamas became a major destination for Americans as mass tourism began and both visitor numbers and revenue from tourism soared during the 1960s and 1970s. By 1968 there were one million international arrivals, and by 1972 one and a half million foreign tourists visited the Bahamas. As elsewhere, the oil crisis of 1973-4 led to a setback in 1974, when international arrivals fell by over 8%. A subsequent steady rise in the number of foreign tourists visiting the Bahamas was briefly interrupted in 1981 as the effects of the world economic depression were felt. This is shown in the figure below. But a speedy recovery the following year saw a resumption of the upward spiral of growth, and there were over two million visitors recorded in 1983, while by 1986 the figure was not far short of three million.

About 50% of these international arrivals use accommodation on the islands, which in the past was largely focused on New Providence, although Grand Bahama and the Family Islands are increasing in importance as destinations, the latter particularly during the summer months. The remaining visitors are cruise passengers. The United States is the dominant originating county, having in 1985 supplied 88% of all visitors. Canadian and European markets fluctuate according to rates of exchange for currency and the condition of their national economies. Although there was an increase of 49% in international arrivals, between 1981 and 1985 the Bahamas total revenue from tourism only rose by 36%. This has been attributed to a higher growth in stop-over tourist arrivals during this period, such tourists tending to spend much less than cruise passengers.

The Bahamas became an important Caribbean destination for North Americans at a time when there were relatively few alternatives. Now, a wider range of competing venues both within and outside the Caribbean has slowed growth. Between 1974 and 1984, the Bahamas continued to command 10% of all United States overseas tourist visits. Two factors could have a significant effect on the tourist growth of the Bahamas. The first is that it is becoming cheaper for Americans to visit other destinations. Secondly, there are economic difficulties in other tourist-generating countries. As the Bahamas is heavily dependent upon tourism, which contributed 70% to GNP in 1984 and 60% to government revenue, the country's tourist industry must engage in active promotion and marketing if stagnation and even decline are to be avoided.

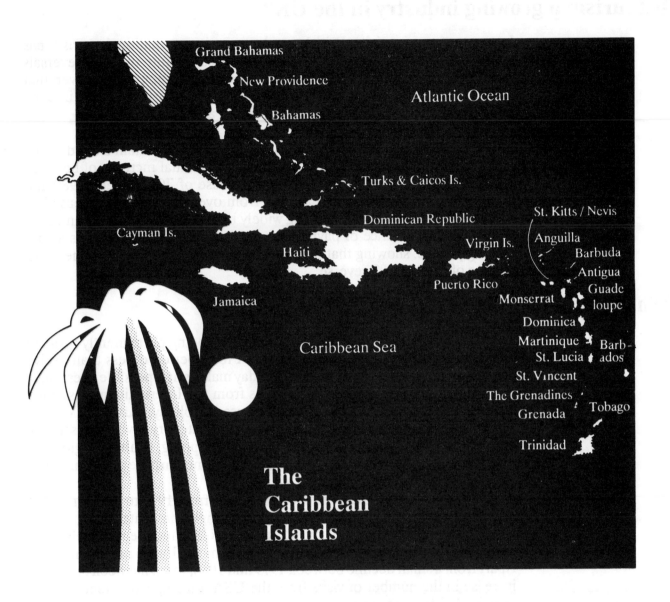

Grand Bahamas

New Providence

Atlantic Ocean

Bahamas

Turks & Caicos Is.

Dominican Republic

St. Kitts / Nevis

Cayman Is.

Virgin Is.

Anguilla

Barbuda

Haiti

Antigua

Puerto Rico

Guade
loupe

Jamaica

Monserrat

Dominica

Caribbean Sea

Martinique

Barb-
ados

St. Lucia

St. Vincent

The Grenadines

Grenada

Tobago

Trinidad

**The
Caribbean
Islands**

# The United Kingdom

## Is tourism a growing industry in the UK?

In terms of tourist visits, British involvement in international tourism has grown rapidly and consistently during the 1980s, in spite of sharp reversals suffered by the overall world trend. It should be remembered, however, that 'tourist visits' are defined as visits from the country of origin and the important question here is: how successful is Britain as a host country?

Figures on visits to the U.K. show that, except where Britain shared in the overall world reversal in 1981-82, there was an annual increase of between 3% and 9%, with an overall estimated increase of 7% between 1980 and 1985. Over the same period, earnings from overseas visitors increased by 84%, with annual increases varying widely between 1% (1980-81) and 25% (1982-83). The balance of payments over the same period presents a contrasting picture, showing that tourism made a slow recovery from the sharp decline of the 1981-82 reverse.

## What about overseas visitors?

An overseas visitor is defined as a person who, being permanently resident in a country outside the UK, visits the UK for a period of less than twelve months. Although not all visitors are holiday makers, it is possible to estimate the numbers of holiday or business visits from the International Passenger Surveys. A four-category classification is used: Holiday; Business; Visiting Friends and Relations; Miscellaneous. (The last category covers visits for the purposes of study, attending sporting events, shopping, health, religious, or other purposes, and includes visits for which no one purpose predominates.)

If we consider visits to the U K over the period from 1979 to 1985 a number of important factors emerge. Until 1985, the single most interesting feature is the increasing importance of visits from the USA and the relatively static picture presented by the numbers of visits from the European Community. Apart from a small decline between 1979 and 1980, there has been an annual increase in the number of visits from the USA, ranging from none at all to over 33%. This uneven increase reflects the complexity of the factors influencing the marketing of tourist destinations, an important example being the role played by tourist images.

The dramatic downturn in the number of visits from the USA in 1986 (from 3,797,000 in 1985 to 2,200,000 in 1986) was associated with terrorist and US military activities in Europe, North Africa and and the Middle East. Further analysis of the number of visits in terms of the four categories mentioned above emphasises the dominance of the USA as a market source. Of the 3,797,000 visits from the USA in 1985, 57% were recorded as holiday visits and only 14% as business trips. It is reasonable to assume that of the 30% visiting relatives or friends, or engaged in miscellaneous activities, a large number included a holiday element in their visits. Therefore, some three-quarters of visits from the USA were likely to be concerned with holidays in one way or another.

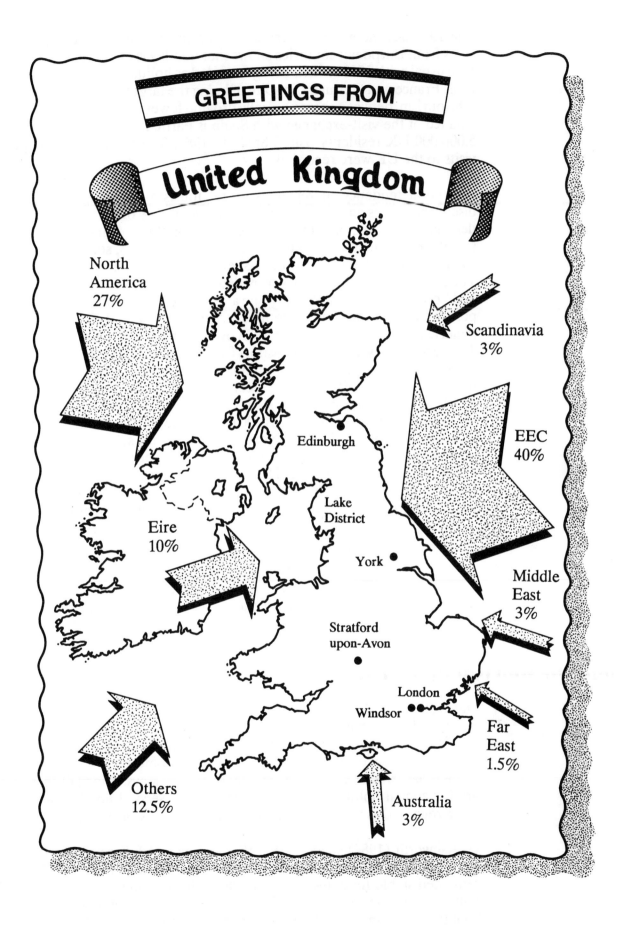

The 1986 decline was very serious for the tourist industry. The picture of visits from Eurpoean countries shows that holiday visits were less dominant than usual, with 35% of visits being recorded as holidays and 25% as business trips. France and Germany, in spite of being the largest EEC contributors to UK tourism, between them normally provide fewer visits than the USA. The balance of the visit-exchange with Spain is particularly striking: while over 5,000,000 UK residents visited Spain in 1984, fewer than 300,000 Spanish visits to the UK were recorded.

A general tendency to regard 'cultural tourism' as being aimed at the discovery of sites and monuments, a distorted image of the geography of the destination region, and the decidedly metropolitan character of modern society may all help to account for the fact that in 1985, some 8.5 million of the 12.4 million overseas visitors visited London for some part of their stay. The European city has always provided a major focus for cultural tourism, and London, along with Paris, Rome and Amsterdam, persistently retains its position among the top five tourist resorts in the world. Of the 3,100,000 American visitors to the UK in 1985 over 2,500,000 (85%) visited London. The percentage was lower for visitors from France and West Germany (51% and 47% respectively), whilst Commonwealth countries seemed to maintain figures of around 70%. Scotland receives 1.2 million visitors a year - a figure which has increased only very slowly since 1980: by contrast, Wales, with about half the number of visitors (600,000 in 1985), has increased its numbers by 80% since 1980. Although Northern Ireland has seen an increase in its number of overseas visitors of some 45% between 1980 and 1985, and although visits from the United States have risen from 44,000 to 62,000 over the same period, the great majority of visitors are still from the Irish Republic. The Euromonitor Report (1986) sums up the situation as follows:

> *On balance, it can be said that the numbers of visits to the United Kingdom by overseas holiday, and other, travellers are on the increase, to the benefit of the UK tourist industry as a whole and to the country's earnings from this industry. England is the greatest beneficiary from this inward traffic but with consistent benefit being gained by Scotland, Northern Ireland and Wales.*

# Domestic tourism in the UK

During the early 1980s domestic tourism fluctuated in the region of 120-140 million trips per annum. A domestic tourist trip is generally accepted as involving an overnight stay in a region outside one's normal home area, but within one's own country. Statistical returns of domestic tourist trips do not include day trips or excursions with no overnight stays. Many of these trips are for annual holidays, and nowadays include second holidays which are often regarded as supplementary to a main overseas vacation.

G. Ashworth (1984) suggests that the tendency of UK residents to take a holiday (about 60%), and to take an overseas holiday (about 20%), have remained stable for some time. In 1980 British residents made about 130 million domestic tourist trips. In 1981 and 1982 this number declined to about 123 million. In 1984 there was a recovery to about 140 million. In spite of the fall to 126 million trips in 1985, British residents spent 6% more on domestic holidays in that year. It is interesting to note that internal trips by overseas visitors (equal to about 10% of the number of domestic trips) result in expenditure which comes close to matching the total spent on domestic tourism. Visits to friends and relatives remain an important purpose for internal journeys (25% of trips by UK residents and 46% of internal trips by overseas visitors in 1985). Since the percentages given for holidays include part visits to friends and relatives, it seems possible that this sort of 'self-help' holiday arrangement may be one of the most common forms of tourism in Britain.

A regional breakdown indicates that the South West of England enjoys 20% of all visits, its closest rivals being Wales (12%), Scotland (11%) and Southern England (11%). The figures for Cumbria (3%) and Northumbria (2%) seem to suggest that there is scope for expansion of domestic tourism in these regions.

An examination of tourist attractions reveals something of the nature of British domestic and internal tourism. It has been suggested by the British Tourist Authority that the seaside still attracts about one third of domestic holiday visitors, with countryside locations and large towns drawing respectively only a quarter and a fifth of the total number. Blackpool Pleasure Beach, the top attraction in England, drew 6,500,000 visitors in 1985, and the leading Welsh resort, Rhyl Suncentre, attracted about 500,000. In spite of the popularity of these novel and spectacular seaside attractions, it is clear that cultural tourism also plays a significant role. The list of the top ten English tourist attractions (all in London) is headed by the British Museum (3,800,000 visitors) and the National Gallery (3,000,000) and also includes the Kensington 'Museum Complex' and the Tower of London. In Scotland, Edinburgh Castle (850,000 visitors) and the Botanical Gardens (720,000) head a list of attractions dominated by monuments and galleries. In Northern Ireland, the Ulster Museum is the top attraction, with the Ulster Folk Museum and the Arrenian Folk Park also in the top six. In Wales, although the Rhyl Suncentre is rivalled only by the National Museum of Wales, Edwardian castles are also significant attractions.

# Short Break Holidays in the United Kingdom

A number of social and economic factors may be cited to explain the fact that short breaks (inclusive packages including accommodation and sometimes transportation) have been the fastest growing features of the domestic holiday market in recent years. The 'Travel and Tourism Analyst' (May 1987) indicates that this sector is estimated to have doubled between 1982 and 1987 and that growth projections are for about 20% per annum for the foreseeable future. A great deal will depend on the continued growth of the disposable incomes of the more effluent socio-economic groups (ABC categories) and at the time of going to press this has been adversely affected by sharp increases in mortgage repayments which have resulted from the government's high interest policy. It is also difficult to be sure to what extent the opening of the Channel Tunnel in 1993 will draw the short break market to nearby European locations. Increased technology and improved booking systems should favour growth.

Research by Middleton and Brien has shown that a distinctive group of short break operators now service a market which is dominated by middle and late middle age customers (over 45 years). A high proportion, probably about 75% take a short break in addition to their main holiday. It is not surprising, therefore, that they are 'off peak' activities with over 50% of short breaks taken during the months of April, May, September and October. Amongst some of the recent developments related to the short breaks sector are the proposals to set up a national network of 200 Little Chef Lodges in the UK by the early 1990s. Middleton and O'Brien suggest that this T.H.F. initiative may be followed by similar moves by Granada, Rank and Accor the French hotel catering group in the provision of low budget, short stay accommodation. A second kind of development is the proposed use of upgraded holiday camps to offer weekend and short breaks linked to a wide range of activities such as fishing, snooker, pottery and windsurfing.

# Chapter 4

# The Structure of the Travel and Tourism Industry

Tourism is an activity in which tourists travel to, and stay at, destinations. As we have seen in Chapter Three this worldwide industry which attempts to satisfy the needs of tourists and encourage the development of tourism, has expanded rapidly in the second half of this century, reflecting an expansion in demand for its products and services. The shape of this modern industry in the U K is the subject of this chapter, which examines its structure, organisation and component sectors. We assess the scale of commercial activity, and finally we consider the value of travel and tourism to the U K.

## Defining the Travel and Tourism Industry

The travel and tourism industry exists as a broad network of commercial and non-commercial organisations, linked together by the common objective of servicing the needs of travellers and tourists. Presenting a formal definition of tourism is problematic, firstly because many of the industry's component enterprises and agencies serve both tourists and resident populations, and secondly because some of the major sectors within the industry are often considered as independent industries with a separate identity. It is necessary, therefore, to identify the different sectors involved in the travel and tourism industry and to recognise the extent and nature of this involvement. By doing so it is possible to view the industry as a distinct entity in which each sector plays its own particular role whilst working with others.

## The Travel and Tourism Industry: Component Sectors

The businesses and organisations concerned with travel and tourism can be classified under the following headings, representing the main industrial sectors.

1. Passenger Transport

   ☐ the means by which tourists reach their destination and have mobility on arrival.

2. Accommodation and Catering

☐ this sector provides the facilities for tourists to eat and stay overnight during their trip.

3. Recreation and Amenity

☐ this industrial sector is concerned with a wide range of provision for tourist activity and enjoyment.

4. Tour Operation and Retail Travel

☐ the organisation of package holidays and sale of inclusive tours or their separate elements to the tourist.

5. Tourism Administration

☐ includes agencies responsible for tourism promotion, marketing and development. These are of an official or semi-official nature.

Together, these different sectors are responsible for devising, operating, selling and developing the range of tourism products. Transport operators and providers of accommodation, catering and amenities sell their services both directly to individual tourists, and indirectly through tour operators and travel agents. In addition, they supply both residents and tourists alike, in contrast to tour operators and retail travel agents, who exist almost solely for the purpose of serving tourists and who occupy a critical role as producers and distributors in the travel and tourism industry. These sectors can thus be categorised as direct providers to the tourist.

In addition to the major sources of direct provision, there are also support services which supply both tourists and the tourist industry. These include publications, insurance and foreign exchange facilities for the tourist; and trade publications, market research consultancy and contract hotel suppliers for the tourism industry. Support services can be both commercial and non-commercial. The activities listed above, together with others, are on the periphery of the industry, but nevertheless represent a significant part of it, and illustrate the expansiveness of tourism.

Although official bodies (often referred to as the public sector) with an interest and involvement in tourism, may act as both direct providers and support services, the Tourism Administration sector represents a distinct category of provision. The public sector includes developers, administrators and promoters active in central and local government. Their perspective on tourism is different from that of the commercial operator. In this field, tourism is seen not only as a business, but also as a planning and policy issue.

The demand for goods and services generated by the movement of tourists is therefore met by a wide range of organisations which form the component sectors of the industry. The table on the next page illustrates the different activities of the travel and tourism industry, and is followed by a review of the key sectors.

## The Component Sectors of the Travel and Tourism Industry

### Passenger Transport

Airlines
Passenger Shipping
Railways
Coach and Bus Companies
Car Hire

### Accommodation and Catering

Hotels, Motels and Guesthouses
Farmhouses, B & B
Holiday Centres, Chalets, Cottages, Apartments
Campsites and Caravans
Timesharing
Restaurants, Cafes, Takeaways

### Recreation and Amenity

Sports and Leisure Facilities
Cultural, Scenic and Heritage attractions
Shops

### Tourism Administration

Central and Local Government
Amenity and Conservation bodies
Tourist bodies and Information Centres

### Tour Operation

Domestic
Incoming
Mass Market
Medium Sized
Small Scale/Specialist Opertors

### Retail Travel

Multiple and
Independent Travel Agencies
Business Houses

# Passenger Transport

Passenger Transport operation is of special significance for the tourism industry because travel is an essential element of the tourist experience. As the railway revolutionised domestic travel in the nineteenth century, so the development of civil aviation in the twentieth century has allowed tourists accessibility to worldwide destinations. Air travel now forms the basis of most overseas package holidays sold in the UK. An increase in car ownership has also changed domestic holiday taking patterns, giving the tourist an independence and mobility not available through the use of public transport.

Private car ownership, however, lies outside the travel and tourism industry, which is concerned with commercial operators offering air, sea, rail and road transport services. Each form of transport, whether purchased independently or as part of a package holiday, has its own particular advantages and disadvantages for the tourist, whose travel decisions are based on cost, convenience, place of origin and destination.

The tourism industry is therefore dependent on the transport sector which has traditionally been characterised by a high degree of state involvement. However, in recent years services have been subject to change as a consequence of deregulation. The changing structure of the transport industry (discussed later) has inevitably made its impact on tourism products.

# Accommodation and Catering

The usual definition of tourism includes reference to a stay at a destination of at least 24 hours. Accommodation is therefore a requirement of the tourist. The commercial response to this demand takes a variety of forms, from large hotels to small guest-houses in terms of serviced accommodation provision, and from camp sites to hired apartments in terms of the provision of self-catering facilities. Holiday centres or villages, which have evolved from the holiday camp concept of the 1930s provide both serviced and self-service accommodation.

Patterns of accommodation usage in the U K have undergone a period of significant change in the past decade. The decline in longer domestic holidays of 1-2 weeks' duration has been accompanied by a growing demand for shorter second holidays and an expansion in the business/conference market. Many hotels, especially outside London, have revised their products and marketing in an attempt to improve occupancy levels. Furthermore, the experience of high standards in hotels abroad has highlighted the deficiencies of the UK's hotel stock.

While the domestic hotel sector has been facing a series of problems, new forms of accommodation, such as farmhouses and time-sharing villas, have been introduced, leading to a new diversity in product range and quality. By comparison, hotels outside the UK have been popular with UK tour operators and tourists, despite increased provision of self-catering accommodation.

# Recreation and Amenities

The recreation and amenities sector of the tourism industry encompasses numerous organisations which provide, or assist in the provision of, attractions and amenities for the use of the tourist. Although often considered less important than the accommodation and transport sectors, the activities supplied by this sector can significantly enhance the tourist's enjoyment and appreciation of the destination(s) visited.

Often, the opportunities and environments for recreation supplied are shared by tourists and residents. In an urban context, operators of theatres, cinemas, museums, shops and sports facilities contribute to this sector, and owners of water and winter sports facilities and caravan sites are active in the countryside. Management of these attractions can be both commercial and non-commercial, with local authorities playing a significant role. At a national level, statutory bodies such as the Forestry Commission, and Countryside Commission together with non-governmental organisations such as the National Trust and the Royal Society for the Protection of Birds make provision for tourists, although this is not their primary function.

As well as being for the use of tourists and local residents, general amenities are also an attraction for day visitors or excursionists. Although not officially tourists, day visitors, in terms of their numbers and spending power are an increasingly important market for some tourism-related enterprises.

# Tour Operation and Retail Travel

Tour operators and travel agents exercise a vital function in the travel and tourism industry. Tour operators buy transport, accommodation and other services and package them into a single holiday product which is sold to the customer directly or, more usually, through a travel agent. Travel agents thus act as the retail outlet for holiday products and for individual travel and tourism services.

The package holiday concept has democratised international tourism since its large scale introduction in the 1960s. In the 1970s, sales of package holidays in the UK quadrupled. The package holiday has developed as a product to include a diverse range of holiday types at destinations throughout the world, although the Mediterranean remains the focus of activity in Europe.

The tour-operating sector thus offers a considerable range of products and caters for many different markets. Mass market and specialist operators provide holidays abroad, whilst within the UK, domestic and incoming operators sell inclusive tours to the resident population and to overseas visitors. Tour operators primarily direct their activities to sending residents abroad, as few tourists travel on package holidays at home. Tourist boards and local authorities try to interest the travel trade (that is operators and agents) in selling the UK as a package holiday destination to the resident population. Whilst such initiatives have met with some success, trade interest will continue to centre on overseas package-holidays.

# Tourism Administration

Although the major contributors to the travel and tourism industry are private sector commercial organisations, public sector organisations play an important role both directly and indirectly by providing services. Indeed it is the government, at central and at local level, that determines the wider political, economic and social environment in which all industries function. Particular departments and semi-official agencies have specific responsibilities regarding tourism.

With the increase in tourist activity and the expansion of the travel and tourism industry, the government has become interested in tourism as a means of income generation and job creation. Foreign exchange considerations, along with the implications of tourism as a foreign currency earner for the balance of payments, have led to a reassessment of tourism's importance, especially in areas of economic decline, where tourism is seen as a possible mechanism for regional development and economic regeneration. However, it needs to be recognised that as a source of income and employment, domestic tourism has limitations and these are discussed below.

The official responsibility for tourism lies with the national and regional tourist boards, the former set up by Act of Parliament in 1969, the latter having evolved since that date into a distinct structure in England, Scotland and Wales. The tourist boards are charged with exercising powers relating to marketing and developing tourism in their areas. The fact that the national boards report to the Secretary of State for Employment underlines the government perception of tourism as a significant employer, both currently and in the future.

# Overview of the Industry

We can recognise that the travel and tourism industry consists of a loose amalgamation of organisations and agencies. Many of these are motivated by wider interests than travel and tourism, but they can be considered an integral part of the industry when they act to meet the needs of travellers and tourists.

It should be emphasised that, in addition to the sectors already mentioned, (which will be examined in detail in later chapters) numerous other businesses play a direct or supporting role in the industry and these are identified in the figure below. As well as being distinctive in terms of its diversity, the travel and tourism industry is unusual in that the public sector forms a partnership with the private sector in the area of tourism promotion and development. It is also an industry which is dynamic and constantly developing. Structural changes are taking place within the tour-operating and retail sectors as large companies come to dominate the industry. The accommodation and transport sectors have also undergone change. New product development and innovation is a central process, as the industry seeks to respond to tourist demand which is itself often unpredictable and vulnerable to events in the external environment.

# The National Industry In An International Context

The structure of the travel and tourism industry described above is found in many developed countries, although clearly national differences do exist. The industry serves the needs of three different tourist groups or markets:

1. Domestic Tourists

☐ Residents travelling and taking holidays within their country of residence;

2. Overseas Tourists

☐ Residents leaving their country of residence;

3. Incoming Tourists

☐ Overseas visitor arrivals from another country.

Demands made on the industry in the U K vary depending upon the group. However, these three branches of the industry, each with its own products, are often supplied by the same source. The transport, accommodation and amenity sectors supply services to domestic and incoming tourists. Tour operators and travel agents sell inclusive tours, mainly to residents travelling abroad, while also making some sales of domestic packages.

The travel and tourism industry obviously has an international dimension. Tourists visiting the UK may rely on non-UK agents, operators and transport carriers. Similarly UK tourists abroad buy foreign products and services both directly and indirectly.

Tourism as an activity and as a business tends to be concentrated in the developed economies of Europe and North America, which together account for over 80% of tourist arrivals and departures. However, there is evidence of its commercial penetration in the developing nations.

## The Economic Significance of the Travel and Tourism Industry

All national economies are subject to long-term structural change. The type of structural change which has taken place within the UK economy since 1945 and particularly since 1979, has involved a substantial decline in manufacturing. The manufacturing sector has shed approximately 2.5 million jobs since 1970. Investment in manufacturing and output have fallen considerably, with damaging consequences for full- time employment, export levels and the balance of payments. In its move away from an industrial base, the UK economy has diversified to take in the so called 'sunrise' sector (based on high technology) and the service industries. Travel and tourism, a major contributor to the service sector, is therefore being taken seriously as an industry with a good performance record and considerable potential. The final section of this chapter discusses the travel and tourism industry as a revenue earner and a source of employment.

# Travel and Tourism as a Revenue Earner

The three main market sectors each make a different set of demands on the travel and tourism industry. In order to reach a total figure for the turnover of the UK tourist industry, it is necessary to add up spending by the following groups:

a. domestic tourists resident in the UK;

b. incoming tourists resident overseas;

c. U.K. residents travelling overseas.

When UK residents travel overseas, clearly only a part of their spending remains within the UK economy. Some revenue is earned by transport carriers, tour operators and travel agents, but the bulk of income generated is in the host or destination country. It has been calculated that, of the total spent by UK residents on travel overseas in 1985, 17.12% remained in the UK, 16.44% was spent on fares to foreign carriers, and the remainder (66.44%) was spent in the countries visited (Professor Rik Medlik, in a paper presented at the Financial Times Conference in 1986 - 'The Prospect for Tourism in Britain').

Over the decade 1978-1988 tourism trips within and to the UK show an overall increase, but the rate of growth has been slow and subject to periodic interruption, a phenomenon characteristic of tourist activity. The number of tourist nights spent in the UK by domestic residents fell, whereas the pattern for overseas visitor nights is irregular. By contrast, tourism out of the UK expanded rapidly, especially at the end of the 1970s, and this expansion is reflected both in the number of tourist nights spent overseas, and in expenditure. Although the figures mask changes that have taken place within different areas, they illustrate the challenges and the competition the UK faces as a tourist destination for its own residents and for overseas visitors.

Despite competition, the industry is important in terms of its total turnover, which in 1986 was made up as follows:

| | |
|---|---|
| £ 7150 million | Domestic tourism |
| £ 5400 million | Incoming tourism |
| £ 1039 | Outgoing tourism (amount remaining within the UK economy) |
| £13589 | Total |

This turnover compares favourably with many other commercial enterprises, and its average annual growth rate of 10% suggests that future prospects are encouraging, even allowing for inflation.

The above figures also indicate tourism's role as an earner of foreign exchange. For countries attracting international visitors, tourist movement represents an export, and for generating countries an import. The British tourist industry has a particularly good record as an exporter and this fact has led to official recognition of its contribution to the balance of payments. At the same time the dramatic expansion in the numbers of UK tourists travelling overseas has generated concern about import payments, which show an increasing tendency to exceed export earnings.

# Travel and Tourism as a Source of Employment

As well as contributing to the national economy by raising revenue and generating income, the travel and tourism industry is often held to be significant in terms of its role as an employer. The provision of services for tourists gives rise to a wide range of jobs in both origin and host countries. The majority of jobs are created at the destination, since such provision necessarily involves a high degree of personal service at the place visited. The UK is both a source of international tourists and a destination for domestic and overseas visitors, and so the industry supports employment in domestic, incoming and outgoing tourist enterprises and organisations.

However, the precise number of jobs created by travel and tourism is difficult to establish. This is partly a function of problems associated with data collection and partly related to the fact that tourism is not yet officially recognised as a separate statistical category.

Employment estimates for the late 1980s put the figure at between 1 million and 1.2 million, the greatest proportion of employees being located in the accommodation and transport sectors. Certainly since the late 1970s, the number of people employed in the travel and tourism industry has increased. In view of its share of total employment within the wider economy, and taking into account the high unemployment figures, the industry has become one of considerable importance. However, some of the claims made for future expansion appear exaggerated and unrealistic.

In summary, an industry of considerable size has emerged in response to the increased numbers of tourists and their growing demand for services and facilities. The industry incorporates many different enterprises and organisations which act together to service the needs of domestic, incoming and outgoing tourists. Such is the scale of activity, that the travel and tourism industry has assumed a new significance as a source of income, foreign exchange and employment. The following chapters will examine the component sectors of this industrial network in more detail.

# Chapter 5

# Transport in Travel and Tourism

## Introduction

Transport is sometimes seen as the 'poor relation' of the travel and tourism industry and yet transport is indispensable to the operation of the industry and a knowledge of its operation is essential to an understanding of the industry. This chapter begins with an examination of the structure of the tourism-related transport industry. Then it considers the regulatory systems which control the industry and concludes with case studies which illustrate why transport plays such a key role in travel and tourism.

## The Importance of Transport

Transport is important to the travel and tourism industry for four reasons.

### 1. Tourism implies travel

Tourism is dependent upon transport, the scale and importance of which is not always appreciated. If we start with the number of passengers passing through the 55 commercial airports in the U.K., the 1987 figure was 86 million, a 14% increase over 1986 and this is predicted to increase to somewhere around 200 million annually by the year 2005.

Quite apart from flying in and out of airports, people have to get to and from them, and currently plans are being implemented for a British Rail link between London (Paddington) and Heathrow, in addition to the existing Underground (Piccadilly line) facility. In 1993, when the new line is scheduled to open, it is expected that 42 million passengers will pass through Heathrow each year. Of these, around 22% would be 'interlining' (changing from one aircraft to another). A quarter of the total, however, would be travelling to or from central London, and of these, slightly under half are expected to use the new rail link - a market of some 5 million passengers each year from the outset.

British Rail of course, does not only carry tourists, but in Europe as a whole railways are estimated to gain about 15% of their revenue from tourism. Total passenger revenue for British Rail in 1987/1988, excluding season tickets, was £1,150 million, and Inter City services carried passengers a total

of 8,250 million kilometres. Many of British Rail's 'provincial' services, for example in western Scotland, mid Wales, and the Leeds-Settle-Carlisle line, now generate more of their income from tourist traffic than from local residents and the scenery and attractions along these routes are being promoted strongly. British Rail has an International Sales department to persuade overseas visitors to use its services, and this generates £34 million in direct income, of which £12 million was from the BritRail pass giving unlimited travel in the U.K..

Returning to the U.K. air travel market, let us consider where people actually travel to and from. Currently, travellers from western Europe predominate, accounting for around 72% of traffic; North America generates 14% and the rest of the world the remaining 14%. Taking all incoming visitors to the U.K. in the month of June 1988, 860,000 came from western Europe, 380,000 from North America, and 270,000 from elsewhere in the world. North America numbers were down by 6% on the year before, although 23% more Britons were travelling to North America. The European figure was a 14% increase on the previous year. All these trends are of great importance to the transport operators, who need to tailor their services accordingly.

A feature which the airlines share with British Rail is that much of the traffic comes from business travellers. Leisure travellers account for 70% of passengers using the U.K.'s airports but, because the fares paid by the 22% of business travellers are higher, they contribute a greater percentage of turnover (50% of British Airways' scheduled revenue is from business travellers). Also, a greater proportion of those originating in the U.K. are on leisure trips than those from overseas; incoming passengers include far more business travellers, and there is a sizeable market in overseas students coming to the U.K. to take English language courses. Some routes and destinations are more important for leisure traffic, whilst others contribute mainly business travel, and this is reflected in the proportions of scheduled and charter traffic. Government policies also have an influence here, and the whole subject is discussed later in the chapter. The following table shows the percentage contributions of scheduled and charter flights to the various destination areas of the world in 1986.

| **Scheduled Charter** | (%) | (%) |
|---|---|---|
| Western Europe | 33 | 37 |
| Eastern Europe | 1 | 2 |
| North America | 13 | 1 |
| South America | 1 | - |
| Africa | 3 | 1 |
| Middle East | 3 | - |
| Indian sub-continent | 1 | - |
| Far East and Australia | 4 | - |
| All areas | 59 | 41 |

# Some of the Major Airports of the U.K.

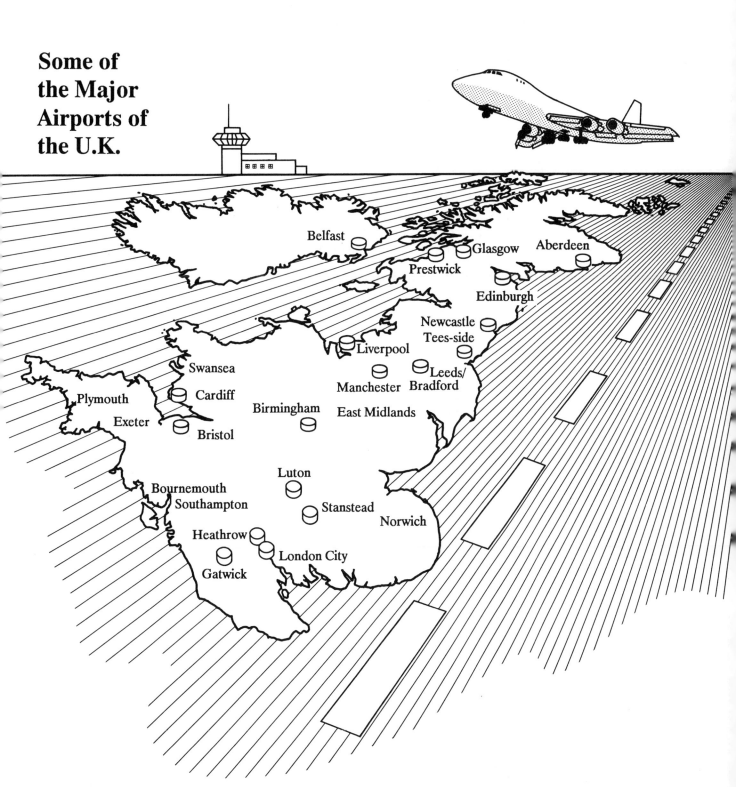

Belfast

Glasgow Aberdeen

Prestwick

Edinburgh

Newcastle
Tees-side

Liverpool

Swansea

Plymouth

Cardiff

Manchester Leeds/
Bradford

Birmingham East Midlands

Exeter

Bristol

Luton

Bournemouth
Southampton

Stanstead

Norwich

Heathrow

London City

Gatwick

It can be seen that charter flights are overwhelmingly within western Europe, but even here there are predictable variations: 85% of traffic to Spain is on charter flights, but only 1% of that to the Netherlands. The importance of that is that most charter flights operate in connection with inclusive tour packages.

Partly because air travel is mainly international, all these passengers are carried by a variety of airlines, large and small, British and non-British. The U.K.'s 'national airline' (though now privately owned) is British Airways, with around 90% of all scheduled traffic carried by British carriers; it also has a subsidiary which specialises in charter operations: Caledonian Airways, set up in 1988 after take-over of British Caledonian. In 1987/88 British Airways' turnover was £3,756 million, on which it made a net profit of £228 million. It carried 23 million passengers and had 42,700 employees - another indication of the scale of transport operations for tourism.

## 2. Transport is a product of the Travel Business

There are other reasons why transport merits attention in a travel and tourism textbook. Travel agents generate a varying, but large, proportion of their income from selling transport services, as distinct from holiday packages - and in particular tickets for the air and rail travel discussed above, together with coach and ferry services. World-wide 75% of all air tickets are sold by travel agents, increasing to 87% in the U.S.A.. Commission is paid on these sales, and it is therefore necessary for the travel agent to know something of the product which is being sold.

## 3. There is overlap between the components of the tourism industry

Some travel agents and tour operators are offshoots of transport companies: the same organisation which puts the package together or sells it may be involved in providing the transport.

## 4. The  quality of transport is important in the travel business

A tour operator contracting hotel accommodation seeks assurances about the standard of rooms, meals and other facilities. The quality of the transport, especially for the tourist visiting a number of locations, may be as important as the quality of the accommodation, food and other facilities. Less attention tends to be given to the choice of transport, and it is rare for transport to be categorised as precisely as hotels. A tour operator contracting seats on an aircraft will probably know the make and model of the aircraft because the number of seats which the aircraft holds is a vital factor in the costing of a package. It is unlikely that the tour operator will know whether the aircraft has equipment for landing in fog (which will affect the reliability of flights), or whether it is noisier than average. In West Germany, a 'star rating' system of the kind used for hotels is applied to coaches. A high number of stars indicates a coach with air-conditioning, toilets, etc. Suggestions that such a system could be adopted in the UK have not,as yet, been taken up, apparently because coach operators are reluctant to commit themselves to providing high-quality coaches.

# The Structure of Tourism Related Transport

The transport industry, in common with the tourism industry in general, involves a range of statutory and commercial organisations operating a variety of management structures. The transport industry can be examined in terms of its external and its internal organisation.

## 1. The External Organisation of the Transport Industry

### (a.) Publicly Owned Transport Operations

Many transport operators are state corporations: nationalised industries such as British Rail, S.N.C.F., and many state-owned national airlines. Local councils usually provide transport in response to social need rather than for leisure purposes. Some local councils, however, operate coach fleets for public hire and an interest by local authorities in the provision of transport contributes to the development of tourism locally. Many regional airports, such as Luton, are owned by companies whose shareholders are the local authorities in their region. Other airports such as Newcastle, are owned by a consortium of local authorities in that region.

### (b.) Transport Operators which are Public Limited Companies

A number of transport operators are public corporations quoted on the Stock Exchange. Some, such as the P & O group with its ferry and cruising interests, have been in existence for a century or more. Others, such as British Airways, came into existence as the result of the sale of nationalised industries. Some countries have chosen a mixture of private and state ownership for their national airlines, Alitalia and Lufthansa being examples of such airlines.

### (c.) Private Transport Operators

At the smallest level of external organisation, there are private firms, which for legal purposes may be either private companies, partnerships or sole traders. The resources of some of these organisations may consist of only one man and a second-hand coach, whereas others are extremely large and may engage in a variety of activities, such as aircraft charter and tour operation. Large tour operators have great market power. The transport sector is similarly dominated by a few large companies, such as International Leisure. The large companies can secure low rates, making for stiff competition, especially where transport is contracted in. However, the small firm enjoys some advantages, particularly if it specialises:

- [ ] low overheads;
- [ ] a high degree of personal commitment;
- [ ] the ability to handle only small numbers of tourists;
- [ ] willingness to accept short bookings rather than whole seasons only;
- [ ] availability to fill gaps in large operators' block bookings;
- [ ] operating in an area remote from the airports and large firms' pick-up points.

Getting to the airport may present, or appear to present, a major problem to the traveller, and the local firm which can build up a reputation by word of mouth and which can offer a door-to-door service, has a strong marketing advantage. Also a small local firm may be able to find a niche in the market which is too small for large companies to be interested in. This is especially true of in-coming tourism, where there are opportunities for 'historic' transport services at heritage museums and the like.

### (d.) Franchising

Franchising involves an administrative organisation planning and marketing a product or service, and contracting out the day-to-day operation to individual firms. This is the form in which the UK company, National Express, operates its long-distance coach business. National Express has recently bought interests in some other companies but most of its fleet is contracted in from other operators on a daily and seasonal basis and fluctuates according to demand. On average 700 coaches are contracted from other coach companies on either a long-term or a trip basis. The contract normally includes the drivers and, in the case of the high quality Rapide services, hostesses. Historically, these companies were all members of the privatised National Bus Company, but increasingly, smaller firms are being used. The coaches are normally painted in the National Express livery, and the rate paid to contractors is lower if this condition is not adhered to.

### (e.) Integrated Transport Systems

Some countries, notably Switzerland, have developed integrated transport systems. Under such systems there is minimal competition between the different forms of public transport In Switzerland all services including rail (owned both by the state and 'private' railway companies), postbuses (owned and operated by the Post Office and private contractors), lake ferries and cable cars (both of which are privately owned) connect with each other and are listed in one comprehensive timetable. The systems are extensively used by tourists, who can buy inclusive tickets allowing travel on any service.

## 2. The Internal Organisation of Transport Operators

There is an important overlap between transport and other tourism sectors. This overlap can take two forms: either horizontal or vertical integration.

### (a.) Horizontal Integration

Horizontal integration occurs when a firm diversifies into a related activity which is not an essential component of its existing market: thus Sea Containers, the owners of Sealink revived the Orient Express, a luxurious train travelling across Europe.

### (b.) Vertical Integration

Vertical integration occurs when a firm develops into another part of the 'chain' involved in the supply of its existing product. This can be seen most clearly in the case of the large tour operators who have developed subsidiary airlines: International Leisure Group which controls Air Europe and Thomson which controls both Britannia Airways and, since its takeover of Horizon, Orion. A lesser-known, but rapidly expanding, organisation is the Pleasu –

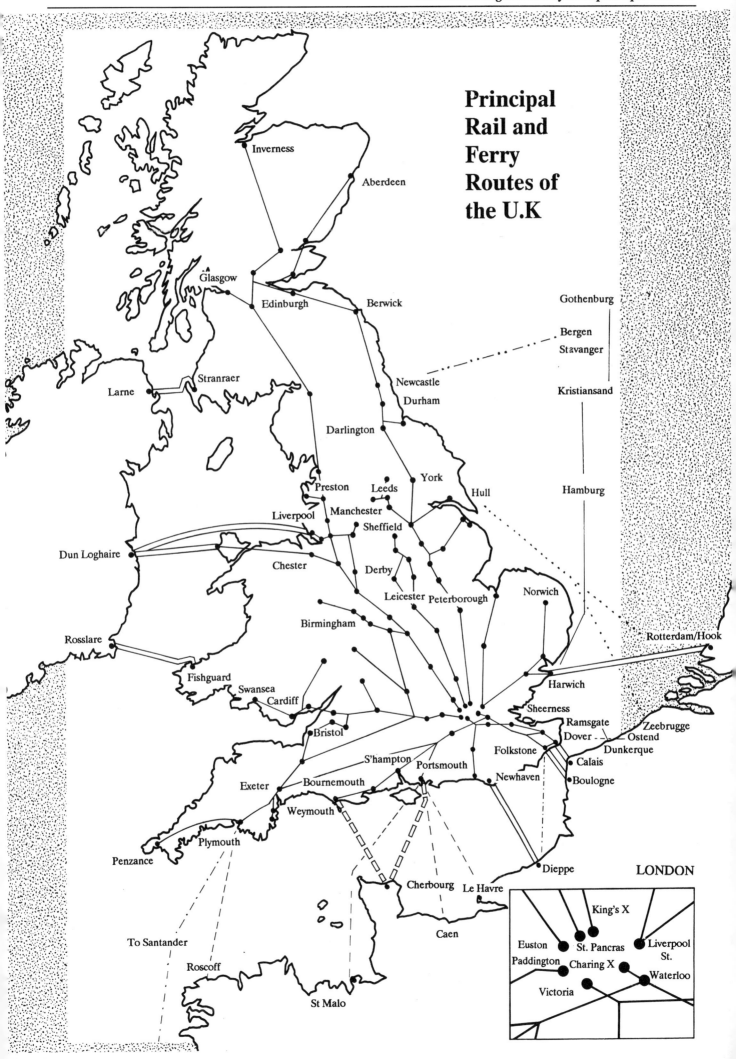

**Principal Rail and Ferry Routes of the U.K**

Inverness

Aberdeen

Gothenburg

Bergen
Stavanger

Kristiansand

Glasgow

Edinburgh

Berwick

Newcastle
Durham

Larne

Stranraer

Darlington

Hamburg

York

Preston

Leeds

Hull

Manchester

Liverpool

Sheffield

Dun Loghaire

Chester

Derby

Norwich

Leicester

Peterborough

Rotterdam/Hook

Rosslare

Birmingham

Fishguard

Harwich

Swansea
Cardiff

Sheerness

Ramsgate

Zeebrugge

Bristol

Dover

Ostend

Dunkerque

Folkstone

Calais

S'hampton

Portsmouth

Newhaven

Boulogne

Exeter

Bournemouth

Weymouth

Plymouth

Penzance

Dieppe

Cherbourg

Le Havre

**LONDON**

Caen

To Santander

Roscoff

St Malo

King's X

Euston

St. Pancras

Liverpool
St.

Paddington

Charing X

Waterloo

Victoria

rama Group, which originally operated casinos. After buying a number of hotels, the group took over a series of small coach-tour operators in Northern England and the Midlands, a purchase which offered both the basis for growth and an obvious area for potential development in conjunction with its hotels. By 1987, the group had become the largest UK coach firm, with over 350 coaches. In that yeart Pleasurama acquired the UK market leader in coach tours, National Holidays. This company, which sold 320,000 holidays annually and had become independent as a result of the privatisation of National Bus, was a franchise operation like National Express. The attraction of National Holidays to Pleasurama was not merely the potential for economies of scale in its existing coach business, but also the possibility of developing a further market for the coach fleet and for the hotel accommodation it already owned. The Pleasurama Group itself has now been taken over by Mecca, with interests in a range of leisure industries.

# The Role of the Transport Operator

The role of the transport provider involves either providing transport for holidays which it organises and sells, or else contracting an external tour operator to do so. This may involve a company providing space on a service it would run anyway (as with British Rail and the ferry companies), or else involve a 'dedicated service', as with coach operators who contract coaches for the full season, and require the coaches to be presented in the livery of the holiday company.

Most transport operators are involved in other markets in addition to the tourist market: ferries carry lorries; railways carry freight; airlines carry more freight in the belly-holds of passenger aircraft than they carry on their freight-only flights; coach operators are often dependent on school contracts and sometimes run local bus services. Indeed, many transport companies have moved into the tourism market in response to a decline in their traditional markets, and as they saw tourism expanding. This joint activity has important implications for the economics of such companies' tourist activities. For example, if certain resources are under-used and therefore available when the tourist market demands them, their incorporation into a tourism operation enables better use to be made of them and improves cost effectiveness. However, once holiday business becomes the transport operator's prime activity the diversion of resources is no longer applicable.

A large part of a transport contractor's work may relate to incoming tourists (on either a national or an international basis), and the extent of this work is often not realised. The British Tourist Authority estimated that in 1984 13.5 million overseas tourists came to the UK, spending £5,000m (including fare payments to British carriers). Although this work is often local, it can, over time, be substantial. For example, skiing holidays in Austria often require coaches to ferry customers to and from the piste. Many skiing holidays fly to and from Munich airport, which is a three-hour coach journey from the resort. Within the UK, firms such as American Express charter coaches to carry incoming Americans from Heathrow on tours of the UK lasting up to two weeks (in addition to more mundane shuttle work between hotels and airports, theatres and so on). Saga Holidays, specialising in tourism for the elderly, offer holidays based in the halls of residence of Durham University colleges outside the undergraduate's term. Saga make block bookings with

British Rail to transport the holiday-makers to Durham. On arrival, a Durham coach firm ferries the holiday-makers from the station to the colleges, and also on day tours around the region.

In each case, the transport provider is geographically remote from the tour operator, and quality control is vital. Whilst it might be possible to specify coaches of a particular quality, a holiday can be spoiled by a poor driver. Training of coach drivers is a neglected area, and, particularly in large cities, good coach drivers are scarce.

# Regulatory Control of Transport

## 1. What is regulation ?

Between 1979 and 1986, the UK government deregulated the UK road passenger transport industry. The terms 'regulation' and 'deregulation' need definition, to show why they are important to tourism. Whilst deregulation is a political issue, and therefore any definition is likely to be either vague, or controversial, or both, the attempt at its definition introduces an examination of the area.

'Transport regulation' might be defined by those in favour of deregulation as 'non-commercial interference with an untethered or free market in the provision of passenger transport services.' Such a wide definition could include within it many unlikely possibilities, for example, government action in fixing wage levels. This later became a topical issue when, in response to their deregulation in the late 1970s, US airlines reduced wages and in some cases introduced a two-tier structure, within which new staff were paid less than those already employed. Usually, however, regulation is concerned with safety (sometimes called 'quality') control, and economic, or quantity, control.

External safety control is generally accepted as socially beneficial. For example, regulation requires of airlines extremely high standards of maintenance and operating procedures. Regulation generally attracts controversy only when it is shown to be absent. For example, the sinking of the *Titanic* in 1912 precipitated a demand for regulation to ensure that every ship carries sufficient lifeboats for all its passengers. The loss of the *Herald of Free Enterprise* at Zeebrugge in March 1987 precipitated discussions concerning the adequacy of safety procedures on ro-ro (roll-on roll-off) car ferries.

'Quality' controls include such matters as the professional qualifications of ships' masters, airline pilots and coach drivers, their working hours and the mechanical condition of the equipment they use.

Economic, or 'quantity', control, is less widely accepted, especially by those people who benefit from the removal of this form of regulation. The commonest types of economic regulation are:

(a.) **Regulation governing initial entry to an activity.**

This is normally introduced for one of two reasons. These are:

(i) to favour one form of transport at the expense of another (for example, West Germany and France discourage road transport in order to favour their comprehensive rail networks).

(ii) to limit competition within a particular sector of the transport industry.

This is usually the reason for bilateral air agreements (discussed below). Such agreements often restrict the number of airlines licensed to operate a particular route to one national airline from each country served.

(b.) **Regulation concerned with the fixing the level of operations or the timetable.**

Again, agreements concerning air services often do this in order to give 'fair shares', to avoid operators continually re-timing their services for competitive reasons and to secure the maximum number of customers.

(c.) **Regulation to establish prices.**

The International Air Transport Association (IATA) establishes prices for scheduled air services over most of the world, although its influence has weakened in Europe and particularly in North America.

Economic regulation may spread to other areas. For example, IATA has attempted to regulate standards of airline catering and seat pitch (the number of inches between the seats).

A further type of regulation is concerned with the quality of the environment. For example, as the result of pressure from residents living beneath airport approach flight paths, limits are placed on night movements of aircraft at airports. This affects the utilisation of aircraft and thus airline economics. Another type of environmental regulation is the imposition of controls on transport operators' premises, limiting where they may be sited and how they might be used.

# 2. Why is regulation important ?

The availability and the price of transport services, as sold by a travel agent or bought through a contract by a tour operator, are critically affected by regulation. Understanding how regulation works helps the travel agent and the tour operator to secure the best deal, since sometimes, the same product can be bought at vastly different prices. Regulation is a constraining factor on management, which is prevented from doing things in the way it might wish. The response of some managers is to search for loopholes and other ways round the regulation, in order to maximise profit. This explains some of the strange practices of the transport industry. For example it is much easier to gain approval to provide charter flights than scheduled air services. The definition of an inclusive tour, for which most charter flights are run, is that accommodation must be provided as a well as travel. Some air operators who were seeking to get round the difficulty of entry and the high scheduled air fares imposed by IATA offered instead packages including very basic accommodation, still well below the scheduled fare and which customers were not seriously expected to use, as a device to get round these rules.

# 3. The case for regulation

(a.) Economic regulation encourages stability. Providing a regular service, especially an air route to a far-off destination, may be profitable only at certain times, and were free entry to the market allowed, a new competitor might choose to run only at profitable times, in the process removing the existing operator's profit and leading to the cancellation of a poorly-used service. It may be important to passengers, and for political or strategic reasons to a government, that the regular frequency is maintained.

(b.) Competition precipitates price wars, eventually leading to bankruptcy for less successful companies. As the passenger often pays substantial amounts of money in advance, the consequence of a travel company going bankrupt is either that the customers are unable to travel, or else that they are left stranded at their destinations. This is generally considered to be socially unacceptable.

(c.) Deregulation of competition and pricing can and often does mean that carriers cannot afford to renew their equipment. As their existing fleet of ferries, coaches or aircraft wears out, the carrier cannot afford replacements. Studies during the late 1980s demonstrate that the age of aircraft in the United States (which deregulated its domestic air traffic in 1979) is not only considerably higher than in European countries with their regulations firmly in tact, but is also in excess of the manufacturers planned life-expectancy. This has profound safety implications, and is a matter of social concern.

(d.) New equipment is generally more efficient and so cheaper to run, quieter and therefore socially more acceptable, and environmentally less damaging. Cutting prices may deprive operators of the opportunity of buying new equipment.

(e.) Sometimes potential traffic is insufficient to support two operators. In a competitive situation only one, or neither, will survive. This appears to be true of ferry services to the Scottish Islands, where attempts to introduce competition have led to the failure of one or the other operator. This phenomenon, known as 'wasteful competition', can also have undesirable social side-effects. Transport vehicles are criticised for the noise, pollution and congestion they cause. To operate, for the sake of competition, significantly more services than actual passenger traffic demands, as was the case with aircraft crossing the North Atlantic in the early 1980s (the passengers involved could be carried in fewer than half the services operated on a typical day) is socially and environmentally objectionable.

(f.) Where an operator services a number of routes, profitable routes can be used to cross-subsidise unprofitable routes which are considered, for one reason or another, necessary. To achieve this, the operator must have a monopoly on the profitable route. In a deregulated market, a competitor has access to the profitable route, with no commitment to the poor route. By charging a lower price, the new operator entices passengers away from the original operator, reducing or eliminating the possibility of cross-subsidy.

(g.) Industries with high capital/technology costs are expensive to enter, and therefore there may be few, if any, competitors. The customers of a company which holds a monopoly needs protection from the complacent habits that may arise as a result of poor service standards, high costs, etc.. Regulation can prevent excessive fares from being charged and can monitor the quality of the service.

# 4. The case against regulation.

(a.) Regulation implies non-commercial interference in an untethered market. Whether society is better served by an unregulated, or a centrally-planned, or a mixed economy is a political issue. Countries in western Europe and North America have economies which are mixed: they range variously along the spectrum between the poles of central planning and an absence of regulation. Operating transport is different from running, say, a grocer's shop, in that disregarding safety standards is likely to have much more serious consequences. Economic deregulation can, therefore, be accompanied by enhanced enforcement of safety standards. Operators which do not comply can be refused authority to operate.

(b.) A regulatory body must be set up to carry out the regulation. Whilst set up with the intention that they be informally run and simple, such bodies inevitably develop precise procedures and set precedents, requiring the employment of specialist lawyers to advance or answer a case. The expense of this is feasible for a large operator, but may be beyond the means of a small firm. Thus, unless steps are taken otherwise, regulation disadvantages small operators.

(c.) In an untethered market, a transport operator may choose to run an unprofitable service for commercial reasons, for instance, to win greater market share. If running an unprofitable service is deemed necessary for social or political reasons, then politicians make the decisions. The contentious issue here is who pays the difference. Should the loss be paid for from public funds ? Or should users of another service be expected to cross-subsidise, when they have little or no choice in the matter? Furthermore, it may be that another operator could run the unprofitable service profitably. This is not to say that cross-subsidy never happens with deregulation, in practice not all routes are contested. However, it is a feature of competitive systems that, even if competition does not exist at the time, an operator must remain efficient, keep down costs, and maximise business. Otherwise the operator will be vulnerable to attack from a competitor. This is known as the 'theory of contestable markets'.

(d.) Regulatory bodies without strict guidelines sometimes expand their terms of reference to include matters less central to the purpose for which they were created. Whilst it is valuable for aircraft passengers to be protected from poor hygiene in the preparation of chilled meals, it is doubtful that it should be the responsibility of a transport regulatory body to lay down guidelines.

(e.) Where conventional competition is not allowed, an operator's desire to maximise market share is channelled into fringe areas. Costs are increased by spending on free drinks, limousines to the airport and expensive promotion. Airlines may also compete for favour with the business traveller by providing a greater frequency of service than is really needed, simply to ensure that a customer is never lost to a rival through an aircraft being full. The significance of this is that the ordinary passenger tends not to be served as well.

(f.) If regulation means that entry by newcomers to a market is severely restricted, those already in the market can form a cartel, which effectively creates a monopoly. Cartels are powerful, generally low-profile, and tend to act against the public interest. There is a danger that a cartel may be more powerful than an industry's regulatory body, and also that a cartel may be able to exert unconstitutional influence over the regulatory body. It is said by some people that intercontinental air transport, with the exception of traffic over the North Atlantic, may be subject to the operation of a cartel.

# 5. Practical effects of deregulation

Conclusions about deregulation can be drawn by considering two practical examples. In 1979-80, long-distance coaches in the UK and domestic airlines in the USA were deregulated.

In both cases it can be said that, since that time, patronage has increased, the quality of the equipment has improved, and competition, together with improvements in productivity and other cost savings, have led to reduced prices for the customer. Whether the outcome has been as desirable for the operators is more debatable, and not all customers have felt the benefit.

It is a maxim in business that the strong get stronger and the weak get weaker. In the transport business this has applied not only to the operators but also to the locations they serve. National Express was predominant in the UK Express Coach market before 1980 and still is, despite competition from large and small operators, which declined in importance during the 1980s. In America the effect of competition has been more complex. Large but weak operators such as Pan Am lost out, as did small low-cost newcomers, such as People Express. Mergers have taken place which, overall, concentrate services into fewer hands (the top eight airlines in 1986 carried 94% of all passengers, as against 17% in 1977), while the number of small regional airlines declined from 263 to 150 between 1978 and 1986.

By 'strong locations are getting stronger' is meant that transport operators tend increasingly to concentrate on major inter-urban flows at the expense of cross country routes and minor destinations. Both air and coach operators have developed the use of 'hubs'; centres where reserve aircraft or coaches are concentrated and passengers' opportunities for reaching given destinations are maximised by their having the possibility of changing from one service to another. In the US, public funds have to be used to retain services to minor destinations which operators would no longer serve by cross-subsidy. In Britain too, small towns and villages have lost coach services. The coaches now ply only fast trunk road system routes, linking many places in Wales and rural England, already deprived of rail services.

Deregulation offers management opportunities to cut operating costs. A case in point is the system operated by regional air services in America. One aspect of this involves 'code-sharing' by large and small airlines. Increasingly, information on service availability is obtained from visual displays on travel agents' counters, and the operator who can project the required information first is most likely to make the sale. Thus, large airlines have an incentive to offer as comprehensive a service as possible, while smaller ones gain from association with the large airlines - a gain which extends to the timetabling of services into and out of the major 'hubs' at suitable connecting times. Such 'code- sharing' brings large and small airlines closer together and will probably lead to more mergers, and therefore fewer operators.

Deregulation has encouraged greater flexibility in pricing, leading to substantially increased sales for the transport operator. In the late 1970s, payment for National Express tickets with Mars Bar wrappers would have sounded ridiculous; today such an offer is conventional marketing strategy, and similar ideas have been used by state monopolies such as British Rail. Operators have learned that indiscriminate price-cutting may take them from profit to loss. Some operators have learned that the way to increased profits is to maintain or increase prices, while improving quality in a way that makes the product unique and more attractive to the customer.

# 6. Who are the Regulators?

Central government carries out some functions directly through its Ministries. In national terms, it determines policy on, for instance, the location of new airports, and the relative status of existing ones; and the lack of coach-parking facilities in major tourist centres, especially in London, and ways of making more available.

The process of international negotiation to introduce air services is carried out at diplomatic level by the respective governments' Foreign Offices.

Governments also set up specific bodies to carry out regulatory functions. In Britain, the Civil Aviation Authority controls air service licensing, has charge of the safety of aircraft and their operators and runs the Air Traffic Control Service, and a number of major airports. The Traffic Commissioners, through local Traffic Areas, issue and monitor operators' licences held by coach firms. These licences are primarily concerned with safety. Now that all road traffic is deregulated, the responsibility of the Traffic Commissioners is not to approve the services, but to keep records of those being run and to exercise quality control over operators. International coach services, on the other hand, cannot be introduced in the same way as UK national ones because other European countries operate regulated systems. It is necessary, therefore, for negotiation to take place through the Department of Transport and its overseas counterpart before a service can be started.

Local government is also able to regulate. Local authorities own many regional airports; control licences for taxis, many of whose users are tourists; in sensitive areas they may lay down routes to be followed by tourist coaches and determine where coaches can park. Being responsible for subsidising local bus services, local authorities are able to determine which unprofitable rural services (which may be oriented towards tourists) will run. For example, Tynedale District Council together with the Countryside Commission and the Northumberland National Park, supports a bus service connecting a number of Roman sites on Hadrian's Wall, in order to improve public access to the sites and to relieve pressure on car parking spaces at the more popular sites.

There are international bodies supported by governments. Principal among these is the International Civil Aviation Organisation (ICAO), a United Nations body to which all members of the UN automatically belong. ICAO is concerned mainly with the technical side of air operation, in particular with the investigation of accidents (in which a number of countries are likely to have an interest), with the improving of technical standards for the benefit of all, and with helping developing countries to match facilities with international standards.

ICAO works closely with  the International Air Transport Association (IATA), which is not a government body but a trade organisation, that is, a body which represents most international airlines. IATA is concerned with technical matters (hence its liaison with ICAO), and also provides legal and financial services for its members. However, it is best known as the body which still decides a great many of the fares to be charged for flights across the world by international airlines, a role which technically is delegated to it by the individual governments.

Transport operators also have national trade associations which may have a regulatory function. The work carried out by the Association of British Travel (ABTA) in setting standards for travel agents is a form of regulation. One of the requirements of ABTA members is that all member companies must place a bond with it. This is a sum of money which acts as an insurance against the financial collapse of a tour operator after customers have paid for holidays. Many smaller coach operators are not ABTA members, because they run from a limited area, selling through direct bookings and a few agents. Nevertheless their trade association, the Bus and Coach Council (BCC) has a similar bonding system, which has not been required to issue payments to passengers, because no member has failed. A similar bonding scheme is operated by the Passenger Shipping Association for the ferry operators.

Airlines which use a given airport normally form a users' committee. These committees are important because they allocate the 'slots' or departure times for flights. With many major airports nearing the maximum number of departures they can handle, it is important that each airline secures the maximum number of 'slots' and obtains a high proportion of them at peak times when passenger demand is greatest.

Before leaving the topic of regulation it is worth noting that the free trade policies of the European Economic Community (EEC), include some deregulation of air services within the community.

# A regulatory system in practice

## 1. London sightseeing tours

How does an operator obtain approval to run sightseeing tours by bus or coach in London? First, the owner of the vehicles must have an Operator's Licence issued by the Metropolitan Traffic Commissioner. If the customers have already been formed into a group beforehand by a tour operator, the vehicle is simply chartered from the bus or coach operator, as this constitutes contract work for which there are few further formalities. The operator is required only to keep a record of the trip. Alternatively, if passengers are picked up in the street and tickets sold on the spot, the position is different. London is an exception to the rest of the UK in that there is still economic regulation of bus services, although this may change in the near future. The operator normally has to obtain a Road Service Licence, also from the Metropolitan Traffic Commissioner. One of the grounds on which the Commissioner can refuse to issue a licence is if severe traffic congestion would be caused. Picking- up and waiting points can be controlled to avoid congestion. As there has been considerable expansion of bus services since licensing was relaxed in 1980, and since congestion has been caused by competing operators' buses occupying space at popular spots such as Piccadilly Circus, the Commissioner is likely to impose conditions regarding waiting. In one case, operators were granted licences subject to there being only one vehicle at the starting point at any one time.

## 2. Air service agreements: Laker Airways and Skytrain

In order to understand the struggle between Laker Airways and the UK government over the former's application to introduce the Skytrain service from the UK to North America, it is necessary to examine the procedure by which an airline obtains a licence. First, a bilateral agreement must be made between the governments of the countries concerned. This agreement specifies the number of airlines that are to operate the service. It is normally either a 'dual designation' in which only two airlines may operate (usually one from each country) or a 'multiple designation' which allows a number of airlines to operate a service. The agreement normally specifies that the fixing of detailed times and fares should be delegated to IATA, subject to government confirmation. It also specifies which of a number of possible 'freedoms' apply. These 'freedoms' grant the airline the following rights.

(a.) Freedom to fly over a country's territory.

(b.) Freedom to land for technical reasons.

(c.) Freedom to set down passengers, mail and freight from the originating country.

(d.) Freedom to pick up passengers, mail and freight from the originating country.

(e.) Freedom to start the flight in the home country (A), pick up passengers, mail and freight in country (B) and convey to country (C).

(f.) Freedom to start in country (A), and operate via the home country (B) to country (C).

The granting of the first and second of these freedoms is normally automatic. The third and fourth are negotiable, although possession of these freedoms normally forms the basis of most international services; while the fifth and sixth freedoms are the least commonly agreed.

An airline wishing to take advantage of a bilateral agreement must next satisfy the licensing requirements of each state involved. Also it may be that two airlines sharing a route agree to pool the revenue on that route, in order to provide a more attractive timetable for the customer.

The above applies to scheduled services, whereas many tourists are carried on charter flights. Each country is entitled to form its own view as to whether to encourage charters. The USA, for example, has a totally deregulated scheduled market, and very few charter operations; whereas in Europe, scheduled services are generally tightly controlled, and charters are encouraged since they are seen as assisting the growth of tourism.

The number of charter flights grew rapidly during the 1960s and early 1970s as an alternative to scheduled services. Their popularity was and is due to the low air fare. This is because the cost per passenger is low. It is worth summarising the reasons for this. First, it can be assumed that a higher percentage of seats on the aircraft will be filled. Tour organisers ensure this by cancelling or consolidating flights. This means that the passengers from two or more flights which are not full may be combined onto a single flight. Second, a larger number of seats is fitted into a given type of aircraft when used for charter flights than is used for scheduled services. Third, most charters are operated by small carriers, whose overheads are low and who spend little on promotion and in-flight service. Fourth, charter flights operate only when commercially justified, there being no obligation to maintain a 'service'. Fifth, one flight might be used by several tour operators, thus minimising the commercial risk to both operator and carrier.

By 1970, the low-cost of charter flights meant that, in some cases, package holiday prices were below IATA approved scheduled fares to the same destination, and this has led to much criticism of those fares. Another effect of the freedom available to charter flight operators was that operators supposedly providing flights for pre-organised clubs and groups in fact sold seats on an individual basis. A further response to the situation was that of Laker Airways, primarily a charter business, which proposed a cheap scheduled service between London and New York along charter lines and with no advance booking. Laker was entitled to do that under the UK's 'Bermuda' bilateral agreement with the US, and a licence was granted by the CAA in 1972.

Under the Bermuda agreement, the Civil Aeronautics Board in the US was entitled to check Laker's suitability as an operator and obtain the President's approval before services could commence. The first of these things was done, but the second was not probably due to pressure from Pan Am and other airlines, and due to the oil crisis of 1973-74. This crisis and the commerce and trade recession which followed affected Britain and British Airways. The two UK General Elections in 1974 returned Labour Governments. These took a different view of competition between airlines from that of the previous Conservative administration. Whilst the application by British Airways' to the CAA to revoke Laker's Licence was unsuccessful, the overtures it made to the government were successful. It was decided that only one British airline would operate across the North Atlantic and British Airways was favoured, and this was followed by the publication of a White Paper confirming the view.

Meanwhile, the CAB withdrew Laker's licence from the list for the Presidential confirmation. It appeared, therefore, that, despite his having complied with licensing requirements, purchased aircraft and trained crews, Laker was not to be permitted to fly Skytrain. A legal action was brought against the Secretary of State for Trade and Industry, (who at the time decided air policy) on the grounds that in withdrawing Laker's permission to operate he had acted outside his powers (ultra vires). The court held that Laker was right, a decision which was confirmed by the Court of Appeal. The British government accepted the court's decision, and Laker commenced operation. This was assisted by a new President in the United States who took a more sympathetic view.

In the short term, Skytrain was embarrassingly successful, leading to long queues at terminals and a change of policy by the government which then allowed advance booking for Skytrain. Competitors were forced to respond to Laker's initiative by introducing low 'stand-by' fares which caused Laker to complain about 'predatory pricing' i.e. charging below their own cost of operation in order to force him out of business. The long-term effect of all this was that the trend was set for more flexible pricing on the North Atlantic and other routes, which, owing to the rise of other low-cost operators such as People Express and Virgin, has continued. Demand for cheap air services is recognised, and failure to provide them on a legitimate scheduled basis can lead to illicit charters such as existed in the 1960s. Air service licensing is highly competitive, and politics, national and international, can have a decisive effect on the outcome of an application.

Laker Airways later collapsed in bankruptcy, as a result of expansion into less successful routes and currency fluctuations.

# The Future

The most important near-term future influence on tourism between Britain and other west European countries will be the opening on the Channel Tunnel in 1993. Passing under the English Channel (la Manche) between Folkestone in England and Sangatte in France, the tunnel will carry rail vehicles of two kinds: 'shuttle' trains carrying cars and coaches, both with their passengers, and heavy goods vehicles; and through trains carrying freight or passengers direct between European cities. It should be possible to travel centre to centre between Brussels and London in about 2hrs:45mins; and between Paris and London within 3 hours based on the French 'TGV' trains (Train à Grande Vitesse), although this running time will be possible only after completion in 1995 of a new rail line between London and Folkestone. Trains running between centres in the U.K. to centres in continental Europe may carry sleeping cars. It is likely that a market which will be developed is the inclusive rail tour traffic, for which carriages, and even whole trains, will be reserved.

Existing transport operators are concerned at the effect the tunnel may have on the viability of their operations. The short sea ferry crossings in the Dover area are likely to be most affected, and it is likely that the number of routes will be reduced. The ferry companies are currently improving the quality of their vessels, in order to make them more attractive, and they can expect to be preferred by many of their customers.

A subject which has received less attention is the effect on shorter air routes. Even the fastest through rail service will be unable to match current airport to airport times, but if centre to centre times are compared, allowing for travel to and from airports and for check-in times, it will probably be quicker to travel between London and Brussels by rail. The issues then will be how far current air passengers will transfer, what new traffic might be generated and how much traffic really is centre to centre. Civil servants attending Euro-meetings in Brussels may well transfer, but much industry and housing has now spread away from city centres. Heathrow, for example, is more easily accessible from the M4 corridor of industrial growth than is central London, and a similar situation can be seen around Paris.

It has been estimated that, by 1995, the airlines might lose 5.4 million of their passengers annually to the Tunnel, increasing to 8 million by 2000. Even so, it is thought that the effect of the development of the European Single Market, a significant part of which will be put into operation at the end of 1992, and also the industrial reorganisation which will follow 1992, could boost air travel, leaving the airlines with an overall increase in business. However, even were this expected increase not to take place, current pressure on airports and air traffic control in south east England is so great that the loss of some short haul European services could be welcomed as a way of allowing growth on other routes!

# Chapter 6

 **Tourist Accommodation**

We can understand accommodation as being 'somewhere to stay away from home'. Clearly, it is one of the most important elements in the tourism product. The success of a holiday may wholly depend upon the quality and type of accommodation offered. It is therefore important that tour operators and travel agents can provide the consumer with the 'right' accommodation. Should the accommodation be inadequate or badly serviced, then ultimately it will be the tour operator who is held responsible.

Accommodation is of course an industry in its own right and a detailed examination of its structure lies beyond the scope of this chapter. However, it is extremely important that those involved in travel and tourism do have some understanding of how the accommodation sector operates.

## History of Accommodation Provision

Chapter 2 examined the history of tourism and noted the importance of the developments in transport. Similarly, in this brief chronological history of the accommodation industry we can trace its development partly as a function of changing modes of travel. We can begin in Roman Times. Scattered along the uniformly straight roads of the Roman Empire were located posting houses or 'Diversoria'. These were perhaps the earliest forms of inns, providing simple shelter and resting places for men and horses.

By the eleventh century, ale houses had spread along the roadsides of Europe, again providing the most basic form of shelter. For those travellers on pilgrimage, accommodation was often provided by religious institutions or private households - the most frequented religious houses establishing separate dormitories or guest-houses.

Traditionally, private households took in both friend and stranger, and from such houses originated inns, auberges and gasthofs. During the twelfth and thirteenth centuries, inns were still comparatively rare. They were called Common Inns, to distinguish them from the town residences of men attending court which were known by the same name (as in the 'Inns of Court' in London). The main hall of the inn would normally serve as both eating and sleeping place. Travellers tended to provide their own food ( essentially the first self-catering tourists), and stabling was available although bought for an additional charge. It was also not uncommon for travellers to have to share their rooms and beds with complete strangers!

In the fourteenth century, the dissolution of the monasteries in England stimulated the development of the 'Common Inn'. These were larger, however, some providing accommodation for 200-300 people with separate sleeping chambers. Guests were still expected to share their chamber and their bed. As well as the roadside posting inns, Common Inns were also situated at the termini points of the stage coach routes in the large cities, and at stage coach stopping places. In the seventeenth century, visitors to spa towns, such as Tunbridge Wells, Epsom, Bath and Buxton were usually accommodated in Common Inns.

It was not until the eighteenth century that the name 'Hotel' began to be used to describe a type of accommodation in which apartments were let, and which employed managers and liveried staff. In France a similar phenomenon occurred with the growth of the 'Hotel Garni'. Hotels also began to spring up in other parts of the continent, particularly in Switzerland, where there were many hotels situated in their resorts.

It was the nineteenth century before developments in North America caught up with those in Europe. The proto-type of the modern purpose built American hotel was Tremont House, opened in Boston. This was followed by the building of Astor House in New York. Such hotels replaced the taverns, in which sleeping four to a bed was still accepted practice. The new hotels had rooms which locked, provided free soap and had the luxury of plumbing. It was from this time that the spread of hotel building moved across America from the east coast to the west.

In Britain the importance of the inn as a form of accommodation declined with the growth of the railways. Hotels were built at railway terminals in London, and alongside provincial stations. Because the railway companies were exempt from the Companies Act 1862 they were able to raise the large amounts of capital needed to build hotels. By the turn of the twentieth century over seventy hotels were owned or controlled by the railway companies.

It was the development of rail and steamship travel which opened the international market. European and American major cities and resorts met the increased demand by building luxury hotels. In London, the Savoy was built in 1889, and Claridges, its great rival, in 1898.

The growth of the railways had given the masses access to the seaside for the first time. Thus it was not surprising that in resorts such as Blackpool and Bournemouth large hotels were constructed adjacent to the railway stations.

The twentieth century saw transport return to the road, as the motor car and coach competed with the railways. At the beginning of the century there evolved a series of roadside 'Trust Houses'. These were free licensed houses created through public trusts, their managers being paid commission. As coach and car touring holidays became more popular, motels were developed alongside the main highways to cater for travellers.

Paid holiday leave became a statutory entitlement in the UK in the 1930's. This stimulated a demand for mass accommodation at a reasonable price. The demand was answered by the development of the holiday camp. Billy Butlin modelled his camp at Skegness on Canadian family camps, and catered for the mass market by offering affordable holidays. At their peak in the late 1940s, 50s and 60s there were over 200 camps in the UK accommodating over 30,000 people each week. Affordable holidays for all were also provided by hostels run by organisations such as the Co-operative Holidays Association, the Holiday Fellowship and the Youth Hostels Association.

Since 1945 increased wealth and leisure time has provided many people with the opportunity to purchase their own holiday accommodation. This may range from a relatively modest caravan to more expensive types of accommodation such as yachts, time-share accommodation, condominiums, villas and apartments. An increase in leisure pursuits and the trend for activity holidays has led to the development of marinas, ski- and sport hotels and holiday-villages.

It is significant to note that as the twentieth century progresses the development of different types of accommodation is still taking its lead from developments in travel. The USA even has plans to rent seats on its space shuttles and given that the predictions are for an increase in demand for activity holidays this may well prove to be a novel and profitable idea. The above outline of developments in accommodation provision highlights the importance of the transport sector.

# Types of Accommodation

There are a variety of ways to categorise types of accommodation. Of these, the distinction based upon whether accommodation is serviced or non-serviced is perhaps the most common. However, no categorisation is easily arrived at, given that many types of accommodation share similar characteristics. Rather than attempt to offer a rigid system of classification for accommodation, we shall consider the various types in turn.

## 1. Hotels

A hotel can be defined as an establishment offering refreshment and accommodation to any traveller who seems able and willing to pay for it. The traveller does not need to make an advance booking and the hotelier is not obliged to provide accommodation.

The law which defines a hotel in Britain derives from the Hotel Proprietors Act 1956, which, confusingly refers to "Hotels" as "Inns". This means that even the most luxurious establishments, such as the Ritz, Hilton and Savoy are classed as Inns! Many of the major tourist receiving countries define a hotel in a similar way, and have some form of legislation to govern the registration and grading of their establishments. Hotels offer guests fully serviced sleeping accommodation and are normally characterised as having public areas for eating and drinking which are open to residents and non-residents.

To cater for a number of particular markets other forms of accommodation have been developed.

# 2. Sport Hotels

Although a relatively new concept in the UK, sport hotels have been established in Europe since the late 1950's. Usually built in conjunction with a sports hall, such as the National Sports Centre at Papendale in the Netherlands, the sports hotel offers both accommodation and refreshment. Furthermore, sports hotels can also offer facilities for conferences, coaching and general leisure use.

At present, the largest sport hotel group in Europe is IHS with 30 'sport-villages' including one recently opened in the U.K. at Norwich.

# 3. Ski-hotels

As the name suggests, this type of hotel was developed specifically to cater for the needs of skiers. Because of the nature of the specialist sport, ski-hotels are seasonal, and are often situated in purpose built ski resorts, such as Isola 2000 in the French Alps. They differ from the Swiss Resort hotels or the Austrian Gasthofs, both of which have extended seasons, catering for a less specific clientele.

# 4. Boatels

In essence a boatel is a floating hotel and this type of hotel is normally associated with:

　　　　a) marina development; or

　　　　b) a floating hotel.

In Egypt, the use of boatels on the Nile, both as a type of accommodation and a tourist attraction has continued to grow, as shown by the following table. However, prolonged periods of drought in recent years, causing low water levels, have raised questions regarding the future use of boatels on the Nile.

**Floating hotels in Egypt 1982-1987**

| Year | Hotels | Rooms | Beds |
|------|--------|-------|------|
| 1982 | 47 | 1,689 | 3,577 |
| 1987 | 61 | 2,308 | 4,632 |

*Horwarth & Horwarth International 1987 Worldwide Hotel Industry*

# 5. Convention Hotels

These hotels are built specifically to cater for conferences, providing large meeting rooms, as well as smaller syndicate rooms. Most hotels of this type also have facilities for pre- and post- convention holidays, and are situated at popular tourist destinations.

# 6. Apartotels

The apartotel was developed by the Melia company of Spain in the 1970s. Such hotels operate and service individually owned apartments, on behalf of their owners. The apartments can also be let by the hotel when they are not being used by their owners. In this case the hotel will act as an agent for the owners. The apartotel has the restaurants, bars and reception facilities expected of any good hotel and will often combine accommodation in apartments with ordinary bedrooms which can be let. The concept of the apartotels is being developed in the UK, although, in this country hoteliers tend to retain ownership of the apartments. The Dalmeny Hotel at Lytham St Annes is an example of a hotel in a traditional seaside resort, successfully operating as an apartotel.

# 7. Motels or Motor Lodges

First developed in America, as a form of low-budget, roadside accommodation, motels are becoming increasingly common in Europe. The French Accor group market motels under the Sofitel, Novotel, Mercury and Formula 1 trade names. Their 'Formula 1' budget-priced motels are being opened at a rate of one per week in France. They will be introduced into Britain from 1989. This chain of hotels operate in a distinctive way. The guests check in and register by credit card on a computer situated outside the hotel. They are given a coded key to gain entry to the hotel and their rooms. All rooms are standard, sleep three persons, and have relatively limited facilities. Groups of four rooms share a toilet and shower, and are serviced as each user leaves. Apart from a continental breakfast, these motels offer no other catering. Rooms in France, at 1989 prices cost approximately £11 per night, though it is anticipated that because of VAT the price in the UK will be slightly higher.

The Automobile Association (AA) has noted the development of such budget-priced accommodation in the UK and lists them as AA Lodges in its 'Hotels and Restaurants in Britain' guidebook. In this country both the Travelodge group, owned by Trusthouse Forte, and Granada Motorway Services have been extremely active in developing such road-side hotels. They offer a standard bedroom which sleeps four people with its own toilet facilities. The motels offer limited catering, but guests may use the facilities of the adjacent restaurant, usually a Little Chef, Happy Eater, or a Granada restaurant. These chains have the significant advantage of being well-known brand names, and can also offer the traveller a straight forward tariff.

# 8. Country House Hotels

These are essentially country houses adapted as hotels. These hotels offer high standards of accommodation and personal service which is reflected in the high prices they levy.

| Country House Hotel Tariffs | | Rate Per Night | |
|---|---|---|---|
| | Number of rooms | Double | Suite |
| Clivedon | 25 | £160-215 | £265-350 |
| Stapleton Park | 23 | £115-172 | £230-373 |
| Chewton Glen | 44 | £137-157 | £242-312 |
| Inverlochy Castle | 16 | £120-145 | £201-272 |

*Source Caterer & Hotel keeper 1988*

# 9. Inns, Auberges and Gasthofs

These traditional types of serviced accommodation are found both in Europe and North America. They are primarily places offering limited accommodation and will normally have a bar, stuberl or restaurant. Inns tend to have few bedrooms, and instead place emphasis on the provision of food and drink for residents and the general public.

# 10. Boarding Houses, Guest Houses and Pensions

In Britain, such establishments are legally defined as 'Private hotels'. Unlike 'Inns' they are able to refuse prospective guests, so it is usually wise to book accommodation in advance. Boarding houses provide serviced accommodation and meals and may have a full table licence for alcohol. They do not normally provide facilities for the general public and residents may find that they have to leave their rooms during certain hours. Most establishments of this type are small - guest houses, for example, are defined as having less than four bedrooms - and are usually independently owned and managed.

# 11. Bed and Breakfast Accommodation and Hotel-garni

Bed and Breakfast accommodation - usually in the form of private houses - tends to be located in rural and resort areas or along holiday routes. As indicated by the name, they offer the tourist a room and breakfast but no main meals.

# 12. Holiday Camps

As previously mentioned, the idea of serviced accommodation for the masses was introduced in the 1930s. The aim of Billy Butlin, Fred Pontin and Harry Warner was to provide low-budget accommodation and entertainment for all the family. The basic idea of the camps still continues, although they have been modified in an attempt to boost their popularity. Although most camps operate seasonally, closing during the winter months, spring and autumn seasons have been extended and there has been a shift from fully-serviced to self-catering, as part of the process to broaden their appeal.

# 13. Holiday Villages

Close to the concept of the holiday camp, is the holiday village idea. Generally located some distance away from existing resorts, holiday villages offer the tourists a geographically concentrated package of accommodation and amenities. Accommodation may be communal or more usually in the form of family units. Also at hand are a range of recreational, sporting and catering facilities.

The holiday village idea is popular in Spain, where villages are regulated and classified by the authorities, and in France where Village Vacances Familles has over 70 villages, providing some 33,000 beds.

# 14. Educational Establishments

Schools and colleges with residential accommodation for their students are increasingly renting this facility out to paying guests over the vacation periods. In some cases the services and facilities may be on par with those offered by hotels. In other cases the accommodation may be better suited to the group travel market. Summer camps such as PGL for young people and SAGA holidays for retired people, widely use accommodation provided by educational establishments.

# 15. Apartments, Villas and Chalets

These are essentially private properties normally occupied by their owners. However, for some parts of the year they may be rented out to guests. Agencies may act on the owners' behalf to find the right clients or the owners of such accommodation may advertise directly through the national newspapers. As a result of growing affluence in Western Europe and North America, more people can now afford a holiday home and demand for this type of holiday accommodation has grown rapidly. The increased availability of charter flights has also made this type of holiday a more feasible proposition as both owners and clients find it easier and cheaper to make independent travel arrangements.

# 16. Camping and Caravan Parks

Once regarded as offering the most basic levels of accommodation and amenities, camping and caravanning have undergone dramatic improvements over the past twenty years. Tents and caravans are now well equipped with the most modern and convenient of appliances, allowing holidays of comfort and ease. Furthermore, camping and caravanning sites have been upgraded. Aside from improved washing facilities, many sites now have shops, supermarkets, swimming pools and other forms of entertainment. Although many sites are open only during the holiday season, where weather permits some are open throughout the year. Most countries now regulate and control camp and caravan sites, either by statute or though private association rules, governing aspects such as capacity, number of pitches, sanitary installations and laundry facilities.

An important development of the 1970s and 1980s has been the growth of holiday packages using tents and caravans as accommodation. Tourists can either make their own travel arrangements, usually travelling by car, or else the tour operator will provide coach, rail or air transport to the holiday destination. The tents or caravans are already on site, and the tour operator services the accommodation during and at the end of each holiday.

# 17. Farmhouses and Gites

There is an increasing market for rural accommodation in farmhouses or 'gites', as they are known in France. Occasionally the farmhouse may be on a working farm, but generally the building has been adapted solely for use as tourist accommodation, offering self catering facilities, bed and breakfast and occasionally full board.

# 18. Condominiums

'Condominium' or 'condo' is an American term referring to groups of apartments or villas which are normally individually owned. The owners share the running costs of the complex as a whole, including the upkeep of the grounds, swimming pools, letting and management fees. The individual owners might use the condo for their own holidays, or may rent it out to other tourists for parts of the year. Real estate companies usually act as agents for the owners, and travel agents may book holidays for their clients through such real estate firms.

# 19. Timeshare Accommodation

Timeshare accommodation as the name suggests involves the purchase of specific time periods relating to a holiday property. Thus, one apartment or villa may have many owners, each with exclusive ownership for one or more weeks in a year for a number of years (in England and Wales this is 80 years). The concept of time sharing has increased in popularity in North America and the Mediterranean Countries. By 1988, Britain had approximately 100 timeshare resorts, situated in Scotland, the Lake District and the South West of England. It is noticeable, however, that prospective timeshare buyers are increasingly looking overseas for their properties. In 1984, 75% of new buyers bought UK timeshares, but by 1987, 75% of new buyers bought timeshares abroad. This change reflects both the growing confidence of people in the timeshare concept and the increasing availability of cheap charter flights. Many timeshare owners can now participate in schemes which allow them to exchange time in their property for time in other properties in another part of the world. This makes time sharing even more attractive to the tourist, as it increases the range of holiday destinations available to the timeshare owner. Companies such as Resort Condominiums International and Interval International make such exchange arrangements for owners.

## 20. Youth Hostels

A traditional form of holiday accommodation which originated in the UK but has since spread world-wide is youth hostelling. The expression 'youth' hostelling is somewhat misleading, for in many countries such accommodation is used by people of all ages. It has, however, tended to retain a rural image, although this is less true today with hostels in major cities and holiday resorts. Hostel accommodation is usually basic and communal, although in some countries many youth hostels now provide more luxurious facilities. Hostels offer low-budget accommodation, and self catering facilities, although breakfast and evening meals can be provided. Accommodation is usually in shared single sex  dormitories, although family rooms have been introduced in some hostels.

## 21. Historic Buildings

In many countries historic buildings are now being used for tourist accommodation. Examples of companies offering this kind of accommodation include the Landmark Trust in the UK and the Spanish Re de Paradores de Estado - a network of state inns. Such buildings may be operated as hotels, as is the case with the Paradores or the Budapest Hilton, or they might be let as self-catering apartments as with Landmark and some National Trust buildings in the U.K. A wide variety of historic buildings are used as holiday accommodation including old mills, warehouses (Christies', the auctioneers, warehouse in London has been developed as a hotel) castles, chateaux and palaces.

# The Classification of Accommodation

Most developed countries with substantial tourist industries have some form of statutory system for the registration and classification of accommodation. Such a system will normally cover hotels through to camping sites. The United Kingdom, however, uses the Standard Industrial Classification, an extract from which is given below. This system of classification separates hotels and residential establishments from other types of catering establishments, and forms a basis on which to compare business activity.

This type of classification may be  satisfactory in terms of allowing analysis of the economic performance of each category but serves no useful purpose as a guide for the consumer.

The Development of Tourism Act 1969  attempted to redress this by proposing a statutory registration scheme for all tourist accommodation. The scheme however, was never fully introduced. Some aspects of the Act were implemented, including the need to provide notification of prices for accommodation, introduced by the Sleeping Accommodation Price Display Order 1977. Until then, providers of accommodation were not required to show their prospective clients how much a room would cost.

Further attempts to introduce statutory registration were made in 1972, when the tourist boards, together with representatives of industry, consumer interests and local authorities, submitted proposals to the Government for a scheme of compulsory registration. In 1974, a voluntary registration scheme was introduced with the support of the accommodation industry and the Regional Tourist Boards. However, in the absence of any means of independent inspection, the register relied solely on the hotelier or guest house - keeper to supply the relevant facts.

The National Tourist Boards set up a consultative committee in 1978 to re-examine statutory registration proposals. Their 1979 report recommended that the Tourist Boards continue with the development of voluntary registration throughout Great Britain, but on a more consistent basis. It also recommended that the matter be kept under review. In 1987 the Tourists Boards for England, Scotland and Wales introduced the Crown Classification Scheme.

It is perhaps useful at this stage to be clear about what is meant by registration and classification.

Registration aims to provide an exhaustive list of the accommodation stock, and was one of the basic functions identified when setting up the National and Regional Tourist Boards.

Classification, on the other hand attempts to:

    (a) categorise the types of accommodation (hotels, motels, campsites etc) using objective criteria;

    (b) specify the physical features of the accommodation type (bath, balcony, etc);

    (c) grade the accommodation according to objective qualities (availability of a night porter, number of courses served at dinner), and subjective qualities (atmosphere and quality of meals etc).

The Crown Classification Scheme, introduced by the English Tourist Board, covers the full range of serviced accommodation.

Classification is optional and is operated on behalf of the English Tourist Board by England's twelve Regional Tourist Boards. In order to participate in the scheme, establishments have to register with the English Tourist Board. Inspectors then visit each establishment, and depending on the level of objective features offered, they are 'listed' and ascribed a number of crowns ranging from one (lowest) to five (highest). Charges are dependent on the number of bedrooms and in 1988 the scale of fees ranged from £22.50 to £90.00.

In Scotland, hotel quality is graded using subjective criteria. During an overnight stay, an inspector assesses the quality of the food and the accommodation, and grades an establishment 'approved', 'commended', or 'highly commended' accordingly. Despite opposition to this 'qualitative' grading system from the British Hotels, Restaurants and Caterers Association, it has also been adopted by the English and Welsh Tourist Boards.

Members of the Regional Tourist Boards are entitled to reduced fees and alternative price arrangements exist for establishments already listed under schemes operated by the AA and the RAC.

One year after its implementation, the English Tourist Board estimates that there are over 18,000 establishments listed under the Crown Classification Scheme, providing the customer with an instant and simple means of comparing services on offer.

In the absence of a comprehensive grading system for accommodation in the UK, a number of independent inspection schemes, operated by a range of organisations, have evolved. These too provide various means of presenting information about an establishment (price and facilities offered), so enabling consumers to make informed choices. Bodies undertaking such schemes are the Automobile Association, the Royal Automobile Club, Michelin and Egon Ronay. In addition, the Good Food Guide and the Good Hotel Guide (both published by the Consumer's Association), provide further information for potential customers.

The AA bases its star ratings on the number and extent of facilities offered and services provided and a subjective assessment of these by its own inspectors. The association grades hotels from 1 to 5 stars. The Egon Ronay guides use a system of percentage marks and award 1, 2 or 3 crowns denoting degrees of luxury. These guides base their grading on an individual rating arrived at after careful testing, inspection and calculation. The hotels are assessed on twenty two factors such as the cleanliness and comfort of their public rooms and bedrooms, the efficiency of reception and the conduct and appearance of their staff. The size of the hotel and the prices charged are not considered in the grading. Inns are not graded as the guide has its own definition of an Inn.

Grading is also carried out by tour operators and by hotel marketing consortia. Consort Hotels, a group of independent hotels, has its own classification system to assist customers in identifying the level of facilities and services provided by each hotel. This system is based on specific criteria which the Hotel must meet in order to qualify for membership. Their classification uses bronze and silver with a crown for hotels of exceptional standard.

Tour operators often accept official ratings and classification schemes, and then add their own ratings in order to compare countries. Thomson have a T rating for facilities, service, food, comfort and location. The scale ranges from 1 to 5 T's with the addition of the Blue Ribbon for hotels of a very high standard. Intasun use 'suns' and have a scale from 1 to 4. Ski-Inghams use the official star rating of the country, but award their own discretionary star when they believe the hotel offers better facilities than suggested by the official rating. They assess self-catering apartments, which normally do not have an official star rating, and award key symbols on a scale of 1 to 4.

The English Tourist Board is now addressing the problem of grading self-catering accommodation, via its Holiday Homes Approval Scheme. This will identify and acknowledge those companies running self-catering holidays that conform to a code of conduct. The scheme is designed to cover a range of self-catering establishments including cottages, flats, chalets and house-boats.

Holiday parks also come under the Tourist Boards grading scheme allowing the public to identify the quality of facilities offered (shops, toilet facilities etc), as being 'acceptable' or 'excellent'.

The English Tourist Board has recently co-operated in an initiative launched by the Brewers Society which seeks to introduce a country-wide standard symbol for pubs with accommodation. The so-called 'Pub Facility Symbols Scheme' requires that accommodation must be registered with the Tourist Board and hence comply with their minimum standards.

At present much of Europe uses a system of stars to rate its accommodation establishments similar to the one used in France. This is as follows:

* Plain but comfortable
** Good average
*** Very comfortable
**** First Class
***** Luxury Hotel

This scheme has however been criticised for attempting to rate too diverse a range of establishments using a single set of standards. Horwarth and Horwarth World Wide (1987) suggest that such a system could utilise some elements of the existing 'star-rating'. Whilst allowing for differences between accommodation types this should make it easier for the consumer to compare like with like.

# The Structure of the Accommodation Industry
## Chains

The accommodation industry in the U.K. traditionally consisted of a large number of small independently-owned hotels and guest houses. While it is true that the majority of establishments are still of this type, since the 1960s the trend has been away from independently owned and operated businesses towards chains of hotels, franchise operations, referral groups and voluntary membership associations or consortia. National and international hotel groups and chains now own a large share of the market. Amongst national and international groups and chains, the purchase and sale of hotels is commonplace. It is interesting to note that ownership of the major hotel chains has switched from railway companies to airlines, then from one airline to another, then from brewery groups with hotel subsidiaries to hotel groups with brewery subsidiaries.

Hotel groups can operate hotels in a number of ways. Some hotels are owned outright by groups, whilst others are leased. In some cases groups can act as an agent, operating the hotel for an independent owner and charging a management fee for their services. Other arrangements include the management of hotels on behalf of independent owners in return for a share in the profits. Some chains can also operate some hotels under franchise agreements, in which the hotel name and image is marketed by one company, who then sell the right to operate that hotel under a particular 'brand name' to the hotel chain.

One of the reasons for hotel chains not owning the hotels they operate lies in the fact that large investments may initially be required for land and building. This is particularly true when hotels are to be located in areas with high land values. A good example of this involves the building firm of McAlpine who became hotel owners in a novel way in the 1930s when they built the Dorchester Hotel in Park Lane, London, an area of exceptionally high land values. As a consequence of the 1930's depression, their clients were unable to pay for the building once it was built, so McAlpine retained it until selling to Middle Eastern interests in the 1970s.

By leasing a hotel, the hotel operator avoids the need for high initial investment. In such circumstances, the land and buildings may continue to be owned by a developer, often as part of a larger project possibly involving shops and leisure facilities. They are then leased back to the hotel group. Where the operator is acting as agent for an owner, high outlay costs are similarly avoided. The hotel management company operates the hotel on behalf of the owner, and receives either a management fee or a share in the profits. Compass Hotels and Crown Hotel Management are two UK groups which operate in this way. Investors, such as builders and insurance companies can purchase the hotel property. There are mutual advantages in this arrangement: the owner has the financial resources and the management company the expertise and ability to operate at a profit.

# Franchising

Franchising originated in the United States. 'Holiday Inns' is the best known hotel company operating under a franchising system. The person or company who buys the franchise (known as the 'franchisee') pays for knowledge, advice and assistance in establishing the business. Most importantly however the franchisee is paying to use a well-known brand name. The other main benefit is that the costs of advertising, promotion and reservations are shared between a large number of hotel units. The seller of the franchise, (the 'franchisor') usually operates hotels or other forms of accommodation under the franchise name. The Holiday Corporation for instance, operates as 'Holiday Inns', Quality International uses the name 'McSleep Inns' and Prime Motor Inns have the franchise for 'Howard Johnson'.

Hotel groups partake in the same advantages and economies of scale enjoyed by any other large company. These include savings in relation to the people they employ, the raising of finance, the marketing of their services and the purchasing of the goods and services they require.

In terms of benefiting from economies of scale, hotel groups offer training schemes for employees, so allowing them to develop skills and expertise, not normally available when working in small independent hotels. Regarding finance, a large chain is able to balance working capital throughout the group and is also able to use the assets of the group as a whole in order to borrow additional capital for expansion. With respect to marketing, large hotel chains are in a position to develop a widely known brand image, and in terms of purchasing goods and supplies, the size of the chain means it can obtain bulk discounts and flexible credit terms.

## The Top 20 Hotel Groups in the U.K.

| Position | | Hotels in UK |
|---|---|---|
| 1 | Trusthouse Forte Hotels | 235 |
| 2 | Mount Charlotte Hotels | 65 |
| 4 | Queens Moat Houses | 73 |
| 3 | Hilton International (including Ladbroke Hotels) | 41 |
| 5 | Crest Hotels (Including 4 Holiday Inns) | 50 |
| 6 | Thistle Hotels | 30 |
| 7 | Holiday Inns | 16 |
| 8 | Swallow Hotels | 32 |
| 9 | Pleasurama | 44 |
| 10 | Embassy Hotels | 43 |
| 11 | Stakis Hotels & Inns | 31 |
| 12 | Imperial London Hotels | 7 |
| 13 | De Vere & GW Hotels | 30 |
| 14 | Rank Hotels | 6 |
| 15 | Metropole Hotels | 5 |
| 16 | Copthorne Hotels | 7 |
| 17 | Kennedy Brookes Hotels | 22 |
| 18 | North British Trust Hotels | 18 |
| 19 | Inter-Continental Hotels Corporation | 4 |
| 20 | Sarova Hotels | 9 |

*(Source: Caterer and Hotel Keeper 7 April 1988.)*

The top hotel groups operating in the UK are shown in the table above. By buying and building new hotels these groups are continuing to take an increasing share of the U.K. accommodation market. Several of the top fifty groups also operate internationally, such as: Trusthouse Forte, the Ladbroke group (who own Hilton International), Queens Moat Houses, Metropole Hotels, and Stakis Hotels and Inns. One interesting trend to note is that the largest increase in the number of hotel rooms built, has been in the budget sector. Trusthouse Forte, Travelodges, Granada Lodges, Hotel Ibis UK, Formula One hotels (both part of the French Accor group) are all developing and running budget-priced accommodation and this trend looks likely to continue.

At the time of writing, Pleasurama Plc are the subject of a takeover bid from Mecca Leisure. In 1987 Pleasurama was listed as three separate hotel groupings. However in 1988, these combined and collectively they are the chart's highest new entry.

Copthorne Hotels is one group which has shown a remarkable growth in recent years and has increased its place in the listing from 46th to 16th. This group is owned by Aer Lingus, the Irish Airline, who acquired it from another airline, British Caledonian. Prior to the purchase of Copthorne, Aer Lingus were already active in the hotel sector, operating the London Tara Hotel, and a subsidiary company, Omni Hotels Corporation, based in New Hampton, USA.

Kennedy Brookes Hotels, the 17th ranked group has recently been taken over by Trusthouse Forte. T.H.F. have also over recent years made several attempts to take over Savoy Hotel Plc, who operate the Savoy, Claridges, the Connaught and other hotels. Grand Metropolitian (Grand Met) have sold Inter-Continental Hotels in order to buy the American food and drink giant Pilsbury, and Bass Plc have bought all of Holiday Inns International operation outside North America to add to its existing Crest and Toby Hotels and Inns. By doing this, Bass has become a major international hotel group.

## Leading hotel groups worldwide.

| No of Hotels | Hotel Group | Headquarters |
|---|---|---|
| 1,832 | Holiday Corporation | Memphis |
| 479 | Sheraton | Boston |
| 742 | Ramada | Arizona |
| 361 | Marriott | Washington |
| 878 | Quality International | Maryland |
| 272 | Hilton Hotel Corporation | California |
| 590 | Day Inns of America Inc. | Atlanta |
| 713 | Accor | Paris |
| 809 | Trusthouse Forte | London |
| 586 | Prime Motor Inns | New Jersey |
| 386 | Balkantourist | Bulgaria |
| 213 | Club Mediterranee | Paris |
| 293 | Bass Hotels | Belgium |
| 431 | Motel 6 | Dallas |
| 89 | Hyatt | Chicago |
| 139 | Sol Hotels | Palma |
| 145 | Ladbroke group Plc | London |
| 157 | Grand Metropolitan Plc | London |
| 158 | Raclisson Hotel Corp | Minneapolis |
| 62 | Westin Hotels & Resorts | Washington |

*(Hotels and Restaurants International. July 1988)*

The above table takes an international perspective and illustrates that with the exceptions of take-overs and the introduction of new brands, the pace of growth is now slowing down. The highest new entry in the 1988 ranking of hotel chains is Bass Hotels, which came into the list at 13th. As part of their corporate rationalisation, Bass have subsequently sold their tour operator subsidiary, Horizon, to Thomson Holidays. Bass provide a good example of how the hotel chains are increasingly becoming internationalised, opening up new markets and allowing faster growth.

Other major changes in ownership have taken place. The Ramada Inn chain ranked third in the world has acquired Rodeway Inns from Ladbroke. In turn, Ladbroke, the 17th largest chain, has acquired Hilton International from Allegis (a combination of United Air Lines, Hertz Car Rental, Westin and Hilton International Hotels). Allegis also sold Westin Hotels, the twentieth ranked chain, to a Japanese construction company, Aoki. Sol Hotels, Spain's major hotel chain and the sixteenth largest in the world has acquired the Madrid-based Melia chain.

Traditionally, as previously mentioned, hotel groups have been subsidiaries of food and drink companies or transport companies - rail and airlines. The following tables show that this trend is continuing.

| Company | Accommodation operations | Airline and Railways | Accommodation operations |
|---|---|---|---|
| Bass | Holiday Inns<br>Toby Hotels and Inns<br>Crest | Wagons - Lit | Pullman International Hotels<br>Arcade Hotels |
| Whitbread | 75% stake in Country Club | Air France | Meridien |
| Grand Met | Recently sold Inter Continental Hotels | Air Lingus | Omni Hotels<br>Copthorne Hotels |
| Scottish and Newcastle | Recently sold Thistle Hotels<br>Langdale Timeshare<br>50% stake in Pontins | Swissair | Swissotel |
| Elders | Sold hotels owned by Courage on takeover | Lufthansa | Penta Hotels |
| Vaux | Swallow Hotels | Finnair | Hotel Berlin Moscow |
| Greenhall Whitley | US Treadway Inns<br>UK De Vere | JAL | Nikko Hotels |
| Boddingtons Hotels | Taittinger Champagne<br>Concorde and Campanile Hotels | Canadian Pacific | C P Hotels |
| Nestle | Stouffer Hotels<br>Swissotel<br>(in conjunction with Swissair) | Nippon Airways | Ana Enterprises |
| Hershey | Hershey Hotels | Nippon Railways | Mikako Hotels |

| Airline and Railways | Accomodation Operations |
|---|---|
| S.A.S. | SAS International Hotels |
| Canadian National Railway Co. | CN Hotels |

The importance and scale of tourism in the Eastern Bloc and Communist countries is reflected by the state-ownership of hotel chains. Other countries such as Spain and Jamaica also have government-owned hotel groups.

Independently owned and operated businesses face many problems in attempting to compete with these large groups. Yet despite many disadvantages, this size of business still operates. Disadvantages include weaker purchasing power, small scale referrals and reservations, lower sales, small marketing budgets and generally fewer opportunities for expansion. There are, however, many advantages in being small. The operation can be managed and run with individuality and flair. Customers tend to remain loyal, which leads to a high degree of repeated business. Some of the limitations mentioned above can also be overcome through co-operation between independent hotels. They are able to join together to form local or national consortia, in order to gain substantial benefits. National consortia of this sort include such groups as Prestige, Best Western, Leading Hotels of the World, Golden Tulip, Interhotels and Consort Hotels. They have central offices, established and financed by members' subscriptions and some also have overseas sales offices, and are able to offer tour operators similar advantages to those offered by the major chains.

Such consortia represent independent hotels over a wide geographical area. Consort, for example, have affiliated hotels in Austria, Holland, Ireland, Spain and Great Britain. Local consortia can operate on a permanent or an ad hoc basis. Competing hotels may also co-operate as resort hotels in order to negotiate preferential discounts on purchases for their guests and for marketing their operations. Ad hoc consortia can also be established to take advantage of particular circumstances. Hotels in the North East of England, for example, are working together and marketing themselves as a whole for the Gateshead Garden Festival in 1990, as did those in south-west Scotland for the Glasgow Garden Festival in 1988.

Access to advertising, public relations, advice, viewdata listing, and referral of groups and individual business are just some of the advantages independents gain by joining a marketing consortium.

## The Referral of Clients to Hotels

Both independent and hotel groups use a variety of methods to have guests referred to them. These include :

1. hotel booking services;

2. ground handlers;

3. hotel representatives.

## 1. Hotel booking services

A hotel booking service is a specialised agency, dealing only with hotel reservations. Such organisations include Expotel, Hotel Bookings International and Concordia. As well as taking bookings by telephone they also have offices at airports and major railway stations. The method of referral normally follows a set pattern. The guest contacts the agent, who then makes a reservation with the hotel. The booking agent then sends confirmation of the arrangements to both the hotel and the guest. The agent will collect commissions from the hotel - usually, commission is charged either the first night only, or for the total stay. In both cases, it is only the accommodation charges which are commissionable, not those in respect of food, drink and other services. Hotel booking agents operate a system known as 'free sale', when they have been allocated a block of rooms by a hotel or a group. This means that they need not confirm availability with the hotel, so allowing reservations to be processed with greater speed.

## 2. Ground Handlers

Organisations referred to as 'ground handlers' specialise in handling incoming groups of visitors from overseas. They deal with travel arrangements and book accommodation and meals. Normally, the travel agent in the tourist's home country books the travel arrangements to a foreign country, and will also arrange for a ground handler to take care of the visitor.

## 3. Hotel Representatives

These companies are retained by hotels to act as local booking agents. For this service they charge an annual fee and commission on all reservations. Hotel representative companies such as UTELL International, Steinenberger and H.R.I. act as intermediaries between the travel agent and the hotel and have national and international offices. Their services are extremely useful to travel agents, saving them both time and money. If a client books through a travel agent via a hotel representative, then it is the hotel which pays the commission to the travel agent and the representative. As a consequence the client is usually charged the full tariff, referred to as the 'rack rate'.

Derek Taylor in 'Hotel and Catering Sales' (Heinemann 1988), makes the point that the use of hotel representatives can save the travel agent money. A hotel, however, will sometimes refuse to pay commission to the travel agent, or may pay the commission by cheque in a foreign currency where the cost of processing the cheque can be greater than its value. To avoid such problems, Taylor suggests that travel agents deduct their commission from the deposit paid to them by the client when the booking is made, rather than wait for the payment from the hotel at the end of the stay.

# The Role of the State in the Development of the Accommodation Industry

The role of the state in the development of hotel and other tourist accommodation depends on a number of factors, including:-

(i) the political and constitutional system of government existing in the country.

(ii) the socio-economic development of the particular country.

(iii) the relative importance of tourism in the economy of the country.

(iv) the developmental stage reached by tourism in that country.

Hotel companies which are state-controlled and are responsible for planning and managing hotels include the following:-

| Company | Country |
|---------|---------|
| Intourist | USSR |
| Balnea & Cedok | Czechoslovakia |
| Balkan tourist | Bulgaria |
| Orbis | Poland |
| Interhotel DDR | Germany |
| Hungar Hotels | Hungary |
| Adm. Auristics Espanola | Spain |

In some countries, government initiatives also exist to promote co-operative organisations among hotel and tourist facilities on a national scale. For example, Finland has the national S.O.K. co-operative for tourism projects and Yugoslavia has H.T.P. Dubrovnik a hotel and tourism enterprise co-operative. In other countries state intervention usually takes the form of planning and co-ordination, legislation and financial investment.

State intervention in Britain with regard to the accommodation sector is largely a product of the Development of Tourism Act which provided the Hotel Development Incentives Scheme. This scheme which ran from 1970-1973 allowed the National Tourist Boards of England, Scotland and Wales to administer grants and loans to finance the building of new hotel rooms, at a rate of £1,000 per bedroom. Until 1970, the hotel stock in Britain had increased by about 2,000 new rooms per year. In the three year period in which the scheme operated 55,000 new hotel rooms were built at an estimated cost of over £60 million. This resulted in a surplus of hotel beds in some areas, while other regions suffered a shortage in hotel bedroom provision. In the late 1980s, the Business Expansion Scheme,was introduced. While not primarily aimed at the accommodation industry, it did offer attractive financing arrangements for hotel development.

# The Economics of Accommodation

An important feature of the accommodation sector in any country is that it needs to cater for both domestic and foreign markets. Countries such as Greece, Portugal and Turkey all have a relatively low volume of internal travel, and few domestic tourists. At the same time, these countries enjoy a high volume of foreign visitors who require serviced accommodation in hotels and motels. In other countries with highly developed domestic markets, such as Belgium, France and Italy, there is more diversity in the accommodation sector, with domestic tourists utilising villas, chalets, apartments etc, as well as hotels. The profitability of all such types of accommodation is clearly dependent on the level of bed usage. Indeed we can describe hotel rooms, rented villas, or camping sites as highly 'perishable' items. An empty bedroom, or a vacant site means a missed sale that can never be recovered. Given that the location of the accommodation is fixed and the time scale is finite, an operator is faced with the obvious fact that if the accommodation is not sold on a particular day revenue is lost.

Just as a transport operator has a 'load factor' which shows the percentage of seats sold on a train, plane or coach, similarly the accommodation operator has an 'occupancy rate'. Like the load factor, the occupancy rate is expressed as a percentage, either of 'room occupancy' or of 'bed (or sleeper) occupancy', as the figure below shows.

$$\frac{\text{number of rooms occupied}}{\text{number of rooms available}} \times 100 = \text{room occupancy rate}$$

$$\frac{\text{number of beds occupied}}{\text{number of beds available}} \times 100 = \text{bed occupancy rate}$$

Bed or sleeper occupancy is usually the more accurate measure of a hotel's performance. If both double and twin rooms can be let as singles this would show a 100% room occupancy whilst having only a 50% bed occupancy rate.

The profitability of a hotel is also dependent on the 'rate' or price which is charged for the room. The hotel's published tariff is called the 'rack rate'. This is the price charged to individuals, but it is usually possible to negotiate a cheaper rate for groups. Such negotiation is possible because accommodation normally shows a higher gross profit than other hotel services, such as meals and drinks.

Hotels usually have a high proportion of fixed costs, and these remain constant regardless of the level of occupancy. These fixed costs include hotel overheads, such as rent for premises, repayment on loans and the fixed wages of staff. Conversely, the marginal costs of occupancy are relatively low in proportion to the fixed costs. Moreover, while the fixed costs remain constant, marginal costs rise proportionately with the level of occupancy. Marginal costs include costs for linen provision, room cleaning, bedroom toiletries and reception stationery. As fixed costs remain constant even during off-peak periods most hotels are prepared to negotiate and reduce prices to attract custom at such times.

In the short-term, most hotel operators can survive if they are earning sufficient revenue from their sales to cover variable costs and make a contribution to the fixed costs. In the long term however, the hotel must earn sufficient revenue to pay all its costs, in order to make a profit. There are situations, however, in which demand for hotel accommodation is inelastic. In such circumstances, even significant price reductions may not result in a corresponding increase in demand. A hotel in the off-season in an unfashionable resort for instance may find that even when prices are halved it is unable to attract many more visitors.

# Price Formation

The competitive nature of the hotel and accommodation industry means that companies must market their services to ensure they have a high level of room occupancy. One of the levels on which hotels compete is price. However, if the prices they are eventually forced to charge are insufficient to cover their costs they will not make a profit.

Even though the accommodation industry is fragmented and dominated by independent units, the large groups and chains exert a disproportionate influence on the prices which are charged by the industry as a whole.

Hotels may set their prices in one of two ways. Firstly, they can adopt an essentially cost-orientated approach. In other words, they calculate their costs for operation and charge a rate which will cover these costs and provide them with a profit. Secondly they may recognise that price is the only marketing variable which generates income. In either case, the pricing of accommodation and meals and drinks are essentially independent exercises.

In the accommodation industry it is common to find that different departments often cross-subsidise. This may be an important consideration relating to the amount of scope or discretion available when pricing hotel operations which varies depending on the relative proportion of fixed and marginal costs. There is considerable scope when pricing rooms since the fixed costs are proportionately high. There is less scope in pricing food and drink, as the variable costs of the commodities are higher, so the prices charged must reflect the hotel's purchasing costs.

# UK Hotel Industry 1989

## Operational data

Departmental operating profit across the UK, as a percentage of revenue, for room sales is approximately 70%, and for food and drink sales it is approximately 30%. This means that the gross profit margins on room sales are higher, and this allows a greater flexibility in pricing. Price, however, is often seen by guests as an indicator of quality. Customers remember and compare prices, and use prices as a guide to quality. Bulk buyers of accommodation, such as tour operators or group organisers, tend to be better informed and consequently more price sensitive than individual buyers. Because of this, bargaining is normal practice. It must be remembered that a price which is set too low, instead of appearing to be a bargain, may well be seen by the customer as an indication of poor quality. German and Japanese visitors to the UK often relate price to quality. However, because they are usually able to pay full prices, reductions are not so appealing.

The season for contracting and selling hotel rooms and facilities is concentrated in the period from April to June, and most hotel groups have a travel sales office with staff who sell to the trade all year. The discounted rates are themselves subject to negotiation, and the price agreed will depend on such factors as the bargaining power of each side, the volume of business and the level of certainty attached to numbers.

As this chapter has shown the accommodation industry plays a key role in travel and tourism. Factors such as availability, quality and price of accommodation figure strongly in the decision making of both individual tourists and tour operators. The increasingly concentrated nature of the hotel industry will also be of importance in determining the shape of future holiday products and it is interesting to note that while many hotel chains are now owned by transport operators and other major companies, the U.K. tour operators have not as yet adopted a policy of buying up hotels. Changes in ABTA guidelines and European legislation which increase the tour operator's liability for the accommodation which is sold as part of a package will mean that it is even more important that those managing the travel business understand the accommodation industry.

# Chapter 7

## ☐ Retail Travel Agency

With their windows filled with holiday posters and special offers, travel agencies are the travel industry's most visible presence on high streets throughout the country. Through these agencies travel and tourism products are sold to the customer. During the winter months retail travel agencies advertise extensively throughout the media, trying to tempt customers with the promise of summer sun. Some agencies are long established household names such as Thomas Cook and Lunn Poly. Others, however, are small local firms working through a single shop but providing a personal service to their regular customers.

Travel agencies are essentially retailers, selling a product in much the same way as Marks and Spencers sell clothes or the local grocer sells tins of beans. However their role is somewhat different to that of a clothes shop or a grocer, in that they act as agents for the industry's 'suppliers' or 'principals'. These principals are the airlines, hotels, tour operators and other providers of travel and tourism products and services. The relationship agencies have with their principals means that travel agents differ both commercially and legally from the general retailer. Unlike most other retailers, they do not generally purchase the holiday or other travel product themselves before re-selling it to the consumer. Instead they exist to serve the travelling public by providing advice and selling travel and tourism products on behalf of principals. In return for acting as a retail outlet, the agents earn their income by receiving commission on sales from the principals, rather than through buying the product wholesale and making a profit by re-selling it at a retail price.

Of course, members of the travelling public could, if they wished, make their own travel arrangements by dealing directly with the principals. Were this to happen both customer and supplier would in effect 'cut out the middle-man'. By saving the agent's commission, the principal might be willing to offer a price reduction to the customer. Despite the seemingly attractive nature of such an arrangement, the 'direct sell' method for most travel products has not really caught on as witnessed by the growth in the number retail travel agencies and the volume of business they now conduct.

In this chapter we will analyse the reasons why travel agents exist, examine the types of agencies which operate in today's market and consider their main sources of income. Finally we will evaluate the market structure which has evolved in retail travel and concentrate particularly on the rapid expansion of the multiple retail chains, known in the industry as the 'March of the Multiples'. This phenomenon is having a profound effect on both the multiples and the smaller independent agents and has been one of the major features of the industry's growth in the last decade.

# Why Do Travel Agents Exist?

To understand why travel agents operate in the first place, it is first necessary to identify those groups in society which benefit from the agents' services. It is possible to categorise these groups under the following headings:

(i) Benefits to the travelling public

(ii) Benfits to the industry principals/suppliers

(iii) Benefits to the business community

(iv) Benefits to the UK economy

## 1. Benefits to the Travelling Public

There are over 7,000 retail travel agencies throughout the UK, offering a unique range of services to the travelling public. By using the expertise of travel agents, the travelling public saves itself time, effort and money.

People visit travel agents when they need the advice of a travel expert. Consequently, agents must build up a wide range of travel expertise. They must have specialist knowledge regarding the prices of holidays, the range and quality of travel products, travel geography and the processes involved in making reservations and issuing tickets.

Since many consumers also look for personalised service when buying their holidays, some travel agents emphasise the 'customer care' factor. Clients recognise the value of this 'face-to-face' service even at the expense of the cheaper prices they could obtain if they were to 'buy direct' from the operator.

If customers approach tour operators directly for information, they will only receive details of that operator's product. In contrast, the travel agent can give the client information about a range of products, and can offer unbiased opinion and guidance on such topics as alternative destinations, hotels and modes of travel; on appropriate dates and times to travel; on means of payment and value for money. The agency should be able to do this because it employs knowledgeable and well trained staff and may have access to computerised information and booking systems. Using up-to-date information technology, such as Viewdata, a travel agent can access huge quantities of rapidly changing information. By placing itself between the principals and the travelling public, a travel agent can therefore serve the needs of both.

As well as selling holidays, the travel agent can also offer clients a range of ancillary services. These include information about passports, visa and health requirements; recommendations and advice concerning insurance, travellers cheques and foreign currency; transportation to the departure point; overnight accommodation; and car hire. Some agents even sell complementary products such as ski wear, luggage and sunbathing preparations.

## 2. Benefits to the Industry Principals and Suppliers

By using travel agents to sell their products, the principals of the travel and tourism industry gain access to a widespread network of outlets. This means that the principals do not have to operate their own sales outlets. Some operators, do however, sell directly to the public and consequently spend substantial amounts of money on direct mail shots and advertising.

For most principals, selling through a travel agent is a convenient way of stimulating sales. In effect, an agency acts as a free advertising site, with brochures, timetables and posters being displayed without charge. Agents allow principals to place displays in their shop windows and arrange for the operators' sales representatives to meet the public for sales promotion. Joint sales promotions are sometimes held, such as holiday exhibitions and film shows.

## 3. Benefits to the Business Community

Many British companies export goods to other parts of the world. In order to secure and maintain such sales, companies send their sales representatives abroad. These representatives need advice regarding, travel and hotel reservations and ancillary services. Whilst some larger companies make their own travel arrangements, contacting principals directly, many businesses prefer to use the services of a travel agent. The agent is well placed to find the best itinerary at the most attractive price level, make all reservations and supply all necessary tickets and vouchers.

Most travel agents offer business clients extended credit, in return for the exclusive handling of an account. Such extended credit is financially attractive to all commercial organisations.

## 4. Benefits to the UK Economy

There are over 3,000 travel agency companies which are members of the Association of British Travel Agents (ABTA). Although many of the products sold by agents involve expenditure overseas, their annual turnover makes an important contribution to the UK economy. In 1988 these companies had over 7,000 retail branches, each office employing an average of five people.

# The Different Types of Travel Agency

Three main characteristics of travel agencies are:

(i) the size of the organisation;

(ii) the type of business it conducts;

(iii) the appointment of the travel agency.

# 1. The Size of the Organisation

To the outsider, the retail travel industry appears to divide into two main categories:

> (a) a number of very large organisations known as 'multiple' travel agents;
>
> (b) numerous small companies known as 'independents'.

## (a.) The Multiples

Multiples can be sub-divided into three categories:

> (i) Multinationals;
>
> (ii) National Multiples;
>
> (iii) Regional Mintiples.

### (i) Multinationals

Multinational agents have offices worldwide. Thomas Cook for example, is represented throughout the world in most European Countries, North America, the Middle East, India, Sri Lanka, the Far East, South Africa, Zimbabwe and Australasia. Its parent company is the Midland Bank. In the United States, American Express is the largest multinational, and is also part of a large banking and financial institution. Both these organisations operate on a worldwide scale and can provide 'on-the-spot' services for their customers which cannot be matched by other travel agents.

### (ii) National Multiples

National Multiples are agencies with offices throughout the UK. Many are household names and are owned by large parent organisations as can be seen from the table below. In the late 1980s, the market leaders, in terms of number of branches, were Lunn Poly and Thomas Cook, carrying approximately 45% of all business conducted. The multiples' share of the market has increased substantially over recent years, and this phenomenon is known as the 'March of the Multiples'. It will be examined in detail later in the chapter.

### (iii) Regional Mintiples

With offices concentrated in one particular region, these mintiples enjoy close connections with the business community and the media, as well as the public. Many are the result of initial one-shop family businesses which have expanded throughout a region. These organisations are often very successful, particularly when their performance is measured against that of the national multiples. However, because they are relatively small in comparison to the national multiples, they are vulnerable to takeovers.

## Types of agency - by size

**Multinationals**
Thomas Cook
American
Express

| National Multiples | Retail Branches | Parent Company |
|---|---|---|
| Lunn Poly | 510 | Thomson Travel |
| Thomas Cook | 370 | Midland Bank |
| Pickfords | 332 | National Freight Corp. |
| Hogg Robinson | 297 | Hogg Robinson Group |
| A T Mays | 275 | Royal Bank of Scotland |
| W H Smith Travel | 201 | W H Smith Group |
| Co-op Travelcare | 142 | CWS Travel Group |

| Regional Mintiples | | Region |
|---|---|---|
| R E Bath | 45 | South and South West |
| Woodcock Travel | 38 | South Yorkshire |
| Hilary (John) Travel | 29 | East Anglia |
| Althams | 28 | North West |
| Everall | 27 | Midlands |
| Transglobe Travelwise (Co-op) | 21 | North East |

## (b.) The Independents

An independent agency normally consists of a single retail unit. However in this category we can also include organisations which have developed a network of up to about six branches. Unlike the multiples, which usually have branches located in prime high street locations in cities and towns, independents can be found almost anywhere, particularly in a suburb or village. Independents tend to be operated by a sole proprietor (or partners), who has either left a multiple to set up in business or by someone who already has an established local business and wishes to diversify. Independents are also vulnerable to takeover, both by regional and by national multiples.

# 2. The type of business conducted

## (a.) General Agent

The term 'general agent' is used to describe an agent who deals with all types of travel products, from inclusive tours to rail and coach tickets. A general agent will normally have all the necessary licences and appointments to trade, including in particular an IATA (International Air Transport Association) licence which permits the agency to sell international airline tickets. Rules regarding the qualifications of staff, turnover and premises make IATA licences difficult to obtain. A general agent should be able to provide customers with comprehensive travel advice and an efficient booking service. For example, it should be possible to book a coach journey from Sunderland to Chester, buy a rail ticket from Sydney to Adelaide, book a theatre seat in London, or arrange car hire in Delhi. This category of general agent covers the majority of multiple agents as well as some well-established independents. The majority of independents, however, concentrate their efforts on operating specifically as holiday agents.

## (b) Holiday Agent

A holiday agent specialises in inclusive package holidays. Many independent travel agents choose to operate as holiday specialists, because they may be unlikely to secure IATA and other licenses. Selling holidays is also attractive because they produce high commission rates. Given limited markets and a fierce level of competition from the multiples, many agencies concentrate on this area simply to survive.

Traditionally, the holiday agent has been identified as the small independent organisation working in the suburbs. Few aspire to expansion into general agent activities, preferring to leave those to the multiples. However, the commercial security of the independents is now being challenged by the decision of some of the multiples to become holiday agents.

## (c) Business Travel Agent

Business travel agencies, which often form part of a multiple or well-established independent firm, derive their business from commercial organisations, as distinct from the general public. They offer a highly specialised and expert service, in addition to providing the entire product range of a full general agent. In some cases, where the value of a client's account is particularly high, the agent takes office space within the client's premises, and is supplied with staff and appropriate equipment. This is termed an 'in-plant operation'.

The Business or Corporate Travel Market is highly competitive. Because it generates impressive profits for those already operating in this sector, clients are jealously guarded, making it difficult for other agents to enter the market. Such barriers to entry are especially difficult for the small independent holiday agent to overcome.

The few organisations which operate purely as business travel agents can be found in Britain's major commercial centres. Prime high street sites are not necessary, and business travel units occupy general office accommodation. They offer a highly specialised service, and do not attempt to diversify into other market areas. Several of the large multiples have formed separate business travel divisions, each with their own structure and management. In so doing, they have given their leisure and business travel activities separate identities and locations.

## Overview

Until the mid-1980s, most large multiple travel agencies were fully licensed general agents, selling the majority of travel products available. Lunn Poly, however, decided to concentrate on the sale of inclusive tours, and to develop its 'Holiday Shop' concept, and consequently sold its business travel unit to

Pickfords. Other multiples have become more selective in the range of products they sell, questioning the value of occupying staff time and effort in low-revenue activity, such as giving general travel advice. Rather than using the term 'general agent', a number of companies have now formed a 'leisure division', thus making a distinction between the sale of holidays and the provision of a business travel service. Leisure shops concentrate on the sale of holidays, although companies such as Pickfords and A.T. Mays advertise their 'all service' travel shops nationally. Whilst it is difficult for independents to act as general agents because of the licensing regulations, there are some excellent single unit organisations offering a full service.

# 3. The Appointment of the Travel Agency

The appointment of an agency refers to the type of licences that it holds. The two major appointments sought by travel agents are the ABTA and IATA licences. The type of business an agency can conduct is often determined by whether or not it holds an ABTA licence, and this distinction produces two categories of agent - the ABTA agent and the non-ABTA agent.

## (a) The ABTA agent

The ABTA agent is one which has applied for, and been accepted into membership of the Association of British Travel Agents. The ABTA agent agrees to abide by the Articles of Association, which include an agreement not to sell the foreign inclusive travel arrangements of any agent not a member of the ABTA Tour Operators Class. As the majority of tour operators are themselves members of ABTA it is almost impossible for a retail agent to trade without joining the Association. Through this agreement, consumer protection schemes have been developed, applicable to all ABTA members, both retail agents and tour operators. Other ABTA rules cover the suitability of owners, the agent's financial stability, the qualifications of the agency's staff and the agent's agreement to abide by the ABTA Code of Conduct, produced in close consultation with the Government's Office of Fair Trading.

## (b) The non-ABTA agent

A non-ABTA agent is one who either prefers the freedom to trade outside ABTA regulations, or else has been rejected by ABTA. Such an agent is not obliged to conform to rules and regulations, other than those imposed by the principals. The agent cannot sell foreign inclusive package arrangements produced by ABTA operators, but is free to sell those produced by non-ABTA operators. Clients of a non-ABTA agent do not enjoy ABTA's consumer protection schemes, but if they are travelling by air on an inclusive foreign package, the Civil Aviation Air Travel Organisers Licence (ATOL) will cover them in the event of a business collapse by their operator. Non-ABTA tour operators using surface travel may also arrange their own customer protection schemes.

## (c) The IATA agent

An IATA agent is one who has successfully applied for membership of the International Air Transport Association. To gain IATA membership, an agency must undergo scrutiny from the IATA Agency Investigation Panel. This involves the examination of various aspects of the agent's business including its financial record and standing, staff qualifications and experience, the identification and accessibility of its premises, its security facilities and the agent's ability to promote and sell international passenger air transportation.

Once IATA has granted its licence, the agency can offer the customer a full service of worldwide air transportation. The majority of multiples and leading independents hold this licence and obviously the IATA licence is essential for agents in the business travel market.

### (d.) The non-IATA agent

Independents and those multiples which primarily sell inclusive package holidays may have little need to be members of IATA. Indeed, if the agent was granted an IATA licence, this could generate new international airline business and consequently the agent may need to employ additional highly qualified and experienced staff. Such extra costs may discourage the agent from applying for IATA membership. Although unable to offer the customer international scheduled air tickets, a non-IATA agent can still sell domestic air services, advance booking charters and European seat-only deals.

## Aspects of Operation

This section examines some of the advantages and disadvantages of operation in the types of agency identified above.

### (a.) The general/leisure agent

One major advantage enjoyed by the general agent, is the ability to meet the whole range of customer requests. Such versatility can greatly enhance an agent's reputation in the eyes of the public. If an agent handles a casual enquiry competently or sells a relatively low value product efficiently, this can often result in the satisfied customer returning to buy a more expensive holiday. Consequently, from the agent's point of view, the result is a more profitable transaction. In providing such an 'all travel' service, the general agent's staff need to be well trained, qualified and create an atmosphere of professionalism. Within the travel trade, general agents are generally highly regarded, and consequently have considerable influence in their dealings with principals.

Because general agents are not totally dependent on the inclusive tour market, they can always fall back on other products and services, should there be slump periods in the sale of package holidays. Another advantage general agents enjoy relating to the diversity of products they sell, is that they have a more even flow of business throughout the year. This helps to reduce cash flow difficulties which are a common problem for holiday agents caused by the seasonal nature of their trade.

Offsetting these advantages for the general agent are problems arising from handling low cost, low revenue products. For example, it would probably take a general agent less time to process a high cost inclusive tour to the Far East than it would to arrange a through rail booking to a European destination.

The revenue generated for the agent by the sale of the rail ticket is of course much less than that earned by selling the long-haul holiday. An associated problem is the time involved to serve customers. For instance, while a customer is waiting to book a holiday in Bermuda, the sales consultant may be attempting to decipher the engineering-works-related re-timetabling for a rail journey from Betws-y-Coed to Chester-le-Street. Clients rarely like to be kept waiting, and if they always feel that this will be the case in the general agent, they may prefer to place the business with a holiday shop specialist.

General agents also face a number of staffing difficulties. In a general agency, a staff member has to be a 'Jack or Jill of all trades', unable to specialise in specific products. This can lead to gaps in his or her knowledge and experience. Training staff for a general agency is expensive because such training must cover a wide range of topics. Furthermore, employing qualified and experienced travel staff inevitably results in high staffing costs.

A criticism, sometimes levelled at general agents, especially the large multiples, is that their service can often seem impersonal. This may be because sales staff feel less loyalty to a company in which there are thousands of employees. To rid themselves of this image, several of the multiples have placed an increased emphasis on the customer contact skills of their staff.

## (b.) The holiday agent

Holiday agents concentrate on selling inclusive package tours and as a consequence their staff are not distracted by the need to understand and sell other products. Staff training in such agencies emphasises tour operations, travel geography, resort information and customer care.

The packages which the holiday agent sells are usually of a high value and the sale of an inclusive tour generates a high level of commission. Furthermore selling it often takes only a few minutes of the sales consultant's time. The introduction of new technology and the increase in computerised booking systems, such as Thomsons' TOP system, makes selling easier and quicker and so helps to create an efficient professional image.

The proprietors of independent holiday agents are often local people, who are well known in their area. They may be members of the local Chamber of Commerce, Rotary Club or golf club. This can help business, since customers like to book with 'people they know'. Local connections may also help in the recruitment of staff. A multiple will advertise the position of branch manager throughout the company and often appoint from outside the locality. However, a local agent will most probably know most of the travel staff working in the area and so can appoint new staff with a greater degree of fore-knowledge and confidence.

Independent holiday agents often enjoy lower overheads than their multiple competitors. They occupy locations away from the high street and employ fewer staff, often paying them salaries lower than those paid by a general agent.

Despite these benefits, holiday agents face a number of disadvantages. One major drawback is the inability of the agents to meet all the requests of their customers. As a consequence, a holiday agent might have to refer an enquirer to a general agent. However, turning away a potential client on one occasion may discourage that person from ever becoming a client.

This inability to provide a full range of products also causes image problems for the holiday agent, not only with the public but also with the trade. Travel industry principals do not view holiday agents in the same way as they view general agents. Consequently, holiday agents are less capable of negotiating high commission deals with the principals. Many independents are so heavily dependent on the sale of inclusive package holidays that a slump in that market hits them badly. Such a downturn in the market can be caused by a number of factors. It may be the result of a worsening economic situation in Britain, although circumstances such as political disturbances and natural disasters abroad can also have a serious effect on bookings. In such situations, holiday agents have little to fall back on and must rely on what financial reserves they have, hoping that the following year will be better.

## (c.) The business travel agent

The business travel agent enjoys a steady flow of business throughout the year, without the peaks and troughs experienced by leisure agents. In addition, business travel is less prone to sudden fluctuations in customer demand. For example, in times of economic recession, the package holiday market tends to be adversely affected as the level of consumers' disposable income falls, but business travel continues as business executives try to maintain or increase their level of trade.

It is the employer, rather than the traveller, who pays for the travel and so the prices charged tend to reflect greater emphasis on service than economy. Most executives travel by air using either first or club class accommodation. They stay in high grade hotels and will often hire cars. All of these high value products generate healthy commission levels for the business travel agent. Establishing a close contact with individual commercial accounts can generate leisure travel business, as business clients may continue to use the agency to book their holiday travel.

Top business agents are highly regarded within the travel industry and this strengthens their negotiating position with principals. In many cases for example, business travel agents enjoy overriding commission facilities from major airlines.

Inevitably there are disadvantages involved in operating in the business travel market, so discouraging companies from entering the market and forcing those engaged in it to review their operations continually. The market is highly competitive, with the major UK multiple travel agents heavily involved. For example, Thomas Cook, with 79 business travel centres and 47 implants, turned over £250m in 1987. Hogg Robinson, with 48 business travel centres and 53 implants, turned over £200m. The second rank of companies such as Pickfords, AA Travel, American Express and A.T. Mays are all trying to expand into a market which, in comparison with the leisure travel market, is experiencing relatively low growth. In response to this intense competition, business travel organisations have had to undertake costly measures such as offering extended credit to customers and discounting the price of travel tickets. Some commercial accounts even demand an incentive payment, based on the amount of business they place with their business travel agent. This makes life extremely difficult for some agents, who are, in effect, having to repay some of their hard-earned commission simply to keep accounts. For a high volume leisure agent to lose a client may be disappointing but when a business travel agent loses a client it may be catastrophic.

Although overheads for premises are low compared with those of high street leisure agents, other costs are comparatively high. Staff for instance, must be highly trained, well qualified and experienced since there is no margin for error in arranging business travel. Sophisticated new technology is also costly. In 1986 for example, the Travicom President system cost £6,000 excluding running costs. The business community must be made aware of the agent's services and this requires advertising, promotions and sales representatives. Business account-holders not only expect a high standard of service, but may also require some the following: ticket delivery; special air fares advice; 24-hour service; free gifts; detailed itineraries; a translation service; airport representation; VIP handling; special business packages; incentive schemes; corporate rate; and reduced rate holidays.

All of the elements listed above plus regular personal contact between the business agent's management and staff and the account's executives and secretaries demand a major commitment on the part of an agent in this sector of the market.

# Travel Agents' Income

Travel agents earn their income primarily from commission. Such commission is paid by the principals when an agent sells their products. The customer however, may not realise that the agent is earning commission from the sale. The price that the customer pays is an overall price, and does not show the agent's rate of commission. When clients pay for a holiday or some other travel product, they make full payment direct to the agent. Before forwarding payment to the principal, the agent deducts the agreed commission. In this way the client is bearing the cost of the agent's services. Rates of commission vary from product to product. For example, car hire might attract up to 30% commission, whereas rail tickets generate only about 7% commission for the agent. Typical base rate levels of commission in 1988 were:

| | |
|---|---|
| Inclusive tours | 10% |
| Air (Domestic) | 7 + % |
| Air (International) | 9% |
| Rail | 7% |
| Coach | 10% |
| Ferries | 10% |
| Cruises | 10% |
| Car Hire | 10-30% |
| Hotels | 8-10% |

Whilst the list above indicates the main sources of commission for a typical agency, there are also a number of secondary sources of income. These include:

      (a.) commission on ancillary services;

      (b.) overriding commission;

      (c.) interest earned on clients' money held on deposit;

      (d.) the sale of the agency's own products;

      (e.) the sale of complementary products.

## (a.) Commission on ancillary services

Most travel agents offer their clients additional facilities to complement the travel product. Insurance sales for instance, are an attractive source of income to agents because they generate high rates of commission (often between 20% and 40%). Travel agents sometimes offer their clients free insurance as an incentive to buy travel or a holiday. In such circumstances, the agent pays the insurance premium, but still receives commission for the 'sale'.

The sale of traveller's cheques and foreign currency is another important source of income for some travel agents. Companies such as Thomas Cook and American Express offer such facilities, from which they receive 1% commission. Many other travel retailers are sub-agents and receive commission of 0.5%. Agencies also make a profit from a mark-up on the purchase and sale of foreign currencies.

A further source of income for some agents is the sale of theatre tickets, especially for popular shows in London's West End. Travel agents obtain such theatre tickets through theatre ticket booking agencies. The theatre ticket booking agent then receives commission from the theatre, and pays commission to the travel agent.

## (b.) Overriding Commission

Principals, in an effort to stimulate sales of their particular product, sometimes offer travel agents 'overriding commission'. This is additional commission paid by the principal only if the agent achieves a set sales target. The larger the agency the greater its strength in negotiating, or even demanding, an override. On average overrides amount to 1-2% above the basic rate of commission. Overrides disadvantage small agencies, which are unlikely to generate sufficient business to be eligible for such attractive deals.

## (c.) Interest

Agents also earn substantial amounts of money from interest. When a client pays for a holiday, the travel agent immediately banks the money. The time lag between the travel agent banking the deposit and paying the operator varies according to the size of the agency. A small, new agency will have to pay the operator almost immediately, whereas a large multiple agency will have negotiated a longer period of credit. This 'pipeline' money can therefore be used as a short-term investment to earn interest. For larger travel agencies, interest is a major source of income. They therefore do not welcome the recently introduced practice of asking clients to pay only a low deposit (such as £5.00 or £10.00) when booking their holidays.

## (d.) Sale of own products

Some travel agents package and market their own products. One of the most popular products is the mini-break. To the client, a mini-break is a short, inexpensive holiday away from home. To a travel agent, a mini-break involves arranging coach/ferry transport and short-stay accommodation. The attraction of the mini-break is that they can reap all the profit. A mini-break might be to a British resort or city, or to a European destination such as Amsterdam, Brussels or Paris. Once an agency's expertise and reputation is established, it can turn its attention to organising 7 and 14 night inclusive tours, particularly in the UK. This is however an extremely competitive business to enter.

## (e.) Sale of complementary services

Many travel agents also sell non-travel products. Some of the large multiples have diversified into other commercial activities. Hogg Robinson, for example, now offer financial services and operate estate agencies. Smaller travel agents use their premises for the sale of complementary products such as suntan oils, bathing costumes, ski wear and baggage. One travel agency even operates a bridal boutique. So after selecting a wedding dress, the happy couple can arrange their honeymoon, all under one roof!

# 'The March of the Multiples'

The 1980's saw the emergence and rapid expansion of large multiple retail agents. This phenomenon was nicknamed 'the March of the Multiples' by the travel trade press. As the table below shows, there was an unprecedented increase in the number of branch offices opened. Organisations such as W.H. Smith and AA Travel, new to retail travel, won significant market shares from Thomas Cook and Pickfords, who for years had dominated the market place. In response, Thomas Cook and Pickfords redefined their market strategy and launched major branch expansion programmes. The so-called 'march' began with the takeover of many small retail chains. Unfortunately some of these chains proved to be unprofitable, and owning them created problems for the parent organisations concerned, some of which were themselves taken over.

**Multiple outlet figures 1970 to 1989 and prediction to 2000**

| Company | 1970 | 1974 | 1979 | 1984 | 1989 | 1992 | 1995 | 2000 |
|---|---|---|---|---|---|---|---|---|
| Thomas Cook | 152 | 180 | 198 | 277 | 370 | n/a | n/a | n/a |
| Pickfords | - | 95 | 118 | 209 | 332 | 380 | n/a | n/a |
| A T Mays | - | 40 | 60 | 146 | 275 | 400 | 450 | 500 |
| Lunn Poly | 60 | 50 | 62 | 180 | 510 | n/a | n/a | n/a |
| Hogg Robinson | 5 | 24 | 51 | 175 | 297 | n/a | n/a | n/a |
| W H Smith | - | 2 | 45 | 99 | 201 | n/a | n/a | 480 |
| Exchange | 12 | 14 | 38 | 56 | 88 | 600 | n/a | n/a |
| AA Travel | - | - | - | - | 183 | 200 | n/a | n/a |
| Co-op Travelcare | - | - | - | - | 142 | 183 | 204 | 250 |

*Figures do not include Business Travel Units.*

The major takeovers and mergers that have taken place since 1980 are shown on the next page. After a lull in 1986, agencies concentrated on new branch openings instead of takeovers. It is anticipated that, by the end of the century, some of the leading multiples will have merged resulting in the market being dominated by about five extremely large companies.

Independent travel agents collectively make up the greater part of the retail network and the 'march' has worried many of them, as competition has intensified and multiples have opened branches just along the street from their own sites. Indeed, the proportion of branch outlets owned by the multiples has risen from 21% in 1975 to 30% in 1986, and it is estimated that this proportion will rise to 40% during the 1990s. The sale of inclusive tours which provides the smaller agents' most important source of income, has been targeted by the multiples, who took 28% of all such bookings in 1983, 32% in 1985 and 45% in 1988.

A number of multiples, led by W.H. Smith (already possessing prime high street locations for their bookshops), have experimented with 'in-store' units. AA Travel expanded their existing AA Members' regional offices and A.T. Mays linked up with Binns department stores, part of the House of Fraser chain. New indoor shopping complexes, such as the Metrocentre at Gateshead on Tyneside, tend to attract the multiples, rather than the independents, as the initial set-up costs are quite high. Multiples also find it easier to meet the appropriate design and operating requirements of such large shopping complexes.

The changes precipitated by the 'March of the Multiples' have drawn comparison with changes which have taken place in other retailing sectors. In the grocery trade, the small shopkeeper has faced increasing competition from supermarkets and it is estimated that, during the late 1980s, the seven largest multiple grocers controlled 64% of that market. In clothes retailing, the independent shop must now compete with large multiple chains such as Next, Dorothy Perkins, Chelsea Girl and Top Shop, all of which operate units in major retailing centres and indoor shopping complexes.

A number of large and powerful organisations have interests in some of the leading multiples. A travel agency is seen as an attractive subsidiary for a commercial bank because the agency will often hold large amounts of client's money prior to paying its principals, and the banks are in a position to profitably use such short term deposits. Agencies also handle both foreign currency and travellers cheques and commercial banks see such business as complementing their own operations. In 1973, the Midland Bank took an initial share in Thomas Cook, and subsequently Cooks have now become a wholly owned subsidiary of the bank. Similarly in 1987, the Royal Bank of Scotland took a controlling interest in A.T. Mays.

The principals themselves see the ownership of travel agencies as a means of getting closer to their consumers. Lunn Poly for example, is a wholly owned subsidiary of Thomson Travel, who also control both Thomson

Holidays and Britannia Airways, and in 1988, British Airways took a share of Hogg Robinson. These complex structures of ownership raise interesting questions for the future. What, for example, would be the consequences if the Midland and Royal Scottish Banks were to open retail travel centres in their own branches? Is Lunn Poly expanding its network in preparation for Thomson to sell its package holidays exclusively through its own agency? Will British Airways offer Hogg Robinson special incentives on its products?

## Takeovers/Mergers in Retail Travel 1980s

Blue Sky }
Frames }       Thomas Cook

James Hill (Yorkshire) }
Norman Richardson (North East) }    Pickfords Travel
Lunn Poly Business Travel }

Ellerman Travel (North) }
Renwicks (South West) }    Lunn Poly

Blue Star }     Wakefield Fortune }   Hogg Robinson
          Exchange }
          (39 locations) }
          Pendle Travel }

Ian Allen Travel }     W H Smith
Kenning Travel }     AA Travel
Ashdown Travel }

# The Motives behind the 'March of the Multiples'

We can understand why the 'March of the Multiples' has come about by looking at some of the benefits the multiples have sought to achieve.

## (a.) Economies of scale

By expanding the number of units they operate the multiples benefit from economies of scale. The opening of a new branch or the takeover of an existing chain will add little to the overhead costs of central administration and accounting. Systems will already exist to support additional units, and only a few additional staff may be required to cope with the extra paperwork. There will come a point, however, when the volume of administration does become too great. Once this point is reached, the company will find it necessary to increase its investment in people and equipment. Indeed, at this point a multiple may question whether it should be expanding at all.

## (b.) An increase in assets

When a takeover takes place, the newly expanded company needs only one head office and so it can close the head office of the company which has been taken over. This benefits the company financially in two ways. Firstly the sale of the premises raises cash for investment and secondly, by employing fewer head office staff, overheads are reduced.

## (c.) Addition of expertise

When a takeover or merger takes place the buyer acquires the existing expertise of the company which is taken over. This may benefit the buying company if they are weak in a particular market segment. Takeover should also enable a strengthening of senior and regional management. For example, the takeover of a chain will probably result in the merged company having two regional managers in each region. As only one is required, the new owners can then select the best person on merit.

## (d.) A reduction in competition

Takeovers reduce competition, increase the market share, raise turnover, and may help to increase profits. The new owner may have more than one office in a town, and is therefore faced with the option of retaining all the properties, or else of selling one or more of them, so reducing competition.

## (e.) Greater bargaining power with principals

Large organisations tend to have more buying and negotiating power than the small organisations. In the retail travel trade, principals such as airlines and tour operators are more willing to discuss deals such as commission overrides or 50/50 advertising campaigns, if the larger organisation is able to meet higher sales targets. Principals are eager to make their products available through large branch networks and are therefore willing to accept terms which are more favourable to the multiples.

## (f.) Enhanced public awareness of the company

The 'march' has heightened public awareness of the multiple companies, and strengthened their respective brand images. Travel multiples such as Thomas Cook, Pickfords and Lunn Poly are now household names. Their brand image is reflected in their shop design and advertising campaigns leading to higher sales, greater turnover and increased profit.

## (g.) Geographical spread

It is essential for a multiple to operate retail units in as many trading centres as possible, so helping to spread its overhead costs. Being able to spread out throughout the country is therefore another explanatory factor behind the 'March of the Multiples'. When it took over Renwicks Travel, Lunn Poly strengthened its presence in the south west of England where it had previously been weak. In a similar way, Pickfords took over Norman Richardson Travel, a regional chain in the North East.

We can see that a central driving force behind the 'March of the Multiples' has been the desire to maximise the profitability of travel companies and their parent organisations. Businesses exist to make a profit and a successful business will seek to grow hoping to improve its profitability. Without the expectation of a reasonable return on initial investments in terms of personnel and capital, there is little reason for the multiples to continue their so-called 'march'.

Despite the expansion of the multiples, increased profits have not always followed. While parent companies may have expected good profits each year, intense competition between the multiples (involving the introduction of low deposits and the practice of discounting) and the costs involved in a rapid expansion of the number of branches, has in fact reduced profits for some of the multiples. Between 1985 and 1986 for example, the multiples suffered a 4% drop in their overall earnings. It is a commercial fact of life that when good profits are not achieved, parent companies tend to sell their holdings.

Such a move could lead to a reduction in the number of travel agencies, thus reducing the level of competition. Special offers and discounts could then be withdrawn, and profits would rise again. It remains to be seen if this series of events comes about.

# Consequences of the 'March of the Multiples'

In this section we shall consider the effects of the 'march' on the retail travel industry, in terms of the effects on the multiples themselves and the effects on the independents who make up the rest of the industry.

## (a) The effects on the multiples

### (i) Corporate image

The leading multiples have been anxious to develop their own individualistic corporate images. This can be seen by the office design and decor adopted by each of the multiples. Every branch of the multiple is fitted out in a similar way using a corporate colour scheme. The same shop fitters are used to refurbish a new branch, or else contractors are required to follow exact specifications. Travel sales consultants must now wear uniforms, whereas until the mid-1970s uniforms were uncommon. National advertising is used to reinforce the corporate image, by employing the house colours and uniformed staff. Marketing campaigns are controlled from head office, and window advertising is co-ordinated nationwide to ensure that all branches reflect the company's sales policy. This image-conscious attitude differs markedly from the days when each office had its own style, staff wore their own clothes, there was no national television advertising and window displays were left to the 'creativity' of the branch manager and staff.

### (ii) The introduction of new technology

Increased competition and the resulting need to offer customers the best and quickest service, has led the multiples to invest heavily in new technology. The multiples are keen for potential clients to view them as professionals. Modern branches are therefore equipped with an array of computer terminals, all on view to the customer. Every sales consultant has access to a computer terminal which can be rotated to enable the customer to see what is happening. The system most widely used is Viewdata, which links the agent, via existing British Telecom telephone lines, to the computers of the principals. British Telecom also operate Prestel, a computer service offering agents thousands of pages of travel-related information. In attempting to provide its staff with the most sophisticated equipment, multiples are finding that they have to change their systems on average every three years, in order to keep pace with technological advances. An innovation introduced in the late 1980s has been the private 'in-house' Viewdata information service, whereby messages can be passed instantaneously between head office and the branches.

### (iii) The need to develop customer service and staff expertise

Since the leading multiples all offer similar products with comparable customer incentives such as low deposits, the only factor that may differentiate them in the eyes of the public, is 'service'. For this reason, the multiples have had to emphasise the importance of 'service' through staff training. Whereas in the past, emphasis was on training in technical skills, such as the ability to read a rail timetable and issue tickets, there is now also emphasis on customer-contact skills. During the recruitment process, potential staff are now assessed on how they are likely to perform with clients. Existing staff are often required to attend a series of selling-skills courses. The successful completion of such training courses may be tied to salary increases, qualified staff moving from company to company, as the multiples each try to offer the best salary and prospects in attempts to recruit the most able personnel.

### (iv) Product discrimination

In a highly competitive environment, the multiples must maximise the potential of their best-selling products. One of the ways of doing this is through product discrimination. This involves the agency emphasising certain products in preference to others. In discriminating between the products they sell, the multiples take into account the sales potential of the product, the level of commission they will earn, the degree of customer satisfaction and their knowledge of the operator's competence. Product discrimination may also involve attempting to enhance a product's image in the eyes of a potential client group. The benefit of product discrimination is that it helps potential clients to recognise the products easily so improving the likelihood of a sale.

Some multiples place these products in distinct categories. Thomas Cook, for example, have a 'Winners' and 'Preferred' list; Pickfords 'Gold', 'Silver' and 'Bronze' awards; A.T. Mays 'Blue Riband'; and so on.

The display of brochures also plays a part in the process of product discrimination. The multiples place brochures with high sales potential in a position on their shelves which immediately attracts the public's attention. The positioning of brochures on the racks is carefully considered with those advertising holidays with a high sales potential usually being placed at eye level. This procedure clearly poses a problem for low-volume specialist tour operators, who complain that their brochures are rarely displayed. However, such a brochure racking policy can earn the multiples powerful negotiating positions when seeking commission overrides from operators. It also allows them to discriminate against those tour operators whose products they believe are not up to standard. A flood of complaints about an operator from clients or a poor level of administrative service when dealing with bookings can lead the multiple to withdraw the brochures from display.

### (v) The increased offer of incentives to customers

When the original ABTA Codes of Conduct were produced, travel agents were prohibited from offering inducements to customers, as it was thought this would destabilise the industry. These rules were subsequently relaxed, however, as they were thought to be against the public interest under the Restrictive Practices Act 1956. ABTA also ruled that its agents were forbidden from reducing prices advertised in the tour operators' brochures. This agreement between agents and operators was ruled unlawful in the Restrictive Practices Court in 1982, after the ABTA policy was challenged by the Office of Fair Trading. Despite this ruling, however, individual tour operators were still free to insist that retail travel agents sold their holidays at the advertised brochure price. In effect, the relationship between operator and agent remained virtually the same, except that agents were now free to offer incentives to customers provided this did not give the impression that the holiday was being sold at a reduced price. Increased competition between the multiples has led to a range of new incentives being offered to customers, including free travel insurance and free transport to the airport.

Other aspects of discounting have led to further assessments of policy. A system of redeemable vouchers was introduced by the Ilkeston Co-op travel agency. On purchasing a holiday, customers were given vouchers by the Co-op which could be used to purchase other goods and services in the store. Some tour operators took the view that this was tantamount to reducing the price of the holiday, thereby undermining the price control agreement. When some operators then refused to allow the Co-op to sell their holidays, Ilkeston Co-op decided to take the matter to the Monopolies and Mergers Commission - an official body which investigates, amongst other things, restrictive commercial practices. The decision, reached in Autumn 1986, was that as long as agents charge the public the holiday price determined by the operator, agents are free to offer whatever 'pecuniary inducements' they wish. The ruling caused an explosion in discounting in the winter of 1986-7 with all the major multiples advertising money-off deals. The development which caused most damage financially to the agents was the introduction of the 'low deposit' incentive. Instead of collecting the standard 40% of the total holiday price as a deposit, multiples asked for a deposit of only 5% if customers booked early. This practice has seriously affected the agents' cash flow as they still have to forward the full deposit of 40% to the operators. The practice has reduced agency profits and has led to calls to end such offers in the interests of a more secure industry.

## (b.) The effects of the 'march' on independent agents

*(i) Excessive competition*

Over the last ten years, the number of travel agency outlets in the UK has increased markedly as can be seen from the table below.

| Year | ABTA Retail Members | Branch Offices | Total | % Increases |
|------|---------------------|----------------|-------|-------------|
| 1978 | 1,807 | 2,182 | 3,989 | |
| 1979 | 1,896 | 2,305 | 4,201 | 5.3 |
| 1980 | 1,950 | 2,448 | 4,398 | 4.6 |
| 1981 | 2,094 | 2,687 | 4,781 | 8.7 |
| 1982 | 2,211 | 2,844 | 5,055 | 5.7 |
| 1983 | 2,396 | 2,903 | 5,299 | 4.8 |
| 1984 | 2,537 | 3,196 | 5,733 | 8.1 |
| 1985 | 2,647 | 3,372 | 6,019 | 4.9 |
| 1986 | 2,806 | 3,657 | 6,463 | 7.3 |
| 1987 | 2,889 | 4,107 | 6,896 | 8.2 |

If you then take into account the fact that the UK population has been growing at a much slower rate than the increase in branches, you can appreciate that each individual branch now has fewer potential customers, as the table below shows.

1971 One agent for every 15,900 of the population

1980 One agent for every 12,720 of the population

1986 One agent for every 8,000 of the population

1987 One agent for every 8,000 of the population

The increase in agency numbers is hitting the independents hardest. Whereas independents previously dominated the market in city suburbs, small towns and villages, there is now likely to be a multiple branch around almost every corner.

*(ii) Smaller market share*

Research by ABTA demonstrates that in the period between 1985 and 1986 the turnover of all travel agents rose 13% to 4.5 billion. However, 51% of this figure has been earned by only 3% of agents. This compares with 69% of agents accounting for only 17% of sales. The majority of independents therefore control only a small, and shrinking, proportion of the total market. This dilution of business will mean that during the late 1980's, independents will face, on average, an annual 10 to 12 per cent fall in their summer holiday bookings.

*(iii) Pressure on profits*

Further evidence regarding how the march is affecting independent agents is provided by ABTA figures which show that retail members with an annual turnover of less than £1m (which includes most small independents) increased their turnover by only 4% while those members with an annual turnover in excess of £100m (assumed to be multiples) enjoyed a record rise in turnover of 45 per cent.

An examination of the accounts of the smaller ABTA members (classified as those with a turnover of less than £1m) yields the following revealing figures:

66% of small agents had a turnover of less than £800,000

50% of small agents had a turnover of less than £500,000

42% of small agents had a turnover of less than £400,000

22% of small agents had a turnover of less than £200,000

Agents make on average 10% commission on overall turnover and so there is little profit left out of £20,000 commission for the smallest agents once salaries, premises and other operating expenses have been covered. For this reason, although new retail offices are still being opened at a rapid rate, the number of agents going out of business has also increased.

This difficulty in generating profits means that independents find it difficult to compete in agency price wars as they cannot afford to offer low deposits, free insurance and other incentives. They operate on small advertising budgets and are only be able to make minimal investments in new technology. Small independents also have to keep staff salaries to a minimum, which means they have difficulty in attracting experienced staff and retaining existing staff.

Despite all these problems, some individual branches of independent agents are more productive than branches of multiples. For example Intasun recently announced that the major multiples were not represented among their top ten agency locations on the basis of sales and Cosmos stated that in 1986 the top ten multiples had failed to increase their share of the sales of its products over 1985 levels, despite a 5% increase in outlets.

*(iv) Consortia*

In a response to the 'March of the Multiples', some independents have linked together to form consortia. Such consortia are similar to those found in the grocery trade where, when faced with the growth of the supermarkets, many small shopkeepers joined with each other under such banners as Spar and VG Stores.

One of the largest such groupings in the travel trade is the National Association of Independent Travel Agents (NAITA), which had 650 retail outlets at the end of 1987. By negotiating collectively, NAITA has been able to obtain some of the benefits enjoyed by the multiples, such as override commissions, joint advertising, a closed-user computer system and an own-brand cruise brochure.

Consortia have also emerged on a regional basis, where small independents have joined to fight collectively for a share in the market. An example from the North East of England is 'Linkline Travel', made up of eight independent agents with fourteen branch offices. By combining with each other, these agents are able to offer free holiday insurance, low deposits and other inducements. Their joint advertising campaign consists of local regional television advertising and advertisements in the newspapers.

*(v) Franchising*

The alternative for the small independent to becoming part of a consortium is to become a franchisee: that is, to link up with a nationally-known retail multiple, yet still retain the ownership of the agency. This trend has grown dramatically in high street retailing in general with many well known names such as Kentuckey Fried Chicken, Body Shop, Prontaprint and Swinton Insurance operating through franchises. By the late 1980s franchising accounted for almost 10% of high street retailing.

The multiple, Exchange Travel, has led the field in franchising. In 1987 it had franchised only 52 retail branches and was in the process of franchising a further 51. By mid-1988 this number had risen to 125, and a target for the early 1990s has been set at over 400 franchised branches.

Franchising offers the small owner-manager immediate access to a national name and product, instant purchasing power and market knowledge, management support and staff training. A fee is payable to enter the scheme, and after that a 1% royalty on turnover.

# Summary

The so-called 'March of the Multiples' is likely to continue until the market is saturated with branch outlets. It is expected that the multiples will emerge as a powerful top-five grouping, bringing more pressure to bear on the independents. Nevertheless, independents have responded by forming consortiums or by joining franchises. Their future potential was summed up by Jack Smith, the President of ABTA, in his convention address in Innsbruck in 1987:

*"There is room, has always been room, and always will be room for well-managed forward-looking agents to make a healthy living in travel by meeting customers' needs. There is room for well-run business of all sizes, and while there is no such thing as easy money or an easy life, companies who know where they are going can prosper. Make a virtue of your size, your independence and your flexibility. Well-run independents can out-perform any typical multiple and the multiples admit this. The small and medium size members are the industry, employing around 40,000 people, and they are its future."*

# Chapter 8

## ☐ Tour Operations

# Introduction

In considering tour operations, we need to begin with the tour operator. The tour operator buys the individual elements that go to make up the travel product (transport, accommodation, etc.) and combines them in such a way that a package of travel, the 'tour', is then sold to clients. The tour operator makes a profit by charging a price for the complete tour which is higher than the cost of the individual elements which go to make up the package.

This basic description of a tour operator is as valid today as it was when Thomas Cook first organised a chartered train to run between Leicester and Loughborough in 1841. From such humble beginnings, Cook went on to develop fully inclusive travel arrangements covering tours to Scotland, Europe and the United States.

It was not until after World War II, however that the travel industry began its rapid development. Major international airlines were at that time re-equipping with modern jets, thus releasing older aircraft for use on non-scheduled routes to developing holiday destinations, particularly in the Mediterranean area. Newly formed travel companies were able to take advantage of recent hotel developments, especially in Spain, and to link these to charter flights. The breakthrough came in 1959, when airlines were allowed to undercut ordinary fares and produce special charter rates, which were combined with charges for accommodation. At that time Universal Sky Tours, for example, were able to offer two centre tours at prices ranging from £28 for 8 days to £37 for 15 days, fully inclusive.

Since then, in spite of inevitable failures and problems connected with the emergence of a new industry the popularity of the package tour has continued to increase, especially since 1970. Even substantial increases in costs resulting from the oil crises of 1973-74 did little to stem this growth.

The number of visits abroad by U.K. residents on inclusive tours has shown remarkable growth. In 1970 there were 2.71 million visits made. By 1980 this had increased to 6.25 million which had a market value of £1.2 billion. The 1980s saw continued expansion so that by 1987 the number of visits had risen to 11.98 million with a market value of £2.6 billion.

Today, a multi-million-pound industry each year takes an estimated 12m package-tour holiday-makers, double the figure for 1980. If one considers that the total outbound figure for all holidays is around 20m, it is clear that package-tour operators have penetrated deeply into the market.

# Industry Structure

The majority of tour operators are members of A B T A , the Association of British Travel Agents. Figures published by the Association show a marked increase in membership over the last ten years. In 1977 there were 306 tour operator class members of ABTA, by 1982 this had risen to 462 and in 1987 to 648.

It should be remembered, however that membership of A B T A is not compulsory, and there are an estimated one hundred or so additional operators who sell direct to the public. It is worth noting too that a high proportion of the total number of operators are very small companies, while the top 30 companies are estimated to account for 80% of the overseas tour market. We shall now move on to consider briefly the major types of operators.

## 1. Mass Market Operators

These operators carry the bulk of all holiday-makers taking package holidays. They usually offer a wide portfolio of products, including for instance summer sun and winter sun holidays, ski holidays, long-haul holidays and short breaks. The largest three operators in this category in 1987 were Thomson with 25% of the mass travel market, International Leisure Group (Intasun), with 13% and Horizon, with 7%. Early in 1989, however the Government permitted the takeover of Horizon holidays by the Thomson group, taking their overall share of the market to an estimated 32%

A number of these mass operators own subsidiaries in other sectors of the industry. This is known as integration. The best example of vertical integration is offered by the Thomson Travel Group.

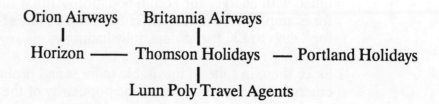

The International Leisure Group (Intasun), is a further example of a company which is integrated horizontally, enabling it to offer holidays in a variety of market segments, e.g. Club 18-30 (the youth market), NAT Holidays (camping/caravanning) and Skiscene (winter sports) holidays.

It is not only Thomson which has an interest in airline operators. Intasun are linked with Air Europe, Redwing with British Airways, Cosmos with Monarch, and Owners Abroad (Falcon/Tjaereborg) with Air 2000.

These large organisations have considerable power in controlling the market. They can obtain substantial discounts on transport and accommodation costs provided through bulk buying. They have special commercial arrangements with their distributors, the travel agents, to ensure maximum exposure of their products at the point of sale. The leaders among them are now in the process of providing agents with self-ticketing, invoicing and administration technology.

# 2. Independent operators

Many of these organisations are involved in specialist markets, in particular market segments. The areas in which they operate can be classified accordingly to various criteria, for example:

(i) Age

☐ schools, youth market, elderly segment.

(ii) Destination

☐ short break, U.K. domestic, short-haul, long-haul.

(iii) Activities

☐ golf, climbing, camping, sailing, wine tasting, etc.

Many of these companies sell direct to the customer by advertising in newspapers, magazines and specialist journals. For them to try to maintain a presence in the 7,000 or so travel agency branches would not be cost effective .

# 3. Direct-sell operators

Although this market consists predominantly of small operators, there are a number of major players. The principle by which they operate is to sell direct to the customer and so pass on the saving, (approximately 10%) achieved by not having to pay the travel agents commission. The top three such operators, Portland, Martin Rooks and Tjaereborg, are estimated to have around 50% of the direct-sell market. A number of specialist villa organisers, such as Beachvillas and Meon Villas, command a further 25%, while some 80 smaller concerns make up the rest.

Again, it is interesting to note that the leading operators in this area are in fact part of much larger groupings already mentioned, Portland being an arm of Thomson, Martin Rooks part of the Redwing/British Airways group, and Tjaereborg part of Owners Abroad, who control Falcon holidays. In 1987, Portland carried 304,000 holiday-makers, and similar numbers were carried by Martin Rooks and Tjaereborg.

The remainder of this chapter gives an outline of the basic methods used to plan and prepare a large-scale, inclusive tour programme.

# Planning an Inclusive Tour Programme

## 1. Overall Objectives

In the case of most large tour operators, planning and preparation is carried out by the marketing department. It is the task of this department to produce a programme which will:

(a.) have the correct capacity;

(b.) be competitively priced;

(c.) appeal to customers;

(d.) produce the required profits.

We shall now consider each of these important criteria in turn.

### (a.) Capacity

Capacity refers to the total number of holidays that the tour operator puts on sale. It is often difficult to predict demand, and failure to predict it accurately will result in either overcapacity or undercapacity. Overcapacity occurs when the operator contracts for more holidays than there is a demand for. All the places are not taken, with the result that the operator must either cancel departures or else consolidate. Consolidating means combining two or more departures to the same destination (for example, flights on a Friday and Saturday afternoon may be merged); alternatively it may mean transferring passengers to an alternative departure point. Using cancellation and/or consolidation to solve overcapacity will have the negative effects of alienating customers and damaging the reputation of the operator. Often it is the retail travel agent who has the unenviable task of advising customers of changes, and operators who persist in this practice soon lose favour with both their customers and their travel agents.

If the operator decides neither to cancel nor to consolidate, selling excess capacity at a discounted rate may be the only alternative. Although attractive to the customer, this can be disastrous for the operator, whose tight profit margin may disappear. Discounting excess capacity has become common in recent years, particularly with leading market operators such as Thomson, ILG and Horizon who are more concerned with improving their market share than increasing their profit.

Undercapacity is the term used when an operator contracts fewer holidays than the market demand later shows could have been sold. Potential customers have to be turned away, and may choose to travel with a competitor instead. This also gives the competitor the bonus of possible repeat bookings. Both overcapacity and undercapacity derive from errors of judgement at the planning stage. Unless the operator is aiming to increase market share however, targets such as turnover and profit will necessarily be met. Furthermore, although difficult to achieve in the high season, extra beds can sometimes be arranged, which gives the operator the opportunity to sell more holidays, and thus match more closely market demand with availability. Retail travel agents dislike being told that a holiday is already fully booked, and like repeated undercapacity even less.

**Volume, turnover and profitability of UK tour operators**

| Year | Number of air ITs taken abroad by UK residents (millions) | Turnover of top 30 air IT operators (£ millions) | Net profit of top 30 air IT operators (% of turnover) |
|------|------|------|------|
| 1981 | 5.2 | £1,120 | 5.1% |
| 1984 | 7.2 | £1,799 | 3.0% |
| 1985 | 6.4 | £1,841 | 3.3% |
| 1986 | 8.3 | £2,132 | 1.7% |

Notes:

1. Totals are IPS figures for ITs abroad by air (excluding Irish Republic).

2. Top 30 figures are CAA data collected from ATOL holders.

## (b.)  Pricing

The UK tour business is extremely competitive, and keen pricing is therefore essential.  Most customers seek good value and a low price.  However, foreign hotel accommodation can vary widely in quality, and sometimes will not meet the expectations of customers.  The dilemma facing the tour operator is obvious.  An operator must either choose quality and face being undercut on price by competitors, or else sacrifice quality for a low price. Large mass-market operators have the advantage of being able to contract at lower rates due to their bulk purchasing power.

If the public perceive a holiday as being overpriced it is unlikely to sell well. An operator who repeatedly overprices holidays will gain an reputation with the public for high prices.  This, however, can be turned into a marketing advantage if the operator is seen  at the same time to be offering a high-quality product.  An alternative response to overpricing is simply to reduce prices.  This might make the operation unprofitable.  By reducing prices and costs, however, the operator may be seen as offering a poor-quality product, and may in time acquire a down-market reputation.

## (c.)  Customer Appeal

Customer appeal  is determined by what is presented, to whom, and how. Destination, accommodation and mode of transport are obvious factors. Others include a range of departure points and times, a variety of resorts and accommodation, and appropriate leisure facilities.  The target group must be clear, e.g. fun-lovers, families, jet- setters or pensioners.  The brochure must have an attractive appearance, both inside and out. In this way customer appeal can be seen to involve the entire product, not only each individual element, but viewed as a whole.

Lack of customer appeal may result from two different types of problem. The first concerns the benefits offered to the customer.  Perhaps Four Star hotels should have been offered instead of, or as well as, Two Star. Perhaps Glasgow should have been included as an alternative departure point.  The second type of problem concerns the way in which the product is presented to the customer. Brochure layout may be muddled, and price panels may be complex, with too many supplements and concessions. If picture reproduction is poor, the entire range of products will have a down-market image. A programme which lacks customer appeal is unattractive to retail travel agents and to customers. Business will be lost to competitors whose programmes have greater customer appeal.

## (d.) Profits

Whatever else a business does, it exists to make a profit. No business can operate indefinitely without the hope of making a profit. Businesses unable to make a profit eventually fail. Profit allows reinvestment to take place in new equipment, new staff and new systems. A tour operator might want to buy aircraft, install a computerised reservation system, recruit staff with different skills or try out alternative marketing techniques. None of this can happen without the expectation of sufficient profit. Realistic profit targets must be planned, set, aimed for, reviewed and reset.

More recently, in offering customers especially good value for money, large tour operators have gone without profit, in order to capture a greater market share. Their hope is that, by effectively starving other operators of business, and therefore making them non-viable, the number of competing operators will be reduced. Having achieved this goal the remaining operators will then be free to increase prices in order to increase profits.

# 2. Time-scale

It is vital that the operator timetables carefully the planning and preparation process for a programme. For instance, advertising, especially on television, must be booked months in advance. Brochures must be published before the advertising campaign begins. Target dates must be set for completion of each stage of the process. Such targets help staff to set their own objectives in order to complete the necessary work within the time-scale.

Overall time-scales vary according to the size of the programme. Three examples will serve to illustrate this point.

**Large Scale** (1,000,000 + holidays)
Departure dates:   Summer 1990.
Start of sales:   August 1989. Planning and preparation = 15 months.
Start of research: June 1988.

**Medium Scale** (500,000 + holidays)
Departure dates:   Winter 1989/90.
Start of sales:   June 1989. Planning and preparation = 11 months.
Start of research: July 1988.

**Small Scale** (Mini-breaks, etc.)
Departure dates:   Winter 1989/90.
Start of sales:   August 1989. Planning and preparation = 9 months.
Start of research: November 1988.

# 3. Principal Stages of Tour Planning

Planning a tour begins with research, and progresses through a number of stages, to brochure publication, media advertising and sales.  At each stage many tasks need to be carried out, such as negotiating aircraft seats, selecting hotels, training couriers and designing the brochure.  Most of these tasks are likely to depend on the immediately preceding tasks having been completed.  For instance, it is possible to book hotels only after a resort has been selected, and booking beds must come after selection of hotels.  The planning process involves a series of tasks which have to be performed in logical sequence.

With so many tasks to be performed by a variety of different personnel in different departments, including those outside the company, the process of planning and preparation needs careful co-ordination.  Co-ordination involves ensuring that all the tasks are performed, in the right order, within the time-scale.  In most companies, the marketing department acts as co-ordinator, operating as the hub of a wheel around which the other departments or personnel are arranged radially.

The staff of a marketing department usually consists of marketing or product managers, and their assistants. In addition to its co-ordinating role, a marketing department researches markets, monitors sales performance, prepares a marketing plan and writes detailed reports on the following:

> (a.) transport requirements (for the transport managers);
>
> (b.) overseas accommodation requirements (for the accommodation managers);
>
> (c.) brochure proposals (for the publications department);
>
> (d.) advertising requests (for the advertising agency).

The marketing department is also involved with final pricing policy, competition, assessing customer response, late sales and discounted fares. All the other  departments (transport, accommodation, publications, personnel, etc.) provide the marketing department with specialist support.  But essentially the entire operation revolves around marketing.

# 4. Research

The purpose of research is to provide a sound basis on which to draw reliable conclusions concerning the market. The main objective of a research team is to predict the total market size, and the type and extent of holiday demands. Bearing in mind that the research may need to begin fifteen months before the first passengers depart, the research team's task of prediction is not easy.

Accurate prediction demands informed judgement, which in turn requires as much relevant data as can be obtained.  In addition to the problems of obtaining accurate data in the first place, and of determining which data is relevant, it must be borne in mind that much data ages rapidly. For example, currency rates fluctuate, natural disasters and strikes occurs and competitors move into or out of a market segment.

There are a number of distinct areas in which research takes place. These include holiday trends; economic, social and demographic trends; and competition. We consider each of these below.

# (a.) Holiday Trends

A research team attempts to forecast changes in customer choice by asking customers how they view the product. By researching customer attitudes, wants and needs, all variable factors, the research team is able to predict more confidently the holiday programme which will most satisfy the market at any given time. The factors the team focuses upon are the five basic ingredients of the inclusive package holiday:

## (i) Destination

Customer preferences regarding which countries to visit are constantly shifting between the main receiving areas, such as Spain, Italy and Greece. New development areas (for example Turkey in 1988) must be identified as early as possible. Preference between resorts tends to shift according to fashion, customer spending power and the facilities each resort has available.

## ( ii) Transport

The majority of package holidays involve air travel. There are however, some years when coach travel is especially popular. Luxury coaches have recently been introduced for continental destinations and this in turn encourages customers towards continental travel. Long and uncomfortable delays at airports, and fare supplements due to aviation fuel price increases, discourage travelling by air. Customer preference concerning departure points (local/ regional/national) has also to be considered.

## (iii) Accommodation

The respective popularity of hotel rooms and apartments/villas shifts with fashion. In years of economic prosperity, the higher grades of hotel (Three, Four and Five Star) are in greater demand. Catering fashions (full-board, half-board, room only, etc.) also change.

## (iv) Duration

The length of inclusive package holidays vary between 7 and 21 nights. One customer might be tempted to take two 7-night holidays separated by several months, instead of a traditional 14-night break in the summer. In times of economic hardship, the customer who annually takes a 21-night holiday might be able to afford only a 10-night holiday. A research team must predict the correct balance to be offered in the programme.

## (v) Holiday Type

Over the last twenty years, the sun, sea and sand package tour to Mediterranean resorts has become a British tradition. Some customers, bored with that tradition, want something different. Alternatives include cruises, cultural tours, long-haul destinations, activity holidays (such as camping, walking, climbing, ski-ing). If an operator wishes to keep up with, or even ahead of, the competition, every holiday opportunity and combination must be explored (examples of some of the more esoteric holidays on offer include wine-tasting in French chateaux, ballooning across the Andes and walking the Great Wall of China).

# Research Methods

Having established the areas to be researched, the marketing team must then decide which methods to use. A variety of such methods are available. They generate differing amounts of data of varying reliability and require different degrees of analysis.

Questionnaires can be designed to determine the customer's preference regarding almost any aspect of a holiday. Such questionnaires are easy to administer, and provide the operator with a large amount of data extremely quickly. Customers returning from a holiday are asked to complete the questionnaire. A research services consultant is then contracted to analyse the data. This may be repeated monthly: Thomson Holidays, for instance, spend over £25,000 each year on questionnaires.

A second source of straightforward data is the tour operator's own staff. All experienced staff have expertise of some kind. Staff placed overseas as representatives can supply up-to-date reports of customer reactions to the various parts of the holiday package. Regional managers and reservations staff can offer statistical data, and, drawing on past experience, their interpretation of the data.

Media reports can also be useful. The researcher should always be on the lookout for articles in trade journals, national newspapers, consumer magazines (such as *Holiday Which*) and television and radio programmes. The importance of such articles may not be so much in the anecdotal detail as in the fact that they play a major role in opinion formation.

A different type of data source is represented by detailed analysis of previous sales performance trends. This involves the close examination of, for example, the number of holidays planned, by country, resort, hotel, etc., and how each of these matches with resulting sales figures. A similar examination of the performance of competitors is also necessary. This type of detailed analysis is best performed by a specialist retail audit company whose charges are likely to be between £20,000 and £30,000 per annum.

Similar to these indicators of sales performance trends are the tourism statistics obtainable from most governments. These are much more general than data specific to an operator, but can offer a broader and longer-term picture. They represent a data source via which it is possible to examine the changing patterns over time in modes of transport, destination, holiday type, etc. The drawback to these statistics is that they are always six months out of date on publication, making forward prediction less secure. This kind of data can reveal useful information about the destinations of U K holiday makers. In the UK, the major continuing statistical analysis is provided by the International Passenger Survey. The principal results of this survey are published in HMSO Business Monitor MQ6, Overseas Travel and Tourism.

**Visits abroad by UK residents**

**Top ten destinations, all modes of travel**

| | 1984 | 1985 | 1986 | 1987p |
|---|---|---|---|---|
| 1 | Spain | France | Spain | Spain |
| 2 | France | Spain | France | France |
| 3 | Eire | Eire | Greece | Greece |
| 4 | W Germany | W Germany | Eire | Eire |
| 5 | Italy | Greece | W Germany | W Germany |
| 6 | Greece | Italy | Italy | Italy |
| 7 | Netherlands | Netherlands | Portugal | Netherlands |
| 8 | Belgium/ Lux | Belgium/Lux | Netherlands | Portugal |
| 9 | Austria | Portugal | Belgium/Lux | Gibr/Malta/Cyp |
| 10 | Portugal | Yugoslavia | Yugoslavia | Yugoslavia |

*p = provisional*

*Source: Business Monitor MQ6 (HMSO)*

**Inclusive tours versus Independent holidays   Western Europe (incl. EEC)**

| **Thousands** | | | |
|---|---|---|---|
| 1984 | 1985 | 1986 | 1987 p |
| **ITs** | | | |
| 8,523 | 7,931 | 9,941 | 11,026 |
| **Independent** | | | |
| 5,437 | 5,720 | 6,405 | 6,675 |

*p = provisional*

*Source: Business Monitor MQ6 (HMSO)*

# (b.)   Economic, Social and Demographic Trends

Holiday trends are influenced both by customer choice and by external change. A number of important factors known as 'tourism determinants' are important in relation to the process of tour planning and preparation. These are as follows:

## (i)   Currency and Commodity Values

The price the customer is willing to pay for a holiday is perhaps the most important determinant of tourism. The price of an overseas holiday is heavily influenced by the currency exchange rates.

The exchange rate of sterling against the currencies of each of the leading tour destinations is important, because the operator pays for accommodation and transfers in local currency. These costs are passed on to the customer through pricing. Of almost equal importance today is the fact that, holiday-makers are concerned about value for money at the resort. Radio and television networks broadcast programmes such as 'the Holiday Programme' and 'Wish You Were Here', identify and illustrate with typical tourist purchases which destinations give good value for money.

The currencies of the leading Mediterranean tourist-receiving countries are popularly known as 'Sunshine Currencies'. Because these currencies fluctuate against sterling, in order to make forward predictions on likely demand for tourism, the researcher must be aware of changes that are occuring or are likely to occur. The table below shows fluctuations in the sterling value of three currencies.

**Sterling against Sunshine Currencies**

|  | Dec.84 | Jun. 85 | Dec. 85 | Jun. 86 | Dec. 86 | Jun. 87 | Jun. 88 | Forward |
|---|---|---|---|---|---|---|---|---|
| **Peseta** | 203.80 | 225.75 | 225.00 | 216.04 | 196.70 | 204.40 | 203.98 | 205.90 |
| **Lire** | 2271.80 | 2518.00 | 2474.00 | 2312.25 | 1980.25 | 2155.00 | 2302.32 | 2308.10 |
| **Drachma** | 151.39 | 175.41 | 216.19 | 212.85 | 203.82 | 225.97 | 247.97 | 257.00 |

From the table it can be seen that over the period from December 1984 to June 1988 sterling increased some 63% in value against the Greek Drachma. This gain in the value of sterling and the increased spending power that this will bring the tourist abroad has to be balanced against possible inflation at the destination and at home. The matter is not straightforward.

To give an example: in January, a family book a month's holiday in South America. They find out the cost of living in that region, and calculate that they will be able to afford their weekly shopping needs. On their arrival in July, however, they discover that steeply rising prices over the past six months have substantially increased the cost of living. Nevertheless, it is likely that these steeply rising prices (and other economic factors) have weakened the currency against Sterling. Therefore, when the family come to buy their holiday money, just before they depart, they get a good exchange rate. On the other hand, towards the end of their holiday, prices have risen so much that the holiday money runs out. (The family could have avoided this problem in one of several ways: buying money locally as they needed it; buying Sterling travellers' cheques, etc.).

## (ii) General economic situation

To predict the total market size, a knowledge and understanding of both national and international economics is necessary. This is so for a number of reasons.

The amount of money a family spends after meeting its 'essentials' (rent/ mortgage, fuel, food, transport, etc.) is termed their discretionary spending.

Discretionary spending is spending on things such as entertainment and holidays, and so, the overall level of national discretionary spending helps to determine the size of the inclusive tour market. (Some people, however, have now come to regard a holiday abroad as essential.) In times of economic prosperity, overall discretionary spending increases, and the inclusive tour market expands. People tend to perceive themselves as being better off, and may be willing to borrow money more readily. In times of economic recession, however, as unemployment soars and real incomes plummet, overall discretionary spending decreases, and the inclusive tour market contracts. Not only do people tend to perceive themselves as being worse off, but low wages and unemployment remove from the market altogether huge numbers of potential tourists.

Industrial disputes, at home and abroad, can affect the inclusive tour market. Domestically, strikes lasting a long time and involving large numbers of key workers (e.g. the strike in 1984 by the National Union of Mineworkers) affect the way in which people perceive their discretionary spending. Disputes involving air or sea traffic staff are of concern to the would-be traveller. Equally important are disputes involving personnel likely to affect the quality of the holiday, such as couriers or hotel staff. General strikes, civil unrest (e.g. in the Lebanon) and deterioration in diplomatic relations (e.g. the bombing of Tripoli in Libya by the United States Air Force) can all seriously affect the size of the tour market.

## (iii) Social and demographic factors

The social make-up of a population is important to the researcher. On a simple level, professional and managerial people (termed socio economic groups A and B, or AB for short) tend to have higher incomes than other people, and would be expected to have more discretionary spending power. On a more sophisticated level, the market for AB holidays may be tiny compared with that for other groups, and may be changing in size.

Age also affects demand; the youth market differs from that for the elderly. The researcher needs to determine how the currently falling birth rate will affect both the size of the youth market and the discretionary spending of families; how the steady expansion of the elderly population affects the elderly market; and in what way better education affects life and leisure expectations.

This kind of information can be gleaned from a variety of sources. The British Tourist Authority produces information and statistics such as those shown in the following table.

**Holiday Tourism Abroad by UK Residents according to social group.**

|  | 1986 | 1987 |
|---|---|---|
| AB Professional and Managerial | 32% | 33% |
| C1 Clerical and Supervisory | 29% | 25% |
| C2 Skilled Manual | 27% | 26% |
| DE Unskilled, pensioner,etc. | 12% | 15% |

*Source: British Tourism Market, BTA.*

## (iv) Competition

It is also important to study the holiday brochures of competing tour companies. Not only might this save hours of desk-top research; it also provides a set of conclusions which can be used to refute or corroborate one's own conclusions.

In summary, research for a holiday programme involves a sequence of activities (obtaining, collating, analysing and synthesising data, and drawing conclusions) in a variety of areas (holiday, economic, social and demographic trends; current affairs; fashion). The conclusions reached from this process are to some extent dependent on experience and are a matter of personal judgement. This is because it is not always possible to know what weighting to give a particular factor. For instance, to use an example from the above, fear that an aircraft would be shot down, bombed or hijacked markedly reduced the number of US citizens visiting Britain in 1986. Apart from the impossibility of predicting events such as the terrorist bombing of an airliner, or the US bombing of Tripoli, it is difficult to calculate how great an effect an event will have. Nevertheless, the better the research, the more accurate are likely to be the conclusions.

# 5. Marketing Plan

Once the research has been completed, and conclusions drawn, the next task is to produce a marketing plan based on the research. The plan must clearly define a corporate strategy and give the detailed objectives for the programme: departure airports, destinations, hotels, durations, prices, market share and profitability. Staff involved in planning, preparation and sales will work from the plan.

Once the strategy has been defined, and approval from the board of directors has been granted, thought must be given to what the operator wishes to communicate, to whom, and how. The main purpose of communication is to sell the holidays in particular markets.

As part of an operator's strategy, marketing communication also has a longer-term purpose: to communicate an image of the operator and the operator's product. The term 'image' can mean here what impression the operator himself wants to project or the subconscious opinion held by travel agents and the public. Factors which affect image include price of holidays, efficiency of the operator, market level and friendliness of sales staff etc. Media reports are important regarding the communication strategy of an operator's Marketing Department. Reports in *Holiday Which*, magazines such as *Action Woman* and national newspapers are treated seriously. The views of travel agents are important because it is they who sell the holiday to the public. An operator's image can make the difference between a brochure being held on the agent's display rack or lying around the office store-room. Over the course of regular visits to an agent, a tour operator's sales representative will assess the agent's views of the operator.

If an operator's image is poor, then the image must either be improved or re-established. To do either will involve attracting and influencing the media at an early stage. Decisions concerning the promotion of an image are part of the marketing plan. The plan may also recommend changes in administration and sales procedures.

# 6 Programme Capacities

Senior management uses the marketing plan in order to help it decide whether to aim at growth in capacity or consolidation of volume and/or profit. Once overall capacity is agreed, individual programmes are apportioned capacity. For example:

Overall capacity = 104,000, comprising:

Summer Sun (Hotels)   62,000

Villas & Apartments   42,000

After this, Product Managers (e.g. of Villas & Apartments) apportion capacity to each destination, taking into account the following factors:

(i)   sales performance of destination

(ii)   sales performance of individual properties

(iii)   brochure presentation profitability – i.e. the number of properties contracted should relate to the number of brochure pages and volumes.

The table below shows an example of programme capacity by destination.

**Villa and Apartment Programme by Destination**

Total Capacity Target: 42,000

| Destination | Capacity |
|---|---|
| Majorca | 5,000 |
| Minorca | 5,500 |
| Ibiza | 4,000 |
| Costa del Sol | 1,000 |
| Tenerife | 1,000 |
| Gran Canaria | 1,000 |
| Lanzarote | 1,000 |
| Algarve | 8,000 |
| Crete | 5,000 |
| Corfu | 5,500 |
| Rhodes | 5,000 |
| **Total** | **42,000** |

Next, destination capacity targets are linked with aircraft or coach seats. This involves discussion between the Product Manager and the Transport Manager. Departure points must be planned, taking into account the following factors:

(i)   the previous year's capacity in relation to sales

(ii)   financial performance of departures

(iii)  target volume for destination

(iv)  UK regional economic factors

(v)  limits on capacity, e.g. aircraft/coach size.

# 7   Flight Contracts

Once destination capacities and departure points have been decided, the Aviation Section arranges seat bookings, either by negotiating directly with the airline, or by using an airline broker, or sometimes by 'buying' seats from another tour operator. Some large operators have their own airlines. For instance:

- ☐ Thomson owns Britannia
- ☐ Horizon owns Orion
- ☐ ILG owns Air Europe

If a whole plane is chartered ('whole plane charter') the tour operator and airline will agree a fixed rate 'per rotation' (i.e., to the destination and back), e.g.

Boeing 737   Manchester to Faro   £11,000

The operator can then calculate the cost of an individual seat.

A whole plane charter contracted for what turns out to be a poorly-selling route can usually be switched to a more profitable route.

If only part of a plane is chartered ('part charter'), the operator buys a block of seats on either a scheduled or a chartered service, e.g.

Birmingham to Palma   Mid-week Night   £80

Birmingham to Palma   Weekend Day   £90

The airlines have already calculated this seat price. Brokers are often used by an airline in arranging part charter, and flights are shared by many operators.

**The Contract**

The operator, when signing the contract, pays a deposit to the airline: usually 10% for Summer programmes and 5% for Winter. The balance of the money becomes payable on or before the 15th of the month prior to the date of travel. The parties (operator and airline) to the contract agree to a sliding scale of cancellation charges. This gives the operator the opportunity to cancel the contract if forward sales are poor.

The airline is usually paid in US dollars at an exchange rate agreed in advance with guidance from the Tour Operators Study Group. Being made in advance, such an agreement is not without risk. The Aviation Manager is carefully advised by the Finance Department. Additionally, the airline reserves the right to increase the price if fuel (purchased in US dollars) costs rise. This in turn leads to the problem of surcharges.

# 8. Flight Plan

Large tour operators with fleets of aircraft plan their own flight schedules, as do operators who use a particular aircraft for a whole season or a year ('time-charter'). It is up to the operator to make the most efficient use of its planes. Other operators use a broker or a charter airline to work the flight list into a flight schedule. In this case, it is up to the airline to make the best use of its fleet.

It is important in flight planning that each aircraft is used as fully as possible, in terms of both seating and time. Apart from statutory servicing (required by law to check the aircraft and keep it safe), during which an aircraft is on the ground, the aircraft should be in flight. An aircraft sitting idle is wasting money. Whenever possible, charter aircraft are used 'back to back': they fly out one group of holiday-makers, and return with a previous group. Although there will be some empty flights (known as empty legs) at the beginning and end of the season, it is possible to build the cost of these into the charter rate. In order to avoid empty legs, many operators try to ensure year-round departures to the most popular destinations.

Unfortunately, as was seen in the Summer of 1988, delays occurring during the very tight 24-hour schedule produce knock-on effects which can seriously affect passengers waiting for later flights.

# 9. Bed Contracts

The Overseas/Continental Department must now begin to contract properties, in accordance with the programme capacity brief. There are two major forms of contract:

## (i) Allotment

This is an allocation of beds without any financial commitment on the part of the operator, except perhaps for the payment of a refundable deposit. The agreement is one of sale or return. Usually the release date can be as close as two to three weeks prior to departure. This type of contract is more commonly used for large higher grade properties where it is easier for the proprietor to re-sell beds or carry the loss. Virtually all accommodation in the Spanish resorts is contracted by allotment. The attraction for the operator is that there is no risk involved. However, contracts will not be exclusive to the operator, and there will be no guarantee on rates. Usually the more beds on allotment, the cheaper the rate.

## (ii) Commitment

In this case the operator pays a deposit and makes a commitment to pay for the beds even if they remain unsold. In return, a cheaper rate is offered than for allotment. This type of contract is more common in smaller, lower grade hotels which cannot afford the risk of unsold beds. Most apartment properties are secured through committed contracts, since to compete effectively in this area the operator has to make exclusive contracts.

**Rates**

Usually three different rates are applied at different periods during the season:

**Low:**     April, May and Late October

**Medium:**  June, and mid September to mid October

**Peak:**    July to mid September

On average, there is a differential of 20% between low and peak-season rates.

# 10. Contracting

Contracting is usually carried out by senior management, led by the Overseas/Continental Manager. Much time is spent abroad, meeting and negotiating terms with hoteliers. In some cases operators rely on agents at the destination who receive a commission for successful contracting, the advantage being that agents have specialised local knowledge.

The major problems facing the contracting team are:

## (i) Price

As contracts can be signed up to twelve months in advance, there can be a risk in respect of exchange rates.

**Example:** Contract for a bed in a Greek hotel, high season:

Drachma 1700 per night.

TOSG rate set twelve months before payment:

Drachma 202.50 = £1. Rate therefore = £8.40 per night.

**But:**

Rate at the time of payment:

Drachma 225.97 = £1. Price therefore = £7.52 per night.

In this case there is no problem, since there is a bonus of 88p for the operator: however, it is just as likely that the reverse could happen.

There are a number of alternatives open to tour operators for allowing for rises in currency values:

        (a)  currency can be bought at the time of payment;

        (b)  the hotelier may accept a Sterling payment as part of the contract;

(c) a bank may agree to buy forward the required currency;

(d) the operator can hold stocks of currency.

## (ii) Number of Rooms

The main concern here is trying to achieve a balance between capacity and the spread of accommodation. While it is necessary to give the customer a choice of various grades of accommodation, prices also need to be kept at a competitive level. The more rooms on allocation in a hotel, the cheaper the rate will be. This creates difficulties for the small operator who has only a low capacity figure at each resort.

## (iii) Competition

Competition is problematic where a number of different operators share the same accommodation. Such a situation especially when each operator offers a different rate, leads to price comparisons by customers and the media. Many operators try to ensure that exclusive rights are built into contracts to protect themselves from competing UK operators. For this to be acceptable, the hotelier may insist on a commitment contract (with its financial risk for the operator) rather than an allotment.

## ( iv) Planning

Once the properties are under contract and the destination resort targets have been met, beds must be correlated both with aircraft seats and with the duration of particular holidays. This is a complex operation which continues throughout the season, since additional capacity, or consolidations and cancellations, all need to be taken into account.

# 11. Brochure Design and Copy

## (a.) Design

Initial design briefs are drawn up by the various Product Managers in consultation with the Marketing Department, designers and consultants. Their individual responsibilities are as follows:

(i) The Product Manager decides on content, information and copy.

(ii) The Marketing Department gives advice on corporate policy relating to image and target markets.

(iii) The Designers present ideas about design, format, colours, print, etc.

(iv) The Consultants offer advice about printing opportunities and problems.

## (b.) Copy

While decisions are still being taken on design, capacity and contracts, the brochure production section will begin work on preparing the proofs. One of the first tasks to be undertaken is the taking of cut-outs from the previous brochure, for the updating of:

## i. Resort Information

The cut-outs are sent to the tour operator's Information Services Section and/or to the operator's representatives abroad.

## ii . Accommodation Information

Newly contracted accommodation providers are asked to complete a detailed form describing their premises. Current providers are sent a copy of the previous brochure description of their premises for comment and updating.

As the information is gathered, the brochure is built up page by page, but the price and departure grids are left blank until just before publication, so that any last-minute changes in pricing may be taken into account.

The accuracy of the copy is of paramount importance, as there are both statutory and voluntary rules and regulations which have to be adhered to.

## Legal Rules

Every brochure published by or in the name of a tour operator must observe the legal requirements of:

- ☐ The Misrepresentation Act 1967     (Civil)
- ☐ The Trade Descriptions Act 1968    (Criminal)
- ☐ The Civil Aviation Act 1971         (ATOL)

The Act which most frequently applies is the Trade Descriptions Act 1968. Section 14 relates to offences regarding statements about services, accommodation or facilities (as opposed to statements concerning goods). This section is directed against any person who, in the course of any trade or business, makes a statement which he knows to be false, or recklessly makes a statement which proves to be false. Actions are taken by the Trading Standards Department.

In the early years of tour operating (up to the late 1960s), many operators had get-out clauses in their booking conditions, so that they could not be held responsible for the actions of the suppliers of their services (i.e. the providers of travel and accommodation). Under the Unfair Contract Terms Act 1977, operators can no longer ignore their responsibilities, especially in cases involving health or injury.

**Example:** In Portugal in the early 1980s, deaths were caused by fumes from gas heaters in self-catering apartments. Tour operators had to accept a measure of responsibility, since it was they who had contracted the accommodation.

## Voluntary Rules

If the tour operator is a member of ABTA, then a Code of Conduct, drawn up with the Office of Fair Trading, must be observed. Many of the Code's clauses relate to brochure content, and particularly to booking conditions. Every operator must submit a copy of its brochure to ABTA for examination before publication. ABTA will report any breaches of the Code to the operator, who will be expected to amend the brochure accordingly. In order to inform consumers about their rights, and to advise on complaint procedures, the Office of Fair Trading has drawn up a leaflet on the issues of statutory and voluntary regulations concerning package holidays.

# 12. Pricing

Pricing is undoubtedly the most important factor in the planning and preparation of a programme. The original marketing strategy will have indicated profit targets to be met, but at this later stage, the final brochure price must take competition into account. Since the demand for package tours is very price-elastic, brochure prices are a closely guarded secret up until launch.

All profits and costs, including fixed and variable overheads, are built into the price of a holiday. Economies of scale can benefit the larger operators for two reasons: there are more holidays over which to spread the fixed overheads; and a greater number of holidays from which to draw profit. Very little profit results from packages with early and late season departures, or from peak season holidays in resorts which attract many operators. High season departures to less popular destinations carry a higher profit margin. When launching a new product or destination, however, operators will sometimes offer holidays which incur a loss – hence the term loss leader.

The basic elements involved in pricing are:

    i. Aircraft seat cost

    ii. Bed contract rate

    iii. Transfers

    iv. Overheads

    v. Profit mark-up

    vi. Agents' commission.

There are numerous ways of calculating inclusive tour prices. The following example assumes one flight series over a Summer period and one hotel under contract.

## (i) Aircraft Seat Cost: Gatwick-Rhodes

To calculate the cost of the aircraft seat, divide the total rotation costs by the total planned capacity, making an adjustment to allow for the break-even load factor. Add any known taxes to the seat cost.

| | |
|---|---|
| **Aircraft:** | Boeing 737 (130 seats) |
| **Rotation Cost:** | £11,000 |
| **Season:** | 27 weeks |
| **Planned Capacity:** | 3280 (allows for empty legs) |
| **Load Factor:** | 90% |

*(a) Rotation Cost*

$$£11,000 \times 27 = £297,000$$

*(b) Load Factor Adjustment*

$$90\% \text{ of } 3280 = 1952$$

$$£297,000 / 1952 = £100.60$$

*(c) Tax*

Gatwick Airport Tax $= £1.35$

Aircraft Seat Cost $= £101.95$

Allowance for Tax $= £102.00$

## (ii) Contract Bed Rate

To arrive at the contract bed rate, multiply the agreed daily rate by the number of nights.

Greek hotel offers basic rate per night:

| | |
|---|---|
| **Low:** | Drachma 1150 |
| **Mid:** | Drachma 1400 |
| **Peak:** | Drachma 1700 |

Rates for 7 and 14 nights using TOSG rate Drachma 202.5 $= £1$

| | **7 Nights** | **14 Nights** |
|---|---|---|
| **Low** | (8,050) £39.75 | (14,100) £79.50 |
| **Mid** | (9,800) £48.39 | (19,600) £96.79 |
| **Peak** | (11,900) £58.76 | (23,800) £117.53 |

## iii Transfers

To arrive at the transfer cost, take the agreed contract rate per head.

Supply of coach transfers to and from airport at Drachma 764.00 per person: £3.77

## (iv) Overheads

To calculate the contribution to the company's overheads which must be made by each customer, add together the fixed and variable costs and divide by the anticipated total capacity for the season. A higher contribution per customer can be levied from tours to destinations for which competition is less fierce. For larger operators, economies of scale can significantly reduce the contribution per customer. Overheads include:

| | |
|---|---|
| Salaries | (including those for reps) |
| Premises | (rent, rates, heating, lighting, etc.) |
| Administration | (stationery, telephone, telex, computer, postage) |
| Marketing | (research, brochures, advertising) |
| Bonding | (ABTA/ATOL) |

## (v) Profit mark-up

Profit mark-up per customer (the amount extra charged per customer holiday on top of all costs) depends on marketing strategy and on competition at the time of pricing. Peak season departures are loaded with a higher profit mark-up. When competition is intense, however, a holiday may have no mark-up at all, and the operator relies on meeting the load factor target.

Example: The marketing strategy demands a profit mark-up of 10% for low season holidays, 15% for mid season, and 20% for peak. Calculate the selling price (excluding agent's commission) for 7 and 14 nights in the three price bands.

**Low**

| | 7 Nights | 14 Nights |
|---|---|---|
| Seat | 102.00 | 102.00 |
| Bed | 39.75 | 79.50 |
| Transfer | 3.77 | 3.77 |
| Contribution | 30.00 | 30.00 |
| | **175.52** | **215.27** |
| + 10% | 17.55 | 21.52 |
| | **193.07** | **236.79** |

**Mid**

| | 7 Nights | 14 Nights |
|---|---|---|
| Seat | 102.00 | 102.00 |
| Bed | 48.39 | 96.79 |
| Transfer | 3.77 | 3.77 |
| Contribution | 30.00 | 30.00 |
| | **184.16** | **232.56** |
| + 15% | 27.62 | 34.88 |
| | **211.78** | **267.44** |

**Peak**

|              | 7 Nights | 14 Nights |
|--------------|----------|-----------|
| Seat         | 102.00   | 102.00    |
| Bed          | 58.76    | 117.53    |
| Transfer     | 3.77     | 3.77      |
| Contribution | 30.00    | 30.00     |
|              | **194.53** | **253.30** |
| +20%         | 38.90    | 50.66     |
|              | **233.43** | **303.96** |

## (vi) Agent's commission

The brochure price of a holiday includes commission for the retail agent (usually 10%, leaving the operator with 90% of the brochure price). Sometimes the agent's commission is built into the profit mark-up. To calculate brochure price, multiply operator price by 1.111 (i.e. add one-ninth) and round off upwards.

**Example:** Calculate brochure price from the operator price, allowing for an agent's commission of 10%, and rounding the figure to the nearest £ above.

|                      | 7 Nights | 14 Nights |
|----------------------|----------|-----------|
| Operator Price       | 193.07   | 236.79    |
| Low Price + Commission | 214.50 | 263.07    |
| Rounded Price        | £215     | £264      |
|                      |          |           |
| Operator Price       | 211.78   | 267.44    |
| Mid Price + Commission | 235.28 | 297.12    |
| Rounded Price        | £236     | £298      |
|                      |          |           |
| Operator Price       | 233.43   | 303.96    |
| Peak Price + Commission | 259.34 | 337.69   |
| Rounded Price        | £260     | £338      |

Once calculations for the entire programme have been made, the programme is evaluated to estimate profitability. Adjustments are made, for example in the brochure, or through relaunches, to take competition into account. Decisions are taken on surcharges, child reductions, special offers, etc.

Brochure launch signals the start of the sales and marketing campaign.

# Chapter 9

## ☐ Government and Tourism

## Introduction

This chapter examines the role and importance of government in influencing the organisation and development of tourism. As Holloway puts it:

> *"For both economic and social reasons, governments take a direct interest in the development of tourism within their countries and the greater the involvement of tourism in a nation, whether incoming or outgoing, the greater is the likelihood of government intervention in the industry." (Holloway, 1985)*

Elsewhere, Elliott (1987) observed that:

> *"The role of government in the development of tourism in any country is crucial, but governments must operate within the given environment and with established factors which continually change and react with each other." (Elliott, 1987)*

As we shall see later in this chapter there is considerable variation between countries not only in the extent of the state's involvement in tourism but also in its purpose and style. An important factor in determining the nature of a government's involvement in tourism is the nature of the country's political system. A distinction is usually drawn between two systems of government:

(i.) The closed, centrally planned economies, typified by countries in eastern Europe, which exert almost total control over the operation of tourism in their countries;

(ii.) The mixed and market-dominated economies typified by Western Europe and North America, in which both public and private sectors are involved in the mixed economy of tourism.

A number of other factors also influence a government's approach to tourism.

(iii.) The structure of the system of government is important. For example, a country with a highly centralised system of government is unlikely to organise its involvement in tourism in the same way as a country in which the system of government is based on a devolved regional structure.

(iv.) The significance of tourism to a country's economy is important. Where tourism is, or it is anticipated that it will be, a major part of the economy, the government is much more likely to be involved in tourism, than in countries where tourism plays an unimportant role in the country's economic life. Generally we find that the greater the importance of tourism for a State's economy, the greater the extent and profile of that government's involvement.

It would be a mistake, however, to regard 'government' or 'the public sector' as a single, easily identified institution. Even within a relatively small, unitary state such as the United Kingdom, on which this chapter focuses, the structure and system of government is complex. To illustrate this complexity, consider the following classification of the major types of agency in British government which is based on that devised by Dunleavy and Rhodes in Drucker (1983):

## (a.) Central Government Departments

These include ministerial departments such as the Department of Trade and Industry and the Department of Education and Science, non-ministerial departments, departmental agencies and security agencies.

## (b.) Quasi-government Agencies

These are generally referred to under the acronym 'quangos'. They are agencies with responsibility for a specific issue or area. Some have specific powers and responsibilities and as such are referred to as 'executive agencies'; examples include the former Manpower Services Commission and the UK Atomic Energy Authority. Other quangos are merely advisory bodies without specific powers; examples include the Health Education Authority (formerly the Health Education Council) and the Sports Council.

## (c.) Public corporations

Included in this category are the nationalised industries such as British Rail and British Coal and individual public corporations such as the BBC.

## (d.) The National Health Service (NHS)

The NHS has a tiered structure of Regional and District Health Authorities.

## (e.) Local Government

Within England and Wales there is a structure of county and district councils, while Scotland and Northern Ireland have their own separate systems.

## (f.) Quasi-elected Local Government Organisations

These bodies may be considered to be secondary local government and include the police authorities, joint boards and partnership agencies.

These organisations and authorities each have different duties, powers and responsibilities. Their relationship with Parliament and the nature of their accountability varies, as does the way in which they are financed. Not all of these types of public body relate to the tourism industry, although a surprising number do. Many have primary functions which are unconnected with tourism such as the Forestry Commission, the Regional Water Authorities and the Ministry of Defence, but organisations such as these undertake activities which influence the level and quality of tourism provision. It is interesting to note that they are often unwisely neglected in discussions of government and tourism. The purpose of this chapter is to consider how the travel and tourism industry is influenced by some of these public authorities and agencies.

# The Historical Framework

As we noted in Chapter 2, travel and tourism has its origins in ancient times and has evolved and developed to its present level over the two thousand years. The involvement of central and local government is, however, a comparatively recent development. The availability of 'leisure time' for an increasing proportion of the population has only become a reality over the past century, and particularly since the Second World War. The consequent significance of tourism for national and local economies has similarly only been recognised during this period. Hence it is only since the Second World War that governments have begun to take much of an interest in tourism.

As the historical development of tourism is covered in Chapter Two, this section is restricted to a review of the background and nature of government actions which have had implications for tourism.

Government involvement with tourism has generally been justified on political, economic and social grounds. This has been manifested by intervention in policy, planning and legislation which has had direct and indirect influences on the development of tourism.

The origins of UK government involvement with tourism can be traced, albeit indirectly, to the political, economic and social changes that occurred during the nineteenth century as a consequence of the industrial revolution. This period saw social pressures and increasing political demands for a reductions in working hours. The period of the 'Industrial Revolution ' saw production shift into large scale factory units and the emergence of organised labour. Workers eventually won from their employers improvements in working conditions and holidays with pay. These changes, combined with legislation such as the 1871 Bank Holiday Act, assisted the development of mass tourism. The 'Wakes Weeks' when Lancashire and Yorkshire mill town factories shut down production and large numbers of people headed for Blackpool illustrates this process. Other contributory factors included the growing demand for escape from the cramped and insanitary urban environment, the expanding railway network and the emergence of specialist travel organisers such as Thomas Cook.

## Education and Literacy

The Victorian period also saw an increasing proportion of the general public exposed to education and literature as a consequence of legislation extending access to schooling.

This growth in literacy, combined with the romanticisation of nature, for instance in the writings of Wordsworth and Walter Scott and the emergence of popular travel literature led more people to appreciate the attractions of places outside their home areas. So one aspect of government policy, the spread of public education, increased interest in travel. Other policies helped to provide the means to travel.

## Leisure and Recreation

The provision of facilities intended for the benefit of local residents has traditionally been a function of local government. However, in some cases, facilities such as municipal parks and gardens and leisure centres - intended primarily for the local population - have become important attractions for visitors.

## Foreign Policy

Government foreign policy and particularly relations with other countries has been an important factor influencing the development of tourism. The decision to impose visa requirements on particular countries is one example. Anther example is the effect of past migrations to and from Britain and former colonies, which have led to a large 'Visiting Friends and Relations' (VFR) market.

These examples illustrate policies, planning and legislation intended for purposes other than the growth of tourism. However, in each case, government actions have had the indirect effect of promoting the expansion of tourism.

# Tourism Organisations

The first recorded case of direct central government involvement with the specific purpose of furthering tourism in the UK was in the 1920s, when the government decided to provide resources to finance the Travel Association of Great Britain and Northern Ireland (TAGBNI). The objective of the Association was to encourage foreign tourists to come to Britain. Central government funding indicated its recognition that the TAGBNI's plan to encourage overseas visitors was worthy of support. During the inter-war years the TAGBNI evolved into the British Travel Association with added responsibilities for promoting domestic tourism. During this period the Association's status remained voluntary, however, and it had limited powers and received no clear policy guidelines from government.

Between the 1950s and 1960s, UK government involvement with tourism remained confined to the provision of grant aid to the voluntary British Travel Association and to local authorities in selected resort areas. Beyond a general acceptance of tourism as a good thing, there were no specific policy objectives, and only one statutory mechanism for implementing policies for tourism in the UK prior to the 1969 Development of Tourism Act: the Development of Tourist Traffic Act (Northern Ireland) of 1948.

The Development of Tourism Act of 1969 was the first piece of national legislation specifically related to tourism. The Act was passed at a time of rising unemployment, a balance of payments crisis and a sterling crisis. It marked the recognition that tourism was a significant 'invisible' source of foreign exchange. The government also recognised that both incoming and domestic tourism had the potential for creating and supporting employment. In short, the Act transformed the voluntary British Travel Association into a statutory body called the British Tourist Authority with broader responsibilities and powers. In addition, national Tourist Boards were established for Scotland, Wales and England. These are discussed below. The Act provided grant aid to accommodation developments and introduced powers for the classification of accommodation. The establishment of the Tourist Boards in 1969 was a turning point in the government's involvement with tourism in Britain. Agencies were now established which were empowered to act as advisors to government on policy and planning matters and as channels for the distribution of government support to tourism-related projects. The Tourist Boards have developed as intermediaries between public and private sectors, channelling resources, informing policy and lobbying for the industry.

# Employment Policy

Since the late 1970s, the British economy has been going through the process of transition from a manufacturing and industrial economy to a service economy. The period has been characterised by major job losses in primary and manufacturing industries, particularly in Northern England, Scotland and Northern Ireland. Increases in employment have tended to come in the service sectors, particularly in southern Britain, including services for tourism. The precise extent of this employment is unclear because of the difficulty of attributing jobs specifically to tourism. Nevertheless, central and local government departments with responsibility for employment and economic development rarely seem to doubt that the provision of attractions and amenities for tourists can form the basis of a strategy for local and regional development. Much vaunted examples of this are the past, present and future National Garden Festivals in Liverpool, Stoke, Glasgow, Gateshead and the Rhondda Valley. Whilst such developments are increasingly led by the private sector, the statutory tourist boards have maintained an important promotional and co-ordinative role.

# Regulation of Transport

As well as direct involvement in the development of tourism in the UK through statutory organisations, central government also plays an important role in regulation, and in some cases State ownership, of sectors which make up the tourism industry. This has been particularly true in relation to transport. Government interest in the provision and control of transport and communications in Britain for social, economic and strategic purposes has been shown in its concern to ensure that transport services are available to fulfil social needs; for instance, the carriage of mail and supplies to remote areas has, in the past, taken precedence over purely commercial objectives. Legislation against monopolies and cartels in the transport sector is further evidence of this intention.

The organisation of the transport industries is covered in Chapter Five and so this section, therefore, is restricted to a review of the key developments in government regulation, control and de-regulation of the UK transport sectors.

The railways in Britain provide a clear example of State regulation and eventual control of a major transport network. The fragmented private ownership of the railways under which the rail system was established was ended during the 1920s under government direction. Nationalisation of the railways under the British Railways Board followed in 1947. Following the 1963 Buchanan Report, the network was drastically reduced, starting with the so-called 'Beeching cuts', reflecting the emphasis on motorway and road construction in national transport policy. British Rail, already with one of the lowest levels of state subsidy to national railways in Europe, is now being directed to reduce further its dependence on state finance. A number of assets have been privatised, including Sealink Ferries and British Transport Hotels. Many valuable station sites have been developed by commercial companies, for example the development of London's Victoria and Liverpool Street Stations.

Coach and bus company operations were originally licensed in London in 1924, with national licensing introduced by the 1930 Road Traffic Act. A state-owned National Bus Company took over the operations of the regional companies with the passing of the 1968 Transport Act. More recently, state ownership has been substantially reduced and licensing of operators considerably relaxed following the 1986 Transport Act

Government involvement with civil aviation in the UK began in 1924, when Imperial Airways was established. The airline received heavy state subsidies because of its strategic importance. The company maintained links with colonial outposts, and its aircraft and pilots could be employed for military purposes during times of emergency. The airline was taken into state ownership and renamed the British Overseas Airways Corporation (BOAC) in 1940. The Civil Aviation Act of 1971 led to the amalgamation of BOAC with British European Airways (BEA) to form the state-owned 'flag carrier' British Airways. This airline was subseqently sold into the private sector in 1986.

The system of airline route licensing was formalised by the Chicago Convention of 1944, which established a process of bilateral treaties to award routes between countries and to specific airlines. This system remains largely intact, although recently there have been attempts to change its procedures. In the UK, the Civil Aviation Authority (CAA) is the statutory organisation which awards licences on the government's behalf. The CAA is also responsible for safety procedures and for the air traffic control system in the UK.

A number of airports in the UK remain in the public sector under local authority management. Examples include Manchester, Luton and Newcastle. Control of several others, however, including Heathrow and Gatwick, passed to the private sector following the government's sale of the British Airports Authority (BAA) in 1987.

Major changes regarding the role of government in the ownership and regulation of transport sectors, therefore, occurred in the 1980s. The disposal of state assets and the reduction of regulations have been part of the political programme of the Thatcher government. In its view, markets must be permitted to allocate resources with minimal interference from the state. It is therefore not surprising that direct state control of these sectors has been considerably diminished. This is most notable in the U.K. and U.S.A., although it can also be seen to a lesser extent in other countries.

The historical development of government involvement with tourism in the UK has therefore been shaped by three distinct but related sets of factors:

1. Social, economic and political pressures have brought about legislation which has had both a direct and indirect influence on the growth of tourism, having led, for instance, to reductions in working time and the imposition and subsequent relaxation of exchange controls. In other cases, legislation has been a consequence of the growth of tourism, for instance following the Development of Tourism Act 1969

2. Central and local government's responsibilities for deciding policies and conducting planning, for example through the Tourist Boards, has influenced the location and type of tourist developments.

3. Central government ownership (in some cases combined with regulation of the various transport networks), originally intended for social, economic and strategic purposes, has also had the effect of creating and directing tourist passenger traffic.

# The Role of Central Government

Holloway (1985) contends that a national government's role in tourism covers a number of aspects. These include:

(i) the planning of tourism;

(ii) the provision of resources to support tourism;

(iii) the supervision and regulation of certain sectors of the tourism industry;

(iv) the direct ownership of key components of the industry;

(v) the promotion of tourism both domestically and overseas.

In the United Kingdom few of these functions are discharged by central government in an integrated, high-profile manner. Many are carried out by the government at arm's length through the operation of other authorities and agencies, often at a regional or local level. There is neither a central government Department of Tourism nor a Minister of Cabinet rank specifically and exclusively responsible for tourism affairs. Traditionally the Department of Trade (and Industry) has been the Department with the primary responsibility for tourism. Accountability to Parliament has been through a (junior) Minister of State outside the Cabinet.

The task of any national government in organising tourism has been well summarised by Burkart and Medlik:

*"At the national level, tourism is in the first instance a government responsibility, to formulate a tourism policy, which may be translated into a plan. Such policy clarifies how tourism is seen in the context of the national economy, what objectives are to be pursued, how tourism enters into national and regional planning; these objectives can be then translated into quantified targets and rates of growth. When the role of tourism is defined, the policy provides a statement of the means by which the objectives are to be attained; the means cover such matters as the administrative arrangements, the respective roles of the private and public sectors and the fiscal arrangements". (Burkart and Medlik, 1981)*

According to Burkart and Medlik, a government, having undertaken such an exercise in policy planning will normally delegate responsibility. This delegation will be to one of the following bodies:

(i.) a governmental department which will be either a Ministry or Department;

(ii.) a semi-governmental organisation such as a statutory body created by government legislation;

(iii.) a non-governmental organisation which may well be voluntary.

The British government has tended to opt for the second option creating the British Tourist Authority and the three English, Scottish and Welsh Tourist Boards by the 1969 Development of Tourism Act. It is argued incidentally, that one of the weaknesses of the 1969 Act is its failure to identify properly the respective role and responsibilities of these four bodies, thereby perpetuating confusion, conflict and duplication. Burkart and Medlik provide an account of the pattern of Government's thinking at that time. They argue that five main options were available to government:

(i.) to extend the powers of the old British Travel Association to include development and perhaps other responsibilities;

(ii.) to allow the British Travel Association to concentrate on promotion and to give powers of development to the then Board of Trade;

(iii.) to allow the British Travel Association to concentrate on promotion and to establish a new development organisation;

(iv.) to combine both development and promotion in a government department;

(v.) to combine both development and promotion in a new statutory body.

As the authors observe:

*"In the end, the fifth alternative, a new statutory organisation outside a government department and combining promotion and development, appeared to present the balance of advantages, and what was*

> *probably the most radical of the five available options*
> *was adopted" (Burkart and Medlik, 1981)*

Despite this pattern of administrative devolution, however, central government has continued to set the tone of policy; in fact government policy messages display a curious degree of uniformity. As a Scottish commentator has put it:

> *"While a good deal of administrative devolution*
> *characterises tourism, this has not been accompanied by*
> *the evolution of distinctive governmental approaches at*
> *Scottish or Welsh levels". (Heeley, 1986 )*

The debate leading up to and including the 1969 Development of Tourism, for example, centred around central government's concern to increase the foreign exchange earnings produced by visitors to Britain. Against the background of an improved balance of payments situation, the Heath Conservative Government concluded in its 1970 review of tourism that the earlier concern to boost foreign earnings had perhaps led to the neglect of regional and local considerations, hence the phasing out of the Hotel Development Incentives (HDI) scheme and the introduction of the Tourist Projects Scheme in 1971-2. The election of a Labour Government in 1974 heralded a further review of tourism within the Department of Trade, leading to ministerial guidelines being produced by Peter Shore, the then responsible minister, in that year. These reiterated that earnings from overseas visitors and consideration of the local tourist economy would remain the twin pillars of tourism policy but sought to attract tourists away from the established and increasingly congested centres such as London and Stratford towards less frequently visited locations. In this way it was hoped that the development of tourism might be seen to assist ailing local economies. Out of this policy sprang the Tourism Growth Points (TGP) of the late 1970s. Designated in areas such as Scarborough and the High Pennines, these experiments attempted to draw up integrated tourism development plans for selected areas. They demonstrated an unusually high degree of direct central government involvement. In 1982 another Conservative Government once again set about a review of tourism culminating in the announcements of Norman Lamont, then junior minister for tourism, in November 1983. These guidelines tended to reverse the move towards decentralism promoted by Labour in the second half of the 1970s. Yet despite this succession of sometimes contradictory government review statements, successive governments have shown a marked disinclination to commit themselves to any systematic plan for tourism. As Heeley puts it:

> *"National tourism policy goals, as defined by national*
> *government in both the Shore and Lamont reviews, are*
> *brief and exhibit a high degree of generality and*
> *ambiguity. There exists no apparent mechanism for their*
> *implementation. They amount to little more than a*
> *statement of good faith in the balance of payments*
> *contribution and the wealth-job creation potential of*
> *tourism, and the desirability of achieving certain specified*
> *and largely uncontentious improvements to the country's*
> *tourist products. They fail to emphasise a linkage with*
> *other policy fields and, in particular, do not reflect the*
> *close ties between tourism, on the one hand, and*

*transport, leisure/recreation, and heritage on the other.*
*Finally, they do not provide the statutory national tourist*
*agencies with the direction necessary to enable them to*
*evolve purposeful strategies. Such direction does not exist*
*in any meaningful form at present ..." (Heeley, 1986)*

# The Role of Local Government

Local authorities throughout Britain are increasingly involved both directly
and indirectly in the development of local frameworks for tourism and in the
provision, supply and operation of tourist facilities. The table below provides
some indication of the financial extent of this involvement:

**Estimated Local Authority Expenditure On, and Income From, Leisure and
Recreation 1985-86**

(see notes 1&2)

| England and Wales (£'000) | Expenditure | Income |
|---|---|---|
| Urban parks and open spaces | 314,084 | 43,784 |
| Indoor sports halls and leisure centres | 220,821 | 103,872 |
| Swimming pools | 137,846 | 45,775 |
| Theatres, halls and arts centres | 102,639 | 42,311 |
| Art galleries and museums | 58,944 | 9,015 |
| Community halls, public halls | 51,291 | 15,359 |
| Outdoor sports facilities | 32,553 | 8,641 |
| Other arts activities and promotions [3] | 32,143 | 4,780 |
| Central or departmental catering | 31,699 | 34,660 |
| Promotion of tourism | 29,445 | 5,236 |
| Country parks, amenity areas, picnic sites and nature reserves | 27,396 | 6,199 |
| Golf courses | 13,632 | 12,669 |
| Allotments | 5,136 | 3,256 |
| Other leisure and recreation facilities and central departmental administration [4] | 324,2800 [5] | |
| Total | 1,381,906 [6] | 335,557 |

(1) The estimates for England and Wales relate to 95 per cent of authorities.
(2) Excludes libraries.
(3) Includes promotions in public libraries and on private premises.
(4) Includes grants and contributions.
(5) Net expenditure.
(6) Includes net expenditure on other leisure and recreation facilities and
central departmental administration.
*Source: Social Trends, 17, 1987*

The terms 'leisure and recreation' and 'tourism' are not synonymous; even
so, the provision of tourism facilities has often been regarded as developing
out of a wider concern in local government for the provision of 'leisure
services'.

This immensely varied range of activities offers a complicated, fragmented, piecemeal picture, which is a consequence of the development of the 'leisure industry' itself and of the development of leisure services within local government. Travis attempted to classify ten 'identifiable sectors within the realm of local authority leisure services'. These are listed below, together with a brief indication of the facilities and services provided under each.

## (a.) Sport and Physical Recreation

sports and leisure centres; sports and leisure pools; playing fields; studios; golf courses; multi-purpose lakes; marinas; sports festivals; promotion of amateur and professional events and tournaments;

## (b.) Informal Outdoor Recreation

playgrounds; urban and coutryside parks, gardens; allotments; beaches; footpaths; national parks;

## (c.) Arts and Cultural

art galleries; art centres; museums; concert halls; theatres and theatre companies; festivals; exhibitions and events; orchestras and concerts; heritage;

## (d.) Libraries

public lending and reference libraries; local archives; reference and specialist libraries; mobile libraries; library events;

## (e.) Entertainment and Catering

multi-purpose halls; restaurants; bars; catering services;

## (f.) Conservation and Interpretation

museums and related restoration and conservation services; archaeology; interpretation and exhibition; conservation areas (urban and rural); historic buildings and sites; nature reserves; interpretation centres; heritage;

## (g.) Tourism

promotion and publicity; infrastructure; information centres; conference facilities; themes; facilities and venues; parks; centres and camps; sites (e.g. caravan and camping); social tourism; heritage;

## (h.) Youth and Community

youth clubs; community centres; outdoor recreation; adventure; play;

## (i.) Adult Education

adult education centres; leisure classes;

## (j.) Social Services

day centres; clubs (e.g. for the elderly and handicapped); social tourism; play.

This classification, although helpful, clearly fails to identify mutually exclusive categories; many of the activities, in addition to those specifically identified under 'Tourism', are clearly of central relevance to the development of tourism in a local area. Nevertheless, it does provide some indication of the scope and extent of local government's involvement, which perhaps official expenditure statistics fail to indicate. In the specific context of tourism, Holloway (1985) has identified the following principal responsibilities of local authorities.

(a.) Provision of leisure facilities for tourists and for residents;

(b.) Planning, physical and policy;

(c.) Powers relating to development control;

(d.) Provision of services and facilities for visitors;

(e.) Car and coach parking;

(f.) Caravan and camping sites;

(g.) Relevant information and statistical data;

(h.) Marketing and promoting the local area;

(i.) Restoration, preservation and maintenance of historic buildings and sites;

(j.) Enforcement of public health and safety legislation.

Some of these are mandatory obligations. For example, county authorities must develop strategic structure plans, in the framework of which district authorities must prepare local plans conforming to them; also compulsory is public and environmental health legislation. The statutory obligations, however, usually relate to more general matters rather than to the specific areas of leisure or tourism; apart from relatively minor legal requirements, provision in this field is almost entirely discretionary, having been developed by local authorities under legislation which permits them to act rather than makes their actions mandatory. Powers are often concurrent rather than specific. The following pieces of legislation are relevant in the development of local government's portfolio of leisure services.

## Education Act, 1944

This major Act imposes a duty upon local education authorities to provide 'leisure time occupation, in such organised cultural training and recreative activities as are suited to their requirements, for any persons over compulsory school age who are able and willing to profit by the facilities provided for that purpose'. This has usually resulted in youth and community/adult education sections within Education Departments.

## Local Government Act, 1948

This permits local authorities to establish information and publicity services for tourism.

## National Parks and Access to the Countryside Act, 1949

Creating the National Parks Commission and the Nature Conservancy, this Act imposed a duty upon appropriate local authorities to manage National Parks as designated.

## Public Libraries and Museums Act, 1964

This act imposes a duty upon the appropriate local authorities to provide arrangements for a public library service, and permitted all local authorities to provide museums and art galleries.

## Countryside Act, 1968

This legislation permits local authorities to provide countryside recreation facilities.

## Local Government Act, 1972

A major piece of legislation creating new, reorganised, county and district authorities in England and Wales and allocating functions to them. It confers mainly discretionary, concurrent powers in the field of leisure services; regarding tourism specifically, the effect was to consolidate the 1948 legislation.

## Local Government (Miscellaneous Provisions) Act, 1976

This Act gives permissive powers to local authorities to provide non-cultural recreational facilities. It also enables the two tiers of local authorities to draw up inter-authority and inter-service agreements.
(Based on Travis et al., 1981 and Travis, 1983).

The relevant legislation, then, is fragmented and piecemeal; there exists no single, comprehensive Local Government (Development of Leisure and Tourism) Act. Even so, many authorities, from Bradford to Bristol, from South Tyneside to Swansea, energetically exploit their discretionary powers within the limit of their resources. This has always been the case even though the underlying rationale and policy intentions have shifted considerably over the years. The origin of local government's involvement in the provision of leisure services lies in a distinctly nineteenth-century conception of civic philanthropy. Thus, public parks were opened in Preston and Birkenhead in 1842 and 1843 respectively, a development consolidated in the Recreational Grounds Act of 1852 as part of an attempt to retrieve a lost ruralism. In the interests of public health, local authorities began to provide facilities such as slipper and swimming baths. By the 1950s a variety of sports facilities were beginning to be developed, a development given additional momentum by the creation of the Sports Council in 1965. Similarly, cultural provision by local authorities benefited from the creation of the Arts Council in 1946 as well as from the emergence of Regional Arts Associations in the 1950s and 1960s.

This shifting policy landscape can be set within the analytic framework outline suggested by Rapoport and Dower (1976). Seeking to analyse the aims and intentions of all bodies involved in the provision of leisure services, Rapoport and Dower identify three main sets of aims to be found among providing organisations:

## (a) requirements of the consumer:

☐ physical fitness
☐ pursuit of excellence

- [ ] entertainment and enjoyment
- [ ] intellectual development
- [ ] social and physical welfare

## (b) concerns of the community:

- [ ] economic benefit
- [ ] reduction of anti-social behaviour
- [ ] conservation of natural beauty and heritage

## (c) interests of the providing organisation:

- [ ] commercial profit
- [ ] organisational image
- [ ] administrative arrangements and interdependencies

The shifting complementarities and interdependencies, as well as the implicit and explicit tensions, between a local authority's support for tourism and its other activities within the field of leisure services and beyond can be sensibly explored in such a scheme.

At present, the policy emphasis is on economic development. Many local authorities value the importance of leisure services, particularly tourism, as part of their economic development strategies; so much so that some practitioners would argue that tourism projects are entirely concerned with economic development and ought not to be seen as part of a wider package of leisure services. The point is debatable. Certainly many authorities emphasise the economic benefits to local communities of incoming tourists; however, the extent to which such benefits can genuinely be divorced from, say, the proper management of heritage or the undeniable attraction of the presence of major artistic organisations (which a local authority may also partly support) is problematic. Interdependencies and externalities, positive or negative, are always difficult to disentangle.

Nevertheless economic development is now given the highest priority, and the contribution of tourism has been eagerly seized upon by central and local government. Martin and Mason (1988) have provided a recent review of the policy stance which sees tourism as:

> *"... a source of economic growth and job creation which can, at least in part, fill the gaps left by declines in older, more traditional industries. As such, it may be one key to the resolution of the social problems caused by the economic decay of inner cities, old industrial towns and rural areas."*
> *(Martin and Mason, 1988)*

North American examples of urban regeneration in which tourism has played a major role include the renovation of the Inner Harbours of Baltimore and Boston. Schemes in both cities have been much publicised in Britain, thus further prompting local authorities in large urban areas to draw up their own comparable programmes of urban redevelopment. In Martin and Mason's analysis, there are, typically, three principal components to such packages:

(a.) the development of new facilities to provide a focal point and catalyst for both local visitors and tourists;

(b.) the upgrading of existing facilities and buildings, usually emphasising any 'heritage' elements and involving systematic and comprehensive thematic interpretation for purposes of publicity and marketing;

(c.) the projection of the city or town as a central launching pad for the exploration and discovery of surrounding geographical areas.

Martin and Mason's cited examples of urban authorities in the U.K. which implement such tourism projects include London (Covent Garden; Dockland; Battersea Power Station), Bristol, Gloucester, Manchester, Liverpool, Bradford, Gateshead and Glasgow (Martin and Mason, 1988, ). Others include Swansea, Cardiff, Wigan, Stoke-on-Trent, Hull and South Tyneside; indeed, it may be increasingly difficult to find authorities without such schemes. The same values and expressions are increasingly to be found in the realm of arts funding and provision. In 1988, for example, the Arts Council formally launched its drive for increased public and private sector co-operation. This was labelled 'An Urban Renaissance: The Role of the Arts in Urban Regeneration', and Sir William Rees-Mogg, Chairman of the Arts Council, launched the strategy as follows:

*"There is little awareness nationally of the important role which the arts are playing in revitalising depressed urban areas. The Arts Council has launched the 'Urban Renaissance' project to inform those involved in redevelopment - policy makers, property developers and inner city agencies - on the ways in which the arts can stimulate economic and social regeneration. Throughout Britain, the Regional Arts Associations are accomplishing much in inner city areas. 'Urban Renaissance' will provide a facility for sharing these successful formulas for regeneration, involving partnerships across the public and private sectors."*
*(Arts Council, 1988)*

In view of the existing fragmented pattern of mainly permissive, concurrent powers, and given the shifting content and messages of policy, it is hardly surprising that the organisation and management of tourism within local authorities is tentative and uncertain. Within leisure services generally, Travis (1983) has been able to document the move away from the organisational fragmentation of the 1970s, which reflected the chaotic scatter of 'relevant' discretionary powers, towards the development of an integrated leisure service with more influence within the authority and perhaps more political impact. A 1985 survey by the Audit Commission, the Local Government Training Board and the Institute of Local Government Studies confirmed the emergence of leisure/recreation groupings in 1982, 78% of appropriate authorities were found to have a committee within this programme area. In 1983, Travis took stock of the emerging situation as follows:

> *"Leisure Services Departments are established, and their*
> *rules are being consolidated, but generally personnel still*
> *act as in introverted, narrow and separate disciplines.*
> *Will one see a single, unified 'Leisure Services Profession'*
> *emerge in the 1980s? Is there still a need for a single*
> *recodified Leisure Services Act - to do for this field what*
> *such legislation did earlier for Town and Country*
> *Planning and for Social Work?"*
> *(Travis, 1983 )*

The management of tourism initiatives in local authorities possibly confirms some of Travis's implied concerns. Tourism projects are frequently accommodated managerially in Planning Departments, Economic Development Units or Chief Executive's offices and their respective Committees. The tension indicates a dilemma: is the promotion of tourism a welfare function or more properly a simple business operation better guided by commercial principles? To what extent should local authorities be involved and what is their proper contribution? Certainly the distinction between public and private sectors is less than clear-cut. Local authorities have always promoted tourism in liaison with other public sector organisations, typically with the appropriate Regional Tourist Board. Increasingly, however, they are developing coalitions and alliances with a wider range of bodies, public and private. As Martin and Mason conclude:

> *"Successful development of an area for tourism requires*
> *co-operation between the public and private sectors and*
> *between the local community and other organizations*
> *involved. It is a process of partnership and there need to*
> *be common and accepted goals."*
> *(Martin and Mason, 1988)*

# Public Agencies and Tourism

In this section, the role of public agencies in the development of tourism in the UK will be considered. In this context the term 'Public Agencies' refer to those organisations established by statute and financed wholly or partly by government for the purpose of research and the development of sectoral interests. In spite of the government's financial interest in them, the governing bodies of and the work undertaken by these agencies arguably remains free of state control and direction. This constitutional position has resulted in such bodies being termed 'Quasi-Autonomous Non-Government Organisations' (QUANGOS).

The specialist QUANGOS established to research and develop tourism in the UK are the Tourist Boards. Owing to the diverse nature of tourism, however, there are other public agencies with varying degrees of interest in tourism which must also be taken into account. It is nevertheless appropriate to consider the background and functions of the specialist bodies first.

Tourist Boards are agencies created specifically for the purpose of researching and developing tourism in a particular geographical area. They also aim to co-ordinate the activities of other organisations which have an interest in tourism. It has already been noted that the Travel Association of Great Britain and Northern Ireland has been in existence since the 1920's. This association was a voluntary one, with limited powers and few clear policy objectives. Following the Second World War, and in particular since the 1960s, increasing prosperity and leisure time have enabled larger numbers of people to travel for recreational purposes. In addition, rising world trade post-war has led to a growth in travel abroad for business purposes. Against this background, the increasing significance of tourism as an 'invisible' item on the current account of the balance of payments and as a generator of employment was recognised. The need for a statutory organisation with defined powers and objectives therefore became apparent.

Such an organisational structure was created by the Development of Tourism Act 1969, with the transformation of the old British Travel Association (formerly TAGBNI) into a statutory British Tourist Authority, with new national Tourist Boards for England, Scotland and Wales.

According to the Development of Tourism Act, the functions of the British Tourist Authority (BTA) are:

> (a.) To encourage people to visit Great Britain and people living in Great Britain to take their holidays here;

> (b.) To encourage the provision and improvement of tourist amenities and facilities in Great Britain.

The Tourist Boards in Scotland, Wales and England have similar functions in their respective territories. So far as powers are concerned, the Tourist Boards can:

> (a.) In accordance with arrangements approved by the relevant Minister and the Treasury, give financial assistance for the carrying out of any project which, in the opinion of the Board, will provide or improve tourist amenities and facilities in the country for which the Board is responsible;

> (b.) With the approval of the relevant Minister and the Treasury, carry out any such project (section 4.1).

Tourist Board activities are therefore constrained by the level of funding allocated following Ministerial and Treasury approval; financial assistance provided by the Tourist Boards may be in the form of grants, loans or subscription (section 4.2).

In addition, the Tourist Boards have a duty to advise government ministers and certain public organisations in respect of tourism (section 5.1). Powers are also available to assist corresponding bodies in the Channel Islands, Isle of Man and Northern Ireland and to provide technical assistance to the Overseas Development Administration in connection with tourism-related aid projects (sections 5.3 and 5.4).

It should be noted that the BTA was originally the only Board empowered to act overseas, and it therefore handled promotions in foreign countries on behalf of the national boards. More recently, however, the Scottish Board has also assumed powers enabling it to operate overseas.

The statutory obligations have been interpreted by the national Tourist Boards as including the following activities (adapted from Holloway, 1985):

## Planning and Management

This includes research and development, conservation of attractions (in co-operation with other organisations), licensing, and involvement with training in co-operation with schools, colleges, polytechnics and universities.

## Marketing

This includes research and forecasting, advertising, the production of literature, special promotions and public relations campaigns; the operation of Tourist Information Centres also comes into this category.

## Financial

Tourist Boards fulfil an advisory role as well as administering the disbursement of government aid.

## Co-ordination

This means they must co-ordinate their activities with other public bodies and with local and regional tourist boards. This function also includes co-operative marketing with private companies selling holidays to and within the UK, plus the organisation of workshops, seminars and conferences.

Following the Development of Tourism Act, a network of regional Tourist Boards was established. These regional Boards are funded partly by their respective national Tourist Boards, and also by local authorities and by private company subscription. Activities undertaken are similar to those described above, but are limited to the regional Board's particular geographical area.

The terms of the Development of Tourism Act indicate the comparatively open brief accorded to the Boards in the interpretation of how tourism may be best developed. This can be seen as a strength of the system, permitting wide-ranging research and allowing the Boards to evolve in the context of contemporary demands. Such leeway can also be seen as a weakness, with Boards open to conflicting demands from different interest groups and proving unable to satisfy any of them. The emphasis of the Boards has certainly changed over time, with the interests shown in the 1970s in social tourism and environmental issues giving way in the 1980s to an interest in economic research into tourism as a generator of employment. Given the proportion of funds coming from Government, however, the extent of autonomy enjoyed by the Boards is debatable.

A large number of other public agencies are also involved to varying degrees in the planning, management and control of tourism. A notable example is the Countryside Commission, which only left direct Civil Service control in 1982. The statutory duty of the Countryside Commission is to promote conservation, and enjoyment, of the countryside in England and Wales. This

**Tourist Boards of England and Wales**

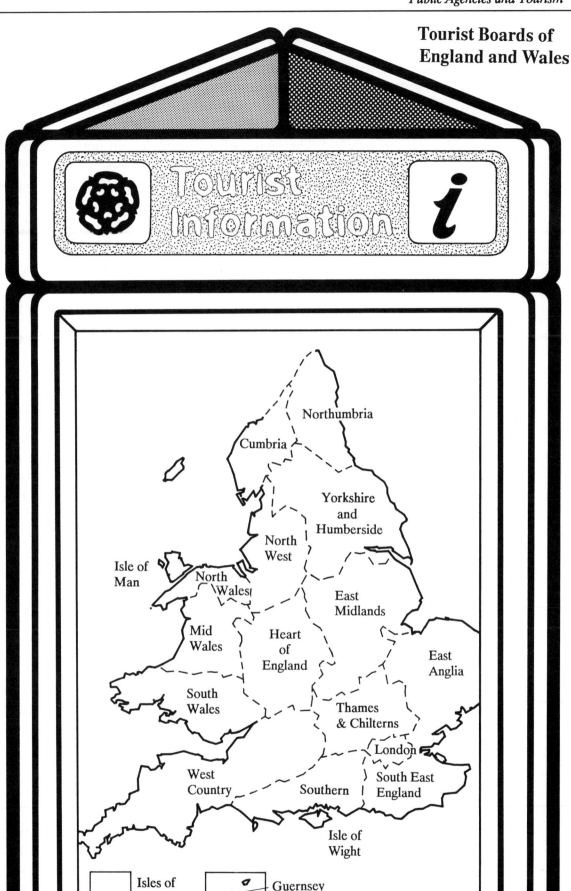

duty clearly marks the Commission as an organisation with a direct interest in reconciling tourism (in the sense of access to sites) with conservation. The three main aspects of the Commission's work, which can be seen as including elements of planning and management for tourism, are as follows:

☐ The giving of policy advice on landscape conservation, countryside recreation and access;

☐ The promotion of action through appropriate funding, and the reconciliation of conflicts;

☐ The designation of natural resources, for instance National Parks and long-distance paths.

Another public agency with an interest in tourism is the Forestry Commission. Arguably the largest landowner in Britain, with responsibility for 3 million acres of forest, the Forestry Commission's primary objective is timber production. It does, however, have the further policy objective of developing its forests for recreation. The main emphasis has been on providing facilities for day visitors, for example car parks, picnic sites,viewpoints, forest walks and visitor centres with information and interpretation materials. The Forestry Commission is also involved with the provision of accommodation services, with caravan and camping sites and cabins being available in some of their 450,000 acres of forest parks.

Other public agencies concerned with specific sectoral interests which can also be seen as having interests in tourism include: the Historic Buildings and Monuments Commission (more commonly referred to as English Heritage); the Arts Council; the Sports Council; the Nature Conservancy Council; and the Water Authorities. The latter organisations are currently in the early stages of preparation for privatisation.

There exist also other public agencies which provide advice and other assistance to specific user groups which may include recommendations relating to tourism. For example, the Agricultural Development and Advisory Service, in suggesting tourism as an activity to a hill farmer, would fit into this category. The Council for Small Industries in Rural Areas is another organisation which might recommend a tourism-related development to people seeking its advice. In these cases the primary role of the agency concerned is advisory, in particular regarding financial management and marketing aspects. Such agencies may also provide financial assistance in the form of loan and/or grant aid.

In addition to the various sectional agencies mentioned above, a number of regional organisations have been established in order to promote the interests of particular geographical areas. Examples include the Welsh and Scottish Development Agencies, the Highlands and Islands Development Board, the Urban Development Corporations and the Northern Development Company. These organisations have been established by central government with private sector interests, either in co-operation with local authorities or bypassing them. The principal objective of these regional agencies is to attract inward investment in order to bring about economic revival in areas of deprivation and high unemployment. The development of tourist attractions and infrastructure is regularly proposed as a strategy. Dockland developments in London, Liverpool and Bristol, though not exclusively concerned with tourism, have been thus presented as likely to attract visitors and tourist spending. The private sector is playing an increasingly important role in such regional bodies, while local authorities have been losing a number of planning and policy-making powers to these development agencies.

The above section has indicated the multiplicity of public and semi-public organisations which are involved to varying degrees in the development and management of tourism. To summarise, these can be broadly categorised as follows:

☐ **Tourist Boards:** organisations specifically equipped with powers and responsibilities for tourism at national, regional and local levels.

☐ **Amenity Agencies:** Other QUANGOS with peripheral involvement in tourism. Examples include the Countryside Commission, the Forestry Commission, the Arts Council, English Heritage.

☐ **Advisory Agencies:** Organisations concerned with specific client groups. Examples include the Agricultural Development and Advisory Service and the Council for Small Industries in Rural Areas.

☐ **Development Agencies:** Organisations involved with economic development in specific geographical areas. Many of these bodies were created in the 1980s, particularly in inner-city locations where private sector corporations are extensively involved.

# The International Dimension

A number of organisations with international interests in the development of tourism exist worldwide. These bodies can be broadly categorised under four headings:

### (a.) International Trade Associations

These are international associations specifically concerned with particular sectoral interests in the tourism industry. The Universal Federation of Travel Agency Associations (UFTAA), for example, is made up of representatives of national private sector tourism industry associations, and acts as a forum to discuss issues of common interest. Membership of these organisations is usually voluntary (the Association of British Travel Agents, ABTA, resigned from UFTAA in 1988). These International Trade Associations generally do not have statutory or regulatory powers beyond their membership rules.

### (b.) International Tourism Organisations

Typically, such organisations emphasise all the tourism interests of a particular 'world region' or major territorial bloc. Territory defines eligibility for membership. Examples of such organisations are the Caribbean Tourism Association, the East Asia Travel Associations and the Pacific Area Travel Association.

Representatives of both private and public sectors participate, with the objective of encouraging co-operation and co-ordination of activities to the mutual advantage of member countries. Regional marketing and product development, with the aim of encouraging international visitors to spread their time between member countries, are typical activities of such organisations.

## (c.) Inter-Governmental Tourism Organisations

Officials and other persons responsible for tourism in member countries' government organisations comprise the membership of these international bodies. The Organisation for Economic Co-operation and Development Tourism Committee and the World Tourism Organisation are the largest groupings in this category, and will be considered in more detail below.

## (d.) Inter-Governmental Economic Unions

A number of attempts at regional economic integration have been made since 1945. The objectives of the Inter-governmental Economic Unions have usually been the encouragement of increased trade between member states by reducing tariff and non-tariff barriers, and the establishment of common agricultural and industrial policies. The operations of these regional groupings can have significant effects, direct and indirect, upon the development of tourism in member countries. The particular case of the European Economic Community (EEC) will be discussed separately.

We are concerned here with the relationships between the public or government sector and the development of tourism, and shall therefore focus on the roles of inter-governmental tourism organisations and Economic Unions, with particular reference to the Organisation for Economic Co-operation and Development (OECD) Tourism Committee, the World Tourism Organisations (WTO) and the European Economic Community (EEC).

## OECD Tourism Committee

The overall policy objectives of the OECD include the following:

- [ ] to achieve the highest sustainable economic growth and employment and a rising standard of living in member countries,

- [ ] to contribute to sound economic expansion in member as well as non-member countries in the process of economic development;

- [ ] to contribute to the expansion of world trade on a multilateral, non-discriminatory basis in accordance with international obligations.

With tourism as an important and increasing component of world trade, it is not surprising that the OECD has established a specialist committee to report on the industry's development and economic significance in member countries. Membership of the OECD is largely drawn from representatives of the 'Free Market' economies namely Austria, Australia, Belgium, Canada, Denmark, Finland, Federal Republic of Germany, Greece, Ireland, Italy, Japan, Luxembourg, the Netherlands, New Zealand, Portugal, Spain, Sweden, Switzerland, Turkey, the United Kingdom and the United States of America. Yugoslavia is also partially involved in the work of organisation.

These nations represent some of the major starting points and destinations of world tourist traffic. The committee's work, then, is intended to inform OECD members and policy makers about the scope, significance and direction of tourism and report on any trade barriers affecting movements. The committee produces an annual publication, entitled Tourism Policy and international Tourism in OECD Member Countries. This publication reports the year-by-year evolution of tourism and is a valuable source of statistics and background information. Government policies and actions relating to tourism are reported from each member country. Trends in tourist flows are charted and balance sheets for receipts and expenditure are drawn up. The publication also reports developments in air, rail, road, and sea transport. Since it has been published since 1961, it provides a valuable source of data for the period of tourism's most rapid growth.

The Statistical Working Party of the OECD Tourism Committee is engaged in the valuable task of studying ways of standardising and improving the quality of statistics of tourist movements and the recording of receipts and expenditures in national accounts.

# World Tourism Organisation

The WTO was established by Resolution 2529 of the 24th session of the United Nations General Assembly in 1975 as a successor to the International Union of Official Tourism Organisations (IUOTO). The WTO is an intergovernmental organisation operating under the auspices of the UN and comprising at the time of writing, 109 member states, 3 associate members and 150 affiliates representing the professional and operational sectors of the industry. Like the OECD's, the WTO's publications are a valuable source of statistical data. The WTO provides the longest continuous record of tourism flows, having (until 1975 in its former guise as the IUOTO) gathered and published figures since 1947. A reliable historical series only applies from 1967, however, due to changes in methods of data collection and interpretation.

Annual publications of the WTO include The World Travel and Tourism Statistics Year-book which reports global tourist movements, use of transport and motivations for travel. The Year-book also includes data on receipts and expenditure, and on accommodation capacity and occupancy.

Since 1978, the WTO has also produced an annual collection of data entitled Domestic Travel and Tourism statistics, which is designed 'specifically to highlight the development of the population travel within their country of residence'. As relatively few countries systematically collect domestic tourism statistics, however, only 46 countries are at present covered by this publication.

The WTO also periodically provides Economic Review of World Tourism. In this publication, tourism is placed in the context of the world economy, and its contributions to the gross domestic product and balance of payments reviewed. The development of demand for tourist facilities and the accommodation and transport sectors are also considered.

Both the OECD and the WTO perform the important function of providing accessible collections of statistics for a large number of countries. The intention is primarily to inform planners and policy-makers concerning global trends in the direction and magnitude of world tourism, but various publications described above also represent useful source material for the student of travel and tourism.

# Inter-Governmental Economic Unions

The Inter-Governmental Tourism organisations described above are concerned exclusively with the collection, dissemination and analysis of data relating to tourism for the use of their relevant member government departments.

There also exist other inter-governmental co-operative bodies which have more broadly defined areas of interest. These (usually regional) groupings are generally involved with forging integration between member countries' economic and industrial policies. To this end, these organisations are endowed with varying degrees of legislative and regulatory powers which often take precedence over national legislation. This issue of autonomy and sovereignty has frequently caused tensions between member governments attempting to place 'national interests' before those of the organisation.

In some cases, these tensions have led to individual countries withdrawing membership and the collapse of the organisation concerned (the East African Community for instance in 1978). Political conflicts between members can also seriously undermine the operations of these organisations. Nevertheless, it is argued that the collective benefits can outweigh individual losses for members of integration schemes, hence their continuing existence.

Four types of such schemes can be identified worldwide. These types are not necessarily fixed, and organisations may switch between them according to their members' interests.

| Type | Characteristics | Examples |
|------|-----------------|----------|
| Free Trade Area | Common internal tariffs, but differing external tariffs | European Free Trade Association (EFTA) |
| Customs Union | Common internal and external tariffs | South African Customs union |
| Common Market | Common tariffs and few restrictions on the mobility of capital and labour | European Economic Community (EEC) |
| Economic Union | Common Monetary Policies | European Monetary System (EMS) |

*Source: Edwards, 'The Fragmented World' (Methuen, 1985)*

The objectives and operations of these organisations clearly go beyond the development of tourism. Nevertheless the policies they approve and implement can have important implications for tourist traffic. The effects (not necessarily representative) regarding tourism for members of one such regional organisation, the E(E)C, are considered below.

# The European (Economic) Community

No detailed and comprehensive analysis of the structure and operation of the EEC can be provided here. Excellent introductory volumes which analyse its structure and operation are already available: (Budd, 1987, Butler, 1986)

The EEC has played a significant role in the development of European tourism, in particular through the evolution of a legislative and regulatory framework and through the provision of funds for the development of locations for tourism. This section will be limited to identifying those elements within the EEC which have specific implications for tourism.

Four main institutions constitute the EEC. These are:

## (a.) The European Commission.

This body acts as the guardian of the treaties underpinning the community. EEC laws, for example, rules concerning competition, are enforced by the Commission. In addition, the Commission has powers to make proposals for community policies and is responsible for monitoring existing polices. Functions of the Commission which relate directly to the implementation of tourism include the study of transport systems within the Community. The commission has powers to direct EEC funds relative to the improvement, integration and elimination of bottlenecks in transport systems, and to simplify cross-border access.

The European Commission is also charged with bringing practices in member countries more into line and with ensuring that they are answerable to EEC rules regarding competition. An example of this responsibility affecting the travel industry is the 1985 'Traveller's Charter', in which the Commission proposed that holiday prices should be frozen within 30 days of departure, and that compensation as well as refunds should be given in the event of late holiday cancellation by tour operators. These proposals have yet to be implemented. The Commission has also in 1986 made proposals for the reform of the system of airline route allocations between airlines and member states. These proposals would liberalise aviation in the EEC. Route-sharing obligations would be removed and new entrants to the market permitted. It is argued that if airlines were allowed to decide their own tariffs (providing operating costs are covered), the resulting increased competition would serve to lower the currently high fares between member states. These proposals, however, have yet to be approved by the European Council. (see below). A further responsibility of the Commission is the organisation and management of development co-operation between the EEC and the signatories to the Lome Convention, the so-called African, Caribbean and Pacific states (ACP). The Convention specifically provides for assistance with tourism projects in these countries in the following areas:

☐ Definition of policies

☐ Development of strategies through financial and technical assistance

☐ Development, maintenance and rehabilitation of tourism assets

☐ Training and professional education

☐ Marketing and promotions

☐ Research and development

☐ Data collection, analysis and dissemination

☐ Encouragement of regional co-operation

The European Commission is therefore the institution most directly involved with policy formulation and execution. Approval of the Commission's proposals, however, rests with a separate institution, the Council.

## (b.) The European Council,

The twice or thrice-yearly meeting of Heads of State, is the principal decision-making body of the Community. Subordinate to this is the Council of Ministers, the meeting of relevant ministers from each member state. It is at the Council's meetings that the Commission's proposals are debated, adopted, amended or rejected.

## (c.) The European Court

The Court enforces the terms of the founding Treaty of Rome; and as a result of the Treaty, subsequent secondary legislation. It presides over hearings brought before it under Community law.

## (d.) The European Parliament

This is a unique institution. It passes no legislation relating to the EEC (that is still held individually by member countries' parliaments), and no central government is responsible to it. What it does is to approve or reject EEC budgets, and it also has powers to sack the European Commission.

The above outline indicates the primary functions of the EEC's major institutions. It is also necessary that we consider the position of four separate sources of capital which come under the umbrella of the EEC.

The European Investment Bank (EIB) provides loans on favourable terms to projects meeting the following criteria:

☐ stimulating the development of less prosperous regions;

☐ serving the common interest of more than one community state;

☐ improving industrial co-operation or communications between member countries.

The Regional Development Fund (RDF) provides grant assistance to projects meeting the above criteria operating in geographical areas requiring urgent assistance. Funds from both the EIB and the RDF have been used across the Community for investments in roads, railways, bridges, ferries, airports and harbours.

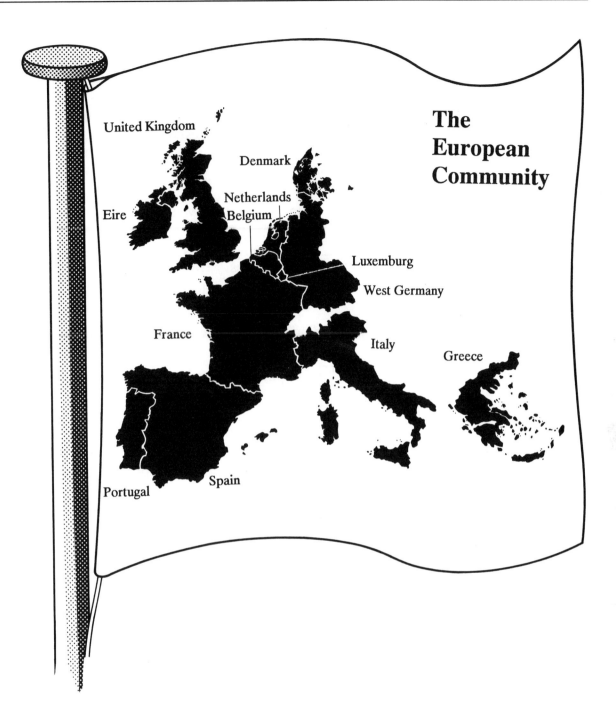

The Social Fund provides assistance for training, retraining, resettlement and job creation. So far as the tourism industry is concerned, preference is given to training programmes that are necessary for modernising the industry.

Finally, The European Agricultural Guidance and Guarantee Fund provides grant aid for tourism, craft industries and conservation projects in Europe's least favoured areas.

## The Future

The EEC appears to be firmly set on the creation of a literal 'Common Market' from 1992. Whether European integration and harmonisation will prevail over perceived national interest remains to be seen: who will lose and gain is another unanswered question. The objectives, however, are clear. They have been summarised by Budd (1987) as follows:

☐ The creation of a 'peoples' Europe, of which its citizens feel a part, and in which frontiers are seen to become less and less necessary.

☐ The removal of barriers to the free movement of goods and services.

☐ Closer standards, access to public contracts, stronger competition policy, more technical co-operation.

Specifically regarding transport, the aims of the open market proposals are as follows:

☐ Simplification and gradual elimination of frontier controls and formalities.

☐ Creation of a Transport Infrastructure Programme facilitating the movement of people and goods throughout the community, including its peripheral areas.

☐ Co-ordination of a European transport market by road, rail, air and sea.

☐ Improvement of safety standards in all aspects of transport.

If carried through, the proposals should create the conditions for strong growth in leisure and business travel markets. Ownership patterns within the industry could also be affected with trans-European transport and distribution corporations entering the market-place.

# Public and Private Sectors: The Mixed Economy of Tourism.

Structurally, tourism is a highly complex business involving a broad spectrum of interests which are not always obviously compatible. It embraces both public and private sectors, in a web of interconnectedness, interrelationships and interdependencies. Both public and private sectors share in the mixed economy of tourism, particularly in the so-called modern, western-type states. Within the structure of government itself, this fragmentation and complexity is replicated. A diverse range of authorities, agencies and organisations is involved, many not obviously or primarily concerned with the development of tourism. For the student of tourism this represents a daunting prospect, yet one not wisely ignored.

# Chapter 10

## ☐ The Marketing of Travel and Tourism

## Introduction

The purpose of this chapter is to discuss the processes of marketing travel and tourism products, and to show how such techniques are employed by the travel and tourism industries. It is extremely important that those involved in the travel and tourism industry are aware of what marketing techniques are available and the benefits they can bring. Before examining the application of marketing to the industry we need to consider exactly what marketing means.

## What is Marketing?

Marketing is a much misunderstood subject. It is therefore important that we define the term clearly at the outset. This however, is no easy task: already over fifty different definitions of marketing have been advanced. These range from 'tongue-in-cheek' definitions such as: 'marketing is selling goods that don't come back to customers that do', to others which are more academic. One definition, widely quoted, is that put forward by the British Institute of Marketing. It is that:

> *'Marketing is the management process which identifies, anticipates, and supplies customer requirements efficiently and profitably.'*

This definition is quite comprehensive. It includes all the major roles of the marketing function from determining consumer needs, the efficient satisfaction of these needs, whilst ensuring the organisation concerned makes a profit out of its activities.

Two inter-related interpretations of marketing can be identified. Firstly, marketing can be seen as a philosophy of business, a way of life for the organisation concerned, where all its activities are centred around meeting the needs of customers. In a competitive marketplace it is important that businesses have a clear picture of who their customers are and an equally clear understanding of what those customers expect from the products they purchase. If the organisation does not supply products that meet customer needs, then its competitors will. Thus, an organisation should aim to be 'customer-oriented'. Secondly, marketing consists of the various techniques available to an organisation's marketing department, which will allow it initially to determine consumer needs and then to motivate the consumer to purchase the products on offer. These techniques can be viewed as a process, a series of steps that an organisation can take which will lead to efficiency and profitability.

## The Marketing Process

Without customers businesses would not exist. This is an obvious fact, but one which is sometimes forgotten. In the current competitive environment, an organisation which can most closely satisfy its customers' needs will best guarantee its survival in the years ahead. Marketing is the management process which is responsible for identifying these needs and making sure that they are satisfied. To help in this process there are six steps an organisation can follow which will increase its level of efficiency in the market place. These six steps are discussed below.

# Step One - Segmenting the Market

The first thing that any organisation concerned with marketing has to do is to segment the market. This means that it must divide the market in which it operates (or wishes to operate) into groups of consumers, all of whom have common needs. Market segmentation is the key to a marketing strategy, since no other decisions can be taken until the company has identified its consumers.

The reason why market segmentation occurs lies in the fact that organisations can no longer regard markets as being uniform, where all consumers wish to purchase the same product. Clearly, for example, different consumers have different tastes in holidays and wish to enjoy different activities when they go on holiday. Young people on an 18-30 holiday will obviously not have the same needs as senior citizens on a Saga holiday. Thus each organisation has to divide the market into clearly defined segments where each segment represents a discrete body of consumers, each of whom will have clearly defined needs which warrant a separate marketing strategy.

When a market has been segmented, each segment should reflect the following important characteristics.

- ☐ each segment should be large enough to justify further investment of time and money by the company;

- ☐ each segment should be 'reachable', in the sense that it should be possible to give the consumers in that segment appropriate information about the company's products;

- ☐ each segment should be measurable, so that the likely demand for travel and tourism products in that segment can be identified.

There is no single way of segmenting a market. Each organisation has to choose bases, or variables, that it thinks are appropriate in respect of its consumers. There are four commonly used 'bases' for market segmentation:

# Figure 1: The six steps of marketing

Segment the market

Develop a profile of the consumers in each market segment

Determine the attractiveness of each market segment

Select the target market(s)

Develop a positioning strategy for each target market

Develop a marketing mix for each target market:

The product
The promotion
The price
The distribution
The personnel
The physical environment

1. descriptive variables;

2. explanatory variables;

3. a combination of descriptive and explanatory variables or 'lifestyle market segmentation';

4. 'geodemographics' which is a relatively new approach, divides consumers into groups depending on residential area.

We shall now consider each of these 'bases' for market segmentation in turn.

# 1. Descriptive Market Segmentation Variables

Descriptive variables are widely used by the travel and tourism industry because they are relatively straightforward to compile, give a reasonably accurate profile, and also provide an indication of the size of the segment. There are four main ways of segmenting a market using descriptive variables. These are by:

(i) Geographic location

(ii) Cultural affiliation

(iii) Demographic segmentation

(iv) Behaviour in the product field

## (i) Geographic location

An organisation may segment its market according to the geographic location of its consumers. Tour operators recognise that consumers living in different parts of the United Kingdom have different needs when they purchase holidays. Most of the leading tour operators now provide regional departure points for tourists, instead of requiring them to make their own way to Luton, Stanstead, Heathrow or Gatwick Airports. In addition, major tour operators, such as Thomson Holidays and Intasun, charge different prices for holidays sold in different parts of the country.

## (ii) Cultural affiliation

In this sense, 'cultural affiliation' refers to a distinctive 'way of life' consumers may practice, as determined, for example, by their religion, their political affiliations, their membership of a particular group or society, or by some other cultural influence. Each cultural group will offer opportunities for the marketer, since members of a specific group will normally conform to a particular way of life which will incorporate common needs or interests and this could lead to them having specific travel requirements.

An example of such market segmentation is Major and Mrs. Holt's Battlefield Tours. These are specifically aimed at consumers with an interest in military history and include comprehensively packaged tours to sites of famous battles in Europe, North America and the Far East. Another example of the use of such segmentation has been the recruitment of Bishop Desmond Tutu by Inter-Church Travel as tour manager and guide for its religious pilgrimage tours to religious shrines and sites in the Holy Land. Indeed, many cultural groups will find that there are tour operators which have developed packages to meet their needs and interests, and which provide specialised tour programmes.

## (iii) Demographic segmentation

Perhaps the most common means of segmenting the market, particularly where the major travel agents and tour operators are concerned, is by using demographic data. These characteristics refer to the age, sex, income, socio-economic group and stage in the family life cycle of the consumer. Demographic data can be obtained from a variety of sources. The British Market Research Bureau conducts an annual questionnaire survey to establish the buying habits of a representative sample of the UK population. In total, some 20,000 people answer their lengthy questionnaires. The results of the survey indicate, for example, which type of consumer purchases a Thomson holiday and which type purchases an Intasun Holiday.

In addition to published sources of data, the company's own records will provide valuable information. When customers complete the booking form in the holiday brochure they have to provide background details of the people in the party, for example, whether there are children going on the holiday, whether the customer is single or married, and sometimes the age of the party members. Analysis of data will help to build a demographic profile of the customer booking a particular holiday.

A further source of demographic data is provided by the National Census of Population, conducted every 10 years in the U.K. This requires all householders to provide details of the people living in their house - their age, sex, stage in family life cycle, occupation and so on. This information could be used to give the tour operator or travel agent an idea of the number of people in each market segment living in a particular geographic area.

A travel agency, for example, will be able to refer to demographic data to obtain particulars of the consumers who might be attracted to buy its holiday. For example, if a travel agency discovers that 70% of its catchment area is made up of households comprising two couples with children under the age of 18 years, where the head of the household falls into socio-economic group A or B and earns over £20,000 per annum, such information will be of use in determining which tour operator's brochures should be displayed. Similarly, some tour operators specialise in providing packages for specific demographic groups. 'Twenty's' and 'Club 18-30' are two tour operators who produce packages especially for young, probably single, consumers from the lower socio-economic groups.

## (iv.) Behaviour in the product field

The fourth demographic variable frequently used for segmenting the market is that of behaviour in the product field. Consumers can be classified according to the brands they chose or company loyalty, whether they are price-conscious, and whether they are frequent or infrequent purchasers of travel or tourism products. Under this category we will consider the following types of consumer:

(a.) Customers who demonstrate brand or company loyalty;

(b.) Customers who are extremely price conscious;

# Figure 2: Demographic market segmentation variables

1. **Socio-Economic Group** - consumers can be segmented according to their occupation. Five broad occupational groups have been identified:

| Socio-Economic Group | Occupation |
|---|---|
| A | Higher managerial, administrative, or professional |
| B | Intermediate managerial, administrative, or professional |
| C1 | Supervisory, clerical, junior administrative, or professional |
| C2 | Skilled manual workers |
| D | Semi-skilled and unskilled manual workers |
| E | State pensioners, widows, casual and lowest grade earners |

2. **Age** - tour operators frequently use this as a segmentation variable.

| Age Group | Products/Companies Offering Holidays to the Age Group |
|---|---|
| Teenagers | PGL Young Adventure; Dolphin Holidays |
| 18-30 | Club 18-30 - International Leisure Group<br>Twentys - Owners Abroad Group<br>Freestyle - Thomson Holidays |
| 30-60 | 'A la Carte' - Thomson Holidays<br>Mountains - Horizon Holidays<br>& Lakes   - Intasun<br>               Thomson Holidays |
| 60 years plus | Saga Holidays<br>'Young at Heart' - Thomson<br>                 Holidays |

3. **Stage-in-the-family-life-cycle** - consumers can be classified according to their martial and family position:

> Young
> Young, single, with no children
> Young couple with child(ren) under six
> Young couple with child(ren) over six
> Couple with children over eighteen living at home
> Older couple with no children living at home
> Older, single person

4. **Income** - the personal disposable income of the consumer can be used as a segmentation variable. Some products are targeted at consumers with high disposable incomes - cruises, flights on Concorde. Other products are aimed at consumers with relatively low disposal incomes - camping/self-catering holidays.

5. **Sex** - some travel and tourism products are specifically designed for either females or males, while others appeal to both sexes.

| **Sex** | **Product** |
|---------|-------------|
| Male | "Night-life holidays to Bangkok" |
| Female | "Beauty-treatment holidays at a health farm" |
| Unisex | "Package holidays to Greece" |

(c.) Frequent travellers such as the business community;

(d.) Infrequent travellers.

### (a.) Customers who demonstrate brand or company loyalty

Some consumers, especially as they become older, may increase their loyalty to certain branded products or certain companies tending to make regular purchases. This is a type of consumer that all companies seek to serve, as it is often easier to satisfy the needs of established customers than to try to win customers from competitors. Travel agents and tour operators recognise the value of encouraging loyalty toward their products and actively encourage repeat purchases by offering special discounts to regular customers or, for example, by establishing a Travel Club which distributes to subscribers, a magazine containing travel information.

### (b.) Customers who are extremely price conscious

While some consumers will be loyal to a brand or company, others will purchase the holiday or set of travel facilities which is the cheapest or which represents the best value for money. The 1970s saw the growth of travel agents who established themselves as 'bucket shops', specialising in selling discounted air-tickets to price-conscious consumers. Young people, particularly students on low incomes, are often the specific target of travel companies, who vie fiercely for their custom. Indeed, in the market for domestic travel in the United Kingdom, bus and coach operators as well as British Rail, recognise students as a discrete market segment and provide clearly defined products and incentives to attract their custom, such as providing special discount cards.

### (c.) Frequent travellers such as business travellers

Consumers may also be segmented according to whether they are frequent or infrequent users of travel or tourism products. The business sector is composed of those who travel frequently. These consumers look for particular advantages from the travel products they purchase, namely reliable services, ease of booking, and comfort while travelling. To cater for these needs, travel agents frequently designate a section of their operations exclusively to serve the business traveller and employ business travel consultants. American Express and Hogg Robinson Travel are prime examples of travel agents which have developed business travel operations. Transport companies positively discriminate towards the business traveller by providing business and first class facilities at the point of embarkation as well as during the flight or on board the train. These are intended to make the journey more relaxing so that the business traveller arrives at his or her destination refreshed and ready for business.

### (d.) Infrequent travellers

Tour operators also identify infrequent travellers and attempt to encourage them to travel more frequently. Solos is a tour operator which provides holidays for single, divorced or separated people. It was felt that people falling into such categories were reluctant to buy conventional holidays aimed at families or couples. To cater for the special needs of people holidaying alone, Solos has developed a range of packages that offer friendship and companionship, as well as travel to popular tourist destinations.

# 2. Explanatory Market Segmentation Variables

Whilst descriptive variables enable the physical and social characteristics of the consumer to be determined, and allow the marketer to establish the size of the market, they do not explain why the consumer acts in a certain way, or buys a particular tourism product. Explanatory variables are needed for this.

Information that explains the consumers' behaviour can be obtained by conducting market research surveys. Such research is important as it allows the marketer to 'look inside the consumer's mind'. Once the research findings have been analysed, the marketer is in a better position to explain why consumers behave in a certain way, or why they buy a particular travel or tourism product. Markets can be segmented by four such explanatory variables:

  (i.) the reasons why people travel;

  (ii.) benefit segmentation;

  (iii) psychographic variables;

  (iv.) reference groups.

## (i.)  The reasons why people travel

Explanatory variables are fundamental to explaining the many different reasons why tourists travel. Business people might have to attend meetings and conferences. Private individuals may travel to holiday destinations in order to relax, or might travel to visit friends and relatives. Young people frequently may travel to other towns and cities to attend college. Each of these different types of traveller will have clearly defined needs that will provide marketing opportunities for travel and tourism companies.

## (ii.) Benefit segmentation

Consumers may be encouraged to buy a product if they recognise that they will benefit from it. For example, people who buy summer sun charter inclusive tours to Spain, are not buying their package holiday simply for the flight on the aeroplane, the stay in the hotel, and the excursions that are arranged for them (which we could describe as the features of the holiday). Rather, the tourists are buying the complete package in order to enjoy the benefits of going away on holiday - two weeks in the sun, the opportunity to sample a foreign culture, to have a change and a break from normal everyday routine, and to meet people and have a generally relaxing time.

Tour operators therefore have to identify the specific benefits that consumers in a particular market segment look for when going on holiday. When identified, the tour operator can devise a holiday package that provides the specific benefits that are attractive to a particular market segment.

In recent years, there has been a proliferation of products that have been launched onto the market, each aiming to provide specific benefits to consumers. A growth area in the 1980s has been the 'Short-Break Holiday Market' which are holidays of less than four nights duration. Companies competing in this market have been devising packages that offer distinct benefits to specific market segments. Ladbroke Hotels, for instance, offer

'Action Extra' holiday programmes where tourists can choose from a number of different sporting activities such as sailing and parachuting. This activity break is designed to offer holidaymakers benefits of excitement and the opportunity of learning a new sport. Other hotel groups offer 'heritage' breaks where holidaymakers can learn about local history, or 'hobby' breaks where the participants are introduced to new leisure pursuits. There has also been a growth in the winter sun holiday market, with retired people in particular enjoying the benefits offered by the milder climates of Mediterranean resorts.

The popularity of holidays to destinations beyond the Mediterranean (the 'long-haul' market) is growing as tourists seek to discover countries and cultures quite different from their own. In addition to this benefit, tourists purchasing the more expensive packages to 'exotic' destinations, may also gain 'psychological and social benefits'. Holidays are ostentatious products. In other words, they 'say something' about the purchaser. For some people this may be the main reason for buying that type of holiday. Here the holiday is regarded as a status symbol, like a certain type of car, expensive clothes and houses. People who purchase expensive holidays such as an exclusive round-the-world cruise on the QE2, or safari holiday to Kenya may be wanting to impress their friends, and be regarded as adventurous, or particularly wealthy.

## (iii.) Psychographic variables

The majority of people do not regard holidays as status symbols. Rather, they are merely seeking to spend two weeks in the sun having as much fun and enjoyment as they can, at the best possible price. When choosing holiday destinations therefore, these tourists might not be motivated by the local culture, but by whether the resort is 'Anglicised'.

Attitudes and motivations, together with beliefs and perceptions, form the 'psychograhic' profile of a consumer. Once the tour operators can understand this profile, they can infer a person's buying behaviour and devise the appropriate tourist products to cater for these segments of the market.

## (iv.) Reference Groups

In recognising the importance of psychographic profiles it is helpful to understand the influence of 'reference groups'. These can be defined as any group to which an individual belongs and which may help to shape his or her basic attitudes, motivations, beliefs and perceptions and ultimately buying behaviour. Reference groups may be formal or informal.

### (a.) Formal reference groups

A 'formal reference group' is one where some form of entry qualification is required to join the group. This might simply mean completing an application such as in joining a club or society, passing examinations to enter a particular profession, or just being an employee of an organisation. When individuals are members of a formal reference group, they will usually conform to the norm behavioural patterns of the group and develop a similar psychographic profile to other members. The implications of this for marketing travel and tourism products are extensive.

If a tour operator can identify formal reference groups with a demand for a certain type of travel product, it could then develop specialist packages to satisfy their needs. A growth market in the 1980s has been that of 'Incentive Travel'. Companies that employ salespeople, for example, encourage the sales force to work harder by offering them incentives. An incentive thought to be particularly motivating to certain salespeople is that of a free overseas holiday, awarded when a certain sales target has been reached. Similarly specialist tour operators devise imaginative holidays for successful sales people, or organise overseas conferences in exotic locations for the sales force.

*(b.) Informal reference groups*

The term 'informal reference group' refers to those groups not formally organised and which do not require people to 'join' in any formal sense. Instead, people are members of a group simply because they belong to the same family, or are friends with other group members. Nevertheless, being a member of an informal reference group can influence a person's buying behaviour. There are often dominant members of friendship groups who might persuade their friends to go on holidays with them. The leader of the group might choose the tour operator, the resort and the accommodation. Indeed, most tour operators recognise the role of these group leaders and offer them a discount, or a free holiday, if for example, they book a holiday with ten other people.

When families choose holidays, the role of various family members in the buying decision process is also of interest to travel companies. Which family member or members visits the travel agent(s) in the first instance to collect brochures? Who decides on the resort? Clearly, there will be many factors which will influence a family's decision when choosing a holiday and it is not possible to make generalised statements. What can be said, however, is that the leading tour operators do conduct market research to learn more about this process. Their findings from such research are then used to group families into different market segments according to their buying behaviour.

Explanatory variables are very important. Not only can they be used to divide the market into groups of consumers with common needs, they also go some way to explaining buyer behaviour. When the consumer's buying behaviour is understood, marketing strategies can be devised that stimulate the consumers to buy a particular tour operator's product, or holiday in a specific resort. The marketing mix variables, to be discussed later in this chapter, provide the techniques that the travel and tourism industry can use to stimulate and manage tourist demand. Whereas most of the descriptive variables can be established from published data, it is likely that the travel and tourism organisations will have to undertake their own research to discover explanatory variables which are relevant to their own products.

## Establishing a Profile of the Consumer

Descriptive market segmentation variables enable the physical characteristics of the consumer to be established, as well as allowing the marketer to determine the size of the market, by referring to Census data. This approach does not, however, give a total profile of the consumer. What is also required is an understanding of why the consumer acts in a certain way, or buys a certain travel or tourism product. Many travel and tourism organisations find that they need to commission market research to provide such information.

Such research can discover the benefits that a person looks for when buying a product, what their beliefs and attitudes are, what perceptions they have of different travel products or companies, and what motivates them to travel or visit a particular tourist attraction. In addition, market research can also establish other reasons why a consumer behaves in a certain way. Is the consumer influenced by a friend or relative to buy a certain product, or do they use a particular travel agent because discounts are available to certain firms or trade union members?

Explanatory market segmentation variables are important to understand because they allow the marketer to look inside the consumer's mind and to determine why the consumer acts in a certain manner. Go-Ahead Northern, one of the United Kingdom's largest, privatised bus and coach operating firms based in Gateshead, Tyne and Wear, has implemented extensive market research questionnaire surveys and has conducted regular group discussions with members of the travelling public to determine what passengers like and dislike about Go-Ahead Northern. Market research has also produced information showing the travelling public's perception of the company. This places the company in a much better position to develop marketing strategies which would encourage more passengers to travel with the firm. In fact, between 1983 and 1987, 13 million more passenger journeys were recorded carried by the company, partly as a result of a better understanding of their passangers and developing new products to meet their needs more closely.

## 3. Lifestyle Market Segmentation

A third approach to market segmentation, one which is becoming increasingly popular, is known as 'lifestyle market segmentation'. This approach is felt to offer a more complete picture of the consumer than other approaches since not only are descriptive variables being considered, but also the all-important explanatory variables. Lifestyle market segmentation divides the market up according to the consumer's way of life. It is this which has resulted in the marketing world labelling segments with acronyms such as 'Yuppies' (standing for young, upwardly mobile professionals), 'Dincs' (double-income, no children), 'Wooppies' (well-off old people) and 'Glammies' (the greying, leisured, affluent, middle-aged sector of the market).

A travel or tour company which has taken a lifestyle approach can develop products that will appeal specifically to people with a particular way of life. For instance, because of the ageing population in the United Kingdom, tour operators such as Saga Holidays are well placed to serve the special needs of senior citizens. As mentioned previously, a growth area in recent years has been the market for extended winter holidays in the Mediterranean for senior citizens. In order to cater for the specialised needs of this group, tour operators have had to build up a complete picture of their lifestyle so as to ensure that all their requirements can be met. As part of the package offered to senior citizens, British nurses are on hand to provide them with health care, non-denominational religious services are held by British priests, special leisure activities are organised for them such as whist drives and old-time dancing, and facilities are arranged so that they can obtain their old-age pensions.

# 4. Geodemographic Market Segmentation

The fourth approach to market segmentation is referred to as 'geodemo graphics'. Geodemographic market segmentation is an approach that classifies consumers according to residential area. People living in similar areas will often have similar social characteristics and lifestyles, and hence similar buying habits so enabling market segmentation.

This method of classification was first developed in the late 1970s by Richard Webber, a college lecturer, (see Webber, 1977) who analysed the Census of Population data. In his original work known as ACORN (A Classification of Residential Neighbourhoods), every parish in the UK with a population of more than fifty people was assigned to one of 36 residential neighbourhood types. These residential neighbourhood types ranged from agricultural villages to inter-war council estates and to better-off retirement areas with wealthy older residents. The 36 residential neighbourhood types were then grouped into eleven broader categories. These ACORN groups are as follows:

## ACORN Groups

A Agricultural areas

B Modern family housing, higher incomes

C Older housing of intermediate status

D Poor quality older terraced housing

E Better-off council estates

F Less well-off council estates

G Poorest council estates

H Multi-racial areas

I High status non-family areas

J Affluent suburban housing

K Better-off retirement areas

*Source: CACI Market Analysis*

Research conducted by Webber, and more recently by CACI Market Analysis (a Market Research Organisation) which has subsequently developed and marketed ACORN on a commercial basis, shows that each of the ACORN groups differs in terms of its buying behaviour. Maps can be produced of rural areas, towns and cities that show the different residential types, (according to the ACORN classification), that are represented. This information can then be used for a number of different purposes.

For example a travel agent when thinking of expanding and locating in a new town could purchase an 'ACORN map' of the town. This will inform the travel agent of the types of residential areas in the vicinity. From this the travel agent can evaluate potential demand for the products which will be sold. If the travel agent discovers that most of the residential areas comprise 'new detached houses, with young families' and 'detached houses in exclusive suburbs' then the agent might conclude that people living in these neighbourhoods will have a high demand for overseas holidays.

Direct-sell tour operators, such as Tjaerborg and Portland Holidays might also use geodemographic market segmentation. These companies have a large database of customer's addresses. An analysis of such data might reveal, for example, that the majority of their customers live in 'inter-war semis, being white collar workers' or live in 'recently acquired private houses, with young families'. When these tour operators send out direct mail letters and brochures to prospective customers, rather than sending out brochures at random, they can use the ACORN system to send their brochures only to families living in these residential areas, rather than people living in 'tenement flats', for example. This method of organising the 'mail-shot' will be more efficient and more cost-effective.

In the 1980s a number of different geodemographic market segmentation systems have been developed. The names given to these systems suggest that this approach to market segmentation allows the marketer to classify consumers into clearly defined segments, for example Pinpoint's 'PiN system' and CCN Systems' 'Mosaic programme'.

It should be clear that an organisation cannot start thinking about what product to offer consumers, the price to charge, or how to promote and distribute the product, until it has divided the market-place into groups of consumers with common needs. Once an organisation has segmented the market in which it wishes to operate, it can then progress to the second step in the marketing process.

# Step Two - Developing a Profile of Each Market Segment

The second step in the marketing process is the development of a comprehensive profile of each of the segments in the market. The marketer should produce a profile that gives as complete a picture as possible of the typical consumer in each segment. A graphic picture should be drawn of each consumer type as well as a brief narrative highlighting the key descriptive and explanatory determinants and emphasising the important lifestyle and geodemographic traits of the consumer.

The profiles developed by Trek America provides a useful example. The company is a specialist tour operator, arranging coast-to-coast adventure camping holidays in North America. Its consumers are primarily single people of both sexes aged from 18 to 40 years, belonging to socio-economic groups B, C1 and C2. It is likely that the 'trekkers' live in privately owned accommodation. While the United Kingdom is an important market, 'trekkers' are also attracted from other developed countries in Europe, South Africa, the Far East and Australasia. The consumer's usual motivation for taking a Trek America holiday is the chance to see as much of America as possible, at a reasonable cost, with like-minded young people. The 'trekkers' enjoy the outdoor life, group-living, and are looking for excitement and adventure on their holiday rather than being simply 'beach-bound'. The 'trekkers' believe that Trek America offers good-value-for money, and is a reliable tour operator. They perceive North America as being a very interesting holiday destination to visit.

This second step in the marketing process is a natural progression from the market segmentation that has been previously completed and involves a synthesis of all the market research data that has been collated. The consumer profiles that have been developed help in the design of the marketing mix, which will be discussed later.

# Step Three - Determining the Attractiveness of Each Market Segment

Modern marketing revolves around the principle that companies cannot produce one product that will appeal to all consumers. Long gone are the days of the standard package tour to Spain that was supposed to attract both young and old, single people and families, rich and poor. Nowadays it is recognised that the most profitable and efficient way to operate a business is to produce clearly defined products for discrete market segments. The task facing the marketer, therefore, is to decide which segments of the market to cater for, and then to specifically target these.

Some companies such as Thomson Holidays, International Leisure Group, Redwing Holidays, and the Owners Abroad Group have the resources to compete in several market segments, and offer a number of separate packages: summer sun holidays, winter sun holidays self-catering holidays, coach tours, and a host of other products. Other companies, however, such as Trek America, do not have the resources to compete in such a large number of market segments, and so specialise in organising holidays for one or two types of consumer. Canvas Holidays is the United Kingdom market leader in continental camping holidays, offering ready erected, fully-equipped family tents on a host of campsites throughout Europe. PGL specialises in organising adventure holidays for children and teenagers.

Each company has to decide in which market segments it will compete. This is a crucial marketing decision, for if the company makes a wrong choice, it might find itself struggling to make a profit. So, how can a company decide which segments it should enter?

Clearly, a systematic approach has to be taken and it should follow a number of stages:

(i) The company must first compile a list of factors considered to be important for its future profitability, and then score each of the market segments against each factor, perhaps on a scale from one (lowest score) to ten (highest score), enabling an aggregate score to be determined for each potential sector. The segment which is found to have the highest aggregate score is then seen as the one for the company to operate in. A slightly more sophisticated approach could involve the company weighting each of the factors in terms of its relative importance.

(ii) Just as a systematic approach is important, so too is the choice of factors that a company uses to measure the attractiveness of each segment. It is important that a company establishes the rate at which each segment of the market is growing, since it needs to ensure that it will be operating in a growth market where there is potential for a new entrant to gain a market share. The number of existing competitors and their current market shares will also be an important factor determining both short-term and long-term success. The company could also examine profitability of companies already operating in the segment over the last few years to establish whether their profit margins are being eroded or increased.

(iii) In addition to assessing the state of the market in each segment, a company considering entering a market segment needs to analyse its own capabilities. Does it have the resources necessary to enter the segment? Is sufficient finance available to launch the new programme? Does it currently employ staff who have the necessary knowledge and expertise to develop the programme? Does that market segment require the company to have a particular type of technology?

(iv) The company must also pay attention to external and uncontrollable factors which could affect that market segment. Is the potential market segment likely to be affected by rising unemployment in the years ahead? Are there any government controls anticipated which may have an adverse affect on the likelihood of consumers purchasing holidays?

Thus, at this stage in the marketing process the company must undertake a comprehensive analysis of market segments so that it can form an objective view of the attractiveness of each. When the company has completed this process of analysis, synthesis and evaluation it can begin to tackle the next stage in the marketing process.

# Step Four - Selecting the Target Market(s)

Once the company has established the attractiveness of each market segment, it has to make a conscious decision as to which to compete in. This stage in the process is known as 'target marketing'. Here, the company's activities are aimed at satisfying the needs of the consumers in each segment which has been targeted.

Target marketing is important, since it means the resources of the company are all intensively channelled in a consistent direction. This should lead to the company operating more efficiently and profitably. The company is no longer wasting resources trying to appeal to all consumers in the market-

# Figure 3: Choosing market segments to target

| Factors import-ant for profit-able operation | Weighting | Rating (1 - poor rating 10 - high rating) | Score (weighting X rating) |
|---|---|---|---|
| 1. The number of existing competitors | 15% | 8 | 1.20 |
| 2. The current profit margins of companies operating in this market segment | 20% | 9 | 1.80 |
| 3. The cost involved in entering this market segment | 10% | 7 | 0.70 |
| 4. The size of the market segment ('000 of population) | 15% | 6 | 0.90 |
| 5. The growth rate of the market segment | 10% | 5 | 0.50 |
| 6. The ease of communicating with the segment | 5% | 8 | 0.40 |
| 7. The segment's price inelasticity of demand | 5% | 8 | 0.40 |
| 8. The threat of unemployment to the market segment | 5% | 1 | 0.05 |
| 9. The susceptibility of exchange rate fluctuations on the price of the product | 5% | 5 | 0.25 |
| 10. The ease of packaging the product: obtaining accommodation, flights, etc. | 10% | 9 | 0.90 |
| | 100% | Total Score | 7.1 |

In this example factor 2 is considered most important for entry into this segment and has been given the highest weighting 20%. It is felt that current profit margins are high and so a rating of 9/10 has been given. The score that is carried forward to make up the total score is: 9 x 20/100 = 1.80.

place, a strategy that would be doomed to failure when its competitors are tailoring their products to meet the needs of clearly defined consumers. Naturally, the company that can produce the package that most closely meets consumer needs will be the most successful, and this requires target marketing.

As previously indicated, the number of segments a company chooses to target depends upon the resources it has available. The three largest tour operators in the United Kingdom, Thomson Holidays, with 40 per cent of the market, International Leisure Group, with 17 per cent, and Redwing with 8 per cent (source of data - Civil Aviation Authority, 1988) operate in a number of market segments. In addition to these leading tour operators, there also exist over 600 other companies, all competing for consumers. The reason all these companies have survived and remain profitable, is that the British market for package holidays has become quite fragmented. The leading tour operators appeal to the mass market, are fiercely competitive, and only gain small profit margins. Many of the smaller tour operators, on the other hand, develop their own 'niches' in the market and specialise in providing products for clearly defined target markets. If competitors are limited in these segments, they can charge premium prices, which result in higher profit margins and so compensate for the smaller market size.

# Step Five - Developing a Positioning Strategy for each Target Market

Irrespective of whether a company is offering products to the mass market or to a more specialised market, the fifth step in the marketing process is how it should 'position' itself and its products on the consumers' perceptual map.

In our discussion of explanatory market segmentation variables we mentioned that consumers develop a particular perception of specific products and companies. All companies aim to ensure that the consumer has a very strong and positive image of it which helps the consumer to differentiate between its own product and those of its competitors.

Product, or company, positioning is the process whereby the company decides upon the image it would like consumers to have of its product or itself. It then develops a strategy that will lead to this desired image being established in the minds of consumers. One important way of positioning a product or company in the consumers' minds is the use of television and press advertising. Here, a single message can be transmitted to the target market at regular intervals. As a result, the consumer might associate the image that is being portrayed by the company with his or her own life-style, and reject the images being developed by competitors. When the consumer has bought the organisation's product this product image will be reinforced if it lives up to expectations, and could develop into brand loyalty, hopefully leading to repeat business in the future.

An example of this has been Thomas Cook's positioning strategy which has been to create the image of providing a 'caring' service, one that even 'looks after teddy'. Another example has been Thomson Holidays' television advertising in the early 1980s which was intended to create the image of Thomson's being a tour operator which carefully controlled the quality of the holidays provided. The advertisements featured a bowler-hatted gentleman bouncing on the beds in the hotel, diving into the swimming pool, water-skiing, and even riding camels on the beach, to show that Thomson thoroughly monitor the quality of the holidays that it sells. In 1988, Thomson's television advertising campaign stressed that holidaymakers, once they have been on a Thomson holiday become loyal to the company, perhaps as a result of the quality of the product, and the good value-for-money it represents.

The positioning strategies of Thomas Cook and Thomson Holidays convey an image to potential customers that helps them to differentiate these companies from their competitors. In a highly competitive market-place such as the travel market, product and company positioning, create a distinct image in the mind of the consumer that is essential.

# Step Six - Developing a Marketing Mix for each Target Market

When the company has decided upon and developed a perceptual image in the mind of the consumer, it can then progress to the final stage of the marketing process - developing a marketing mix for each target market. The marketing mix comprises all those controllable variables which enable the marketer to influence the demand for the product. Traditionally, the marketing mix is referred to as the 'four Ps'. These are

1. the **Product** itself;

2. the ways in which the product is **Promoted**;

3. the **Price** that is charged for the product;

4. the **Place** of the product, that is, how the product is distributed to the consumer, or the points-of-sale where customers can buy the product.

With the growth in the service sector and a greater awareness of the special circumstances of travel and tourism marketing, additional variables have been included in the marketing mix. These additional 'P's are:

5. the **Personnel** employed by the company;

6. the **Physical environment** in which the company operates;

7. the **Procedures** which the company adopts to satisfy consumer needs.

(These were explained by Cowell, 1984).

These additional 'P's have been included because in the service sector, where the product is not a tangible physical object, it is often considered important that the company should pay careful attention to all the variables that might help to create a favourable corporate image. As we shall show later, these additional three 'P's can all be positively controlled by the company to help establish the all-important perceptual image to help influence the consumers' buying behaviour.

No matter what the company considers its marketing mix to be made up of, an important point to remember is that for each market segment a company targets, a separate marketing mix will be needed to stimulate consumer demand. One single marketing mix will not appeal to all market segments.

When designing the marketing mix certain key decisions have to be taken. We will now consider such decisions as they relate to each element of the marketing mix.

# 1. The Product

The product that the consumer purchases is the most important element of the marketing mix, as it is this which is bought to satisfy consumer needs. Importantly of course it is the sale of the product which provides sales revenue for the company. If a consumer buys a package from one tour operator and is satisfied with that holiday, then he or she may decide to book again with the same tour operator in the future. Therefore, the company must pay careful attention to all facets of the product to make sure that it lives up to consumers' expectations and leads to brand and or company loyalty.

When thinking about travel and tourism products you must recognise that the 'product' does not just include the actual holiday that is purchased, or the visit to the tourist attraction, for example. The product is in fact all those elements that make up the experience enjoyed by the customer. Indeed, Kotler (1984) recommends that marketers recognise the product as being made up of three levels:

> (i.) the core product;
>
> (ii.) the tangible product;
>
> (iii.) the augmented product.

## (i.) The Core Product

The core product is the main benefit, or service, that the customer gains when purchasing the product. For example, when a holidaymaker goes to Turkey on holiday, the core product may be relaxation and rest, or the chance to explore a newly developed tourist region.

## (ii.) The Tangible Product

The tangible product really refers to the features of the holiday that are purchased. In our example these would include the flight to Turkey, 14 nights half-board accommodation in the hotel, and transfers to and from the airport. All the features that comprise the holiday, including the holiday brochure, are part of the tangible product.

# The Product

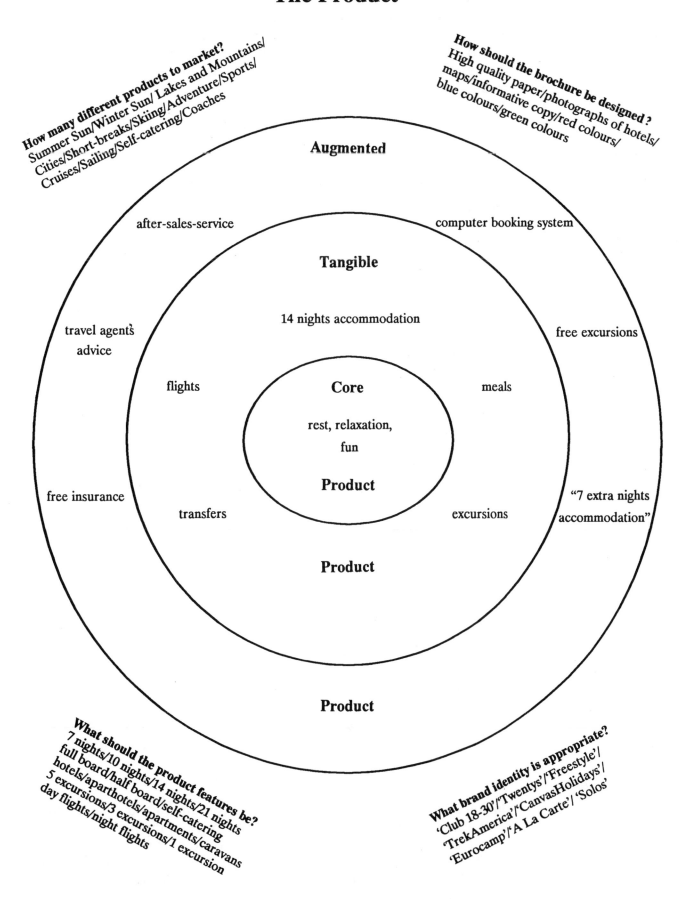

**How many different products to market?**
Summer Sun/Winter Sun/ Lakes and Mountains/
Cities/Short-breaks/Skiing/Adventure/Sports/
Cruises/Sailing/Self-catering/Coaches

**How should the brochure be designed ?**
High quality paper/photographs of hotels/
maps/informative copy/red colours/
blue colours/green colours

**Augmented**

after-sales-service

computer booking system

**Tangible**

14 nights accommodation

travel agents
advice

free excursions

flights

**Core**

meals

rest, relaxation,
fun

**Product**

free insurance

transfers

excursions

"7 extra nights
accommodation"

**Product**

**Product**

**What should the product features be?**
7 nights/10 nights/14 nights/21 nights
full board/half board/self-catering
hotels/aparthotels/apartments/caravans
5 excursions/3 excursions/1 excursion
day flights/night flights

**What brand identity is appropriate?**
'Club 18-30'/'Twentys'/'Freestyle'/
'TrekAmerica'/'CanvasHolidays'/
'Eurocamp'/'A La Carte'/ 'Solos'

## (iii.) The Augmented Product

The augmented product refers to all the other aspects of the holiday that have not been mentioned so far. The staff in the travel agency who arrange the booking, the computer booking systems used by the tour operator, the tour operator's customer services department who handle queries and complaints - in fact all the other services that 'add value' to the holiday.

The task for the marketer is to consider all three levels of the product to ensure that his or her product is suited to the target market's needs.

To be successful in business, companies have to continually review their products to make sure that they are superior to competitors. We shall now consider some of the decisions that marketers have to take with regard to their products. These are:

(a.) deciding on the number of different products to market?

(b.) determining the features of the product

(c.) developing the brand identity

(d.) 'packaging' the product

### (a.) Deciding on the number of different products to market?

All companies need to decide on an optimum number of different products to offer consumers. Should the tour operator offer only inclusive air tours to Spain, or should packages also be developed for Italy, Yugoslavia and Greece? Should the travel agent stock mainly long haul specialised products, or products that will have more of a mass market appeal?

The answers to these questions will depend upon factors such as the resources available to the business, the market segments to be targeted, and the needs of the consumers. The company however, must be wary of not only considering the present situation. Consumer tastes change, and traditional tourist destinations go out of favour as new resorts are developed. The company must therefore pay attention to the future and to new products that could be launched onto the market in the years ahead. Indeed, a far sighted company will incorporate a new product development programme into its marketing strategy as a matter of course, rather than face a crisis following the realisation that existing products are no longer selling.

Controlling the company's range of products, the so called 'product portfolio', and phasing in new products as established ones decline, is an important function of the marketing manager. In addition to taking decisions regarding the number of products to market, the marketing manager has also to take decisions concerning the features that will be included in each product.

### (b.) Determining the features of the product

Buying a holiday is similar to buying other consumer goods. The customer will be interested in what is included in the price of the holiday. Does the price include transport to the point of departure in the United Kingdom? Are free water sports available? How many excursions does the holiday include? Will the hotel be a three-star or a four-star one? How far is the hotel from the beach?

By examining competing products, the tour operator will have some idea of what is essential for inclusion in the package, while market research will discover what additional features consumers would like to see incorporated into their holiday. It is perhaps at this stage of the marketing process that a company can build a unique selling point into its product offering, or in other words create a 'differential advantage'.

Each company must try to develop a differential advantage and thereby attempt to provide the customer with a reason for purchasing its product rather than that of a competitor. Club Mediterranee's differential advantage is that once the price of the holiday has been paid, the holidaymaker has no further major expenses as meals, entertainment, sports and some alcoholic drinks are included in the holiday price. This allows the consumer to accurately work out how much the holiday will cost, and so reduces the need to carry large amounts of cash and travellers cheques abroad.

### (c.) Developing the brand identity

Once it has decided what features to include in the product, the company can then develop a brand identity. It is important to create a brand identity, as this will help to differentiate the company's product from that of a competitor. Brand identities are not only created by memorable brand names, but also by symbols, caricatures, or a combination of these.

Strong brand identity gives the product an individuality which might influence the consumers' buying decision. If the brand identity reflects the quality or consistency of the product, this might encourage the consumer to be brand loyal, and thus be highly valued by all companies.

The Club 18-30 brand identity conjures up images of sun, sea, sand and fun, for young carefree single people. Holidaymakers buying this particular product go abroad feeling confident that they will be holidaying with a company that is highly skilled in organising packages that will meet their needs. To encourage brand loyalty, and hence repeat purchases, Club 18-30 organises reunion parties during the winter months at venues around the United Kingdom, giving 'clubbers' the opportunity of rekindling holiday friendships, and also enabling the company to promote the next season's holidays. Club 18-30 is a subsidiary company of the International Leisure Group, and has been so successful that its brand name - Club '18-30' is now used to refer to all holidays of that type.

Similar to the brand identity concept, distinctive company identities can also be created. Companies with strong and well-respected identities, such as Club 18-30, benefit from the fact that customers can confidently expect a known level of quality. In addition, it will be easier to launch new products since consumers will already have a favourable attitude towards the company and will buy the new product in the belief that they are doing business with a reputable firm.

The Virgin Atlantic airline and Virgin Holidays can attribute some of their early success to the strength of the Virgin empire's corporate identity. Richard Branson's music, broadcasting and publishing companies created an image of value-for-money products and an efficient service in the minds of their target customers. When the airline and tour-operating companies were established under the Virgin name, this immediately gave them a certain credibility. Customers felt that they could buy Virgin's new travel products confidently because they were dealing with a reliable and trustworthy operator.

Although strong brand names and corporate identities are valuable weapons in any company's marketing arsenal, they can, however, involve a substantial investment of both time and money.

## (d.) 'Packaging' the product

Another part of the product element of the marketing mix is how the product is to be packaged. The package, or container, in which consumer goods are sold plays an important role in encouraging consumers to purchase the product, particularly when the consumer is not brand loyal and is being offered a broad choice of products from which to select. Indeed, the product's container adds to the brand identity, displaying the brand name and company logo. The container also displays important information about the product such as its ingredients, features and price.

Of course, holiday products are not stored or displayed in protective containers in the same way as other consumer goods. They exist as intangible combinations of various elements, such as seats on aeroplanes, hotel bedrooms and memorable experiences. Nevertheless, travel agents still have to display the holiday product to potential customers and these customers need information to help them choose the most suitable holiday. Thus, we can regard the travel brochure as the holiday product's container. The travel brochure performs all the functions mentioned above: it displays the company and brand name, cites the product's features and ingredients (such as departure points and dates), and shows the potential purchaser the price of the holiday. In this way it not only communicates information to the customer but also contributes to the corporate identity. Before the holiday, the travel brochure alone represents the actual product that the consumer is purchasing.

Because of the important role the travel brochure plays, tour operators need to pay careful attention to its design and production to ensure it creates an image that will encourage the potential customer to purchase the product. This requires skilful work on the part of all of those who contribute to the production of the brochure. Such people include graphic designers, copy writers, photographers and the marketing team. They have to make decisions about the typefaces to be used; the layout of the text; the photographs and maps to be used; the copy to be included; the colours of the text and pages; the lead-in offer on the front cover (for example, many brochures highlight an inexpensive holiday on the brochure's front cover in order to encourage the reader to open it and read further, this holiday may even be a 'loss leader'); the size of the print run; the lifespan of the brochure; and when the brochure is to be launched, or relaunched, onto the market.

Typically, the majority of photographs in the 'Summer Sun' brochures feature the hotels where the holidays are based. This is because the hotel is a very important factor in the holiday product which consumers take into account when choosing their holidays. Brochures for the more expensive holidays, for example to long-haul destinations, often use better quality paper and feature more photographs of the local culture and landscape, than do the short-haul brochures.

The timing of the launch of the brochure is very important. As brochures are often launched six to twelve months before the holiday season, the tour operator has to bear in mind that there could be changes in the cost of the holiday, relating for instance, to exchange rate fluctuations. It might therefore be necessary to incorporate possible cost increases into the published prices. If the tour operator makes mistakes or unforeseen eventualities arise, then it might be necessary to levy surcharges, which naturally the consumer will not like.

The importance tour operators attach to their brochures is reflected in the considerable resources they invest in them. The leading, mass market tour operators in the UK estimate that it costs them at least £1 to produce each Summer Sun brochure. When some 4 or 5 million brochures are produced by each tour operator each year, the operator must make sure that the brochure is as effective as possible in converting interested, potential customers into actual customers.

# 2. Promotion

Once the holiday product has been designed, the next stage is to promote it and establish how it should be placed before the target market, or 'target audience'.

There are four main ways in which a company can communicate with its target market. The company can use:

(i.) advertisements;

(ii.) sales promotions;

(iii.) publicity;

(iv.) personal selling.

## Promotion

| Advertising | Sales Promotions | Publicity | Personal Selling |
|---|---|---|---|
| Television | Competitions | Press releases | Sales reps |
| Press | Free gifts | Editorial stories | Travel agents |
| Direct mail | Cash discounts | Exhibitions | Telephone sales |
| Posters | Extra holiday features | Publicity stunts | |
| Radio | Price reductions | Free 'give aways' | |
| | Free travel insurance | Film shows | |
| | Free car hire | Sponsorships | |

We shall now discuss each of these in turn.

# (i.) Advertising

Advertising is a form of communication. A company can purchase space in the media in order to convey a message to its target audience. Newspaper and magazine advertising are the main channels through which travel and tour companies communicate with potential customers. Indeed, most of the national newspapers contain specific sections for such advertisements.

Types of advertising that a travel company can use to promote its products are:

(a.) National Newspapers and Magazines

(b.) The Local Press

(c.) Commercial Radio

(d.) Television Advertising

(e.) Poster Advertising

(f.) Direct Mail

## (a.) National Newspapers and Magazines

The Sunday Times, the Guardian, and the Sunday Express are just three examples of newspapers which tour operators use for advertising their products. The sunday papers provide extensive classified and display sections which group the advertisers by market segment. For example, the Sunday Times has advertising sections devoted to winter sports holidays, holidays afloat, special interest holidays and holidays in self-catering accommodation.

A glance at a selection of magazines during the months of December to May will reveal a host of travel advertisers trying to attract the customer's attention. Each magazine is carefully chosen so that its readership profile matches the profile of the consumer that the travel company has targeted. Travel or tourism companies with target markets in the A or B socio-economic groups might advertise, for example, in the *Observer Magazine* or *The Sunday Times Magazine*. Those aiming to attract the middle to lower socio-economic groups, the C1s, C2s or Ds, might advertise in the *News of the World*'s colour supplement or that of the *Sunday Express* or the *Mail on Sunday*.

## (b.) The Local Press

Travel companies that serve local or regional markets will tend to use regional or local newspapers and magazines for their advertising instead of the national press. Once again, the advertiser can choose between display or classified advertising. The rates for both of these in the local press are considerably less than for the national press, but naturally the readership is smaller. Press advertising, however, is restrictive, in that it only allows for a printed message to be sent to the target audience, whereas radio advertising, allows an audio message to be used.

### (c.) Commercial Radio

Using commercial radio stations as a means of communicating with local audiences is becoming increasingly popular. The advertiser can choose at what time of day the advertisements will be transmitted, thus allowing for a certain degree of target marketing since different types of people listen to the radio at different times of the day. The production of a memorable advertisement for a travel company with a catchy jingle, played at frequent intervals during the main holiday-buying months, will be a useful means of supporting the other elements of its advertising campaign.

### (d.) Television Advertising

If the company does have a large advertising budget and is aiming at the mass, national market, television advertising is a possibility. There are many advantages to running a national television advertising campaign: a large audience is reached; the advertiser can create a favourable image of itself and its products by the use of well-produced advertisements; and the message is transmitted visually as well as verbally. The main restrictive factor on television advertising is however the cost. Actually producing the advertisement is in itself expensive. Hiring the director, actors, film crew, and post-production staff, and using an advertising agency to write the copy line and buy space on the television channels is a costly business.

There are however, less expensive ways of advertising on television. Advertising on Teletext via the Oracle network is quite inexpensive, although the audience is limited Nevertheless, this type of advertising is useful for communicating 'last-minute bargains' to both consumers and travel agents.

### (e.) Poster Advertising

Another inexpensive way of advertising is by using posters. These are useful for displaying short messages, such as price reductions or last-minute vacancies. Posters can be displayed in travel agents' windows or at sites which enjoy large pedestrian flows, such as underground tube stations or railway stations.

### (f.) Direct Mail

A recent growth area in advertising has been the use of direct mail, where companies write directly to identified individuals, informing them of products which the company considers to be suitable for their needs. Mailing lists can be derived from previous and existing customers, from refering to Electoral Registers, and by buying them from companies specialising in their production. Once a company has established a computer data bank of names and addresses, it can then send direct mail letters and brochures at regular intervals to prospective customers.

If a company segments its market geodemographically, then an important method of communicating with target groups will be by direct mail. Direct mail has grown rapidly because of its cost effectiveness. The company can communicate directly with its target market without having to buy advertising space in the media. For direct mail to be successful, however, a company has to carefully plan the design of the letter. It needs to attract the immediate attention of the reader, create interest in the products on offer, stimulate demand, and lead the consumer to actually purchase the product.

# Factors determining the choice of Advertising Media

Clearly, one factor which will influence a company in deciding which advertising media to use will be the level of finance available. If considerable funds are at hand, the company could use a combination of television, radio, press and poster advertising. If, however, there is little cash to spend, it might be that the only form of advertising that is used is the holiday brochure itself.

Another factor which determines the type of advertising used relates to the market a company has targetted. If the company is aiming to attract a national market then it will use the national press and a number of television stations. On the other hand, if its market is a regional or local one, it will be applicable to use local or regional media.

# The Objectives of Advertising

When devising an advertising campaign, it has to be borne in mind that the advertisements alone cannot sell the product. Advertisements are felt to be capable of achieving three main objectives of:

(a.) informing the target audience;

(b.) persuading the target audience;

(c.) reminding the target audience of the products available to them.

## (a.) Informing the Target Audience

Informative advertisements are designed to provide the target audience with facts of which they might be unaware, such as that the company has opened a new travel agency, new destinations have been introduced into the tour programme or prices have been reduced. As a result, such advertisements tend to have a great deal of copy which is factual and technical as opposed to being rich in flowery phrases.

## (b.) Persuading the Target Audience

A second objective of an advertising campaign is to persuade consumers to purchase the company's products instead of those of a competing firm. Advertisements which aim to do this usually try to establish a distinct identity for the product. Thomson Holidays' bowler-hatted quality controller is one example, as is the British Airways' television advertising campaigns, which persuade the consumer to fly with the airline because of the superior service it provides both in the air, as well as on the ground. Advertisers sometimes take persuasive advertising a stage further, by writing what is known as 'knocking-copy'. In such adverts one company implicitly criticises a competitor's product or shows it to be inferior. In so doing, the advertiser hopes that the consumer will be persuaded to buy their superior product. In developing such campaigns, however, the advertiser must ensure that all the claims made are true and can be substantiated, and that the advert complies with the ABTA Code of Conduct.

## (c.) Reminding the Target Audience of the Products which are Available

This forms a third type of advertising. Reminder campaigns are used to keep the company's name or its products at the forefront of the consumer's mind. Simple, repetitive messages and jingles typify this form of advertising, and are used to reinforce and maintain brand or company identities.

Before leaving advertising it is worth noting that not everyone believes adverts increase sales and there is still considerable debate as to its cost effectiveness.

# (ii) Sales promotions

Promotions are a means of boosting the sales of the product. Sales promotions offer the consumer particular incentives to buy the product. Their use has grown considerably in recent years, although it is difficult to quote expenditure figures as no publicly available records are kept. For this reason sales promotions are referred to as 'below-the-line' expenditure, whereas advertising is referred to as 'above-the-line' expenditure since monthly records are kept. We now consider sales promotions aimed at the consumer and the trade.

## (a.) Sales Promotions aimed at the Consumer

Companies use sales promotions to increase sales of their products in the short term. With a sophisticated sales promotions industry developing in the United Kingdom, there is now a whole range of different techniques available to companies. Competitions, free gifts, cash discounts, extra holiday features and price reductions are just some of the forms sales promotions might take. It is recognised that sales promotions are usually effective, but with only a short-term impact, as the consumer quickly becomes bored with one particular promotion. Whilst advertising campaigns can be thought of as building up brand loyalty, sales promotions can be viewed as the reverse, helping to break down competitors brand loyalty. Similarly, advertisements are very much individual creations, whereas sales promotions are very easily replicated by competing firms.

Travel and tourism companies make extensive use of sales promotions in their promotional mixes. In 1986 and 1987, the major British tour operators to the Mediterranean offered a small number of packages to early bookers for £50 in order to stimulate demand for their products. Other operators offer free flight bags, travel insurance and travel guide books.

## (b.) Sales Promotions aimed at the Trade.

The examples given above are incentives aimed at the consumer. Tour operators also devise sales promotions for travel agents, encouraging them to sell more of the tour operator's products.

Most of the leading tour operators, with the exception of Thomson Holidays, offer 'override' or 'bonus' commissions to travel agents who sell more than a specified number of holidays. For example, if the standard commission paid to the travel agent for selling holidays is 10% of the brochure price of the holiday, should that travel agent sell more than 500 holidays, the commission level might be increased to 12.5%.

A further type of sales promotion offered to travel agents is that of free holidays, or as they are sometimes termed an 'educational'. In 1988, Silk Cut Faraway Holidays (a long-haul tour operator) introduced a sales promotion whereby any travel agency selling eight of its holidays in the season would be entitled to receive one free holiday for a member of staff. 'Educationals' are another form of sales promotion, but not normally tied to the sales level of a particular product. With educationals the tour operator takes a party of travel agents to an overseas resort to 'educate' the agents on the facilities and amenities offered to tourists. It is hoped that as a result of the educational, the travel agents will be in a better position to recommend key resorts, hopefully those promoted by the tour operator organising the educational.

Sales promotions can also be offered to the company's own employees. The staff working in a tour operator's 'reservations' department, for example, handling incoming telephone calls from travel agents and customers, can be encouraged to recommend certain holidays by being offered an incentive. The member of staff in reservations might receive a free flight, or a discount off the price of a particular holiday, should he or she sell a particular number of holidays or flights.

As you can see, companies use sales promotions in different ways. They are a very popular method of stimulating demand for the product because of the immediate effect they have on sales. With advertisements on the other hand, sales tend to increase only after a period of time has elapsed.

# (iii) Publicity

Publicity is the way in which a company communicates with its target audience but without buying space in media, and hence at little or no cost to itself. There are two types of publicity-using either

(a.) the media; or

(b.) non-media methods.

## (a.) The Media

Media publicity occurs when a newspaper, magazine, radio station or television programme produces an article or programme about a company. It can be extremely beneficial as it tends to have a high level of credibility. This is because it is not the company itself that is commenting on how good the products are but a respected third party - a journalist or television presenter. In addition, this publicity may reach an extremely large audience depending upon the circulation figures for the newspaper or the viewing levels for the television programme. Of course the company does not have to pay for such widespread media exposure. There is, however, some cost involved. This is because good publicity stories need to be generated, and the company will have to employ someone to write and distribute press releases to news editors.

Some companies even embark on publicity stunts to capture the media's interest. Richard Branson has used dare devil exploits to publicise his Virgin Atlantic airline. In 1986 he broke the trans-Atlantic power boat record at the second attempt in Virgin Challenger, while in 1987 he took to the air in a hot-air balloon to become the first balloonist to fly the Atlantic. On both occasions his exploits attracted world-wide media interest, ensuring prime-time television news coverage and the appearance of the Virgin logo on the front pages of national newspapers.

While Virgin Atlantic gained from some very favourable publicity on these occasions, one drawback when using media publicity as a means of communicating with the target audience is that the actual message which is published cannot be controlled. For example if a travel company provides poor service then articles telling of disappointed holiday makers may appear in the press. Television programmes, such as Esther Rantzen's 'That's Life', sometimes publicise holidaymakers who feel that they have been let down by their travel agent or tour operator. Of course bad publicity such as this can do a company irreparable damage.

Another means of generating media publicity is for the firm to invite a journalist from a newspaper or magazine, or a production team from a television programme such as the'Holiday' programme, or 'Wish You Were Here', to try out the holiday, in the hope that they will write a good report about it. Indeed, newspapers, magazines and the television channels run regular holiday features in the winter and spring of each year.

## (b.) Non-Media Publicity

Non-media publicity is really a catch-all term for a plethora of other possibilities available to a company wishing to communicate with its target audience and is sometimes referred to as public relations. Included under this heading might be the following:

- ☐ the production of 'give-aways' such as badges, tee-shirts and key rings;
- ☐ attendance at exhibitions and travel shows;
- ☐ the organising of seminars and film shows;
- ☐ the sponsorship of specific events.

Such methods of communication will inevitably involve a certain amount of expense, but will increase the public's awareness of the company.

Some of the smaller travel companies concentrate more on non-media publicity than other forms of promotion. Explore Worldwide and Exodus Expeditions, two adventure tour operators, organise regular slide and video shows in central London for prospective clients in order to provide information on the tours they have available. The World Travel Fair, held each December, in London is the world's largest travel and tourism exhibition, where tour operators and principals, (such as hotel groups and airlines), can meet in order to establish and maintain links with each other as well as exchange contracts.

Publicity, no matter what form it takes, is an important element of the promotional mix, and should be carefully planned and implemented by the company to make sure that maximum exposure is obtained from every media story or publicity event. As with advertising, however, publicity does not really sell the product. All it can do is to increase the consumers' awareness. It is personal selling, the final element of the promotional mix, which represents the most effective way of selling the product.

## (iv.) Personal selling

The best method of finally persuading the consumer to buy a product is to use personal selling, where the seller meets the purchaser on a face-to-face basis.

Personal selling is effective because it enables the seller to fully understand the needs of the buyer. In a travel agency, the booking clerk could use a series of questions, to discover exactly what type of holiday and resort the customer is looking for. Once the clerk has established what the customer wants, the clerk can then offer the customer a range of alternative holidays. In order to encourage the customer to buy a particular holiday, the clerk will, of course, need to emphasise the benefits of buying that holiday as opposed to any other.

During the conversation, the travel clerk can reassure the customer about the reliability and quality of the holiday company which has been selected. Personal selling is the only means of selling which is interactive and allows an immediate response and feedback to the customer. To become proficient at personal selling, the travel clerk needs appropriate training. This should allow the clerk to gain experience in reading the buying signals which the customer gives and enable him or her to react to such signals in the best possible manner.

It is not just travel agents who recruit and train salespeople. Tour operators may also use personal selling. If the tour operator uses 'direct-sell' techniques, it will need a telephone sales force to deal directly with customers. Alternatively, if the tour operator sells its holidays through travel agents, it will still need a sales force to sell the product to the agents, and to encourage them not simply to carry its holidays in the agency but also to give a prominent position to its brochures on their display shelves.

In managing its promotional mix a company has to achieve a balance between each of the four elements of advertising, sales promotion, publicity and personal selling. Each constituent part has advantages and disadvantages and the travel or tour company needs to find the most appropriate mix for its product and its chosen target market.

## 3. The Price

The third element of the marketing mix we need to consider is that of price. In other words, how much should a company charge for its products. Pricing decisions are crucial since ultimately the price that is charged for the product, in relation to the company's costs, will determine the profit or loss that is made. The price is also important in what it tells the consumer about the product. The price should give the consumer some indication of the quality of the holiday. Price will also play a part in creating the company's corporate identity. Companies should, therefore, regard pricing decisions as an inherent part of their marketing strategy. The price should not be set simply as a result of analysing the various costs involved in putting the holiday package together and then adding on a fixed percentage to represent a profit margin. Rather, there are a number of other steps that a travel company needs to take when pricing a product.

## (i.) Determine the likely level of demand for the product

As market demand will set the upper limit of the price that can be charged, it is important to establish the likely demand for the product. If the price is set too high, consumers will be unable or unwilling to purchase the product. Market research surveys can be used to gauge an idea of the likely demand for a product. In addition, previous sales of the product can be used to forecast potential demand in the future.

## (ii.) Determine the price elasticity of demand in each of the market segments in which it operates

This, as we shall see may be extremely useful when deciding upon price changes. Some market segments will have inelastic price demand. By the term 'inelastic' we mean that increases or decreases in the price charged will have little effect on the amount of the product that the consumers wish to buy. For example, a tour operator may find that demand for one particular destination is price inelastic and so increases prices confident that demand will not be greatly reduced. Luxury holidays are more likely to be demand inelastic for two reasons. Some of their appeal is created by their exclusive nature which is itself, of course, generated in part by the high price (cruises on the QE2 or flights on Concorde are examples). The second reason is that the consumers of luxury goods are usually more affluent and as such are less likely to be deterred if the price of the holiday rises.

In other market segments, demand will be price 'elastic'. This means that changes in the price of the holiday will have a significant effect on the level of sales. If prices are increased, the tour operator will find that sales drop dramatically. Conversely, if there is even a relatively slight price cut, demand will show a substantial rise. Holidays which appeal to the mass market fall into this category, as consumers of such holidays tend to be less affluent and much more price conscious.

The elasticity of demand is not always obvious and companies will vary their prices to 'test the market' before making major policy decisions. Price elasticity is also liable to change as fashions dictate the buying habits of consumers. An understanding of the current state of demand in the marketplace, therefore, plays an important part in the pricing decision.

## (iii.) Establish the Costs of Production

Whilst the demand existing in a market segment determines the highest price (or ceiling price) a company can charge, the costs involved in producing the holiday sets the lowest price (the floor price). In essence, this is the least amount that the company can sell the holiday for and still cover its costs. The company, therefore, needs to have a full knowledge of both its fixed and variable costs, together with an understanding of how these costs are to be apportioned over the range of products it sells. We shall illustrate this using the example of the costs of an inclusive air charter package.

The costs that have to be taken into account when pricing the holiday include:

- [ ] flight costs;
- [ ] accommodation costs;
- [ ] transfer costs (from the overseas airport to the accommodation and vice versa);
- [ ] airport taxes (both in the UK and overseas);
- [ ] overseas destination costs (such as excursions);
- [ ] overseas representative costs;
- [ ] an allowance for contribution to the company's fixed costs;
- [ ] the company's profit margin;
- [ ] a commission to be paid to the travel agent for selling the holiday.

In 1988, the costs for a short-haul holiday to a Mediterranean resort, for a mass market tour operator, were approximately as follows:

| Cost element | Percentage of selling Price |
|---|---|
| The flight | 38% |
| Hotel accommodation | 42% |
| Contribution to fixed costs and administration | 7% |
| Resort costs and transfers | 2% |
| Travel agents commission | 10% |
| Tour operator's profit margin | 1% |
| | 100% |

This illustrates the highly competitive nature of the short haul market, where the leading tour operators such as Thomsons, Intasun, and Redwing only achieve small profit margins for each holiday sold. There are a number of other major factors which a travel company should consider when establishing the price of its product. A consideration of these helps to establish where between the ceiling price and floor price, the actual price to be charged should be pitched:

(a.) The  effects of fluctuating exchange rates

(b.) Perceptual pricing

(c.) Price discrimination

(d.) Seasonal pricing

(e.) The company's sales history

(f.) Competitor's prices

(g.) Discount pricing

(h.) Promotional pricing

(i.) Booking periods

(j.) Group discounts

## (a.) The effects of fluctuating exchange rates

The pricing decision of tour operators is complicated by fluctuating exchange rates. Various elements of the cost of the holiday such as accommodation, resort costs and transfers will have to be paid for in a foreign currency. Furthermore, as we have already noted, holiday brochures are produced many months before the holiday is taken. The tour operators, therefore, have to forecast how exchange rates will fluctuate, and allow for such fluctuations, in the prices they charge. When these fluctuations are in excess of those which the tour operator had allowed for then the alternatives are to levy a currency surcharge on the customer or for the operator to carry the extra costs itself. Again both choices are obviously undesirable.

## (b.) Perceptual pricing

Once the company has established ceiling and floor prices, it can start to consider other factors likely to influence the price it can charge. One important consideration is that of 'perceptual pricing'. By this is meant charging a price directly related to the price the consumer thinks the holiday is worth. Can the company charge a higher price for the product because the consumer perceives it to be of higher value or higher quality than competing products? Will the consumer be prepared to pay a higher price for the holiday because the destination is perceived as being exotic and only recently commercialised? Holiday trips to China sell at premium prices, partly as a result of the mystique arising from China's recent isolation from the Western world.

## (c.) Price discrimination

As well as taking into account the possibility of perceptual pricing, a travel company might also consider price discrimination. This occurs when the same product is sold to different consumers at different prices. For example, certain groups of consumers such as students or senior citizens have smaller incomes than other sections of society. Tour operators wishing to attract such less affluent consumers might offer them reduced prices to encourage them to travel. British Rail provides a good example of an organisation operating price discrimination with its range of concessionary and 'Saver' tickets.

## (d.) Seasonal pricing

Another type of discount that could be operated is 'seasonal pricing'. At certain times of the year when demand is low, the price of a holiday can be reduced to encourage customers to purchase it. Similarly, at times of peak demand the price can be increased. The company therefore gains revenue which will compensate for the reduced revenue received during off-peak periods. If you look at British travel brochures you can see that prices for Mediterranean holidays or flights are lower in May and June and again in September and October. These are the 'shoulder' months. Prices rise in the months of July and August which are the peak months of demand.

## (e.) The company's sales history

The level of sales of the product which the company has enjoyed in the past will also be useful in determining what price to charge. If the tour operator found that during the last season, when the price of its holidays were reduced, that sales increased dramatically, then it may decide not to increase the price of the product above this level for fear of losing demand.

## (f.) Competitors' prices

The prices charged by competitors are always of concern to holiday companies. When a competitor launches a brochure, the other tour operators compare the prices charged with their own to see if there are any major price differentials that might cause customers to choose the lower priced product. Should one competitor undercut the prices charged by other tour operators offering similar holidays, then the higher priced operators may have to reduce their prices. This is especially so in those market segments where customers are very price sensitive and are looking to buy the holiday that represents the best-value-for-money.

## (g.) Discount pricing

Last-minute discounts, where holidays that have not been sold just prior to departure are offered at reduced prices, are another feature of the British travel scene. Such discounts are attractive to a particular type of consumer, who frequently leave booking holidays until the last possible moment.

Usually about six weeks before a holiday is due to commence, tour operators advertise any unsold holidays at discount prices. It is important that they sell as much of their capacity as possible since overseas accommodation, and seats on aircraft are often paid for by tour operators on a seasonal basis. If a holiday is not sold, the tour operator still has to pay for the accommodation and the flight. To avoid this, discounts are offered to 'late-bookers' to encourage them to buy particular, unsold holidays.

## (h.) Promotional pricing

The practice of promotional pricing is similar to above, but instead of a last-minute discount being offered, a discount is offered to early bookers. A limited number of holidays may also be offered for sale at a discount in order to provide incentives for customers to visit travel agents and book early.

## (i.) Booking periods

You may have gathered from the above that there are three distinct booking periods for holidays:

- ☐ the pre-Christmas period from October to December;
- ☐ the post-Christmas period from January to March;
- ☐ the late-booking period in the six weeks preceding the start of the holiday.

Tour operators and travel agents recognise these distinct periods and devise their pricing strategies accordingly to encourage maximum booking of holidays in the two earlier periods.

## (j.) Group discounts

Finally, most tour operators offer group discounts to people who book the same holiday and travel together. Indeed, group leaders are often offered a free holiday if there are ten other full-fare-paying passengers travelling in the party.

The British travel industry is extremely price competitive. The leading tour operators seek to sell as many holidays as they can, in order to benefit from economies of scale. The more seats that are reserved on an aircraft, or the more hotel bedrooms that are booked, the greater the discount the tour operator will be able to negotiate with the supplier. Holidays, to some extent, can be thought of as 'commodity products', with consumers often believing that whoever the tour operator is, the holiday will be largely the same. This makes it difficult to build a differential advantage into the marketing of the holiday and leaves price as the main element to attract the customer. When companies compete against each other on price however, their profit margins tumble. This in essence is what has happened to British tour operators in the 1980s.

# 4. The Place

Once a company has decided on the promotion and pricing of the product, the next stage of the decision-making process relates to the 'place' element of the marketing mix. In other words, how to distribute the product to the consumer, and which points-of-sale to use in order to help consumer purchase. We shall see that there are two main ways of selling holiday and travel products:

> (i.) through travel agents;
>
> (ii.) by direct sell.

## (i.) The Sale of Holidays through Travel Agents

Distributing the holiday product to consumers is significantly different to distributing a physical product, in that the travel agent does not hold 'stocks' of the product, only the holiday brochures. Thus, the travel agent or tour operator does not need extensive stock-rooms and hence avoids holding costs.

## The Role of ABTA

A major feature in the distribution of travel products in the United Kingdom is the role of the Association of British Travel Agents (ABTA). ABTA strictly controls the travel industry and lays down clearly defined regulations to which its members have to conform. One of the main regulations is that travel agents and tour operators as ABTA members can only transact business with other ABTA members. To become a member of ABTA however, a travel company has to meet certain criteria.

Every year, the audited accounts of the travel company have to be submitted to ABTA for scrutiny. The company must also provide a bond in the form of a percentage of the travel company's annual turnover. This is set aside in a frozen bank account and used to reimburse holidaymakers or help with their repatriation should the travel company with whom they are dealing cease trading.

As well as meeting financial criteria, the travel company has to allow its premises to be open for inspection by ABTA to ensure that they are of a suitable standard. This means, among other things, that they must be fully open to the public, that the company name must be clearly displayed outside, that inside there is adequate office funiture that there are at least two external telephone lines and that there is display space for brochures. Travel companies wishing to apply for ABTA membership must also ensure that the staff they employ meet ABTA's guidelines with regard to the previous training and experience of staff.

Tour operators that sell their holidays through travel agents have to pay commission to the travel agent for each holiday sold. This is often the main source of income for the travel agent, and travel agents obviously seek to gain as high a level of commission as possible. In practice however, the level of commission averages 10% of the holiday's selling price. Tour operators selling new products, or products for which a special sales drive is being organised, might increase the level of commission. The higher levels of commission are known as 'over-rides'.

An estimated breakdown of the source of a travel agent's sales turnover is given in the following table:

**Source of a Travel Agents Sales Turnover**

| Source | % |
|---|---|
| Inclusive pack-age holidays | 55 |
| Air tickets | 31 |
| Rail tickets | 3 |
| Ferry tickets | 2 |
| Insurance | 1 |
| Car hire | 0.3 |
| Other | 7.7 |
| | 100% |

*Source: Adapted from Mintel/Trade estimates 'Travel Agents' Mintel Market Intelligence, April 1988*

The role of ABTA in the British travel industry is an important one, and the control that ABTA exerts is wide-ranging from helping to maintain and improve the reputation of the industry to safeguarding the interests of members of the public. It is within the context of such protection and influence that the distribution of the holiday product takes place.

If a tour operator is a member of ABTA, it can use the 6,000-plus travel agents who are also ABTA members. If a tour operator has substantial resources, such as Thomson Holidays does, then it might also consider establishing its own chain of travel agents. Thomsons, for example own the Lunn Poly group of agents. Alternatively, instead of, or in addition to using, travel agents, the tour operator may decide to sell direct to consumers, without using any intermediaries. This is a method used by tour operators who are not members of ABTA.

## (ii.) Direct Selling

If the tour operator is not an ABTA member, the main way to reach potential customers is to operate on a direct-sell basis. This can be achieved by establishing a specialist travel agency to sell the operator's own products, or by using a wide variety of promotional techniques such as direct mail shots and direct response advertisements in the press. Such publicity techniques entails the company communicating directly with its target market, so by-passing the need for the travel agents.

Canvas Holidays is an example of a tour operator which is not a member of ABTA and which trades on a direct sell basis. The administrative headquarters of the company is in Hertfordshire. This acts as the reservations centre, where a team of trained telephonists with expert knowledge of the company's products deal with all customer enquiries and bookings. Customers wishing to speak in person to the reservations department are welcome to visit the headquarters.

In direct selling, press advertising is a useful technique. As Canvas Holidays appeal to families in the B and C socio-economic groups throughout the United Kingdom, it uses the 'quality' mass media (the Observer, the Sunday Times, the Sunday Telegraph, and the popular dailies) as its sales venue. The company has extensive sites in Western Europe and enjoys a high degree of brand-loyalty. The company has found that once customers have found the 'Canvas Experience' meets their needs, they often book subsequent holidays but in a different part of Europe.

Satisfied customers also help the company through word-of-mouth recommendations to friends and relatives who might not have heard of Canvas Holidays. In this way, more people become aware of the holiday possibilities available to them. By operating a variety of marketing approaches, Canvas Holidays is able to prosper on a direct sell basis, and feels it has no need of ABTA membership.

For a company involved in the UK travel and tourism industry, whether or not to join ABTA is an important decision. One advantage of joining lies in the access a company has to a nationwide network of travel agents and the increased credibility membership brings. This dimension of possessing a responsive and reliable reputation is likely to give a company added appeal in the market place. The main drawback to ABTA membership is the initial cost of meeting the membership criteria.

In addition to the four traditional elements of the marketing mix, given the growth of the service sector in general, and the travel and tourism sector in particular, we will now look at three additional elements:

☐ the organisation's personnel;

☐ the physical environment in which the company operates; and

☐ the processes involved in satisfying consumer needs.

# 5. Personnel

The personnel that a travel or tour company employs should be regarded as a strategic element of the marketing mix. Sales staff are instrumental in selling the product to the consumer and the resort staff must ensure that the consumer enjoys the holiday. If the sales personnel do not have adequate knowledge of the product or lack selling skills, consumers will have a very poor impression of the company and so may choose not to buy its products. Similarly, if the operational staff have no customer relation skills or no awareness of the importance for the company of satisfying the consumer, the holiday-maker might not enjoy the holiday and as a consequence might not book again next year.

## The Importance of staff training

It is vital, therefore, that the company takes account of staff training when planning its marketing strategy. If the organisation's employees are not creating the appropriate image for the consumers, then the other components of the marketing strategy could be rendered ineffective. For this reason, travel agents, tour operators, organisations running tourist attractions hotels and transport operators, invest a great deal of time and money in training their staff.

In the early 1980s, British Airways conducted market research which showed that passengers had a relatively low opinion of the attitudes and competence of their ground and air crews. It was consequently felt by BA, that their staff crews were creating a poor image with the passengers. The company decided that such a situation had to be rectified, otherwise the number of passengers carried would decline further as customers might chose to travel with airlines that took more care of their passengers. To overcome this problem, extensive customer- relations training was organised by British Airways aimed at improving the level of service offered to passengers. The training paid off, and British Airways is now highly respected for the way it treats its passengers, and in 1987 it was voted the world's number one airline by business travellers.

Training programmes for operational personnel should also cover areas other than customer relation skills. In 1986, Go-Ahead Northern, developed an innovative idea for the bus industry, by re-launching their bus inspectors as 'Product Group Leaders'. Previously, the bus inspectors acted as the 'police officers of the bus industry' looking for fare-dodgers and vandals. After the deregulation of the industry in October 1986 the company felt that the inspectors would be better deployed as public relations ambassadors, helping to encourage more passengers to use Northern's buses, rather than deterring them. To make the Product Group Leaders idea a success, a comprehensive training course was organised, which introduced them to marketing, leadership skills, time-management skills, public speaking skills and communication skills, as well as customer relations training. Following the training and the adoption of a new, more informal uniform of blazer and slacks, the Product Group Leaders have proved very successful.

Indeed, part of the image that is created by employees is generated by their appearance and grooming, as well as by their communication skills. Attention, therefore, has to be given in the marketing strategy to a consideration of the uniforms to be used by employees.

# 6. The Physical Environment

Another aspect of the organisation's operation which can help to influence the demand for its product is the physical environment within which the company operates. The first impressions that a potential customer receives about the company are extremely important in determining whether the customer chooses to buy or not. The external condition of the premises creates an image in the minds of customers, either encouraging them to enter or go elsewhere. The notepaper and letterheads that are used in correspondence contribute to the corporate image. The decor inside the company premises helps to create a favourable atmosphere in which to conduct business. The manner in which the telephonist handles telephone enquiries can deter or encourage business. All of these factors, plus many more, help to create the physical environment within which the business is operating.

A company needs to pay great attention to all of these things to make sure that its physical environment is as welcoming as possible to potential customers and that a welcoming corporate image is conveyed.

## The Design of Travel Offices

The leading multiples devote considerable attention to the design of their agencies. The new branches that are being opened by companies such as Lunn Poly, Thomas Cook, W H Smith Travel and Hogg Robinson Travel are all adopting similar styles. Large, open-plan offices are used, decorated in colours that are light and pleasing to the eye. Huge plate glass windows, enable customers to see directly into the retail unit. There is strong emphasis on the role of personal selling with only a modest number of brochures being displayed. The ones which are displayed are those of the leading tour operators, for which demand is high. Those travel agencies that have large stocks of brochures in the customer area will find that customers have a tendency to pick up brochures and then walk out of the agency without speaking to the sales staff. Each time this occurs, a potential sale is lost. To overcome this problem, customers are encouraged to ask the salesperson for brochures and information rather than pick them up themselves. Once the customer and the salesperson are in conversation, the process of direct selling has begun and the trained salesperson can find out what the customer is actually looking for.

## Merchandising

'Merchandising dynamics', a term borrowed from retailers, is now a buzz word in the travel agency world. This concept involves presenting the product to the consumer in the best possible way. The positioning of brochures on the racks in the travel agency can influence customer demand for the product. Those brochures, and hence products, that are frequently sought by customers are positioned within easy reach, while those brochures that might not be so popular are either at a higher, or lower level, than those frequently demanded.

In-store displays by tour operators, known as 'point-of-sale' material is also carefully designed and positioned. If a tour operator is running a special promotion, the brochures featuring this might be displayed separately, using a special stand in a prominent position away from the display racks. This will attract the attention of customers.

Television sets, showing videos of overseas destinations are another means of displaying the product to potential customers. These enable more information to be provided about the resort and the activities that can be enjoyed on arrival.

# 7. The Processes

Consumers will also be encouraged to do business with a company if the processes involved in buying the holiday create a favourable first impression. The ways in which the company operates can be considered to be part of the marketing mix. If the consumer perceives the company as being inefficient, they may choose to book with a competitor who appears more business-like.

## The Importance of New Technology

It is important that travel companies should be at the forefront of new developments in technology.

Far-sighted companies are continually reviewing and updating their computerised systems and are keen to capitalise on the best available information technology. In this way a company may be able to stimulate further demand for its products, hence its relevance to the overall marketing mix.

Most of the leading tour operators in the UK have developed their own data banks and on-line direct booking systems. The Thomson system is known as TOPS, while the Intasun is called INTA. These systems allow travel agents to check the availability of a holiday while the customer waits to book it immediately if it is still available. This saves a time consuming and expensive process.

Furthermore, on-line direct booking systems mean that the tour operator can communicate important information directly to travel agents using the available information technology. For example, if the tour operator decides to introduce a new product, or reduces the price of an existing one, this information can be transmitted to the travel agents by the computer booking system. Before the travel agent enters the TOPS system, for instance, a message is displayed on the terminal screen, informing the agent of any new developments.

In the near future, direct debiting of customer accounts is to be introduced, along with other innovations that will make booking and paying for travel facilities much easier. The challenge for the travel agent or tour operator is to keep abreast of these developments by investing in new technology as it becomes available. If the service offered to the consumer can be improved, then the company could see increases in its customer loyalty.

Another approach that some agencies are adopting, is for counter staff to have access, via their computer terminals, to the previous sales history of clients. Therefore, when a customer enters the agency and wishes to book a holiday, the salesperson will have the full particulars of that customer's previous holidays immediately available. This not only helps in deciding what type of product will satisfy the customer's needs, (based on their previous experiences) but also enables a good rapport to be established with the customer. Before the salesperson establishes the current needs of customers, a few minutes can be spent chatting about how they enjoyed their previous holiday to Spain, and how they found the Hotel Del Sol.

Travel agents are also beginning to equip coaches with computer booking facilities. The coach is then used as a mobile booking office, visiting residential areas or rural areas poorly served by travel agents. This method allows careful target marketing as the travel agent can locate the coach in those areas most likely to have consumers who will want to book holidays. By simplifying the booking process and being generally innovative, the travel agent can create a further differential advantage.

## The Importance of Marketing the Differential Advantage

The marketing mix, as discussed above, comprises all those controllable elements that can influence consumer demand. A company has to develop a compatible, and coordinated marketing mix for each market segment that it seeks to target. In designing the marketing mix, however, it is vital to build in a differential advantage. A company should seek a unique selling point and thus give the customer a reason for purchasing its product rather than a product of a competitor.

In creating a differential advantage a company should try and make its product better than that of its competitors. The company can generate important questions such as:

☐ Can new tourist destinations and resorts be included in the programme?

☐ Is it possible to upgrade the quality of the product?

☐ Can the number of departure points in the United Kingdom be increased?

After a careful review of the product, the company should then pay attention to its promotional mix.

☐ What is the current corporate or brand image?

☐ Can this image be enhanced further by improved advertising, more favourable publicity, or the instigation of a sales promotion campaign?

☐ How distinctive is the promotional mix?

☐ Is it positioning the product or the company appropriately?

The company needs to evaluate its own channels of distribution to see whether they can be improved in any way. An analysis has to be made of the channels that competitors are using to determine whether they have any weaknesses that could be exploited. The company should assess whether its personnel are fully trained and are aware of their role in the marketing strategy, making sure that it has skilfully designed its physical environment and processes.

If a company finds that a differential advantage cannot be created in any of these areas then the only element of the marketing mix which is left for it to compete on is the price. Should the travel company find itself competing on price then its profit margins will be eroded, perhaps to the stage where the company is making a loss. Indeed, this is relatively common in the United Kingdom, where there are many companies competing against each other, all offering virtually identical products to the consumer. In fact Thomas Cook decided to withdraw from the short-haul European market and concentrate on the long-haul market for its tour operating activities. It is estimated that the leading tour operators in the short -haul market make only 1% or 2% profit from each holiday sold. In the long-haul market this profit margin is considerably greater, particularly if the destination is a Third World country where the supply costs of the tourism industry are relatively low.

When price wars take place there are inevitable casualties with tour operators going out of business and their customers left stranded overseas or out-of-pocket at home. To safeguard themselves from such a position a company needs to follow the six steps discussed above. By systematically developing a marketing strategy, which is translated into a marketing plan and then implemented, a company can minimise the risks of operating in a notoriously risky business.

The high risk nature of the travel industry can partly be explained by understanding the context within which the industry operates.

# The Context of the Industry

There are a number of features, distinct to the travel and tourism industries which do need to be taken into account by the marketing team when devising their marketing strategy. These are:

1. Perishability

2. Intangibility

3. Inseparability

4. Ease of entry to the industry

# 1. Perishability

The travel and tourism product cannot be stored for future sale. If there are unsold seats when the aeroplane takes off then the airline has lost revenue it will not be able to recover. In a similar way, if a hotel can accommodate 1000 people every night and only achieves sales of 500, then revenue is also irretrievably lost. The marketing challenge, therefore, is to make sure that the company is operating at full capacity for as much of the time as possible. To be successful, the company will need carefully designed marketing strategies to stimulate demand. Such strategies, hopefully do not simply involve price reductions to sell the vacant capacity, but are based on other elements of the marketing mix.

Madame Tussauds has successfully adopted marketing strategies, resulting in increased numbers of visitors being attracted. The whole experience of visiting Madame Tussauds has been made more fun and informal. Visitors are now allowed to stand close to the wax work models, and can take photographs, a practice which previously was prohibited. An improved promotional mix has been designed which features television advertising, and brochures being distributed to hotels as well as tourist information centres. Pricing packages designed to attract visitors have also been developed for specific target markets. As a result of this new marketing approach Madame Tussauds is now one of the leading tourist attractions in the United Kingdom.

# 2. Intangibility

The fact that the holiday product is not a physical object but an amalgam of 'invisible' services does create certain problems for tour operators and travel agents. To overcome this intangibility, tour operators attempt to create some form of tangible offering that potential customers can relate to. With the growth in the home ownership of video-recorders, tour operators are now able to record the features of their holidays on video for home viewing by potential customers, thus taking away some of the uncertainty the customer may have when buying a holiday.

Silk Cut Faraway Holidays has adopted this approach as well as developing a less expensive means of communicating with the consumer. Recorded interviews have been made between Graham Phillips, Silk Cut's General Manager and Allison Rice, a travel writer and broadcaster. Each recorded audio tape refers to a particular destination that Silk Cut features in its programme. The tape depicts an interview in which Allison Rice asks Graham Phillips a series of questions about the tourist destination under consideration. Potential customers can play the tape on their own cassette players and find out more about Silk Cut Holidays and the tourist destinations.

Travel brochures also help to overcome the intangibility problem and this is why so much effort, expense and creativity is devoted to their design. Indeed, for 50 weeks during the year, when the customer is at home, the travel brochure represents the product that might be purchased.

# 3. Inseparability

Holidays are 'people orientated'. The enjoyment gained from a holiday cannot be separated from the personalities who go to make up that holiday - the personnel employed in the travel agency, the airline crew, the hotel staff, the tour operator's overseas representative, and of course, the holidaymaker. All of these have a role to play in ensuring that the holiday lives up to the customer's expectations. Human behaviour, however, is highly variable and it is difficult for a company to ensure that its employees display good customer relation skills all of the time. Similarly, the company has no influence over the behaviour of the customer when on holiday, but it will be the customer's attitudes and behaviour that also contributes to the pleasure gained from the holiday. This means that there is an uncontrollable element inherent in the production of the travel or tourism product which can lead to the holidaymaker being disappointed with the holiday. To take account of this problem, it is important that as much information as possible is provided in advance to the potential customer, both by the tour operator and the travel agent. This will reduce the risk of the customer purchasing an unsuitable holiday at the outset. Special attention has also to be paid to the personnel who will deal with the client on a face-to face basis to make certain that they have suitable personalities for dealing with the public.

# 4. Ease of entry to the Industry

It is relatively easy for a tour operator or travel agent to set up in business. For a tour operator, most of the travel services included in the holidays are leased, or are purchased as and when required. The greatest cost involved lies in producing the brochure and marketing the holidays to travel agents and the public. Similarly travel agents do not purchase products from tour operators until the customer pays for them, and so do not incur the risk of unsold stock or stock-holding costs. Therefore, entry to the industry might be considered to be relatively straightforward and this means that if one company is seen to be successful in a particular segment of the market then it is not difficult for a competitor to offer a similar product. A related point is that it is difficult to establish a non-price related differential advantage, which also allows easy entry to the industry. The conclusion that can be drawn, is that tour operators and travel agents must have marketing skills of the highest order to keep them well-ahead of their competitors and not simply rely on competing on prices.

# Conclusion

From the points covered in this chapter, you should now be aware of the special circumstances that surround the marketing of travel and tourism. The marketing skills and techniques discussed have largely been developed for consumer goods, so although they may have some relevance, the special circumstances of the travel and tourism industries cannot be forgotten. The mark of skill for the marketer is the creation of a differential advantage for a product. However, devising a unique selling point in the travel and tourism industries is no easy task. Indeed, it is a fact that many companies are painfully becoming aware of.

# ☐ Case Studies

☐ Continental Coach Holidays after 1980
*by David Holding*

☐ Strategy Changes at Sealink after Privatisation
*by David Holding*

☐ British Airways Air Fares and Liberalisation in Europe
*by David Holding*

☐ Westworld Travel
*by Joan Henderson*

☐ The Neilson Leisure Group
*by Amanda Greason*

☐ Miles Better
*by Joan Henderson*

☐ The North of England Open Air Museum at Beamish
*by Ken Harrop*

The following section of this book contains a number of case studies which have been designed to provide students of Travel and Tourism with an insight into the operation and practice of the industry. The subject matter of the case studies has been chosen to reflect the diverse nature of the industry and includes an examination of the development and operation of individual travel and tourism organisations, an analysis of specific issues and a consideration of a particular sector of the industry. The case studies are in the main factually based, apart from Westworld Travel, a fictitious organisation, which nevertheless faces realistic problems. In addition to being of value as a source of information to the student, they may also be used as the basis for a series of practical assignments.

# Continental Coach Holidays after 1980

This first case study deals with an interesting subject which has received little coverage in textbooks and articles - the rise and fall in 'economy' coach holidays during the 1980s.

The deregulation of express coach services in the UK, applied also to coach-based holidays in the UK and travelling overseas. Prior to 1980, the market was dominated by a relatively small number of operators, such as National and Wallace Arnold, and a newcomer wishing to enter was required to prove a need for the additional facilities he was proposing to introduce against objections from those companies already licensed. Almost all holidays were of the touring variety, holiday-makers staying overnight at a number of hotels over a period of 10 to 14 days.

Deregulation had a number of indirect effects. One was that anomalies in operators' catchment areas were ironed out. Previously, operators might have been restrained by competitors' objections from picking up in particular towns, whereas now any tour can pick up anywhere that is considered worthwhile. Secondly, deregulation transferred the right to organise the holiday from the operator alone (who had to obtain the licence from the Traffic Commissioner) to anyone choosing to act as a broker and charter coaches as required. There have been two major consequences of this: one is the appearance of 'direct-sell' holidays, organised by sometimes rather anonymous firms and often sold through local newspapers, and the other is the mounting of tour programmes and single-centred holidays by travel agencies and hotel groups who, again, charter coaches as required.

The major focus of this case study, however, is on the rapid growth of cheap continental holidays, which involve overnight travel by coach. Most of these holidays use self-catering accommodation in Spain or the South of France, but some operators of 'Lakes-and-Mountains' type touring holidays have also adopted the overnight pattern. When tour operators do not stop en route a saving of up to £100 can be achieved in the price of the holiday by eliminating the cost of hotel accommodation during the journey. It should be noted, however, that part of that saving may be the result of using lower quality hotels at the final destination and furthermore, overnight travel does incur certain additional costs for the tour operator as it necessitates either carrying additional drivers or the establishment of staging points with relief drivers en route.

Most of the growth in overnight coach holidays was in self-catering 'sun, sea and sand' type holidays. It is worth considering why such a sudden growth and subsequent decline took place. Firstly, of course, deregulation allowed existing operators to develop their businesses more easily and attracted other companies to enter the market. Many did, on a modest scale, and agencies, tour operators and accommodation-providers could put together their own packages. In particular, however, the large coach tour firms were aware of the impending free entry of smaller competitors into the easily organised hotel market; they therefore had to provide something different. The de-regulation of coach operation which occurred in 1980 came soon after the second oil crisis of 1978-9, which led to sharp increases in oil prices and therefore in air operating costs. At the time, also, the pound was strong against European currencies, and these factors, combined with a series of poor summers in Britain, made cheap continental holidays very attractive to those holiday makers who had traditionally taken a week or two by the coast in Britain. Finally, road improvements both in Britain and Europe, together with faster and more luxurious coaches, made the journey to the Mediterranean for the first time relatively painless.

During 1980 and 1981 this type of holiday was a major growth area for coach operators. In the North East of England, for instance, Nat, Siesta, Sun Travel, Target and Zebra Holidays all mounted sizeable programmes of overnight holidays to the Mediterranean. In other areas the coach fleets of Parks of Hamilton and Trathens of Plymouth each grew from a few coaches to over 100, either as a result of a growth in their own holidays or because of an increase in charters to other tour operators.

By 1983 a decline in the demand for overnight coach holidays set in. This was probably due in part to customers experiencing this type of holiday once and deciding as a result not to try it again! (Many were undoubtedly satisfied, particularly at the price charged. An interesting example of the trade-off between quality and price and people's different priorities.) Another reason was that the airlines were forced to reduce prices for air charters. Initially they had responded to oil price rises in 1978-9 by increasing fares, but now, finding themselves with empty aircraft, they were prepared to cut prices again, narrowing the differential between coach and air charges. Lastly, the coach operators were finding from experience that tight scheduling (usually two return coach trips to Spain each week) and high reliability were necessary for financial survival. The same is true still of air charter operations, which explains why simple problems with aircraft when demand is highest at summer weekends can lead to the familiar delays to passengers at airports. Small coach companies had been tempted into a new sphere of operation by the promise of high returns, but were now faced with high interest rate repayments on loans they had taken out for the purchase of coaches costing up to £120,000 each. As the market declined, supply of coaches exceeded demand and tour organisers were able to impose low rates on operators prepared to accept any income rather than have vehicles idle. In this way organisers were able to keep prices competitive, but coach operators suffered acute financial problems, Trathens, for instance going into liquidation. A particular difficulty was that the high-specification coaches were unsuitable for other work and so could not be 'cascaded' to lower-level use. Nor did any demand exist in the second-hand market.

# ☐ Strategy Changes at Sealink after Privatisation

Sealink was the trading name chosen for the ferry operations run by British Rail along with the State railway organisations of Belgium, France and Holland. Sealink UK was by far the largest partner, owning at the time of its separation from British Rail 38 ships, compared with 15 held by the other organisations put together. This was largely because Sealink had inherited ferries that sailed not only across the English Channel and North Sea but also to the Isle of Wight, the Isle of Man, Ireland and even on Windermere in the Lake District. Historically, its services were connected with and dependent upon those of the railways, carrying what are still known as 'classic foot passengers' and providing the link in rail services such as the London-Dover-Calais-Paris and London-Harwich-Hook of Holland-Amsterdam routes. Before air travel grew in the 1960s, Sealink represented the principal means of travel to Europe. Passenger-only ferries were gradually supplanted by roll-on roll-off (ro-ro) ships carrying cars, coaches and heavy goods vehicles.

We should not forget the importance of the private car in all forms of tourism. Not only is virtually every car used at some time for family trips to the coast or country, but 20% of all cars in the U.K. are now taken abroad for holidays. This has brought tremendous growth in camping and caravanning holidays as well as other self-catering and hotel based trips - shared, of course with fellow-Europeans. Until the Channel Tunnel is opened, the ferry operators have a near-captive market for this business.

From the early 1960s, British Rail, as Sealink's predecessor, operated a price-fixing cartel on the important English Channel services along with the only other passenger carrier, Townsend (later Townsend Thoresen and then P & O European Ferries). This came under threat from the mid-1970s as, following British entry into the EEC and an increase in traffic to Europe, new operators such as the Olau Line, Sally Line, P & O and Brittany Ferries, crossed the channel but although competition increased to some extent, the cartel largely survived. When the UK government proposed the sale of Sealink as part of its privatisation programme Townsend Thoresen entered a bid, which was rejected following examination by the Monopolies and Mergers Commission; following this Townsend Thoresen purchased the small-scale Channel operations of P & O, while Sealink was sold in 1984 to the Bermuda-based company Sea Containers. This case study concentrates on the changes introduced by Sealink since its change of ownership, but it is worth noting that Townsend Thoresen itself was subsequently purchased by the P & O group, shortly before the loss of its 'Herald of Free Enterprise' at Zeebrugge in March 1987.

Before considering the actual changes made by Sealink, we should look first at the background and the reasons for the changes. Firstly, the ferry and rail operations of BR had assisted each other, and a direct loss sustained by one might have been worth bearing if that operation was assisting the other to make money; with separation from BR this became irrelevant. Secondly, BR, as a nationalised industry in receipt of a public subsidy to meet a Public Service Object (PSO), can be required to maintain services for political or social reasons, but Sealink, as a privately owned and commercial body, cannot. Thirdly, it might have been possible, for just such political or social reasons, to cross-subsidise poor services from profit made by good ones, but quite apart from the absence of a political remit, the increasingly competitive situation on the English Channel routes removed any possibility of this: every route must now stand or fall by itself. Finally, it is fair to say that Sealink's financial performance in the years before its sale when it was still in the public sector as part of British Rail would not have been regarded as satisfactory in a private company. In 1981 Sealink suffered a loss of £9.6m; in 1982 and 1983 it made profits (before tax and interest) of £2.9m and £12.8m, but these were related to turnover of £232m and £265m and were achieved partly owing to the company's failure to invest in new equipment since it knew that the sale was to take place.

On privatisation, Sealink needed to make substantial changes overall in both its objectives and its general operations. More specifically, it also needed to adopt appropriate strategies for particular routes. In general terms, it had inherited high levels of staffing and poor productivity compared with its rivals, and there was also a clear over-dependence on traditional markets that were in decline. For example, its Irish routes no longer carried large numbers of emigrant workers making return visits to their families. On the other hand, there appeared to be a large untapped market for package holidays in Ireland.

Let us now look at the action taken by the Sealink management in particular areas. On the Straits of Dover the number of routes operated was reduced. Dover-Boulogne, which Townsend Thoresen also operated, was closed, and Dover-Ostend was handed over entirely to the Belgian partner, RTM. A further problem here has been the probable opening of the Channel Tunnel in 1993 to which traffic on the short sea routes is especially vulnerable. Sealink would probably have ceased operating from Folkestone (to Boulogne) entirely in the light of this and of losses being made on the route, had not a decision by BR to develop Folkestone as a rail passenger terminal kept it open for the time being.

Further along the channel, the Newhaven-Dieppe route was making a loss due both to a longer crossing time (hence fewer round trips per day) and to an agreement with the SNCF and the Belgian RTM that standardised fares should be charged on all the Channel routes. Also, Sealink was penalised by an agreement that existed to pool revenue and divide it according to the number of sailings. Sealink operated larger ships and so carried more traffic, but only received the same income as SNCF for its smaller vessels. It was decided, again, to cease operations on this route and it was now operated only by SNCF but using the name 'Sealink Dieppe Ferries'.

Services to the Isle of Man were terminated, and regarding the Irish Sea an agreement was reached with the Irish company, B & I Shipping, to pool services so that the surplus then existing could be reduced. However, B & I has since been experiencing problems of its own, and these arrangements may not yet have resulted in stability.

Regarding the Channel Islands a more positive approach was taken. It was felt that demand existed for a service from the European mainland to the Channel Islands, and the existing service from Weymouth was linked with that to Cherbourg in France to make this possible. However, it was also felt that the wealthy Channel Islanders would be willing to pay approximately double the existing fare for travel of a '5-star' standard, and the ships were refurbished for the purpose, but this turned out to be a mistake. Many chose to make the much quicker journey by air for a slightly higher price, while Brittany Ferries combined with Huelin, a Guernsey-based company, to operate a basic shipping force at lower fares. Following, this Sealink proposed closure of all sailings from Weymouth, and suffered damaging industrial action over the redundancies that would arise. Finally, agreement was reached with Huelin-Brittany to run a combined service as British Channnel Island Ferries, from Portsmouth all the year round and from Weymouth during the summer. Further changes have taken place since.

Even before these setbacks and the threat from the Channel Tunnel arose, Sealink clearly needed some new successful activities. The parent company Sea Containers had already re-introduced the Orient Express train between Boulogne and Venice, using Sealink's Folkestone-Boulogne ferries and a separate BR vintage Pullman train from London as connections. For 1986, a connecting luxury ferry was introduced between Venice and Piraeus, Istanbul and Kusudasi in Turkey, using a Sealink vessel and crews.

The Hoverspeed hovercraft operation from Dover to Calais was purchased from its management. This operation, itself the result of a merger between Hoverlloyd and the BR-owned Seaspeed, was financially weak and seemed likely to be an early victim of the Tunnel. However, it was already developing a motorists' package holiday programme based on its crossings, and it seems likely that this will be expanded, along with Sealink's own brochure, as a hedge against possible further closures.

Sealink has undoubtedly been something of a disappointment to its new owners, partly because anticipated cost-and-revenue improvements have proved harder to obtain than expected. However, while continuing uncertainty about the effect of the Channel Tunnel must be discouraging, the hard decisions may by now all have been implemented, investment is going ahead (for example in conference facilities on the Harwich-Hook route), and the motoring holiday programme is likely to expand.

# British Airways Air Fares and Liberalisation in Europe

In Chapter 5 the effects of total deregulation of air services in the United States were discussed, and mention was also made of the trend towards more flexible pricing of air transport, generally. However, although the EEC has a policy of removing all internal barriers to trade, including transport, by 1993, it is still the case that air services within Europe operate very much as if the EEC did not exist, in other words, bilateral agreements are made between individual members, whose airlines can only fly between their home states and the partners to those agreements. We shall now examine the progress so far in removing these barriers, and the political factors that stand in the way here too.

Although air fares in Europe are still controlled by IATA and are relatively high, discount fares of various kinds have been available since problems arose with charter flights in the early 1970s. The most important of these are APEX or SUPER-APEX return fares, offered by the national airlines such as British Airways (BA) or Lufthansa, which first appeared on trans-Atlantic routes and gradually spread to Europe, and most recently to the Far East. The APEX fare is designed to fill spare capacity without the airline losing revenue as a result of its attracting business travellers who would be willing to pay the full fare. For this purpose conditions are attached which are reasonable for the leisure traveller but which the businessman often cannot comply with. These are usually that:

(a) it is not possible to cancel and obtain a refund - as one can with full fares;

(b) the ticket must be bought two or three weeks in advance;

(c) the passenger must spend at least one Saturday night at the destination;

(d) the reduction is only available for a limited number of seats on specific, less popular flights.

Two further points should be made. One is that, apart from APEX fares, many seats in Economy Class (as opposed to the Business Class which airlines have introduced over the last few years) are sold in blocks at a discount to tour operators, and so on some routes there may not be many passengers paying the Economy fare at all. The other is that, in addition to APEX fares, some cheap fares are available from airlines who hold Fifth or Sixth Freedom rights within Europe; many of these are the cheap flight offers seen in small advertisements in newspapers, though some are sold by European airlines making seats for unpopular flights available in blocks at a discount through 'bucket shops'. For example, in January 1988 the IATA economy fare from London to Frankfurt was £125 single and £250 return; but it was possible to buy an APEX return for £88, travelling by British Airways or Lufthansa or to travel by a Far Eastern airline for slightly less. The EEC has long held the view that fares within Europe were kept artificially high by the limits on entry, but some members have strong views about their national sovereignty, and this has prevented the market from being opened up. The European Commission published a report in May 1984, entitled 'Developing a Community Air Transport Policy', which accepted that the total deregulation achieved within one country by the USA would not be achievable within Europe, and that Europe must settle for more modest measures. It proposed that parties to bilateral agreements should not necessarily share traffic equally between the two countries, that airlines should have more freedom to charge what fare they liked within a set range, and that revenue-pooling arrangements should be open to examination.

More importantly, the EEC made it clear that its sympathies lay with lower air fares, and it was possible for the more liberally-minded member countries to modify their bilateral agreements. Britain and Holland did this, leading to a greater availability of lower fares and the entry of new operators. Perhaps the most important consequence of the agreement change by Britain and Holland, however, was its effect on neighbouring countries who were less willing to change. If a traveller from Germany to Britain finds that by making the easy journey over the Dutch border instead of going to Frankfurt he can halve his air fare, he will do so and the effect is to put pressure on German airlines to charge competitive fares. However, it has been argued that Holland does better out of the agreement, since it enables its airline KLM to carry, on a 'Sixth freedom' basis, passengers from the UK to the Far East via Amsterdam. Such passengers would previously have travelled by BA and in this case KLM gain a substantial increase in passenger traffic without BA gaining a comparable benefit.

The EEC initiative also encouraged the use of smaller aircraft as a means of connecting regional centres away from the main traffic routes. This was intended as a boost to minor airlines, but of course the number of routes where such operation is profitable are limited, and the EEC made clear its opposition to countries subsidising their airlines.

Meanwhile, BA, like Sealink before it, was being prepared for privatisation by the UK government. BA's value on the stock market depended on the profitability of its services, and it was argued that, since the European routes were among BA's best and since that resulting profit would have been endangered by greater competition, the Government had a vested interest in delaying liberalisation. The EEC's next move came when the Commissioner for Competition started to require airlines to give satisfactory answers regarding anti-competitive practices, action on their failure to supply answers being suspended subject to the member countries producing an agreement which would create the required competition.

The sale of BA had gone through by the time the EEC transport ministers met to make this agreement, in June 1987. Implementation of the policy was delayed further until December 1987, because of disagreement between Britain and Spain over whether Gibraltar Airport was to be considered British or Spanish - an example of an external diplomatic issue being dragged into transport matters. When this was dealt with and the agreement finally confirmed in December 1987, it provided as follows:

(1) that the restricting conditions on APEX fares should be lifted, although the 'Saturday night' rule would still apply;

(2) that the rules on percentage shares of traffic between states should be relaxed, encouraging airlines to increase their traffic;

(3) that smaller aircraft should be able to connect regional and major airports without restriction;

(4) that airlines should be able to carry 'Fifth Freedom' traffic between cities in the Community where services existed;

(5) that members should be able to designate additional airlines (multiple designation) to operate a route without reference to the partner state, within the number of flights permitted by the bilateral agreement.

The ministers did not reach a final consensus on all the details of the agreement and it will be noticed that the changes that have been made are all within the limits of the existing bilateral agreements. On the other hand, it is hoped that the relaxation of rules and the provision of easier access to the market will increase competition and so reduce fares overall when the agreement takes effect. Where discount fares exist there will probably be little change, but they should be introduced at times and places where they are not now available.

Simultaneously with the EEC Transport Ministers' meeting, the future of British Caledonian Airways was being decided, and it is worth discussing BCAL's connections with the licensing system and the likely future effect of its sale. BCAL was set up in 1971, at the same time as British Airways was formed from the old BEA and BOAC, to act as a privately owned 'second force' that would provide effective competition between British airlines. However, given the difficulty in setting up new routes under the system of bilateral agreements the relatively small BCAL was never able to create a satisfactory network; its eventual need to be taken over arose because the route pattern with which it was stuck did not consistently produce profitable traffic. It was unhappy about the effect of BA, which then had over 80% of the UK scheduled market, being privatised and so freed from government control at a time when the liberalisation of the market removed the protection other operators had enjoyed. BCAL's overtures to the government were unsuccessful, perhaps again due to the government's desire to maximise BA's attractiveness on the stock market. When BA made its bid for BCAL, it was argued by some politicians and economists that the reduction in competition in British aviation was less important than strengthening the position of BA against 'mega-carriers' from the USA and the Far East. The proposal was examined by the Monopolies and Mergers Commission, which recommended that the merger could go ahead subject to a number of conditions. These related mainly to BCAL surrendering the licences for its services within Europe so that other airlines, including BA, could apply for them.

Other airlines were also interested in BCAL, including International Leisure's Air Europe and the Scandinavian airline SAS, but problems would have arisen here over the need to demonstrate British ownership for the purpose of bilateral agreements (ILG is 49% New-Zealand-owned). BA finally made an offer , which was recommended to share holders for acceptance by a group of the BCAL board who controlled a majority of the shares. The reasons for the interest of ILG and SAS, however, are worth considering. Air Europe had recently been granted licences to operate between Gatwick and eight European destinations, some shared with BCAL, and an appeal by BCAL against the granting of these licences was still outstanding. Air Europe is clearly interested in developing scheduled European traffic, perhaps because progressive liberalisation may undermine the charter market on which it has depended up to now. It may also have been interested in BCAL's control over a large proportion of departure slots at Gatwick at a time when airport congestion in London is increasing. The interest of SAS also reflects liberalisation, in that small carriers lacking economies of scale will be vulnerable, and mergers between them are likely to meet the 'mega-carrier' threat. One reason for Governments having defended the system of bilateral agreements and high fares is that small countries cannot develop their national airlines beyond a certain point, and in a free market they would be unable to compete with larger airlines from abroad; protection of their national routes and high fares enable the airlines (usually state-owned) to carry reasonable numbers and earn satisfactory revenues.

# ☐ Westworld Travel

## Introduction

Westmead is a major commercial and industrial centre (population 1 million) in the south west of England. There are some heavy engineering plants to the north of the city, but most people are employed in the light industry and commercial sectors. The University is another important employer. Most recent developments have been the opening of a new shopping centre (the Caxton Centre), the Exhibition Centre and an airport. The airport deals mainly with domestic flights, although there are a limited number of services to European capital cities.

Unemployment, at 8%, is lower than might be expected, probably because of the Exhibition Centre, which has been a source of temporary employment. However, average earnings are lower than the national average, due to the high student population at the University, the low salaries of employees in the retail shopping complexes, and the increased tendency for companies to put their employees on short time working.

At present there are ten travel agencies in the city, the locations of which are marked on the map overleaf, along with other significant features. Most of the agencies are small independent retailers, but Thomas Cook, Lunn Poly, Pickfords and W. H. Smith all have branches there, while Westworld is part of a regional chain of ten retail outlets.

The ten travel agents in Westmead are scattered throughout the city, though most are situated in and around the shopping and commercial centre. All are ABTA licensed, and seven carry additional licences such as IATA and British Rail. They employ between four and fifteen members of staff each, the exact figure tending to reflect geographical location and, consequently, trade. This factor also appears to affect the levels of automation with which the travel agents are equipped; the three outlets having no computerised system are less accessible than those which have adopted Prestel (and, in four cases, Travicom) automation. Five of the travel agents hold the major accounts of local companies, the most successful in the Business Travel Service (BTS) being Pickfords Travel, Travel Away and Thomas Cook. Those not servicing major firms tend to specialise in the holiday market, offering - for example - package tours and coach trips. The travel agents open for business for between eight and nine-and-a-half hours a day, and for either five, five-and-a-half or six days a week.

Advertising strategies vary according to the finances and strategies of each travel agent. Six of the ten advertise frequently (at least once a month), though this is sometimes dependent on season, and most promotion is aimed at selling one particular product. Local newspapers (such as the *Westmead Messenger* favoured by Westworld Travel) and radio supply the usual forums for advertising. Some employ other methods as well, such as the distribution of leaflets. Travel Away are unique in promoting themselves at the functions of local companies and societies. In-store advertising, such as window displays, is also used.

The size and location of premises cause difficulties affecting several of the outlets. While rapid expansion has created problems of heavy investment for Travel Away, Lunn Poly predicts the possibility of confinement within small premises. Lack of passing trade adversely affects Pickfords Travel and Merrytime Travel. Some of the travel agents could compete more effectively for trade if the efficiency of their staff was improved, as in the case of W. H. Smith. Manor Travel, in contrast, boasts knowledgeable employees but lacks the financial resources necessary for expansion.

It is clear that while several of the travel agents are becoming stronger and more successful - such as Westworld Travel and Travel Away - others have performed poorly over the last few years, including Crouch Travel and Merrytime Travel.

# Westworld Travel

It is proposed to examine in some detail the operation of Westworld Travel, including consideration of its Market Profile and Business Plan.

## Market profile of Westworld Travel (1988/89 season)

The profile includes key facts and figures relating to the business of the agency and the market it serves. The material has been collected for the purposes of planning and formulating a long term strategy. It is summarised under five headings;

    (i)   General Travel

    (ii)  Business Travel

    (iii) Groups, Conferences and Incentives

    (iv) Foreign Exchange

    (v)  General Trading Environment

# Map of Westmead

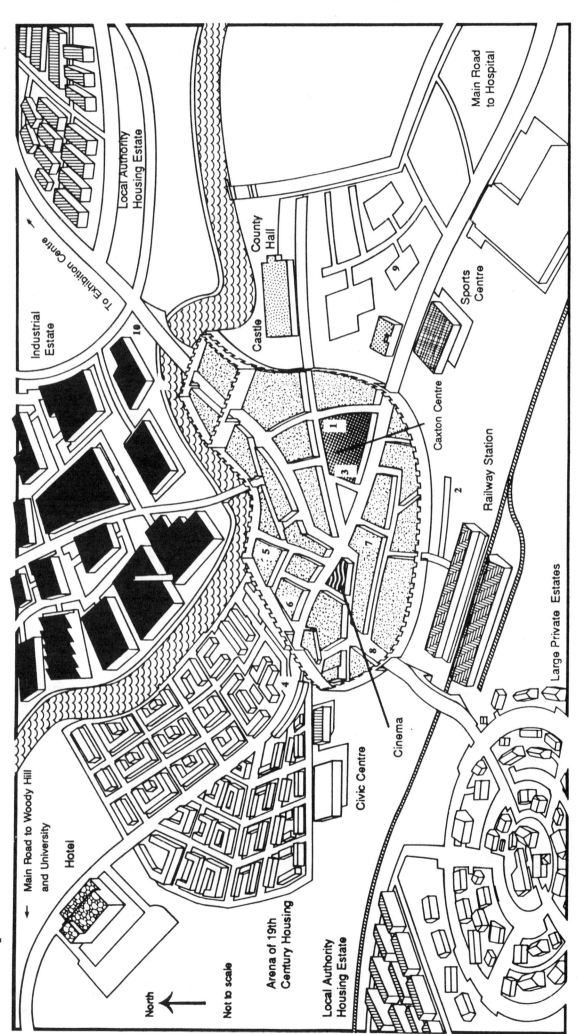

| Name | Licences | Location | No. of Employees | Automation | Major Accounts They Service | Specialism | Hours of Opening | Trading Days |
|---|---|---|---|---|---|---|---|---|
| 1. Lumn Poly | ABTA, IATA, BR, Continental Rail | Good Position in Caxton Centre | 10 | Prestel/Travicom | | Mainly some holiday Market | 0900 to 1730 | 6 days |
| 2. Pickford Travel | ABTA, BR | Poor Situation away from Town near station | 4 | Prestel | Spay Tools, Spartan Electric, Trenley Lifts | Package Holidays and to a Lesser Extent BTS | 0900 to 1730 | 5.5 days |
| 3. W.H. Smith | ABTA | Caxton Shopping Centre | 5 | Prestel | None | Package Holidays | 0900 to 1730 | 6 days |
| 4. Westworld Travel | ABTA, IATA, BR & Continental Rail | Modern premises central position | 7 | Prestel/Travicom | Tollgate Links | Mainly some package BTS market | 0830 to 1700 | 6 days |
| 5. Travel Away | ABTA, IATA, BR | Good Location | 12 | Prestel/Travicom | Sigmone Ltd. Teletone products. Dartmont & Bell (Engineering) | BTS has been their big push this year | 0830 to 1730 | 5 days |
| 6. Crouch Travel | ABTA, IATA | Reasonable position | 8 | Prestel | None | Only holiday market | 0900 to 1700 | 6 days |
| 7. Manor Travel | ABTA | Poor location down side | 5 | None | None | Blub flights coach Tours | 0900 to 1730 | 5.5 days |
| 8. Thomas Cook | IATA, ABTA, BR, Continental Rail | Newly decorated reasonable passing trade | 15 | Travicom/Prestel | Sotex Player Rite. Moulded Electrachip | BTS and General Travel | 0830 to 1730 | 6 days In peak booking. 5.5 days other wise |
| 9. Merrytime Travel | ABTA, BR, Coach Licences | On way out of town Poor frontage plastered with posters | 6 | None | None | Mainly holiday market | 0900 to 1730 | 5.5 days |
| 10. Westmead Coaches | ABTA | Garage situated near coach station | 10 | None | None | Coach holidays | 0800 to 1730 | 6 days |

## 1. General Travel

### a. Average value of booking

| | Summer £ | Winter £ |
|---|---|---|
| Average Value per booking | 620 | 610 |
| Average Value per passenger | 270 | 300 |

### b. Sales by tour operator

| Principal | % total package holiday sales |
|---|---|
| Thomson | 29 |
| Intasun | 21 |
| Horizon | 10 |
| Cosmos | 8 |
| Sovereign/Enterprise | 8 |
| Others | 24 |

### c. Most popular departure airport

| Airport | % leisure customers using airport |
|---|---|
| Luton | 40 |
| Heathrow | 25 |
| Gatwick | 25 |

### d. Occupational groups present in catchment area

| Occupational Group | Comments |
|---|---|
| Senior professionals/administrators & managers<br>Other professionals/administrators & managers<br>Clerical (e.g. Civil servants & shop assistants) | High because shop is in centre of the town |
| Skilled manual workers | Mainly light and heavy industry within the catchment area |
| Semi and unskilled manual workers<br>Pensioners<br>Students | Westmead University 10,000 students |
| Others | Some farmers from surrounding countryside |

**e.   Business accounts with potential for holiday sales**

| Names | No. of employees | Comments |
|---|---|---|
| Slipper Pharmaceuticals | 12,000 | Large sports section. Also own social club |
| Hovingham Group | 9,000 | Social club situated away from centre |
| Bon Fab Ltd. | 6,000 | Social club. Do some travel with another agent |
| Trent 300 | 3,500 | No social club |
| Parry, W. J. | 3,000 | No information |
| Richard Simon | 2,000 | Company has a production/incentive scheme for workers (dept v dept) |
| Winster Products | 2,000 | Social club recently set up - sports teams |
| Pole-Pope Merchant | 1,700 | |
| Benley Machinery | 1,500 | |
| Martin Emprex | 1,400 | |

**2. Business Travel**

**a.   Business travel by sector**

| | % |
|---|---|
| Light industry | 45 |
| Heavy industry | 17.5 |
| Agriculture, Forestry and Fishing | 7.5 |
| Construction | 7.5 |
| Finance | 7.5 |
| Retail | 5 |
| Transport | 5 |
| Education | 2.5 |
| Wholesale | 2.5 |

b. **Business travel by major accounts (and associated problems)**

| Account | Annual sales value | Problems |
|---|---|---|
| Bon Fab Ltd. | £34,290 | Tickets and F/E to be issued immediately reservation requested. May change and cancel. |
| Leisure Products | £15,420 | Poor accountancy procedure - poorly organised - poor payers. |
| Panner Fitzpatric | £8,070 | Poor payers - constantly have to write to them every month |
| Westmead University | £80,730 | Always problems identifying department who will pay or whether individual will pay |
| Hovingham Group | £219,260 | Conflict between their management and travellers. Management want cheapest, travellers want most convenient. This creates problems when chasing them for payment. |

## 3. Groups, Conferences and Incentives

a. **Groups (20 + people) booked during current financial year**

| Group | Reason for travel | Destin-nation | No. in group | Total Value | Revenue as % of sales |
|---|---|---|---|---|---|
| Westmead Netball Team | Netball competition | Milan | 20 | 6000 | 10% |
| Phelps Thomson Group | Family and Friends | Tenerife | 25 | 8240 | 10% |
| Thorn group | Thorn Social | Munich | 22 | 3020 | 10% |

**b. Clubs and societies not currently dealt with, but potential source of business**

| Club Name | Chairman/Secretary | Membership | Former Trips |
|---|---|---|---|
| Westmead Conservative | A. Galton-Tibbs | 2800 | No knowledge |
| Westmead Rugby Club | J. P. Palmer | 1000 | Tours in UK, with occasional travel to Europe |
| Slipper Sports and Social Club | D. Maynes | 12000 | Generally nothing organised by the club, although sporting and social groups organised own travel |
| Westmead Women's Guild | Ms. G. F. Featherton | 400 | Annual group trip abroad, plus delegates visit annual or bi-annual conferences |
| Born Brook Social Club | S. Bradley | 4000 | Actively pursue group travel abroad and in the UK to sporty and other destinations |

**c. Large companies which might be interested in conference incentives or buying gift vouchers**

| Company | No. of employees | Comments |
|---|---|---|
| Lindley & Lindley | 600 | gift vouchers |
| Timberland Household Stores | 1350 | gift vouchers |
| Hovingham Group | 10500 | conference |
| Royal Marketing Assoc. | 1000 | conference and gift vouchers |
| Leisure Products | 400 | gift vouchers |
| Topping Group (car sales) | 300 | conference and gift vouchers |
| Licensed Victuallers Assoc. | 200 | conference |
| Westmead and District Hotels Assoc | 100 | conference |
| Martin (gift catalogue) | 60 | gift vouchers |
| Westmead Preservation Society | 70 | conference or group travel |

### 4. Foreign Exchange

### a. Categories of clients and value of transactions

| Type of Client | Buy | Sell | Total Transaction | Comments |
|---|---|---|---|---|
| Hotels | 4,000 | - | 4,000 | Could be very much bigger with airport bringing more visitors |
| Individuals | 8,000 | 45,000 | 53,000 | |
| Groups | 10,000 | 40,000 | 50,000 | |
| Schools | 200 | 5,000 | 5,200 | |
| Other Business Houses | 20,000 | 80,000 | 100,000 | Still many new accounts yet to be approached |
| Westmead University | - | 10,000 | 10,000 | Mainly two professors - Geography department |

### 5. General Trading Environment

### a. Groups/organisations with international contracts

| Group/ Organisation | Country Involved | Nature of Involvement | Size of Potential Market |
|---|---|---|---|
| Restaurants | Hong Kong | Transfer of money | 8 Restaurants |
| University | World wide | Conferences | not defined |
| Road Haulage | Europe | Transport goods to Europe | 2 companies |
| Hospitals/Solicitors/ Banks/Hotels/ Schools/Religious Groups/Ethnic Groups/Clubs/ Coach Firms | European Cities | Coach Holidays | 2 companies in Westmead |
| Consultants/ Newspapers/ Wholesalers/ Exporters | Europe | Export of goods | Hovingham Group |

**b.   Special events involving incoming/outgoing international travel**

| Event | Comments |
|---|---|
| Exchange visit to West Germany (Manheim) | Yearly visit. Approximately 50 people every year. Contact Mrs. P. Trackle |
| International Conference on Third World Farming | Contact Professor J. Topham - Westmead University - Approx. 150 delegates |

**c.   Strengths and weaknesses of branch**

| Strengths | Weaknesses |
|---|---|
| Prime site. Next to larger retail outlet. Large number of people passing shop. Best location of any travel agency. Large window display area. Near car park, Bailey's Department Store and Caxton Centre | Sign not really prominent. Narrow pavement just outside branch. |

**d. Main local publications**

| Name of publication | Circulation | Distribution | Cost of Advertising |
|---|---|---|---|
| Westmead Telegraph | 180,000 | Westmead and District | £80 |
| Stoneville Herald | 6,000 | Stoneville and District | £70 |
| Westmead Messenger | 150,000 | Westmead and District | £60 |
| Chamber of Commerce Magazine | 4,000 | Westmead and District | £120 |
| Wansdyke and District Farmers Weekly | 1,000 | Wansdyke Westmead | £20 |
| Westmead Tourist Guide | 20,000 | Countrywide | £50 |
| Westmead Advertiser | 40,000 | Westmead and District | £45 |
| Westmead Business Club Newsletter | 50,000 | Westmead and District | £20 |
| Westmead University Magazine | 10,000 | University Campus | £20 |
| Northfield Ratepayers Newsletter | 2,000 | Northfields and District | £20 |

# Business Plan 1989/90

Having reviewed the Branch's performance in 1988/89, Head Office has produced a Business Plan for the next year. The planned results and assumptions underlying the set targets are presented below.

| | | 1988/89 | | 1989/90 | |
|---|---|---|---|---|---|
| | | (£thousands) | | | |
| **Sales** | | | | | |
| | General Travel | 1386.03 | | 1622.21 | |
| | BTS Travel | 1244.78 | | 1484.77 | |
| | **Travel Total** | **2630.81** | | **3106.98** | |
| | Foreign Exchange | 348.49 | | 439.34 | |
| | **Total** | **2979.30** | | **3546.32** | |

| | | | Ratio to sales | | Ratio to sales |
|---|---|---|---|---|---|
| **Revenue** | | | | | |
| | Travel | 253.08 | 9.62% | 315.07 | 9.74% |
| | Foreign Exchange | 4.70 | 1.35% | 7.91 | 1.80% |
| | **Total** | **259.78** | **8.72%** | **322.98** | **6.87%** |
| **Costs** | | | | | |
| | Payroll | 116.50 | | 131.83 | |
| | Other | 68.32 | | 78.57 | |
| | **Total** | **184.32** | | **210.40** | |
| Productivity Ratio | | 2.33 | | 2.45 | |

## Principal Objectives

1. Increase sales in travel and foreign exchange.

   (a) 17.04% increase in general travel

   (b) 19.28% increase in business travel

   (c) 26.07% increase in foreign exchange

2. To obtain five new business house accounts worth more than £15,000 each.

3. To increase package holiday sales by at least 15%.

4. To obtain increased productivity from each staff member thereby achieving a productivity ratio of 2.45%.

## Assumptions underlying the Business Plan

Business travel is expected to continue to increase, but not sustaining the rate of growth experienced last year, when we gained ten new accounts. We hope to obtain five more as a result of a big sales drive early in 1989, though this will involve competing against Travel Away.

According to local business sources, the employment situation seems likely to improve next year owing to the expansion of light industries. We therefore anticipate some growth in sales of package tours and low cost holidays generally. There will probably be even greater demand amongst some sectors of the market for long haul holidays and travel to the United States.

Our foreign exchange (FE) operation is expected to have a big impact next year as a result of aggressive advertising. We now have greater campaign expertise within the branch which will provide an FE service not to be bettered in Westmead.

Developments at Westmead Airport should benefit the branch by encouraging more business representatives and members of the public to travel by air. New tour operators will be providing flights from Westmead next year, and the number of overseas visitors should increase. There will be an open day held at the airport in November and we will be organising a display there for all our Westmead branches.

# ☐ The Neilson Leisure Group

This case study looks at the development of the Neilson Leisure Group from its origins in 1968 until 1987 when it faced a major turning point. The case study is divided into two parts: the first looks at the history and evolution of the company and the second describes its product base and analyses some aspects of its operation.

## The origins and development of the Neilson Leisure Group

The origins of the Neilson Leisure Group can be traced back to 1968 when an Australian couple, Warren and Loraine Sandral, arrived in Britain and started a company called Winterline Coaches which operated camping tours around Europe. The target market, during the late 1960s/early 1970s, was young Australasians benefiting from a scheme operating in New Zealand and Australia which enabled individuals to take long leaves of absence with their jobs guaranteed on return.

Despite an unprofessional marketing approach in which the Sandrals touted for business outside Australia House in London, the initial business idea was successful. The first tour was a seven week camping trip through North Africa, for which Warren drove the minibus while Loraine worked in their office in London and because of the tour's destination the Sandral's decided to change the company's name to Nord Afrik Travel Limited. An association developed between the company and an Austrian, Manfred Ebner, which led to the operation of skiing trips to Kolsass, and subsequently to other Austrian resorts.

The tours were designed so that a client could see as much of Europe as possible in 5-6 months. There was a nine week tour of Europe, a five week tour of North Africa and a five week tour of Scandinavia and Russia. By taking each one consecutively a client could see virtually all of Europe in nineteen weeks.

Because the tours were by this time no longer restricted to North Africa, the company name was again changed, in 1973, to NAT Eurotours Limited. This reflected the "Swingers from NAT" label adopted by the clients. The company also became more professional in its methods of promotion, featuring:

(i) by 1975, four offices in Australia, located at Sydney, Melbourne, Brisbane and Perth;

(ii) a brochure, distributed through Australian travel agents.

NAT aimed to offer an all round service, and therefore to complement the European tours, it provided NAT Euroclub membership costing £3.50 per year in 1973-4. The benefits of the Euroclub membership included:

(i) preferential rates for their London hotel. This was opened in 1975 with accommodation for 250 people and a range of facilities such as a bar and disco. A second hotel accommodated 300 people with similar facilities. NAT tours commenced and terminated at the hotels;

(ii) access to the UK Employment Bureau, helping to arrange temporary employment for the young Australasians while they were in London;

(iii) a Euroclub mailing address for the clients on tour or staying in London;

(iv) day and weekend tours in Britain free of charge;

(v) the NAT Flight Deck (a travel service) which arranged for low cost travel between the UK and Australia.

Meanwhile the programme had been extended to include conventional package holidays to Europe aimed at the British travel market. Between 1974 and 1977 other new products were added, including a three week tour of six countries (Belgium, East Germany, West Germany, Poland, Russia and Czechoslovakia), a nine week Grand European tour, a five week Northern Africa tour incorporating a Mediterranean cruise, and a 22 day Scandinavian tour. Also, from 1976-7, Winter European tours were offered; for example, 18 days visiting France, Italy, Austria, Switzerland, Germany and the Netherlands.

The company continued to extend its promotional efforts, seeking clients from South Africa, Canada and the US and at the same time the NAT offices in Australia were endeavouring to establish a transportation business bringing young Australians to London. By late 1975 a ship-jet operation was set up with stopovers in Singapore and Tokyo which added another facet to the NAT product. One aspect of its operations which the company prided itself on was the quality of its rising number of staff, whose youth and enthusiasm made them well suited to devising and providing a product for the younger generation.

However, at the end of 1978 two measures were introduced which had a dramatic effect on NAT.

(i) new visa regulations meant that Australians could obtain only a three month visa for Europe.

(ii) the system whereby individuals could take long leaves of absence and have their jobs guaranteed for their return ended.

The effect on NAT Eurotours was catastrophic. Their major source of business disappeared, and the company was forced to formulate plans for its future survival. Two principal measures were taken:

(i) the Australian offices, one of the London hotels and the Flight Deck were closed.

(ii) in 1979 application for membership of the Association of British Travel Agents (ABTA) was approved and in so doing the first steps were taken to firmly establish the name NAT Holidays within the British travel trade.

From this point the company developed and altered its existing tour programmes to suit the British market, specialising particularly in static or one destination camping holidays to major European holiday areas. NAT quickly became established as the market leader in this field. The placing of NAT Holidays on the winners list of the UK's leading travel agent, Thomas Cook, helped to make the name synonymous with camping holidays of high quality and value.

Over the following years, 1980-1, the camping programme developed to include self-drive holidays and holidays by air. A further new dimension was created when, in 1982, NAT Holidays purchased a company called Sunsaver Holidays. Also a camping specialist, Sunsaver's caravan programme added another variation to the product, and NAT adopted their Express coach travel as an alternative to the stopover service. In 1983 NAT began to offer coach departures from provincial points.

By 1984 NAT Holidays had become the number one operator for camping. Its products had been developed to incorporate express coach, self-drive and air transport to a variety of countries and resorts in the Mediterranean. Similarly, coach, fly-drive and air holidays were offered to a range of countries - including Spain, Yugoslavia, Italy and Austria - based on hotel and apartment accommodation.

Meanwhile efforts were being made to develop the winter programme into a serious part of the company's overall product range. The emphasis on the fun side of winter sports, that had proven popular with the young Australian market, was retained. In addition to Kolsass, resorts in France, Spain, Italy and other parts of Austria were added, and the programme grew considerably. The winter sports programme was never considered a major profit centre for the company, but was viewed as making a useful contribution to the overall business.

In 1983 the company moved its headquarters from London to Leeds and in April 1986 it took over the name and products of Neilson Holidays from Nationwide Leisure and became the Neilson Leisure Group. The separate product names were maintained, so that the company operated NAT Holidays (summer), NAT Ski, Neilson Ski, Neilson Lakes and Mountains (summer), Villaseekers and French Life.

Despite initial optimism several problems arose from the takeover. Increased administrative pressure made it necessary to expand its premises and instal new computer and telephone systems. As a consequence the company was more vulnerable to technical problems. A prime example was a computer malfunction during the booking season of summer 1987 which caused great disruption. In addition pressure on staff increased for two major reasons.

(a) The acquisition of the Neilson ski programme removed the breathing space previously used by the accounts department to sort out summer problems. In addition, accounts personnel had to cope with the unfamiliar procedures practised by Neilson.

(b) The Neilson products were aimed at a very different market to the NAT holidays and staff in reservations and administration had to get to know the new product very quickly. For example, the Neilson ski programme was aimed at the serious, experienced skier while the NAT programme had always emphasised the 'fun' elements. As a consequence a Sales and Marketing Director was appointed (the only major change in the management structure).

Nevertheless, the company benefited in several ways. Most notably:

(i) the Neilson Ski Training Programme was developed and implemented. This training programme aimed at travel agency staff was designed to improve the sales techniques needed to sell skiing holidays. Staff members nominated by travel agents attended the courses.

(ii) this training programme became the company's major promotional tool aimed at travel agents. During 1986/7 1500 travel agency staff participated in the training scheme, rising to 2000 in 1987/8 (the training programme was promoted at the annual ABTA YTS Conference and resulted in about 500 ABTA YTS trainees per year joining the programme).

In terms of both sales and turnover, 1986 proved to be a successful year. This was despite a massive price war between the two largest tour operators in the UK, Thomson Holidays and Intasun Leisure Group, which forced many other tour operators out of business. Thomson Holidays slashed the lower end of the market so that they were charging similar prices for air holidays equivalent to NAT coach holidays. NAT responded by reducing prices but was unable to undercut Thomson totally, so its profits were affected despite good sales figures. The company chose to retain the margins on price which ensured reasonable profitability per head rather than reduce prices below these margins to reduce competition from Thomson. Sales in high seasons were generally always good regardless of price.

Holidays using overseas rail transportation were introduced in 1987, proving popular as an alternative to coach travel. The trains had NAT staff acting as couriers. By the end of this summer season, however, the programmes were enjoying varying degrees of success.

1. The NAT Holiday summer programme did not sell well during the high season. The pricing strategy (of subsidising early and late season price reductions from high season bookings) proved unsuccessful.

2. The Summer Neilson Lakes and Mountains programme was dropped because it had carried insufficient passengers. A small part of the programme was incorporated into the NAT Holidays brochure.

3. French Life was successful in 1987 and was expected to contribute a profit to the Neilson Leisure Group.

4. Villaseekers was rather unsuccessful, since its accommodation had to be guaranteed financially whether sold or not. Sales were poor and losses were expected.

By mid-1987, Neilson Leisure Group was experiencing the crisis faced by many other tour operators at the same time. Overall holidays for midsummer had not sold particularly well, and the price war was continuing. Medium-sized operators like the Neilson Leisure Group could not sustain either losses or low profits even in the short-term.

The management team consisted of the same young, vigorous, forward-thinking individuals who had been with the company since the early days. Clearly some decisions had to be made about the company's future, and they felt personally responsible for the 200 staff in the UK and 500 in Europe. Further capital was obtained from Investment in Industry and Capital for Companies, and an attempt (which failed) was made to float the company. A meeting of all the Directors was called for the autumn of 1987, which Warren Sandral opened with the question, "Where do we go from here?"

# The Neilson Leisure Group Products

### NAT Holidays

This programme offered a variety of package holidays in France, Italy, Spain, Portugal, Yugoslavia, Corfu, Austria and Malta. Several types of accommodation were featured, including camping and caravanning (in mobile homes, chalets and bungalow tents), hotels and apartments, and the 'Summer Houses' and Gasthofs which had previously been part of the Neilson Lakes and Mountains programme.

Holidaymakers wanting the independence of their own car were catered for, with NAT arranging cross channel ferries and hotels en route, and supplying maps and GB stickers to those opting for self-drive. Alternatively clients could fly from five UK airports, with Gatwick and Manchester offering all destinations. Those travelling by coach had a choice of 80 regional departure points, with all vehicles staffed by experienced NAT drivers and couriers. The journey from Calais to Cap d'Agde and Canet Plage, and the Costa Brava, could be made by train. This was also staffed by NAT couriers and featured bars, food, couchettes and a disco.

Child and group reductions, and other special deals, were offered.

### Villaseekers

Clients could choose from over thirty-five resorts across Europe (in, for example, Spain, Portugal, France and the Greek islands) and a wide selection of villas and apartments. These ranged from two person studios to luxurious villas accommodating ten, many of which were away from commercialised resorts. Transportation was by air or self-drive, with NAT offering a money-saving service on car hire. Three week holidays, child and group reductions, and free places for children on early departures, were available.

## French Life

This programme was designed to provide "the simple pleasures of country life". It offered motoring holidays to France with accommodation in mobile homes, chalets, tents, gites, farmhouses, villas and apartments. Destinations were offered in Brittany and Normandy, Dordogne and Lot, and on the Atlantic and Mediterranean coasts.

The two 'holiday villages', with good sporting facilities, were particularly recommended for families. A special facility for children - the 'French Life Bon Bon Club' -was offered at many sites, and all sites had the 'French Life Game Pack'.

## Ski NAT

This programme offered a variety of wintersports holidays by air, coach and self-drive to resorts in Austria, France, Switzerland and Spain.

Most of the resorts were suitable for beginners and intermediate skiers, while some suited advanced skiers. All were chosen, in addition, for their apres-ski facilities, an aspect of wintersports holidays for which Ski NAT had become famous. Ski packs (including lessons, lift pass, ski hire and boot hire) were available at all resorts. Many resorts offered Ski Kindergartens and Kolsass Weer provided a free Mini-club for children. Learn-to-ski weeks and ski weekends were also available.

A programme of excursions and activities for clients not wishing to ski was offered at each resort.

## Neilson Ski

This programme offered departures by air, coach and self-drive to over 40 European resorts (in France, Switzerland, Italy, Yugoslavia and Austria).

The philosophy behind the Neilson Ski programme differed from that behind the NAT Ski programme, featuring dedication to excellence and promoting Neilson as the 'ultimate ski operator'. BASI-qualified Ski Guides were employed to act as group leaders and organise skiing expeditions. Resorts were chosen for their suitability for all standards of skier, and ski packs were offered for each resort.

Reductions for groups and children, teenage specials, Haute Cuisine at selected hotels, and Ski-Senior weeks were available. Refunds were promised to those new to the sport whose enthusiasm proved short-lived.

## For all Products

Booking conditions were contained in the 'Promise of Fair Trading'. Clients were urged to book through their local ABTA travel agents. Insurance offers were included in the brochures; insurance was compulsory for skiers.

## Operations

The operations department was one of the most important developments in Neilson Leisure. It had two sections:

*(1) Aviation*

This section liaised with airlines, advised resorts of anticipated arrival and departure times, dealt with flight manifests and organised export representation.

*(2) Coaching*

The operation of the coaching section was rather more involved, since Neilson Leisure ran sixteen coaches of their own in 1987, and often handled many more when demand required it. It was not uncommon for more than thirty coaches to be operating on one departure date. During 1987 the coaching department handled NAT Summer Holidays, NAT Ski and Neilson Ski. Its functions included:

(a) on advice from the reservations department of the requirements for each departure, the allocation of vehicles, drivers, caterers and couriers to the appropriate regional departure points. This was organised through the Traffic Department (for drivers) and through Express Couriers and Coaching (Couriers were responsible for the control of food and drinks stock on their coach). The coaching department organised and monitored each journey, though Mediterranean Express handled the train operation;

(b) ensuring that clients were allocated to the correct regional and resort coaches;

(c) advising Sealink of final numbers and booking extra spaces when required. The company's relationship with Sealink was excellent: on a high season departure a ferry might carry 40 Neilson Leisure and NAT coaches (over 2000 passengers);

(d) minor functions, such as organising ferry crossings for self-drive passengers for NAT French Life and Villaseekers; booking accommodation for drivers, couriers and operations staff; and producing the manifests and paperwork for the couriers.

The organisation and style of the coach journey had been improved over the years. Initially - for example - a London coach terminal served as the interchange point, being replaced by motorway service stations and, finally, Dover Port. The company had progressed to operating luxury coaches with superb facilities, and the Traffic Department recruited and trained drivers. Neilson Leisure prided itself on the efficiency of its coach operation and the operations team, but problems were inevitably encountered through bad weather, mechanical failure of vehicles, strikes by ferry companies and poor traffic conditions.

# Marketing

Since becoming members of ABTA the company saw the retail travel trade as their major source of business, and the bulk of their sales promotion was directed at travel agents.

Various methods of promoting the Neilson products were employed:

(i) Incentive commission rates were negotiated with travel agents, particularly the multiples (who had clear marketing and brochure racking principles).

(ii) By 1987 a sales force had been developed which consisted of seven sales representatives and a Sales Manager. It covered the whole of England and Scotland, organising joint promotions with travel agents and offering a good back up service.

(iii) Press advertising was carried out in the travel trade newspapers, public newspapers, magazines (e.g. TV Times) and on television. When required to by the agents, the company got involved in 50/50 advertising.

The Neilson Ski Training Programme was the biggest marketing thrust for the winter products, but the range of products offered was wide and appealed to various client types. The company was keen for products to be developed and adjusted; this was based on the analysis of client questionnaires and feedback from resort staff.

Both product and price were influenced by the competition.

The pricing policy of Neilson Leisure was totally market led. A balance had to be sustained between reasonable profit margins and competitive prices, and in practice it was often tipped in favour of the latter. Pricing had to take into account the things that the travel market had learned to expect - free holidays for children, low season reductions, etc. A computerised reservations system and competent staff, who knew the product well, facilitated booking.

The Neilson Leisure aim, highlighted in the brochures, was to, "Give you (the client) the best possible holiday for your money without cutting any corners. We know we can offer quality holidays at prices we know you'll love".

## Neilson Leisure Personnel

The company's key personnel team was comprised of directors in the following departments; Marketing, Group Operations, Operations, Finance, and Administrations. There were, in addition, managers in Group Marketing and Overseas Personnel.

Staff required in the resorts were area managers, representatives (for hotels, apartments and camp sites), camp site managers, bar staff, maintenance staff, catering assistants, and a security team. Couriers for trains and coaches were also needed.

The recruitment and selection process began in October, and went through the following stages:

(i) In October it was ascertained how many of the current staff wanted to remain with the company for the next season. They were allocated to a particular position based on their own preferences and on appraisals completed the previous season.

Approximately 60 + % of representatives returned the following year (most other operators were lucky to get 20%). The representatives were made offers by January.

(ii) The number of new staff required and the positions they would fill were assessed. Advertising for recruits, through newspapers, was arranged.

(iii) Application forms were assessed by Personnel staff. Factors considered important were the presentation of the form, previous work experience, extent of personal travel abroad, age, and (helpful but not essential) foreign language skills. An interest in dealing with people was of paramount importance.

(iv) Group interviews were held in January/February, to judge how applicants related to each other and interacted. The more successful candidates were interviewed individually, and offers made within a fortnight.

Success in selection was seen to mean success in training. It was recognised that the products provided by Neilson Leisure were essentially similar to those offered by other tour operators, and that the difference came in the nature and quality of the overseas representation. Consequently great emphasis was placed on the training scheme, and six different programmes were devised. These covered the training of new representatives, area managers, coach couriers, train couriers, camp site managers and second year representatives. Two examples follow:

(a) New Representative Training Course

This typically began in early April, and consisted of a coach journey to Cap d'Agde. Aspects of the product covered included transportation, duties in resort, public speaking, client departure and arrival procedure, and company. Fostering loyalty and commitment to the company was seen as an important objective of the training.

(b) Courier Training Course

This was designed to test the stamina of potential couriers who, if successful, would spend the greater part of their working lives on the move. The training was therefore carried out on a coach, so that trainees could become familiar with coach duties (such as use of a microphone) and routes to resorts.

When the training programmes had been completed all the overseas personnel involved collected at Cap d'Agde for a company seminar.

# ☐ Miles Better

This case study traces the development of Glasgow as a tourist centre leading to its successful bid to host the 1988 Garden Festival and its acquisition of the European City of Culture title. In particular, emphasis is placed upon an examination of the role of the various bodies involved in promoting tourism in the city.

Greater Glasgow forms part of Strathclyde Region which was established by the 1973 Local Government (Scotland) Act. The Region extends from the southern lowlands of Ayrshire to the mountains of Glencoe in the north, and from the west coast islands to Lanark. It has a population of around two-and-a-half million (almost half the total population of Scotland), most living in Glasgow and the surrounding towns. The City of Glasgow itself, excluding outlying districts, had a population of three-quarters of a million in 1981.

## The History of Tourism in Glasgow

Industrial expansion in the nineteenth and twentieth centuries saw the heyday of Glasgow. But those heavy industries, such as shipbuilding along the banks of the River Clyde, have long since declined, giving rise to recession and the associated problems of unemployment and declining investment. There still remains much evidence of Glasgow's industrial heritage, including some heavy industry and newly-developed light industry. The City has continued to be an important commercial and financial centre in addition to housing a number of central government agencies.

Unlike Edinburgh, which boasts a great many historical, cultural and recreational facilities, Glasgow was not perceived as a tourist attraction. By contrast, it had the dubious distinction of a dirty, depressed, deprived and violent city. This was in spite of notable features such as parklands, cultural amenities and events, shopping facilities, and architecture. These leisure tourist resources were largely unexploited, although business travel was recognised as important to the city.

Things changed during the 1980s. Glasgow emerged as a major visitor destination which now rivals Edinburgh in terms of trips and bednights (though the capital continues to attract more overseas tourists). In 1982 Glasgow had 700,000 visitors, a figure which had risen to more than two million three years later.

# Glasgow's Development Programme

Behind this success was a one billion pound investment programme funded by a partnership between the public and private sectors. Its most significant specific achievements have been:

(i) the opening of the Burrell Collection in 1983;

(ii) the construction of the Scottish Exhibition and Conference Centre in 1985 at a cost of over £36 million; and

(iii) the hosting of the National Garden Festival in 1988. The designation of Glasgow as European City of Culture for 1990 will contribute to its continued regeneration.

There was little official or popular interest in Glasgow's tourism until the late 1970s, despite a busy information centre in the heart of the city. This changed in 1979 when:

(a) the post of Conference Officer was created in the City's Public Relations department; and

(b) an Association of Conference and Tourism Services was established.

These resulted from increased recognition in the public and private sectors of the potential for tourism.

Two further developments in 1982/3 benefited the scheme.

## Greater Glasgow Tourist Board

The Local Government (Scotland) Act gave District Councils the responsibility for promoting tourism. Area Tourist Boards were established, in the form of tripartite organisations representing District Councils, the Scottish Tourist Board and industry, working in association with the British Tourist Authority. Area Tourist Boards now cover most of Scotland, with the Greater Glasgow Tourist Board (GGTB) created in 1983.

The GGTB's objectives are to:

(i) increase the number of leisure and business tourists;

(ii) extend visitors' length of stay;

(iii) increase tourist expenditure; and

(iv) provide an excellent information service.

The measures employed include the establishment of a network of information centres, the distribution of brochures, and the encouragement of events attractive to tourists. The GGTB represents the area at expeditions and trade fairs, participating in joint marketing initiatives.

Funding comes from constituent local authorities (currently Glasgow, Inverclyde, Monklands, Strathkelvin and Clydebank District Councils), the Scottish Tourist Board, membership fees, and the revenue raised by the

**Area Tourist Boards In Scotland**

**Key**

1. Angus
2. Aviemore and Spey Valley
3. Ayrshire and Burns Country
4. Ayrshire Valleys
5. Banff and Buchan
6. Caithness
7. City of Aberdeen
8. City of Dundee
9. Clyde Valley
10. Dumfries and Galloway
11. Dunoon
12. East Lothian
13. Forth Valley
14. Fort William
15. Gordon District
16. Greater Glasgow
17. Inverness. Loch Ness
18. Isle of Arran
19. Isle of Sky and South West Ross
20. Kincardine and Deeside
21. Loch Lomond. Stirling and Trossachs
22. Mid Argyll. Kintyre and Islay
23. Oban. Mull and District
24. Orkney
25. Outer Hebrides
26. Perthshire
27. Ross and Cromarty
28. Rothesay and Isle of Bute
29. Scottish Borders
30. Shetland
31. St. Andrews and North East Fife
32. Sutherland
33. City of Edinburgh
34. Cunninghame
35. Kirkcaldy
36. Morey
37. Cumbernauld and Kilsyth
38. East Kilbride
39. Eastwood
40. Inverclyde
41. Midlothian
42. Monklands

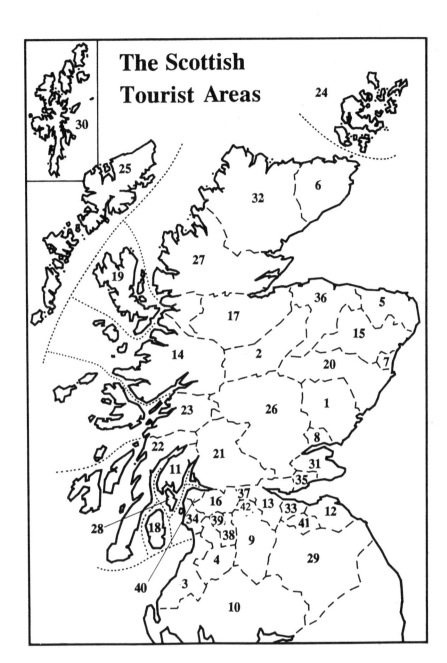

Bureau de Change and theatre ticket sales outlet at the central information centre.Early in 1987 the Greater Glasgow Convention Bureau, funded by the Glasgow and Strathclyde Councils, was set up as part of the GGTB. It had special responsibility for promoting Glasgow as a conference and exhibition centre. By March 1988, 750 requests for information had been answered, and 37 out of a total of 52 formal bids for conferences had been successful. The GGTB's affairs are administered by an Executive Committee. In 1986/7 it consisted of twenty-seven members; thirteen local authority representatives, thirteen trade members and one representative of the Scottish Tourist Board. A statement of income and expenditure for the Greater Glasgow Tourist Board is given below to illustrate the nature and scale of its activity.

# GGTB income and expenditure (from Annual Report and Accounts 1986/7):

## Leisure Tourism:

### a. Expenditure

|  | Actual 1985/6 | Actual 1986/7 | Estimate 1987/8 |
|---|---|---|---|
| Marketing | 95450 | 108978 | 105000 |
| Merchandise | 28559 | 33180 | 30000 |
| Employees | 201575 | 178023 | 233000 |
| Rents and Rates | 72791 | 72594 | 77 000 |
| Other costs | 89498 | 84857 | 73 600 |
| **Total Expenditure** | 487873 | 477632 | 508600 |
| Surplus(Deficit) for year | (52079) | 42486 | 1050 |
| **Total** | **435794** | **520118** | **509650** |

(Other costs includes upkeep of property, postage and telephone, staff travel etc.)

### b. Income

|  | | | |
|---|---|---|---|
| Glasgow District Council | 225800 | 260900 | 260900 |
| Other District Councils | 78800 | 101900 | 91 000 |
| Scottish Tourist Board | 52000 | 54000 | 57 750 |
| Membership fees | 19377 | 22532 | 25 000 |
| Other income | 59817 | 80786 | 75 000 |
| **Total** | **435 794** | **520 118** | **509 650** |

(Other income comes from sales and booking fees, temporary loan interest and advertising).

**Convention Bureau:**

### a. Expenditure

|  | Estimate 1986/87 | Actual 1986/87 |
|---|---|---|
| Marketing | 158000 | 79 326 |
| Computerisation | 0 | 14 674 |
| Employees | 15000 | 22224 |
| Other | 11000 | 421 |
| **Total Expenditure** | 184000 | 116665 |
| Surplus for year | 0 | 42 510 |
| **Total** | **184000** | **74155** |

### b. Income

|  | Estimate 1986/87 | Actual 1986/87 |
|---|---|---|
| Glasgow District Council | 70000 | 70000 |
| Strathclyde Regional Council | 70000 | 70000 |
| Trade | 44000 | 19175 |
| **Total Income** | **184000** | **159175** |

# Surveys And Reports

The Planning Department of the City Council organised a series of surveys to examine existing levels of tourism and to assess its role in the economy, with recommendations for improvements being made.

At the same time the Scottish Development Agency commissioned consultants Pannell, Kerr and Foster to draw up a strategy for the economic development of Glasgow city centre. Their final report, published in 1983, was entitled 'A Tourism Development Study of Glasgow'. It advised that the existing product be improved and the city marketed as a tourist destination, with major new attractions, unique to Glasgow, being developed. Many elements of the strategy have since been implemented, although much of it now requires revision in view of subsequent developments.

# The Roles Of The Various Bodies Involved In The Programme

## 1. The Scottish Development Agency

The Scottish Development Agency, with its policy of supporting the development of major new facilities throughout the country, has been an important source of funds for various Glaswegian projects. Most of the initiatives it backs are large scale and long-term (lasting 3-5 years before completion) with a considerable amount of financial and market assessment necessary in the planning phase.

Projects are only assisted if at least fifty percent of investment comes from private sources, and if they are expected to generate profits. The Agency has currently invested over £34 million in the Garden Festival and is part funding a series of environmental improvement schemes. These include work on the Cathedral precinct area, the Sauchiehall Street pedestrianisation, the Clyde walkway extension, the Forth/Clyde Canal regeneration programme and stone cleaning throughout the city.

# 2. The District Councils

The District Councils have also played an important role in the development and promotion of tourism in their areas. That of the City of Glasgow has been particularly active - a reflection of its size and resources. Within the Council many departments have an interest in tourism, such as Parks and Recreation, Museums and Art Galleries, and Planning. Tourism also impinges on the work of other committees, such as those tackling Economic Development, Employment, and Policy and Resources.

In 1982/3 Glasgow District Council organised the first tourist promotion campaign to be targeted at a specific market. Entitled 'Welcome to Glasgow' it aimed to attract former Glaswegians, especially those resident in the United States, back to visit their native city. It drew an estimated ten thousand extra tourists during 1983.

It was in that year that the 'Glasgow's Miles Better' campaign was conceived in association with Struthers Advertising, and partly funded by the private sector. It was directed at improving the city's image and encouraging investment. Surveys suggest that the perception of Glasgow, particularly in the south-east of England, has greatly improved, and consequently the 'Miles Better' theme has been retained.

Having led successful bids for the 1988 Garden Festival and the European City of Culture title, the role of the District Council declined. The Greater Glasgow Tourist Board (GGTB) instead devised its own strategy for developing tourism (described in the annual reports). A key element of the Board's marketing activity has been to use the above achievements as the platform for advertising campaigns. All the local authorities which support the GGTB have undertaken a range of smaller scale promotional activities. Local facilities such as parks, museums and art galleries were made more accessible by the distribution of posters and leaflets, publicising, for example, heritage trails.

Much of the information is directed at residents as well as tourists, and was designed to increase awareness and an appreciation of local history and heritage.

A strategy for tourism development was prepared by the Planning Department of Glasgow District Council in 1984. Entitled 'A Location Strategy for Tourism in Glasgow', it recommended that:

(i) attention should be concentrated on the three areas of the city which already boasted a variety of facilities (the city centre, the west end, and the south west around Pollock Park);

(ii) a tourist development and promotional programme should be drawn up for each area; and

(iii) tourist facilities outside these clusters should continue to be improved, linking them to the clusters where appropriate.

One of the main objectives behind the strategy was to overcome the dispersion of facilities throughout the city, and make each cluster more attractive and accessible. The report's conclusions have determined much of the District Council's subsequent investment programme. This includes part financing the transfer of the Transport Museum from south of the river to the Kelvin Hall, and the construction of a major indoor athletics arena in the same complex, designed to enhance the west end of the city. Tourism has become an essential element of Glasgow City's economic planning. The current Economic Development Plan (number seven) outlines some of the projects in progress, ranging from the Kelvin Hall conservation scheme to the expansion of accommodation facilities. Specific events, such as the Mayfest Arts Festival and a new Yulefest, are also being supported; a substantial grant to the four major performing arts companies of Glasgow was given in 1986. A Festivals Unit has been established to promote events in the period following the Garden Festival, concentrating on the 1990 European City of Culture activities. The budget allocation for parts of the programme is listed below, with funds being drawn from the Economic Development, Employment, and Policy and Resources Committees (though the Council represents only one of the sources of finance).

## (a.) Promotional Initiatives

(i) £475 000 to the GGTB.

(ii) £220 000 to support the Convention Bureau, and £50 000 towards a conference subvention fund.

(iii) £15 000 on the production of promotional material.

## (b.) Current Projects

(i) £6.3 million towards the Kelvin Hall conversion.

(ii) £700 000 on environmental projects.

(iii) £300 000 on stone cleaning and floodlighting.

## (c.) Planned Projects

(i) Contribution to a new concert hall, costing an estimated £24 million.

(ii) £25 million towards canal improvements, and £180 000 on river boating facilities.

(iii) £330 000 on improved facilities at Pollock Park, and £580 000 on amenities at People's Palace Museum.

**(d.)  Events and Activities**

(i) £150 000 to support the Mayfest, and £100 000 on a Yulefest at Christmas.

(ii) £224 000 to the Scottish National Orchestra, Scottish Opera, Scottish Ballet, and Scottish Chamber Orchestra.

(iii) £605 000 to support activities complementary to the Garden Festival.

*(Economic Development Plan [number 7], Glasgow District Council.)*

# Collaboration Between Development Bodies

Promoting existing tourist facilities and developing new projects in Glasgow has, therefore, involved these bodies;

☐ Regional and District Councils

☐ Scottish Development Agency

☐ Scottish Tourist Board

☐ Greater Glasgow Tourist Board

☐ Convention Bureau

Additional funding has been provided by the private sector and, where appropriate, the EEC. Most major projects have been made possible by a co-operative effort. The Glasgow Ark initiative is an interesting example of collaboration between Glasgow District Council and Glasgow Action (a consortium of public sector agencies, including the Scottish Development Agency, and business community interests; it is leading a campaign to regenerate the inner city through a £300 million programme). Glasgow Ark aims to create a unique visitor attraction based on the city's heritage, and it is anticipated that the 3.5 million pounds estimated cost will be met by loans and grants from the public sector and private venture capital. The growth of tourism in Glasgow is due to the effective co-operation of many different agencies, although there has been a degree of conflict between the Scottish Tourist Board and the Scottish Development Agency over their respective responsibilities. Working relations were improved by a government committee, which recognised the Tourist Board as the principal tourism marketing body (with some development functions) and the Development Agency as the main provider of funding and expertise for large-scale projects.

## Conclusion

Glasgow's experience of the tourism industry covers a comparatively short period, but has been marked by considerable success in devising and implementing a comprehensive product development and marketing strategy. The challenge for the future lies in its ability to sustain the momentum.

# ☐ The North of England Open Air Museum at Beamish

## Introduction

With the exception of Durham Cathedral, the North of England Open Air Museum at Beamish is the North East's biggest tourist attraction. Voted Museum of the Year in 1986 and European Museum of the Year in 1987, Beamish currently attracts almost 400,000 visitors annually. Beamish, like Durham Cathedral itself, is more than just a mere 'tourist attraction'. It is principally and unashamedly a museum  albeit a living museum  with the purpose of

> *"studying, collecting, preserving and exhibiting buildings, machinery, objects and information illustrating the development of industry and way of life in the North of England."*

Its brief is not phrased primarily in terms of the promotion of tourism. Beamish is neither a Disneyland, nor a Flamingoland, nor an Alton Towers. Nor has the museum been developed specifically for incoming tourists. As the brass plate in the Visitor Centre proudly proclaims, Beamish is *"A Museum of Living History for the North East Region and its People"*. The museum is a regional record, a celebration, neither of the 'good old days' nor the 'bad old days', but simply of the 'old days' or at least as accurately as we can reconstruct them. Yet, despite its serious purpose, Beamish is popular. Despite generous local authority and other public support, two-thirds of its income is derived in the form of entrance fees from visitors. Despite its explicit regional orientation, many of these visitors are incoming tourists.

For the student of tourism studies, Beamish well illustrates a complicated set of interrelationships and interdependencies often encountered in the complex business of tourism. The intention of this case study is to provide a descriptive framework within which aspects of this interconnectedness might be further explored.

## Origins And Development

The extent of radical innovation at Beamish can sometimes be forgotten. Within the past thirty years, developments at Beamish itself, imitations and successors elsewhere and developments within the museums profession as a whole have all combined to dim memories of its early eccentric radicalism. All glory, land and honour came its way - it was not ever thus.

The first ever bold steps towards the creation of an open air museum portraying North-East England's social history were taken by Durham County Council in 1958, when it commenced the

> *"collection of material relevant to the social and industrial history of the area."*
> (1987 Development Plan, Para 1.1)

The initial intention was to locate these collections on the outskirts of Durham City at Aykley Heads. Subsequently, however, the early collections became stored first at Barford camp near Barnard Castle, then at Brancepeth Camp, the former home of the Durham Light Infantry. In its early conception, the debt to the pioneering open air museums of Scandanavia was explicitly acknowledged. By 1966 the concept had become enlarged and the decision was taken to establish the proposed open air museum as a regional project. Reflecting this broader status it would be resourced and administered by a consortium of local authorities. The First Report of that subsequent consortium would later relate this history.

> *"After several years of collecting and planning, using the Bowes Museum as a base, the project was almost ready for implementation in 1966. At that point it was decided by Durham County Council that the project could be seen as being of regional importance, and consequently a meeting was called by the Chairman of the County Council in May, 1966. To that meeting all the top tier Local Authorities of the Northern Region were invited (i.e. within the geographical counties of Cumberland, Westmorland, Northumberland, Durham and the North Riding of Yorkshire) and most attended. The result was a working party which subsequently operated until late 1968, when an initial joint committee was established, though still without firm financial commitment."*

(The First Report of the North of England Open Air Museum Joint Committee, 1978 p.6)

From the thirty possible locations identified, reduced to a short-list of five, a site at Beamish was selected and purchased in 1968. Planning permission was granted by the appropriate authorities in June 1969. Located near Stanley along the northern boundary of County Durham, the site has been variously described as a *"peaceful saucer-shaped valley"* (Hewison, BBC TV, 1968) and as a typical landscape complementing the project's museological purpose. Magnusson's film of 1968 preserves a visual record of its agricultural character at that time. In summary, the site is well described in the 1987 Development Plan:

> *"The Museum is located on the northern boundary of County Durham in a well contained 'bowl' of land forming the lower section of the Beamish Burn valley. Covering 100 hectares (250 acres), most of the site lies to the south of the Burn. The topography ranges from steep slopes around the edge of the bowl to gentler, more undulating land in the valley bottom. Glacial*

*deposits around Pockerley to the east and the golf course to the west have left significant local knolls within the valley. Woodlands clothe the upper slopes of the bowl and virtually surround the site."*

(1987 Development Plan, Para 2.1)

In the north west corner of the site stands Beamish Hall, a Grade 2 listed building of architectural and historic significance, once the home of the Eden family and partly dating back to medieval times. It is surrounded by early nineteenth century parkland.

Administrative arrangements for the management and control of the new project developed in parallel to the site acquisition and the accumulation of collections. Reflecting the local government origins of the initiative, these arrangements centred on the joint committee of elected councillors representing the consortium of local authorities which, in 1970, had entered into the joint agreement. These authorities, eight initially, were the County Councils of Durham and Northumberland and the County Borough Councils of Darlington, Gateshead, Hartlepool, Newcastle, South Shields and Teesside. (Interestingly this Agreement was based on a similar one previously drafted by many of the same partners in connection with the developments of a major travel facility in the region, Newcastle Airport; again this would be supervised by a local authority consortium in the form of a Joint Committee).

The following year, 1972, saw the addition of Sunderland County Borough Council to the list of signatories. It also witnessed, on 19 May 1972, the formal opening of the museum by Lord Eccles, then Minister for the Arts, a reflection, no doubt, of its serious museological purpose. The signatories to the 1970 Joint Agreement continued to nominate the members of the Joint Committee until local government reorganisation in 1974, when a new Joint Committee was created. This latter committee comprised elected members representing the four funding county councils: Cleveland County Council, Durham County Council, Northumberland County Council and Tyne and Wear Metropolitan County Council. This arrangement continued until the abolition of Tyne and Wear (along with five other 'Mets' nationally and the Greater London Council), whereupon membership in the Tyne and Wear area returned to the constituent district authorities.

Within fifteen years of opening, Beamish had received the seal of international recognition as European Museum of the Year. For Kenneth Hudson, its achievements merited inclusion in his inventory of "museums of influence". From around 50,000 visitors in 1972, attendance increased eightfold by 1988. In 1987-88, for the first time, the majority of visitors came from outside the boundaries of the North-East. A calculation of its market share index has indicated a virtual doubling since 1974 (Johnson and Thomas, 1989). This overall pattern of growth, however, masks a significant period during which attendances fell; the early 1980s marked a period of waning popularity which bottomed out in 1984-85. A comprehensively documented and annotated analysis of the development of Beamish has been provided by Johnson and Thomas (1989), who organise their material in the following sequence:

| *Developing the Concept,* | *November 1958 - September 1966* |
| *Towards a Regional Open Air Museum,* | *October 1966 - February 1970* |
| *Preparations for Opening,* | *March 1970 - March 1972* |
| *Establishing the Museum,* | *April 1972 - March 1980* |
| *Greater Independence* | *April 1977 - March 1980* |
| *The Downward Slide,* | *April 1980 - March 1985* |
| *Recovery,* | *April 1985 - March 1988".* |

(Johnson and Thomas, 1989 )

For those seeking a detailed account of the development of the museum since its early beginnings, their narrative is to be recommended and cannot be repeated in this introductory case study.

# Role and Purpose: Diverse Expectations

Beamish is explicitly and unequivocally a museum, of international and national as well as local significance, though for many visitors the word 'museum' is unlikely to appear in their description of the visit. Beamish is simply Beamish, not usually Beamish Museum (though road signs thus indicate in order to distinguish from the village of the same name) and hardly ever the North of England Open Air Museum. Yet its purpose is clear enough. This was defined in 1970 as

> *"studying, collecting, preserving and exhibiting buildings, machinery, objects and information illustrating the development of industry and way of life in the North of England."*

Buildings, machinery and objects which shaped that way of life in the nineteenth and early twentieth centuries are gathered together on a single site; here the museum's collections are intended for preservation and exhibition "in the form of complete historical settings". Its displays are supported by the collection of other materials relevant to the focus of Beamish. These include the recordings, photographic archives and a library of documentary and printed evidence. The collections at Beamish are of a 'typical', 'representative' nature, rather than large-scale comparative. The 'Town' area, for example, seeks to show a townscape

> *"typical of a North east market town of the 1920s",*
> *Rowley railway station depicts "a typical country station,*
> *as it would have been around 1910".*

Home Farm gives an impression of mid-nineteenth century agriculture, the colliery shows a North-East coalmine as it would have been about 1913, while the row of pit cottages traces the changing pattern of household culture from the 1890s through to the 1930s.

Beamish, symbolized by its cauldron or black coal wagon, is unashamedly a museum. Appropriately enough the person who, more than any other, stamped his mark on its development was drawn from a museological background. This man was Frank Atkinson, formerly Director of the Durham County Museum Service based at the Bowes Museum and Director of Beamish from 1970 - 1987. Elevated in Robert Hewison's 1986 BBC TV film to the heady status of *"The Man Who Made Beamish"*, Atkinson had already marketed his media personality to Magnus Magnusson in a television film some twenty years earlier. For Hewison, Atkinson brought all the skills, the panache, the flair and the patter of the showman to a serious museological mission. The self-styled *"unselective collector"* (Atkinson,1985) or *"sublimated kleptomaniac"* was fondly described by other museum figures elsewhere in the UK as *"a nutter with an idea"* (Ian Walden) and *"surely the most single minded museum visionary that ever lived"* (Richard Foster). Yet for all his showmanship, Atkinson remained a *"museum man"*. When the needs of managing a large organisation probably outstripped his taste for management, it was to his professional roots that Atkinson retired setting about building up the Bewick Birthplace Museum at Cherryburn in the Tyne Valley.

Interestingly, his successor at Beamish brought financial and management skills from a large private sector retailing company; suggestive perhaps of a shift in the patterns of emphasis and priority. Yet the tension between museological values and other considerations has been inherent in the concept of Beamish since its very early days. In the Joint Committee's First Report of 1978, for example, one reads that:

> *"......if the museum is to develop fully it must seek many sources of income, be these visitors, grant-aiding bodies, commercial sources, or hiring of facilities. In this way this Local Authority controlled museum is breaking new ground; yet the proper functions of the museum in terms of conservation and visitor services are in no way impaired: rather, they are better financed.*
>
> *In short, this is an exiting new venture in so many ways: Local Government regional consortium and financial experiment, an 'experience' for adults and children, a tourist attraction, and a regional record and repository for future generations."*

(First Report of the North of England Open Air Museum Joint Committee, 1978, p.5)

The Chairman of the Joint Committee at that time, Stan Heatlie, captured the ambiguities, paradoxes and tensions:

> *"Beamish is about people, how they worked, played, lived and died. It is about struggles and tragedies, gaiety and laughter, toughness and tenacity, inventiveness and ingenuity. It is a unique way of interpreting the past, but bringing it back to life so that it can be 'experienced', thus helping us all to understand our past and that of our region. If this is exciting for those born here,*

*how much more so it may be for those who know little of the North East.*

*Yet it is not just a preserver of the region's past though it certainly is that. And it is not just a leisure activity though it undoubtedly is that too. Rather it is a way of encouraging the region to take a pride in its own past; to see 'how it was' and thereby to gain a glimpse of how it may be".*

(Chairman's Note of Welcome, First Report of the North of England Open Air Museum Joint Committee, 1978, p.4).

Beamish sits at the centre of a network of sometimes complementary, sometimes conflicting interests. In the mission of the prime movers behind its development, Beamish is primarily and essentially a serious museum. Even so its attractiveness to visitors was acknowledged at an early date, indeed exploited in order to secure popular support, especially locally and regionally. From the outset Beamish was not only a museum but a popular attraction, in the early days an afternoon out. As the first Beamish Report acknowledges, without all the publicity the concept of a regional open air museum may never have come to fruition. In 1971, a year before the formal opening, a temporary exhibition entitled 'Museum in the Making' was opened during summer weekends. In only 20 weekends, it attracted more than 50,000 visitors. According to Atkinson, certain public holiday attendances exceeded those for the aggregate of all other museums and galleries in the region (Johnson and Thomas 1989,p.13). Pragmatism recognised the opportunity. As Johnson and Thomas point out in their analysis of the role of Atkinson and his staff in the development of the museum:

*"He was able to adapt to changing circumstances and opportunities while retaining his underlying commitment to the fundamental concept of a Museum designed to provide a 'living' portrayal of the Region's heritage. For example, he saw and exploited the increasing potential for fund raising that lay in the promotion of Beamish as a tourist attraction even though he himself would have rejected the latter term as accurately reflecting the concept underlying the formation and development of the museum."*

(Johnson and Thomas, 1989. pp.42-3)

By 1972-73, Beamish was attracting 80,000 visitors, the majority in the summer of 1972. Its apparent local popularity assisted the overwhelmingly Labour sponsoring local authorities in maintaining support. Its potential for tourism development was also recognised by the English Tourist Board by the mid - 1970s. For example:

*"Although Beamish was originally envisaged as a regional scheme, for the enjoyment and education of the North East, it is now becoming much more that this, as a survey undertaken for the English Tourist Board in 1975 showed ... 60% of those surveyed were tourists to the region ... 12% were tourists from abroad. Moreover it was calculated that these tourists spent over £300,000 within an eight mile radius of Beamish, thus contributing more to the region than was spent that year on the*

> *upkeep and development of the museum by its constituent Authorities."*

(First Report of the North of England Open Air Museum Joint Committee, 1978, p.11).

In recognition of Beamish's growing significance for tourism, and vice versa, closer links were forged between the Joint Committee and the ETB; indicative of this developing relationship was the appointment of an ETB representative onto the Joint Committee. By 1977 modest attempts were being made at marketing the museum as a summer tourist attraction. Funding bodies extended beyond the sponsoring local authorities and included, for example, ETB, the Countryside Commission and the European Regional Development Fund. When visitor numbers fell dramatically in the early 1980s the museum sought to address the problem in terms of market shares and competitors. The main aims of the current capital programme are articulated in terms of tourist development:

> *"The main aims of the programme relate to the museum's role as a tourist attraction.*
>
> *(a) By creating further 'all-weather' displays of European quality, and marketing these, increase visitors to both the region and to Beamish.*
>
> *(b) By marketing a 'Two-Day Beamish Ticket' for the enlarged displays, encourage the conversion of day visitors and passing tourists into extra hotel 'bed nights' within the region.*
>
> *(c) By providing regional displays, encourage tourists to remain longer in the region to enjoy its unique culture, landscapes and heritage.*
>
> *(d) To provide, directly and indirectly, increased employment and spending power within the region.*
>
> *The developments will consolidate Beamish's position as a premier tourist attraction for the region and the museum would expect to share in the growth predicted in the English Tourist Board's strategic document 'A Vision for England' which would give visitor figures of well over 400,000 in the 1990s...."*

(North of England Open Air Museum, Six-Year Capital Programme 1988-1994, 1987).

The emphasis here is clearly expressed in terms of the business of tourism; the museological focus has apparently been displaced.

Beamish is, and recognises itself as, a major tourist attraction. Yet other traits and ambitions are also evident in its personality and behaviour. Take education, for example. The Museum's educative role was emphasised in Beamish One. The Museum's 1987 Development Plan, a decade later, also expressed its educational role, though by now the interest is expressed explicitly in terms of visitor numbering:

> *"With schools accounting for about one fifth of the visitors to the Museum, Beamish has a significant role as an educational*

> *resource within the Region. Basic material and worksheets are*
> *produced to assist teachers making use of the Museum."*

(1987 Development Plan, Para 1.2).

Other considerations are also important. For example the museum is a significant source of local employment, especially on schemes organised under the auspices of the former Manpower Services Commission. The situation however is plain enough without developing the discussion further. Beamish is a serious museum of international reputation, despite its regional focus. At the same time it is a major tourist attraction, a place of enjoyment and leisure, an educational resource and a home of scholarship. All these activities form part of the so called Beamish Experience. As with so many other tourist destinations, however, the encouragement of large numbers of visitors may in fact change the very nature and character of that experience which constituted the attraction in the first place.

Certainly the diverse range of activities and interests may not always be accommodated. As Johnson and Thomas have put it in the recent assessment:

> *".....a museum like Beamish faces considerable difficulties in*
> *reconciling a multiplicity of objectives. Beamish has served a*
> *wide variety of purposes: the preservation and display of*
> *'heritage'; conservation and scholarship; education; the*
> *encouragement of a regional 'identity' and pride in the past; the*
> *provision of an enjoyable experience for local people and others*
> *from outside the region; and the generation of economic activity*
> *and employment. It is not difficult to see possible conflicts*
> *between these objectives. The resource trade-off between these*
> *objectives is a major task of management."*

(Johnson and Thomas, 1989, p.60).

# Bibliography

Albury, P, 1975, The Story of the Bahamas, Macmillan London

Allcock, J B, 1986 Yugoslavia's Tourist Trade: Pot of Gold or Pig in a Poke?, *Annals of Tourism Research*, Vol 13, No 4, pp565-588

Armitage, J, 1977, Man at Play, Frederick Warne & Co Ltd London

Arts Council, 1988, An Urban Renaissance, The Role of the Arts in Urban Regeneration

Atkinson, F, 1968, Regional Museums, *Museums Journal*, Vol 2, pp74-77

Atkinson, F, 1985, The Unselective Collector, *Museums Journal*, Vol 1, pp9-11

Badal, F N, 1984, El Turismo en Baleares: 1960-81, El Campo, pp81-84

Baker, M J, 1985, Marketing: An Introductory Text, 4th ed, MacMillan London

Baldwin, R, 1985, Regulating the Airlines, Oxford University Press

Barke, M, and France, L, 1986, Tourist Accommodation in Spain 1971-1981, *Tourism Management*, Vol.7, No.3, Sept. pp181-196

Bastin, R, 1984, Small Island Tourism: Development or Dependency?, *Development Policy Review* 2,1 pp79-90

Bryden, J, M, 1973, Tourism and Development, Cambridge University Press Cambridge

Burkart, A J, and Medlik, S, 1985, Tourism Past, Present and Future, Heinemann

Caribbean Tourism Research and Development Centre, 1987, Pocket Guide to Carribbean Tourism Ctrc Barbados

Casson, L, 1974, Travel in the Ancient World, Allen and Unwin London

Choy, D J L, Gee, C Y, 1983, Tourism in the PRC - Five Years After China Opens its Gates, *Tourism Management*, Vol 4, No 2, pp85-93

Choy, D J L, Dong, G L, Wen, Z, 1986, Tourism in PR China: Market Trends and Changing Policies, *Tourism Management*, Vol 7, No 3, pp197-201

Chubb, M, & Chubb, H R, 1981, One Third of Our Time? John Wiley & Sons: London

City of Glasgow District Council, Department of Planning, 1984, A Locational Strategy for Tourism in Glasgow

City of Glasgow District Council, 1987, Economic Plan 7

CM Law Urban Tourism, 1985, Selected British Case Studies, University of Salford

Cohen, E, 1972, Towards a Sociology of International Tourism *Social Research*, pp164-82

Comunitat Autonoma de les Illes Balears, 1985, El Turisme a Les Illes Balears, Conselleria de Turisme, Mallorca

Cowell, D, 1984, The Marketing of Services, Heinemann London

de Kadt, E, ed, 1976, Tourism. Passport to Development?, Oxford University Press: New York

Dicken, G, Guangrui, Z, 1983, China's Tourism: Policy and Practice, *Tourism Management*, Vol 4, No 1, pp75-84

Dunleary, P, and Rhodes, R A W, 1983, Beyond Whitehall in H Drucker, P Dunleary, A Gamble and G Peel eds, Developments in British Politics, Macmillan

Economist Intelligence Unit, 1982, *International Tourism Quarterly*, Report 4, Yugoslavia

Edwards, A, 1985, International Tourism Forecasts to 1995, *Economist*

Elliott, J, 1987, Government Management of Tourism D A Thai Case Study, *Tourism Management*, Vol.8, No.3, Sept 1987, pp223-32

Greater Glasgow Tourist Board and Convention Bureau, 1986/87, Annual Report and Accounts

Guangrui, Z, 1985, China Ready for New Prospect for Tourism Development, *Tourism Management*, Vol 6, No 2, pp141-143

Hairui, L, 1987, PR China's Tourism Industry Today and its Future Development, *Tourism Management*, Vol 8, No 2, pp90-91

Heape, R, 1983, Tour Operating Planning in Thomson Holidays UK, *Tourism Management*, 1983

Heeley, J, 1985, Scottish Hotel School, University of Strathclyde, A Tale of Two Cities and Tourism, *Economic Perspective* 1

Heeley, J, 1986, An Overview of the Structure of Tourism Administration in Scotland, L Houston ed, Strategy and Opportunities for Tourism Development, Glasgow Planning Exchange, Occasional Paper 22

Holloway, J C, 1985, The Business of Tourism, 2nd ed, Pitman

Hunt, E D, 1984, Holy Land Pilgrimage in the Late Roman Empire AD312-460, Clarendon Press Oxford

Johnson, P, and Thomas, B, 1989, The Development of Beamish: An Assessment, University of Durham Department of Economics, Tourism Working Paper 3

Kotler, P, 1989, Marketing Management, Analysis, Planning and Control, Pretice-Hall

Lambert, R S, 1950, The Fortunate Traveller, Melrose London

Leiper, N, 1979, The framework of Tourism: Towards a Definition of Tourism, Tourist and the Tourist Industry, *Annals of Tourism Research*, pp390-407

Lewis, R, 1980 Seaside Holiday Resorts in the United States and Britain : A Review, *Urban History Yearbook*

Liberalisation of Air Transport in Europe, 1987, *Travel and Tourism Analyst*, Economist Publications, March 1987

Martin, B, and Mason, S, 1988, Current Trends in Leisure, *Leisure Studies*, Vol 7, pp75-80

Mathieson, A, & Wall, G, 1982, Tourism. Economic, Physical and Social Impacts, Longman London and New York

Mazi, M, 1972, Development of Tourism Since the War, *Yugoslav Survey*, Vol 13, No 4,

Mead, W E, 1914, The Grand Tour in the Eighteenth Century, Houghton Mifflin New York

Middleton, V T C, 1988, Marketing in Travel and Tourism, Heinemann London

Mok, H, 1985, Tourist Expenditures in Guangzhon, PR China, *Tourism Management*, pp272-279

Murphy, P E, 1985, Tourism. A Community Approach, Methuen New York and London

Nash, D, 1978, Tourism as a Form of Imperialism in Smith, V L, ed Hosts and Guests, Blackwell Oxford

National Tourism Administration, 1985, PR China, The Yearbook of China Tourism Statistics

Naylon, J, 1967, Tourism - Spain's Most Important Industry, *Geography,* Vol.52, pp23-40

North of England Open Air Museum, 1978, Beamish One: The First Report of the North of England Open Air Museum, First Committee, Spring 1978

North of England Open Air Museum, 1987, Beamish, North of England Open Air Museum, Development Plan, September 1987

OECD, 1986, Tourism Policy and International Tourism in EOCD Member Countries

Pannell, Kerr, Forster Associates, 1983, Tourism Development Study of Glasgow

Papadopoulos, S.I, and Mirza, I, 1985, Foreign Tourism in Greece, *Tourism Management* Vol 6 No 2 June, pp125

Papadopoulos, S I, 1987, World Tourism: an Economic Analysis', Revue de Tourisme, No.1, pp2-13

Pearce, P L, 1982, Social Psychology of Tourist Behaviour, Pergamon Oxford

Pimlott, J A R, 1947, The Englishman's Holiday: A Social History, Faber and Faber London

Plog, S C, 1972, Why Destination Areas Rise and Fall in Popularity in Murphy, P E, 1985, Tourism. A Community Approach, Methuen New York and London

Pollard, H J, 1976, Geographical Variation Within the Tourist Trade of the Caribbean, *Journal of Tropical Geography,* Vol.43, pp49-62

Prunsten, J, and Socher, K, 1983, The World Recession and the Future of Tourism, *AIEST*, 24, pp145-156

Recent Trends in International Air Transport Regulations, 1984, *Tourism Management,* December 1984

Regional Airlines in the USA, 1987, *Travel and Tourism Analyst*, Economist Publications, May 1987

Rapoport, R, and Dower, M, 1976, Leisure Provision and Human Need, Institute of Family and Environmental Research and the Dartington Amenity Research Trust

Salman, K, 1985, National Report No.103, Spain, *International Tourism Quarterly*, Vol.2, pp20-41

Sallnow, J, 1985, Yugoslavia: Tourism in a Socialist Federal State, *Tourism Management*, 6, 2, pp113-124

Sea Ferry Travel and Short Cruises, 1987, *Travel and Tourism Analyst*, Economist Publications, Jan 1987

Sealey, N E, 1982, Tourism in the Caribbean, Hodder and Stoughton

Shaw, S, 1985, Airline Marketing and Management, Pitman

Simmons, J, 1984, Railways, Hotels and Tourism in Great Britain, 1839-1914, *Journal of Contemporary History*, pp201-222

Swinglehurst, E, 1982, Cook's Tours: The Story of Popular Travel Poole, Blandford Press

Tamameo, R, and Revuelta J M, 1982, El Pais, Anuario, Madrid

Travis, A S, Veal, A J, Duesbury, K, and White, J, 1981, The Role of Central Government in Relation to the Provision of Leisure Services in England and Wales, University of Birmingham, Centre for Urban and Regional Studies, Research Memorandum No. 86

Travis, A S, 1983, Leisure Services in England and Wales D A Retrospective and Prospective Review, *Local Government Policy Making*, Vol. 9, No 3, Spring 1983

The Changing Role of IATA, 1986, *Tourism Management*, Dec 1986

Towner, J, 1985, The Grand Tour: A Key Phase in the History of Tourism, *Annals of Tourism Research*, Vol 15, No 1, pp297-333

Towner, J, 1988, Approaches to Tourism History, *Annals of Tourism Research*

Travis, A S, 1982, Leisure, tourism and recreation in Western Europe, *Tourism Management*, Vol.3, No.1, pp3-15

UK Economist Intelligence Unit, 1982, National Report No.72, Spain, *International Tourism Quarterly*, Vol.1, pp35-53

UK Economist Intelligence Unit, 1984, The Carbibbean as a Tourist Destination, *International Tourism Quarterly*, Special Report No.49, No.1, pp37-55

UK Economist Intelligence Unit, 1986, National Report No.119, Greece, *International Tourism Quarterly* No.3. pp45-55

UK Economist Intelligence Unit, 1986, *International Tourism Quarterly,* National Report No.144, Bahamas, No.2, pp43-51

Uysal, M, Wei, L, Reid, L M, 1986 Development of International Tourism in PR China, *Tourism Management*, Vol 7, No 2, pp113-119

Valenzuela, M, 1985, Everything Under the Sun, *Geography,*. Vol.57, No.5, pp274-278

Valenzuela, M, 1987, Tourism in Spain Unpublished Paper to Colloquium on Tourism and Development: Geographical Perspectives on the Western European Experience, May 1-3, 1987, University of Exeter

Vukonic, B, 1986, Foreign Tourist Expenditures in Yugoslavia, *Annals of Tourism Research*, Vol 13, No 1, pp59-78

Wahab, S, Crampon, L J, and Rothfield, L M, 1986, Tourism Marketing, Tourism International Press London

Walton, J K, 1981, The Demand for Working-Class Seaside Holidays in Victorian England, *Economic History Review*, Vol 34, No 2, pp249-265

Walton, J K, 1983, The English Seaside Resort. A Social History 1750-1914, Leicester University Press

Webber, R J, 1977 The National Classification of Residential Neighbour-hoods, An Introduction to the Classification of Words and Parishes, PRAG Technical Papers

Withyman, M, 1985, The Ins and Outs of International Travel and Tourism Data, Economist Intelligence Unit, Special Report 55

Wolfe, R I, 1962, The Summer Resorts of Ontario in the Nineteenth Century, *Ontario History*, pp149-160

World Tourism Organisation, 1984, Economic Review of World Tourism, World Tourism Organisation, Madrid

# Index

The following books are also published by Business Education Publishers Limited and can be obtained either from your local bookshop or direct from the publisher by photocopying the order on the next page or by telephoning 091 567 4963

## THE BTEC SERIES FOR STUDENTS

**Core Studies for BTEC (2nd Edition)**
Aug 1989   £16.50
Paperback 608pp A4 format

*The first edition of this text was published in 1986 to cover the first and second year core areas of BTEC National Courses in Business, Finance and Public Administration. With its substantial coverage of the core areas, Organisation in its Environment, Finance and People in Organisations and its case study based assignments, it has proved to be the most popular book used on BTEC courses nationally. The new edition is an updated version of the first book retaining a large number of its most popular features.*

**Business Law for BTEC**
Nov 1987   £14.95
Paperback 368pp A4 format

*This book provides a comprehensive coverage of Business Law taught on BTEC courses at National and Higher levels. It incorporates a range of assignments for which a lecturer's manual is available to Educational Institutions free of charge from the publishers.*

**Marketing for BTEC**
July 1989   £16.50
Paperback 352pp A4 format

*This is a new text suitable for students studying marketing as an option module on BTEC National level courses or marketing as a full or part unit on BTEC Higher National level courses.*

**Information Processing for BTEC**
Nov 1987   £12.50
Paperback 256pp A4 format

*A popular text which covers the BTEC Information Processing Option Modules one and two. It incorporates a range of assignments for which a lecturer's manual is available free of charge from the publishers.*

**Transferable Personal Skills for BTEC**
Feb 1989   £12.50
Paperback 311pp A4 format

*A new text which covers the range of personal skills identified by BTEC in its statement of common skills. It is written in an easy to read style which students will find stimulating and informative. The text facilitates the development of a transferable personal skills training programme.*

**Computer Studies for BTEC**
Oct 1987   £14.95
Paperback 432pp A4 format

*The book was written specially for the first year core areas of the BTEC National Computing course. A lecturer's manual is available free of charge from the publishers to cover the range of assignments included in this book.*

**Small Business Computing Systems for BTEC**
Aug 1989   £12.50
Paperback 256pp A4 format

*A new book designed to cover the SBCS module on the second year of BTEC National Computing courses. The book contains a range of practical skills based assignments which can be used to form the basis of an assignment programme.*

**Getting Started with Information Technology**
Oct 1988   £11.50
Paperback 302pp A4 format

*Aimed at students who are new to information technology, this practical book takes a step by step approach to introducing word processing, data bases, spreadsheets, accounting and integrated packages.*

## THE BTEC SERIES FOR LECTURERS/TUTORS

**Core Studies:**
**A Tutor's Guide**
Aug 1989 £18.50
590pp A4 format

**Transferable Personal Skills**
**: A Tutor's Guide**
Feb 1989 £16.95
500pp A4 format

**Marketing :**
**A Tutor's Guide**
Sept 1989 £17.95
400pp A4 format

**Small Business Computing**
**Systems : A Tutor's Guide**
Sept 1989 £15.50
320pp A4 format

## OTHER PUBLICATIONS

**Transferable**
**Personal Skills :**
**A Student Guide**
Jan 1989 £12.50
311pp A4 format

**Law for Housing**
**Managers** £14.95
468pp A5 format

**Community Health Services**
Sept 1989 £16.95
500pp A5 format

**An Introduction to Market-**
ing Sept 1989 £16.50
352 pp A4 format

## Business Education Publishers Limited

10 Grange Crescent Stockton Road
Sunderland SR2 7BN
Tel 091 567 4963

# ORDER FORM

| THE BTEC SERIES FOR STUDENTS | Retail Price | Quantity Required |
|---|---|---|
| Core Studies for BTEC (2nd Edition) 1989 | £16.50 | |
| Business Law for BTEC 1987 | £14.95 | |
| Marketing for BTEC 1989 | £16.50 | |
| Information Processing for BTEC 1987 | £12.50 | |
| Transferable Personal Skills for BTEC 1989 | £12.50 | |
| Computer Studies for BTEC 1987 | £14.95 | |
| Small Business Computing Systems for BTEC 1989 | £12.50 | |
| Travel and Tourism 1989 | £16.50 | |
| Getting Started with Information Technology 1988 | £11.50 | |

| THE BTEC SERIES FOR LECTURERS/TEACHERS/TUTORS | | |
|---|---|---|
| Core Studies for BTEC - A Tutor's Guide 1989 | £18.50 | |
| Transferable Personal Skills - A Tutor's Guide 1989 | £16.95 | |
| Marketing for BTEC - A Tutor's Guide 1989 | £17.95 | |
| The Abbotsfield File - A Business in Action 1984 | £39.95 | |
| Small Business Computing Systems - A Tutor's Guide 1989 | £15.95 | |

| OTHER PUBLICATIONS | | |
|---|---|---|
| Community Health Services 1989 | £16.95 | |
| Law for Housing Managers (2nd Edition) 1986 | £14.95 | |
| An Introduction to Marketing 1989 | £16.50 | |
| Transferable Personal Skills - A Student's Guide 1989 | £12.50 | |

Surname

Initials                Mr /Mrs / Miss / Ms

Organisation

Tick Box as appropriate

Please Invoice :

☐ Individual

☐ Organisation (Please quote order number or reference)

Post Code
Tel:

* *All books are available by placing an order directly with the publisher (B.E.P.) or through any bookshop.*
* *For orders received from any Educational Establishment for books in the BTEC series an additional book will be supplied free of charge for every ten books ordered.*
* *For all books supplied postage is paid by the publisher (B.E.P.) .*
* *All invoices are payable within 30 days.*
* *For further information ring the publisher on 091 567 4963*